Flying Tigers

BOOKS BY DANIEL FORD

Flying Tigers

Michael's War

The Lady and the Tigers (editor)

The Only War We've Got

Remains

Glen Edwards

The Country Northward

The High Country Illuminator

Incident at Muc Wa (Go Tell the Spartans)

Now Comes Theodora

Flying Tigers

Claire Chennault and

His American Volunteers,

1941-1942

UPDATED AND REVISED EDITION

Daniel Ford

Smithsonian Books

Collins
An Imprint of HarperCollinsPublishers

For

KATHARINE FORD LAIRD AND HER DAUGHTERS,

three bright lights of my life

Flying Tigers: Claire Chennault and His American Volunteers
published by Smithsonian Institution Press 1991; 2nd printing with
corrections 1992; 7th printing with additions 2003. The new edition
published by HarperCollins / Smithsonian Books 2007

Permission to reprint copyrighted material granted by Charles
R. Bond Jr. and Terry Anderson for *A Flying Tiger's Diary* © 1984;
Kojinsha for *Hayabusa sentotai cho Kato* © 1987; Konnichi no
Wadaisha for *Hien tai Guramen* © 1973; Brad Smith for
photographs from the R.T. Smith collection; Robert T. Smith
for *Tale of a Tiger* © 1986; and Tab Books for *With Chennault
in China: A Flying Tiger's Diary* © 1984

Permission to quote from unpublished documents granted by
Helen Burgard, Anna Chennault, James Donovan, David Lee Hill,
James Howard, Robert Keeton, Robert Layher, Charles Mott, Robert
Neale, Charles Older, Anne Marie Prescott, Donald Rodewald,
Wilfred Schaper, Eriksen Shilling, and Thomas Trumble

Calligraphy by Eileen Chow

Designed by Jennifer Daddio

The Library of Congress has cataloged the original edition as:
Ford, Daniel, 1931–
Flying Tigers: Claire Chennault and his American volunteers,
1941–1942 / Daniel Ford
cm.
Includes bibliographical references and index.
ISBN 1-56098-011-7 (cloth);—ISBN 1-56098-541-0 (paper)
1. World War, 1939–1945—Aerial operations, American.
2. Chennault, Claire Lee, 1893–1958. 3. China. K'ung
chun. American Volunteer Group—History. I. Title.
D790.F584 1991
940.54'5973.dc20

978-0-06-124655-5

Manufactured in the United States of America

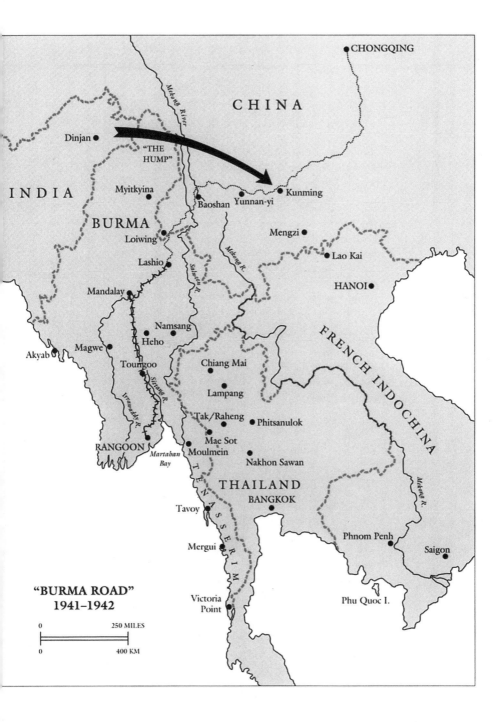

CHONGQING

CHINA

Dinjan

"THE
HUMP"

INDIA

Myitkyina

Baoshan Yunnan-yi Kunming

BURMA

Mengzi

Loiwing

Lashio

Lao Kai

Mandalay

HANOI

Namsang

Heho

Magwe

Akyab

Toungoo

Chiang Mai

FRENCH INDOCHINA

Lampang

Tak/Raheng
Phitsanulok

Mae Sot

RANGOON

Martaban
Bay

Moulmein

Nakhon Sawan

THAILAND

BANGKOK

Tavoy

Mergui

Phnom Penh

Saigon

"BURMA ROAD"
1941–1942

Victoria
Point

Phu Quoc I.

0   250 MILES

0   400 KM

Mekong River

Salween R.

Mekong R.

Irrawaddy R.

Sittang R.

TENASSERIM

Mekong R.

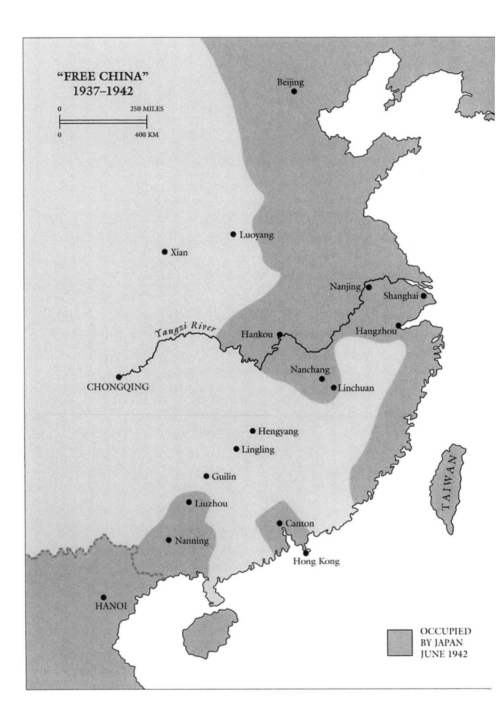

"FREE CHINA"
1937–1942

0   250 MILES

0   400 KM

Beijing

Luoyang

Xian

Nanjing

Shanghai

Yangzi River

Hankou

Hangzhou

Nanchang

CHONGQING

Linchuan

Hengyang

Lingling

Guilin

TAIWAN

Liuzhou

Canton

Nanning

Hong Kong

HANOI

OCCUPIED
BY JAPAN
JUNE 1942

Contents

Preface to the New Edition

For a scholarly look at events that happened a long time ago, *Flying Tigers: Claire Chennault and the American Volunteer Group* was met by an astonishing amount of flak when the Smithsonian Institution Press published it in 1991. Author, publisher, and even the grave old Institution—we all found ourselves accused of having sold out to the Japanese.

Our sin, of course, was to bring the news that there's a discrepancy between Flying Tiger combat claims and the losses actually suffered by Japanese air units in Southeast Asia and southwestern China. In its simplest and most defensible version, the Flying Tiger legend holds that sixty-seven volunteers, flying obsolete planes with Chinese markings, destroyed almost three hundred Japanese aircraft in the air and on the ground, while losing only four men in air-to-air combat.

But wait! As it's most often published, the legend goes on to say that the official tally includes only wrecks located on the ground or otherwise proven, and that the number must be doubled to account for planes that fell behind enemy lines or that lie forever uncounted in the rain forest or beneath the waters of Martaban Bay. And if you were lucky enough to get the Flying Tigers in an expansive mood, as I did for their 1989 reunion at Ojai, California, you'd be assured that Claire Chennault went to Tokyo at the end of the war and learned in Japanese records that they'd lost *one thousand* planes to the men he commanded in Burma and China from December 1941 to July 1942. Indeed, the reunion program that year contained an even more cheerful version of the AVG legend, claiming 299 planes shot down "by official count," plus "another known 240 Japanese aircraft," plus "upwards of a thousand aircraft which could not be confirmed officially." More than 1,500 aircraft!

There are three things wrong with these reckonings. First, Chennault didn't visit Japan after the war. Second, he couldn't have studied Japanese records, because they were in poor shape and he didn't know the language. And third, the Japanese Army Air Force went to war in Southeast Asia with fewer than 750 planes—with which it had to defeat the Flying Tigers and the Royal Air Force in Burma and China while also fighting (in concert with naval air forces) British Commonwealth squadrons in Malaya, Dutch squadrons on Java and Borneo, and U.S. and Filipino squadrons on Luzon. The JAAF couldn't have lost 1,000 or 1,500 aircraft to the AVG, because it didn't have that many to lose.

In fact, Japanese losses to the Flying Tigers amounted to 115, give or take a handful—a finding that shouldn't surprise anyone. Every World War II air force, in every theater of war, came home believing it had inflicted far more damage on the enemy than it had actually accomplished. As a matter of fact, Japanese airmen in Southeast Asia put in claims far more spectacular than those of the Flying Tigers—typically five to one. At the other extreme, Royal Air Force pilots in the Battle of Britain, equipped with gun cameras and fighting over open fields and pastures, inflated their kills by a mere 56 percent.

How could it have been otherwise? Aerial combat in World War II was a struggle in three dimensions, with the hard-pressed pilot doing his best to dive away or lose himself in a cloud, and often with two or three attackers firing at him. Opponents closed on one another at speeds of up to 700 mph. Win or lose, if he had any sense at all, the pilot was frightened half out of his skin. The wonder isn't that he saw things wrongly, even to the point of attacking friendly forces—the wonder is that it didn't happen more often. In the case of Allied squadrons in Burma and China, their difficulties were compounded by the fact that they often fought over enemy territory, or above the rain forest or open water, making wrecks impossible to find.

As for using Japanese sources, after more than half a century a writer shouldn't have to apologize for that. No such skepticism is shown toward German reports of their losses in the Battle of Britain, for example. And though I was the first to compare Flying Tiger combat reports to those of their opponents, I certainly wasn't the first to work with Japanese records. American researcher John Lundstrom made just such an analysis for U.S. Navy pilots in the opening months of the Pacific War. And the eminent British aviation writer Christopher Shores and his colleagues did it repeatedly for RAF pilots and their adversaries in Europe, North Africa, and the Pacific. (As a result of his findings, Shores was moved to write "A Radical Reassessment" for *Air Classics* magazine, urging his fellow aviation writers to stop using such formulations as "*X* Squadron sent fifteen of the Zeros crashing to the ground," when all we really know is that *X* Squadron claimed that many planes. Ironically, the same magazine led the charge in attacking *Flying Tigers* as Japanese-sponsored revisionism.) But those books were met with less fury, probably because they involved a larger canvas, with many squadrons and hundreds of pilots. With the Flying Tigers, each Japanese plane that I traced back to its base in Thailand or Vietnam was a victory that might be subtracted from somebody's bonus account.

Then too, the U.S. military refused to recognize those combat victories when the Tigers rejoined the armed forces in the summer of 1942. Nor did it count their months with the Chinese Air Force as qualifying time for promotion, retirement, or veterans' benefits. That snub remained a hot-button issue for Flying Tiger veterans for half a century, until it was partly remedied in the 1990s.

In any event, with a few good-hearted exceptions, the surviving Tigers—then numbering twenty pilots, plus eighty of the men and

This iconic portrait of three American Volunteer Group fighter planes was taken from the cockpit of Tomahawk No. 77 by its pilot while on a combat patrol over Baoshan, near the China-Burma border, in April 1942. (R. T. Smith photo by permission of Brad Smith)

women who'd supported them on the ground—roundly condemned the book, as a defamation of Claire Chennault and the fighter group he readied for combat in the fall of 1941.

I don't agree. In my opinion, they emerge from the pages of this book as more genuine heroes than the cardboard cutouts of earlier romances, knocking down Zeros with such ease that we can only wonder: with supermen like these, why did the United States need four years, two atomic bombs, and a Russian invasion to defeat the Empire of the Sun? To point out that the Japanese army had a formidable air force, with maneuverable planes and skilled pilots, doesn't diminish the Flying Tigers. Quite the opposite, I should think.

The Japanese accounts are solid; they're convincing; they have the kind of unambiguous detail that can't be faked. Indeed, I'll go further and say that in literally thousands of combat reports—Japanese, American, and British—I found no important instance where a survivor seemed to be lying about what happened. The pilots were often mistaken, but they rarely lied.

That on April 10, 1942, Chuck Older and Duke Hedman engaged Yasuda Yoshito in close combat is a fact that can't be denied by anyone who compares their accounts, which validate one another like overlays on a chart. They met, they fought, and the two Americans split a $500 bounty for shooting down Sergeant Yasuda. But they were mistaken: the Japanese pilot returned to his airfield in Thailand, exhausted but unhurt. All three men were still alive when I began this research in the 1980s, and I talked or corresponded with all of them, in Los Angeles, Reno, and Tokyo.

It's a pity the Tigers focused so narrowly on the question of combat victories, because it obscures the more important point: in 1941–1942, over Burma and China, they compiled a record without equal in the annals of aerial warfare. They fought magnificently in a losing battle. And they provided heroes at a time when we needed heroes as never before in our history, and never since.

Sixty-four years have passed since the Tigers disbanded, yet fresh stories by and about them come along at regular intervals. I fear I'll make no new friends among AVG veterans when I address one of these accounts, published by Christopher Shores in 1993. In the second volume of his meticulous series about the air war in Southeast Asia, published under the title *Bloody Shambles,* he came close to accusing the Flying Tigers of "acquiring" victories from their colleagues in the Royal Air Force, in order to split the combat bonuses paid out by the Chinese government. I take up this prickly subject in chapter 11, with respect to the conflicting stories of Allied raids on Moulmein, Burma, in February 1942, though the accusations aren't limited to a single day.

For the new edition, I've also had the benefit of recently published studies by Alan Armstrong, Terrill Clements, Neil Frances, Umemoto Hiroshi, Ray Wagner, and Daniel Whitney; and memoirs by Chuck

Baisden, Tex Hill, Frank Losonsky, and Muriel Sue Upfill. And I'm indebted to several individuals who corrected errors or supplied new information. They include Martha Byrd, who wrote the definitive biography of Chennault; Joan Corcoran, who was present when the Flying Tigers got their name; Alicia Schweizer, sister of the enigmatic Olga Greenlaw; Suzuki Goichi, who flew against the Tigers in their first combat; Tom Trumble, the Old Man's friend and secretary for many years; and Walter Tydon, project engineer for the P-40. Firsthand information and critiques came—in sometimes fiery form—from history buffs Dave Dunlap, Rick Dunn, Corey Jordan, Kirk Setzer, and Brad Smith, and from AVG pilots Charlie Bond, Joe Rosbert, and especially the late Erik Shilling. (Not the least of my debts to Erik is that he goaded me into taking up flight training at the age of sixty-six, and eventually becoming a certificated pilot.)

While folding in the new material, and making amends for earlier sins of omission and commission, I took the opportunity to shorten and simplify my original text. In that task, I was aided by Sally Ford, formerly my editor, now more nearly my coauthor. In the interest of brevity, I include only limited source notes, posting detailed notes, bibliography, and background material online at www.flyingtigersbook.com.

Throughout the text, I follow the standards of measurements in common use in 1941–1942. Distances are given in land (statute) miles, speeds in miles per hour, and altitudes in feet.

I use the postwar Pinyin system for rendering Chinese place names— so it's *Beijing*, not *Peiking*; *Guilin*, not *Kweilin*—because Pinyin gives a better idea of how a word is pronounced, but I retain the older spelling for historical figures like Chiang Kai-shek. For Japanese words, I use a simplified Hepburn system for rendering them in the western alphabet. Note that the Japanese, like most Asians, put the family name first, followed by an individual's given name; I respect that practice in this new edition, though I didn't in the first.

Burma now calls itself Myanmar. Though grateful for the freedom I enjoyed to travel in that country, I don't feel bound by a dictatorship's preferences, so the country remains Burma—and its capital, Rangoon— in the pages that follow.

Finally, today's U.S. dollar is but a shadow of the greenback of the

1930s and 1940s. Taking average wages as the standard of comparison, you can safely multiply dollar figures in this book by twenty to find their value in our much-devalued currency. The young person who wrote the dust-jacket copy for *Flying Tigers* in 1991 took pains to note that they'd volunteered to fly for China for "only" $600 a month. It was with some difficulty that I persuaded her that they were rather well paid, their stipend being the equivalent, in our dollars, of $144,000 a year.

—Daniel Ford, Durham, New Hampshire, January 2007

Chapter 1

Presenting
Colonel Chennault

The man behind the Flying Tigers was born in Commerce, Texas, on September 6, 1893—or was he? Commerce is right, though there's no documentary proof of Claire Lee Chennault's birth there or anywhere else. As the story is told, his father left Louisiana after a horse trader tried to sell him an unbroken mustang as good farm stock. Mr. Chennault shot a hole through the man's hat, and a sojourn in Texas was thought advisable while the matter cooled.

For most of his life, Claire Chennault gave his birth year as 1890, and not until after his death did his widow set the record straight. As a young man, he needed to seem older than his chronological age, and—in a time and a place that had scant use for vital statistics—he made the change and was stuck with it. And he always did look older than his years: not for nothing did his associates call him "Old Leatherface."

It's a small matter, this business of Claire Chennault's birth year, but suggestive of the ambiguities that marked his career. He was a great man and a flawed one. It can be argued that the American Volunteer Group wasn't his idea, that another man did as much as he did to create it, that he didn't invent its tactics (or at least not exclusively), and that when it was fighting most desperately, he was generally elsewhere. However that may be, it's also true that the AVG would never have succeeded without his passion and his remarkable ability to inspire devotion in young men—and women.

According to family legend, the first Chennault came from France in 1778 to fight for American independence under the Marquis de Lafayette. He stayed to plant tobacco in Virginia, and his descendants moved westward with the country. In the fourth generation, John Chennault grew up in Louisiana and married Jessie Lee. They settled in her hometown of Gilbert—bayou country, woven with swampy tributaries of the Mississippi and forever threatening to return to wilderness. Mr. Chennault farmed cotton, served as sheriff, and fathered two sons. Mrs. Chennault died of tuberculosis in 1901, and the boys were reared thereafter by her sister, Louise Chase. Claire formed "an instant, strong attachment for his young aunt," and her sons became like brothers to him.

In some ways, his was an idyllic boyhood—Tom Sawyerish—though by his own account he was a loner, happiest by himself or with younger boys willing to follow his lead. He quickly made his way through the one-room Gilbert school, and in January 1909 matriculated at Louisiana State University in Baton Rouge, in a class of 146 men and 8 women. The university required incoming students to be sixteen "at nearest birthday," so Chennault tweaked his birth month back to June, which is how it still appears on LSU records. At the same time, he said, he applied to West Point and Annapolis, and during spring break took the train east to sit for the entrance exam for the Naval Academy. This may have been his occasion for falsifying the year of his birth. (Annapolis has no record of this application.) Chennault submitted a blank paper, he said, after considering what life would be like inside those grim walls. But why be dismayed by the regimentation of Annapolis? He was no stranger to drill: like all men living "in barracks" at LSU, he belonged to the Reserve Officer Training Corps and wore his ROTC garrison cap, high-buttoned tunic, and striped uniform trousers to class.

Of his own volition, he joined the Graham Literary Society, and he apparently showed some talent in that direction. "I remember his writing perfectly," recalled his English teacher, Mercedes Garig. "It had character and slanted to the right. It impressed you as though he knew what he wanted to say and how to say it." Not that he spoke very often: "He would just sit and look and I never knew whether it was reserve or shyness. It seemed to me that it may have been just belief in himself—that he didn't have to go outside himself.

"He was slender," Garig went on, "with dark hair and an olive complexion. But the most noticeable thing about him was his silence. I never got close to Chennault, mainly because his work was usually so good that I never had to have many conferences with him."

He was an "aggie," taking eighteen classroom hours each week in English, algebra, botany, comparative physiology, farm accounting, and elementary agriculture. LSU also encouraged students to sign up for sports, and Chennault recalled that he competed in track, basketball, and baseball.

That summer, he farmed a cotton patch to earn money for his sophomore year, but he dropped out of LSU in favor of a teacher preparation course at the State Normal School at Natchitoches. In September 1910, at the age of seventeen, he went to work as teacher-principal of a school in Athens, not far from Shreveport. When the school year was over, he attended commencement exercises at Winnsboro High, where the valedictorian (and only graduate) was Nellie Thompson, plump and pretty. They were married on Christmas Day, 1911. As a family man, Chennault required more lucrative employment than presiding over an ungraded country school: by the time the United States declared war on Germany in April 1917, he was working in a Goodyear tire factory.

Chennault resettled his family near the home place in Gilbert, joined the U.S. Army, and earned the silver bars of a first lieutenant. He was assigned to the 90th Infantry Division at Fort Travis, Texas. On the other side of San Antonio was Kelly Field, a former cotton plantation where the Signal Corps taught cadets to fly. Kelly asked Travis for the loan of an infantry officer, and Lieutenant Chennault joyfully accepted what he assumed was a billet in aviation, only to be told to lead the cadets in parade-ground drill. No matter. If it wasn't flying, it was close, and he could take flying lessons on the sly. And he dressed the part: a 1917 photograph shows him togged out in puttees, riding breeches, shirt, tie, leather helmet, and round-lensed goggles like those worn on the Western Front. The man in the photo is strikingly handsome, though with narrowed eyes and an uncompromising mouth. His companion, by contrast, smiles affably at the camera.

The war ended without Chennault's taking part in it, but peace brought the orders he'd longed for, sending him back to Kelly Field as a flying cadet. Alas, his bootleg lessons had left him with habits that, combined with a rebellious temperament, caused him to be washed out by his civilian flight instructor. Chennault went up in the "washing machine" for the traditional second opinion by a military pilot. This was Lieutenant Ernest Allison, who gave him a second chance: "This man can be taught to fly."

Chennault earned his wings on April 9, 1919. His only flying assignment was a stint on the Mexican border, and he was routinely discharged at the end of his tour. He went home to Gilbert, planted a field to cotton, and pined for the wings he'd lost: "I have tasted of the air," he wrote to his father, "and I cannot get it out of my craw." Happily for him, the National Defense Act of 1920 made the Army Air Service a specialty like the infantry or artillery. Before his crops were in, Chennault applied for one of the newly opened slots for flying officers. On September 14, he again received pilot's wings and lieutenant's bars— a reservist no longer, but an officer in the regular army. Again he spent most of his time in nonflying assignments. By 1922, when he joined the 1st Pursuit Group at Ellington Field, Texas, he'd logged only sixty-three hours in the air.

Chennault was assigned to the 94th Squadron, whose planes bore the hat-in-the-ring insignia made famous by Eddie Rickenbacker, America's "ace of aces" in the war against Germany. In this congenial environment, Chennault became the superlative pilot nature had intended him to be, and in time he went to Hawaii as commander of the 19th Squadron. It was a happy billet for Chennault, now thirty and the father of six sons and a daughter. He sported a waxed-tip mustache, luxuriant and black. His station was Ford Island in the middle of Pearl Harbor, America's mightiest naval base. During a war scare in 1925, Chennault ordered aerial patrols off the coast of Hawaii, and he improvised an early-warning system by posting men with binoculars on top of a water tower. By now he was becoming deaf, an affliction common among pilots of the time, seated in an open cockpit amid the airstream and the roar of an unmuffled engine. He was obliged to fly on a medical waiver, but fly he did, logging 1,353 hours by the time he left Hawaii.

In 1929, the army promoted him to captain, and a year later sent him to the Air Corps Tactical School, where future generals were trained. Among his instructors was Captain Clayton Bissell, three years

A clean-shaven Captain Claire Chennault, in a photograph probably taken in the fall of 1930, when he was tapped for the Air Corps Tactical School. He was thirty-seven but looked a decade older. (National Air and Space Museum)

his junior but credited with shooting down five German aircraft on the Western Front. As Chennault told the story, Bissell believed that the only way to destroy the fast, heavily armed bombers of the 1930s was for interceptors to fly overhead and dangle a ball-and-chain device to snare their engines.

When the Tactical School got a permanent campus at Maxwell Field, Alabama, Chennault joined the faculty. The school was more than an in-service academy: its sixteen-man faculty also served as an incubator for air force doctrine. Chennault tried to devise something more effective than dangling chains to snare enemy bombers. This he did in the air over the town of Waterproof, Louisiana. His cousin Ben Chase had settled there, and Chennault would fly in for the weekend to fish, hunt, and practice aerobatics. Ben had served in the Naval Air Service, and sometimes his friends flew in from Pensacola, where the navy had a stunt-flying team called the Helldivers.

In 1929, the United States had adopted a "pursuit" plane to replace its war-vintage machines. Built by Boeing, this darling biplane was known to the army as the P-12. Its cowling bulged like the head of a clothespin, and its landing gear and upper wing were so far forward they almost met the engine, a 525-horsepower Wasp that drove the Boeing through the air at 190 mph—the fastest and most maneuverable fighter in the world.

When the Tactical School's commander saw the Helldivers perform in 1932, he asked Chennault to create a similar team for the army. For wingmen, Chennault picked Lieutenant Haywood (Possum) Hansell and Sergeant John (Luke) Williamson. After their first performance, letting off steam in a Mississippi tavern, they sang the rollicking verse: "He floats through the air with the greatest of ease / That daring young man on a flying trapeze." Forthwith, they became the Three Men on a Flying Trapeze. Their stunts included a "collision" that brought the aircraft within eight feet of one another, and at times they flew tied together with twenty-foot lengths of control cable—taking off, stunting, and landing again with the tethers intact. The results were awesome. "Chennault's 'Men on a Flying Trapeze' performed feats heretofore considered impossible," wrote a correspondent for the *Air Corps News Letter*. "Wingovers, slow and snap rolls, Immelmanns, and finally

The Three Men on a Flying Trapeze leaning against a Boeing P-12 fighter, about 1935. Chennault's wingmen were Billy McDonald (left) and Luke Williamson (right), sergeant-pilots who resigned and sailed for China after they were turned down for commissions in the Army Air Corps. (National Air and Space Museum)

a turn and a half spin were executed with such precision and perfection that it seemed as if the three planes were activated by a single mind."

The Three Men were indeed activated by a single mind: Chennault's, mimicked to perfection by Luke Williamson and Possum Hansell. When Lieutenant Hansell left the act, he was replaced by Sergeant Billy McDonald. Photographed leaning against the lower wing of a Boeing P-12, they are three remarkably handsome men—all of a height, all of an age, all dressed in leather helmets, leather flight jackets, and sheepskin-lined leather coveralls held up by suspenders—and all happy. Even Chennault is grinning, although his smile is guarded, as if ready for an unfriendly move on the photographer's part.

But the day of the fighter seemed to be ending. In Italy, General Giulio Douhet argued that no city was safe from aerial bombardment, because no means existed by which a bomber could be stopped before reaching its target. Even if intercepted, Douhet argued, a heavily armed "battleplane" could outgun the puny fighters of the day. At the Tactical School, Douhet's writings were translated, mimeographed, and used as a text. In the war games of 1931, the 1st Pursuit Group failed to catch a single bomber, prompting General Walter Frank to declare: "It is impossible for fighters to intercept bombers."

The Boeing company had already designed the monster that would become the B-17 Flying Fortress. It weighed twenty-two tons; its four engines developed 3,720 horsepower and drove it through the air at 256 mph; and it was defended by machine guns at the nose, back, belly, and flanks. (The best American fighter, the new Boeing P-26 monoplane, boasted a top speed of 230 mph and mounted only two machine guns.) With the advent of the B-17 and sophisticated bombsights, air force doctrine became fixated on daylight precision bombing. "American Army or Navy planes," went the mantra, "can drop a bomb into a pickle barrel from 18,000 feet up." Altitude would protect them from antiaircraft fire, and their speed, close-formation flying, and mutually supporting gunners would fend off any enemy fighters that managed to find them in the vastness of the sky.

Chennault wasn't convinced. Applying the lessons of the Flying Trapeze, he argued that the fighter's deficiencies could be overcome through teamwork, esprit, concentration of firepower, and the speed built up in a dive. If a pilot "took the high perch," he could make a screaming pass through an enemy formation, climb back to altitude, and do it again. Chennault also believed that a fighter pilot shouldn't have to keep track of more than one friendly aircraft at a time, and that a sensible commander would keep fighters in reserve, to be dispatched as the situation changed. Above all, fighter defense required a continuous flow of information: observers should be strung around the target and linked by telephone to a command post where enemy bombers could be plotted on a map, enabling the commander to know where and when to intercept. Drawing upon his service in Hawaii, Chennault even suggested how to protect an island from attack: put the observers on picket boats or submarines.

Chennault served on the Pursuit Development Board that drew up specifications for the nation's first 300-mph fighter. Modeled upon the sports racers of the day, it would be a low-wing monoplane with an air-cooled radial engine, retractable landing gear, and a stressed-aluminum skin that provided much of its strength. Chennault flew the competing designs in August 1935, and he agreed with the other members of the board that the army should adopt the Seversky P-35 as its next-generation fighter.

They were wrong: a competing design from the Curtiss-Wright company would eventually prove to be faster, more reliable, easier to fly, and easier to maintain. Curtiss had a tradition of naming its planes "Hawk," and this entry was Hawk-75. The U.S. Army would eventually adopt it as the P-36. To recoup its investment, Curtiss worked up a cheaper version of the H-75, with a smaller engine and nonretractable landing gear, to sell to foreign countries.

Meanwhile, the Three Men gave their last performance at the All-American Air Races in Miami in December 1935. Among the spectators was Mao Pang-chu of the Chinese Air Force—a dashing figure, his face chubby and handsome beneath a wavy shock of hair, his uniform splendidly tailored and beribboned. Also in attendance was William Pawley, a salesman for Curtiss-Wright in China. Pawley was in Miami to recruit flight instructors for the Chinese Air Force and to inspect his company's new export fighter. He threw a party on a yacht in Miami harbor, to which he invited Colonel Mao and the Three Men. Mao offered them lucrative jobs at a flight school in Hangzhou, and the two sergeant-pilots "bought up" the time remaining on their enlistments and sailed for China in July 1936.

Even as *Empress of Russia* took his friends to Asia, Chennault understood that his argument was lost, his career in the air force effectively finished. Now wearing the gold oak leaves of a major, he was assigned as executive officer of the 20th Pursuit Group at Barksdale Field, Louisiana. He was forty-two. His face was pocked; crow's-feet radiated from the corners of his glittering black eyes; his nose was almost perfectly aquiline; razor-cut seams dropped from the corners of his mouth. Altogether, Chennault had the look of a weary eagle. He was an uncomfortable presence—demanding and passionate—kind to subordinates but impatient and sharp-tongued with superiors.

"It is well to avoid a reputation for eccentricity," wrote Henry (Hap)

Arnold in a manual to guide the young aviator from lieutenant's bars to general's stars. He may have been thinking of Chennault. When he read the latter's critique of the West Coast games, he supposedly snapped: "Who is this damned fellow Chennault?" General Arnold believed in bombers—"winged, long-range artillery," he called them. "They can no more be completely stopped once they have taken the air than the big shell can be stopped once it has left the muzzle." A major doesn't advance his career by arguing with the commanding general.

Then there was Chennault's health. He was tremendously active, tremendously eager, always ready for a roughhouse or a pickup baseball game with his sons or subordinates. But he was regularly laid low by bronchitis, the penalty for his addiction to Camel cigarettes. (He smoked up to three packs in twenty-four hours, chain-smoking through the day and sometimes the night.) For years he'd been flying on a waiver for deafness; now, at Barksdale, flight surgeons declared him unfit to fly. They sent him to the Army-Navy General Hospital to be treated for what appears to have been a physical and mental breakdown. In February 1937, the army suggested that he retire at his permanent rank of captain.

The Chennaults had bought a farm near Waterproof. The house was a one-story bungalow, shaded by pines. There was an RFD mailbox, a white board fence, a black cook, and a pier reaching out into Lake St. John. Nellie took to rural life. She was now a portly woman with a perm, metal-rimmed glasses, black dress, and sensible shoes, wearing the benevolent but formidable expression of a Sunday school teacher . . . which she was, as well as president of the Waterproof Methodist Women's Society.

But Chennault had no intention of rusticating. Since meeting Colonel Mao on Bill Pawley's yacht, he'd been bargaining with the Chinese. His assignment, as it finally evolved, was a three-month survey of the CAF at a salary of $1,000 a month, three times what he earned as a major on active duty. On April 30, 1937, he retired from the U.S. Army. Next day he boarded the train to San Francisco, and from there set out across the Pacific on *President Garfield*. He started a diary when he embarked upon the "Great Adventure," but except for that revealing phrase it contains only a recital of the day's events, with few personal reflections and no comment on world affairs. So we don't know what he thought of the news that German and Italian bombers had destroyed the city of Guernica, Spain, killing a thousand or more civilians in history's first terror bombing—the Douhet doctrine come to terrible reality.

Chennault's first stop in Asia was Kobe, on the Japanese main island of Honshu, where Billy McDonald met him for a day and a night of amateur espionage. (Chennault took note of the damage incendiary bombs could inflict upon Japanese houses, built—as they seemed to him—of matchsticks and paper.) *Garfield* then took them to Shanghai, a "treaty port" governed and garrisoned by Britain, the United States, Japan, France, and Italy. The foreigners had their own police, courts, and prisons in Shanghai and every other city in reach of their gunboats—even Nanjing, 200 miles inland, where Chiang Kai-shek supposedly ruled China. In fact, his domain was limited mostly to the valley of the Yangtse River. Japan occupied Manchuria; the Soviet Union controlled Mongolia and Xinjiang; a Communist government held sway in Shanxi; and foreigners ran the treaty ports. Much of the rest was given over to warlords who levied their own taxes and fielded their own armies. In this fractured empire, Chiang was merely "Generalissimo"—the ultimate warlord.

That Thursday—June 3, 1937—may have been the most important day in Chennault's life, for it began his lifelong association with the first family of China. "One sultry afternoon," as he told the story in his 1949 autobiography, "Roy Holbrook appeared and drove me to the high-walled compound in Shanghai's French Concession to meet my new employer—Madame Chiang Kai-shek. We were told she was out and ushered into a dim cool interior to wait. Suddenly a vivacious young girl clad in a modish Paris frock tripped into the room, bubbling with energy and enthusiasm. I assumed it was some young friend of Roy's and remained seated. . . . Roy poked me and said, 'Madame Chiang, may I present Colonel Chennault?' "

Madame enchanted Americans from many backgrounds. They were impressed by her power, awed by her beauty, reassured by her Wellesley diploma, and charmed by her Southern drawl (as Chennault and others have characterized her voice, though in recordings it sounds clipped, authoritative, and unaccented). She was a chameleon who could charm even a soldier of fortune. Among the American pilots hiring out to Chinese warlords in the 1930s was Royal Leonard, who flew the Chiangs to safety after a kidnapping that ended with the Generalissimo promising to lead Communists, warlords, and his Nationalist army in a united front against the Japanese. Madame impressed Leonard as "the most beautiful Chinese woman I had ever seen," and he threw in his lot with the Chiangs. The Generalissimo was a medieval man who never felt entirely comfortable in his "flying palace." But Madame was a modernist. She acquired a plane of her own and had herself appointed secretary-general of China's Aeronautical Commission, in which capacity she was interviewing Chennault.

His account of their meeting is notable in another respect. He was a retired captain who'd never held a rank higher than major. If Holbrook introduced him as "colonel," the title either came from the Chinese or was cooked up by the Americans. The latter seems to be the case. Chinese officers who worked with Chennault in the 1930s were unanimous in agreeing that he was never commissioned in the CAF.

His next interview was in Nanjing, where he met General Chou Chih-jou, a somber-faced infantry leader who'd been sacked by the Generalissimo for losing a battle with the Communists, then given command of the air force. Chou's Italian adviser, General Silvio Scaroni, was there to brief the newcomer. Chennault next went to Hangzhou, where the CAF primary flight school was staffed by Americans, including Luke Williamson and Billy McDonald. After a "wallah-wallah" in their quarters, he set off on a tour of airfields at Nanchang, Canton (Guangzhou), Hankou, and finally Luoyang—Scaroni's domain, where Italian airmen ran an intermediate flight school, assembled kit-built warplanes, and kept the Communists from breaking out of their base in Shanxi.

At Luoyang, Chennault heard that Japanese and Chinese troops were fighting at the Marco Polo Bridge near Beijing. The cause was obscure: Japanese troops on maneuvers, shells exploding in their bivouac area, and Private Shimura Kikujiro vanishing on piss-call. The supposed casualty returned to duty next day, but the Japanese commander was determined to eject Chinese troops from the area. The offensive came as a surprise to the government in Tokyo. However, as they'd done with the earlier occupation of Manchuria, the politicians bowed to the wisdom of the generals, giving Chiang Kai-shek the choice of surrendering Beijing or going to war.

Chennault fired off a telegram to the Aeronautical Commission, offering his services, and was told to go to Nanchang and take charge of final combat training for the Chinese Air Force. The training school was commanded by Mao Pang-chu, the curly-haired officer who'd recruited the Three Men in Miami. Now a brigadier (one-star) general, he tactfully removed himself to the capital when Chennault arrived, leaving the front-line squadrons of the CAF in the control of a man who'd been in the country for six weeks, and who didn't (and never would) speak the language.

Nanchang was a dusty city in the interior, where the Chinese pilots proved so inept that many couldn't be trusted in a biplane trainer, never mind a Boeing P-26. (As the story is told, they were the sons of Chiang's bankers, generals, and legislators, and Scaroni hadn't thought it politic to refuse them wings.) Chennault vented his dismay in a letter to Billy McDonald: "What should I do, Mac, solo them on the Boeing and see if they break their necks or have them think I'm holding out on them? If the Commission is going to keep up sending greenhorns like these, it's no wonder the planes are all wrecks."

On July 23, he went to Nanjing to brief Chiang Kai-shek on the war readiness of the CAF. Chennault's report wasn't reassuring: of up-to-date warplanes, China had ten Boeing P-26 fighters and twenty-one Heinkel, Savoia-Marchetti, and Martin bombers. The backbone of the CAF was a U.S. Navy biplane, the Curtiss Hawk. Bill Pawley had sold the design to China, to be assembled at his factory in Hangzhou. Grandly called Central Aircraft Manufacturing Company (CAMCO), this plant had been assembling the tubby biplanes since 1933, and one hundred were in service with the CAF, doing duty as fighters and bombers.

On July 31, Chiang made his decision. He'd fight—but not at Beijing, where the Japanese could call upon their reserves in Manchuria. Instead he sent his German-trained 87th and 88th divisions into action at Shanghai, against Japanese marines dependent on the navy for supply, reinforcement, heavy guns, and air support. It was a clever move, except that it pitted the fledgling CAF against the Japanese Navy Air

Force (JNAF). The Japanese army regarded the Soviet Union as its most likely foe, so it acquired planes that could fight in the cold and barren reaches of Manchuria, in cooperation with the infantry. The navy, by contrast, expected to fight the United States. It therefore developed planes that could fly great distances, over water, in a tropical climate—the very qualities needed at Shanghai.

Chennault's first job was to silence the guns shelling Chiang's divisions. The order came on Friday the thirteenth. As he told the story, he and Billy McDonald stayed up until 4 AM to plan a raid that would send CAF bombers against the flagship *Idzumo*, anchored in the river off the Japanese consulate.

The sky on August 14 was filled with rags of low-lying clouds, forerunners of the typhoon that was sweeping the coast. Scattered by the storm, the CAF bombers reached Shanghai in flights of two or three. (Japanese warplanes, scheduled for raids that morning on Chinese airfields, were kept on their aircraft carriers by "raging winds.") At 10 AM, *Idzumo*'s antiaircraft guns began to fire, alerting foreign newsmen in the Cathay and Palace hotels, who saw three aircraft over the city. The planes "dived and loosed one bomb each," wrote one reporter, "the explosions reverberating through the city and engulfing [*Idzumo*] in smoke."

They missed. As Chennault explained the disaster, his pilots came in low because of the clouds, but didn't adjust their sights for the new altitude. As a result, their bombs landed in the city itself, wounding and killing more than three thousand civilians. "Oh, it was the most bloody catastrophe," recalled Tom Trumble, a young American seaman on *USS Augusta*. "There were arms, legs, torsos. The streets were running with blood."

Nor did Japanese airmen cover themselves with glory. That afternoon, eighteen Mitsubishi G3M navy bombers took off from the island of Taiwan to bomb the Chinese airfields. (See appendix 1 for Japanese aircraft nomenclature.) The round-trip distance was 1,250 miles, most of it over open ocean—a raid that wouldn't have been attempted by any other air force in the world. At Hangzhou, however, they were ambushed by the squadrons Chennault had trained. Without loss to themselves, the CAMCO-built Hawks shot down two of the fast, twin-engine bombers and damaged a third so badly it crashed on the way home.

On Sunday, sixteen G3Ms appeared in the sky over Nanjing. Without fighter escort, they were "easy meat" for the defenders, as Chennault exultantly noted—and despite the predictions of Clayton Bissell, Guilio Douhet, and Hap Arnold. CAF Boeings and Hawks tore into the G3Ms over Nanjing, shooting down four and damaging six. A Japanese airman confessed to his diary: "We have lost 30 men. . . . I wish to jump out and die with them, but how? My life is not mine. What can I do? The only thing I can do is hold the plane tight and pray God silently." In three days of transocean raids, nine of the modern, twin-engine bombers were shot down and eleven badly damaged, leaving only eighteen still in service. Even worse losses were suffered by the carrier-based planes: on the same Sunday, a squadron of twelve biplane B2Ms attacked Hangzhou, with only one getting back to the aircraft carrier *Kaga.*

By the end of August, however, the first Japanese escort fighters appeared over Nanjing. "Jap pursuit reported superior in performance to Hawks," Chennault wrote. "Chinese pilots are most properly afraid of them." Like most westerners, he didn't believe that the Japanese could have built anything so formidable, and he identified the new fighters as French Dewoitines. (Similarly, the *New York Times* had identified the G3Ms over Nanjing as German-built Heinkels.) In fact, Chennault was seeing the combat debut of the Mitsubishi A5M, an open-cockpit fighter with fixed landing gear and two rifle-caliber machine guns firing through the propeller arc—rather like the Boeing P-26, though faster and more agile.

On September 1, Chiang Kai-shek put Chennault in charge of Nanjing's air defenses. He set up shop at the athletic stadium with five Chinese officers including Lieutenant Lee Cheng-yuan, who helped him develop a control system for the CAF fighters. They put a radio in the leader's aircraft and linked the stadium to an observer network consisting of a few army field radios and many hand-cranked telephones. Chennault configured them in a manner that Lee called "the spider in the web," each radioman serving as the center for a circle of eight or ten observers who reported to him by telephone. The radioman summarized the information and forwarded it to the Nanjing stadium, where it was plotted on a map, with flags indicating the type, quantity, and direction of the enemy planes. The details were simpleminded to begin with: *much noise / little noise; one engine / two engines.* In time the observers became more sophisticated, and the system was expanded to Shanghai and Hangzhou.

With Japanese fighters ruling the daylight sky, Chennault switched to attacks at dusk and dawn. He mocked up *Idzumo* with lanterns on the Nanjing runway and drilled his pilots against this winking target from 3,500 feet. Then the CAF tried it live. Sure enough, the Japanese outlined their ships with searchlights and muzzle flashes, enabling Chinese bombardiers to damage some, though not the charmed *Idzumo*. The sudden increase in accuracy aroused the suspicions of the American consul. "Recent Chinese night air raids over Shanghai are reported to have been carried out by pilots obviously more skilled than Chinese," the consul cabled Washington. "One raider flew very low over foreign area to escape Japanese anti-aircraft fire and when passing over American Country Club dipped his plane and flashed on and off his lights. There is strong suspicion this plane was piloted by one of the American aviators [here]."

Aboard *Augusta*, Tom Trumble saw dispatches identifying Chennault as a CAF adviser. "The name stuck," Trumble recalled, "and for a long time I thought that Chennault was the mysterious 'Mr. Wu' that used to fly by the *Augusta* at dusk every evening and try to bomb the *Idzumo*." Trumble later had a chance to question Billy McDonald on this point. No, McDonald assured him; Chennault was never the bomber pilot, only an observer. For this duty, he flew a fixed-gear Curtiss H-75, brought to China by Bill Pawley in hopes of selling a new generation of fighters to Chiang Kai-shek.

Chennault never mentioned these flights in his diary, but he hinted at them in a September 14 letter to Possum Hansell. "While there is *no* war going on at present," he wrote his former wingman, "some 2,000 Japanese airplanes are doing their annual bombing maneuvers all over China. . . . In view of this Jap activity, Chinese pursuit is conducting its annual gunnery practice." In their first interception over Nanjing, CAF fighters tore into the Japanese bombers and "had six of them burning in just 2 minutes, all six being visible from one spot in the sky." Was he saying that *he* was the airborne observer—or even one of the shooters? Chennault has often been depicted as a mercenary pilot in China, credited with shooting down as many as fifty Japanese planes. A closer observer, James McHugh of the U.S. embassy, afterward recalled that McDonald and Chennault "had a [Curtiss fighter] for their personal use, which they employed in watching the performance of the Japs around Shanghai," adding: "I always suspected them of a clash or two with the Japs." But CAF veterans denied that Chennault performed any more hazardous duty than scouting enemy positions, and his age and health made him an unlikely candidate for aerial combat.

Chennault's letter to Possum Hansell ended with a boast that in time became an obsession: "Boy, if the Chinese only had 100 good pursuit planes and 100 fair pilots, they'd exterminate the Jap air force!" In that sentence, he sketched the outline of the American Volunteer Group he'd bring to Asia in 1941.

The Chinese fought with suicidal gallantry at Shanghai, losing 270,000 men before retreating along the railroad to Nanjing. By the time they captured the capital, Japanese losses were nearly as great. The victors embarked upon an "orgy of looting, raping, drinking, and murder," in the words of an American diplomat. At least 100,000 died, and perhaps twice or three times that number, making the Rape of Nanjing one of the bloodiest events of World War II—and for nothing, because Chiang simply moved his government upriver. Bureaucrats and soldiers, bankers and industrialists, teachers and students, peasants and workers: they moved up the mile-wide Yangtse, scuttling boats behind them to slow the Japanese advance. The Central Aircraft Manufacturing Company was part of this immense hegira. At Hankou, CAMCO reconstituted itself in the shadow of the Japanese Concession, and from this haven repaired warplanes for the CAF, delivering them to the airfield in the morning and dragging them back at sundown, to make good the damage sustained during the day.

Bill Pawley's order book was brimming: sixty Hawk III biplanes, thirty Curtiss H-75 monoplane fighters like the one flown by Chennault, thirty monoplane Vultee light bombers. With Shanghai lost, the aircraft came in through the British colony of Hong Kong, then by rail to the dusty city of Hengyang, where Pawley built a satellite factory to assemble them. Also operating out of Hengyang in the winter of 1937–1938 was Harvey Greenlaw, a former flight instructor at Hangzhou who was assembling training planes for A. L. (Pat) Patterson. The factories became the target of Japanese raids, and Olga Greenlaw recalled how Chennault and her husband would sit on her garden wall, "oblivious of shrapnel falling near them, and discuss the Japanese [bombing] methods."

Mercenary pilots flocked to China with claims of combat experience on the Western Front. At Madame Chiang's request, Chennault organized them into the CAF 14th Squadron, to be equipped with the Vultees Bill Pawley was assembling in Hengyang. Chennault spent the winter shuttling between the combat squadrons at Nanchang and the Vultee base at Hankou. (In whipping the 14th Squadron into shape, he had the help of Ernie Allison, who in 1919 had given him a second chance to become a military pilot.) The mercenaries had more zest for drinking than for fighting; Chinese pilots refused to work with them; Chinese bombardiers proved unable to "hit a city even"—and the planes kept breaking down. The squadron flew its first mission on January 23, 1938. Four Vultees took off; one crashed, two turned back, and the last couldn't find its target. Not long after, the Japanese attacked Hankou when the Vultees were gassed and armed for a raid; a bomb exploded under one of them, and the entire row blew up in a ghastly crescendo. The squadron was then sent to Chengdu, in the far west of China, where the foreigners were to train their own replacements from among CAF pilots.

Chiang fired his Italian and German advisers and turned instead to the Soviet Union. The Russian fighters, battle-tested in the Spanish Civil War, were the Polikarpov I-15 biplane and I-16 monoplane; the bomber was the speedy, twin-engine Tupelov SB. They came by the Trans-Siberian Railway to Xinjiang province, thence by truck along the old Silk Caravan Route, 1,700 miles to the Chinese railhead at Lanzhou. Returning, the trucks carried furs, antimony ore, tung oil, silk, and tea to pay for the Soviet aid. In this fashion, three hundred planes arrived in the winter of 1937–1938. Half were handed over to the CAF; the others came in the form of combat-ready units with their own pilots and mechanics.

Japan protested the presence of foreign pilots in the country—a complaint that might more reasonably have been lodged by the Chinese.

The Russians paid no attention, but the U.S. State Department was more easily intimidated. Consular officers stopped American pilots from entering China and urged those already in the country to leave it. Luke Williamson was among those who went home. More and more, the air defense of China depended on Russian "volunteers." Chennault's diary reveals him steaming over episodes when they refused missions or "sought safety in flight," but publicly he spoke well of them: "A fighting unit would go on duty just before dawn and would stay on duty all day long . . . without lunch or any sort of rest except in the seats of their planes. The mechanics . . . stayed on duty with each of the fighters, in front of the wing, prepared to start the engine at any moment."

As he told the story, four high-ranking officers—Asanov of the Soviet Union, Chou and Mao of China, and Chennault of the United States—worked together in the defense of Hankou. His young communications officer remembered it differently. "The Russians didn't like Chennault," Lee Cheng-yuan told me, adding that the Russians wouldn't speak to Chou when the American was around, for fear he'd learn their secrets. They preferred to deal with Mao Pang-chu, who'd learned to fly in the Soviet Union.

Asanov was right to be suspicious: Chennault sent regular bulletins to the army adjutant general in Washington. In May 1938, he forwarded drawings and specifications of the open-cockpit Mitsubishi A5M, and when the Japanese army introduced a new fighter to China—the Nakajima Ki-27—Chennault filed a report on that as well. As Asanov feared, he also wrote about Soviet equipment and tactics. In a dogfight, he reported, a Japanese pilot would glue himself to the Russian's tail, from which position nothing could shake him. The Russians soon learned to put their Polikarpovs into a power dive when hard-pressed by the nimble Japanese, then zoom back to altitude and attack from above—a tactic very similar to the one Chennault had proposed for use against fast bombers.

A somewhat jaundiced portrait of Chennault in 1938 was sketched by Paul Frillmann, an American missionary at Hankou. They met at a July Fourth baseball game between British and American teams. "He was a smallish man . . . with a silk aviator's neck-scarf and other accessories," Frillmann recalled. "He was standing with a court of ambiguous-looking

men—semi-adventurous, semi-commercial types whom I later found
to be his perennial cronies." Chennault put Frillmann in left field and
himself on the pitcher's mound. As the missionary told the story, the
airman made a great show of spitting on his glove and putting flour-
ishes on the ball, only to have the British players smash his pitches all
over the lot, and especially into left field. Frillmann valiantly ran them
down, until he finally missed one. "The glare Chennault sent me from
his dark hawk face," he wrote, "was something I remembered years
later."

Chou Chih-jou had become CAF commander after losing an infantry
battle; now Chiang fired him from the Aeronautical Commission
because he couldn't defend Hankou from Japanese air attack. He was
sent to the far-west province of Yunnan, bordering the British colony
of Burma, to build a new flight school. Chennault went with him into
exile, as did Billy McDonald and Boatner (Butch) Carney—one of those
"ambiguous-looking men." Carney had a widow's peak, dainty mustache,
and long, disreputable face. But he came from Louisiana, and Chennault
enjoyed his company.

Yunnan was a high and desolate country of brown mountains, green
fields, and blue lakes. With one hundred thousand residents, Kunming
was its principal city. Mountains guarded it to the south, north, and west,
and the air was so clear that every wrinkle in their flanks could be seen
from the city. Poplars bordered the road to the airfield. This road, with
wooden-wheeled carts creaking along it in the mist of morning, reminded
Europeans of France. This was no accident, for Kunming had long
served as a hill station for the French colony of Indochina—Vietnam,
principally, but also including present-day Cambodia and Laos. The
French had muscled a narrow-gauge railway over the mountains to Kunming, whose 6,200-foot altitude made it a splendid retreat from the heat
and humidity of Hanoi. Along this track ran a small rubber-tired train
called the Michelin.

The Chinese gave Chennault a house in the European district, half
a mile outside the wall, near Green Lake and the Hotel Grand du Lac.
Later he acquired quarters at the CAF academy nearby. This was a

beautiful building with redbrick walls, two stories to the eaves, with a ridgeline as high again above that, and a dragon-tail dormer over the entrance. The CAF had commandeered it from the Advancing Intelligence Society, a fraternity of students and professors who'd migrated to Kunming and there become part of Southwest Union University.

Chennault's new job was "chief flying instructor" under General Chou. He established a primary flight school at Yunnan-yi (Nanhua), 100 miles west on the road to Burma; an intermediate school at Mengzi on the Vietnam border; and an advanced school at Wujiaba airport outside Kunming. Eighteen Americans worked for Chennault over the next two years. Among the newcomers was C. B. (Skip) Adair, who came out with his wife to run the primary school at Yunnan-yi. Another was a radioman named John Williams, whom Chennault had known at Maxwell Field.

Kunming was a bitter pill for Chennault, who until the Russians arrived had been Chiang Kai-shek's factotum of the air. His health suffered in the chilly winters and damp summers, and he often took to his bed with bronchitis, colds, or pleurisy, whereupon Joseph Lee, a CAF flight surgeon, dosed him with sulfa drugs. Sick or well, Chennault played bridge, dominoes, mah-jongg, cribbage, and poker. He drank bourbon, sometimes to the point where he ended in a wrestling match in the early hours of the morning. In season, he hunted for ducks and doves. He played tennis obsessively—seven sets even on days when he was teaching cadets to fly. And he went wenching. Chennault in China was known as an "enviable cocksman," whose conquests included Rose Mok (Carney's wife or girlfriend) and the wife of another instructor, Harry Sutter.

Flying was a never-failing solace. Chennault flew beautifully, whether driving a twin-engine Douglas transport to Chongqing or stunting a Curtiss H-75 over Wujiaba—the latter, especially, a pretty thing to see. "Nobody flies a fighter like the Old Man," Butch Carney said. To John Williams, Chennault seemed to be the H-75's animating force, rather than its Wright Cyclone engine. "When he strapped on that plane," Williams told me, "he just seemed to lift it into the air."

The Japanese captured Canton and Hankou in the fall of 1938, and the Sino-Japanese War fell into stalemate along a no-man's-land 1,000 miles wide and 100 miles deep. Chiang's troops tore up the railroads, destroyed the bridges, and cratered the roads—the traditional Chinese response to invasion, in contrast to the set-piece battles at Shanghai, Nanjing, and Hankou. On the coastal side of the roadless zone was a Japanese army of 750,000 men. Inland was a Nationalist army far larger in size but woefully lacking in training, leadership, weapons, and morale.

Chiang's final capital was Chongqing in Sichuan province, northeast of Kunming. He brought the wealth of the nation with him: scores of banks and government bureaus, four hundred factories, forty thousand university students, millions of soldiers, and more millions of refugees. Before they arrived, Sichuan had a population of 50 million—a Britain or a France—and its principal city had two hundred thousand residents. What did they know of Chiang Kai-shek and the Sino-Japanese War? They learned soon enough, as Chongqing's population reached a million and the Japanese bombers arrived. The city's awakening was witnessed by Theodore White, a young Harvard graduate working for Chiang's Ministry of Information. The Chongqingese, he wrote, were "peasants born in the Middle Ages to die in the twentieth century." The city was shrouded in mist throughout its six-month winter; when spring came, the fog lifted and the planes came over like vultures that had waited all winter to feed. The date was May 3, 1939. "The bombers came from the north," wrote Teddy White, "out of the dusk, in serene, unbroken line-abreast formation, wing tip to wing tip, and laced their pattern through the very heart of the old city." Five thousand people burned to death—at the time, the most successful massacre in the history of aerial warfare.

Twenty raids followed. The twin-engine G3Ms came and went without escort, for the A5M fighter was too short-legged to make the trip and return to their base at Hankou.

Teddy White sometimes dined with Chennault at the Methodist mission in Chongqing. Like Olga Greenlaw, he noted that Chennault— "taciturn and courtly"—refused to take shelter when the bombers came over, but stood in the open and studied the Japanese formations "as a football coach studies films of a team he expects soon to meet in the field." The details went into Chennault's notebooks, and he fed them to James McHugh, a Marine Corps major who served as the naval attaché in Chongqing. McHugh in turn sent them to the Navy Department, where they met the same bureaucratic fate as Chennault's reports to the adjutant general.

Among the industries following Chiang Kai-shek to the west was CAMCO. Bill Pawley loaded his machine tools onto flatcars and sent them down to Hong Kong, thence by steamer to Hanoi in Vietnam. The Michelin was to have taken them to Kunming, but the French closed the railroad under Japanese pressure. Pawley shifted everything to Burma, and from Rangoon it traveled by barge, rail, plane, truck, and elephant-back to a lovely plateau at Loiwing, across the Chinese border in Yunnan province.

This route was now China's lifeline. From the Burmese railhead at Lashio, a track used by Marco Polo in the twelfth century had been straightened, widened, and paved with stone, by hundreds of thousands

With hand tools and muscle, conscripted laborers built the "Burma Road" across China's mountainous western border. For three years it was the most famous section of a lifeline stretching 2,000 miles from the British port of Rangoon to the Chinese capital at Chongqing. (National Archives)

of forced laborers. Journalists called it the Burma Road: 700 twisting mountain miles from Lashio to Kunming, over mountains that rose to 9,000 feet, through the mile-deep gorges of the Mekong and Salween rivers. Crude but lovely chain suspension bridges were thrown across the rivers; on either side, climbing in and out of the gorges, the road folded upon itself like Christmas candy, with terrifying turnouts at the outside of each loop.

At Loiwing, six thousand workmen built another factory, financed by China but owned in part by Bill Pawley, to whom the Aeronautical Commission awarded a contract for 55 H-75 fighters, 75 Vultee attack planes, and 33 CW-21 interceptors—Pawley's latest export marvel, a warplane derived from a Curtiss sport-racer.

After spending $4 million on the factory and $5.25 million on aircraft assemblies, Chiang hedged the bet by ordering a fleet of U.S.-built planes from Pat Patterson. Chennault regularly flew to Chongqing to work on this contract, which finally included 120 trainers, 25 dive bombers, and 54 Seversky P-35 fighters, for $8.8 million. But Pawley (as Patterson told me) sabotaged the deal, and in the process bankrupted the Seversky company. In the end, only the trainers reached Rangoon, and those too late, as Harvey Greenlaw discovered when he shifted his base of operations to Burma. The British were as nervous as the French, and as reluctant to offend the Japanese by letting their de facto colony become a supply route for China. The trainers remained in their crates on the Rangoon wharf, among growing piles of war matériel intended for Lashio and Kunming.

Still hedging, Chiang asked Pawley to scout the possibility of hiring U.S. pilots to replace the Russian "volunteers." The spokesman was Bruce Leighton, a retired naval officer whom Pawley had hired as vice president of his personal holding company, called Intercontinent. Leighton wangled an interview with Harold Stark, chief of naval operations. He argued that it was in America's interest to frustrate the Japanese occupation of China, which could be done by giving Chiang Kai-shek an air force of one hundred fighters, one hundred bombers, and fifty pilots, supplemented by the cadets Chennault was training in Kunming. The

Pawley family would handle the affair as a commercial enterprise, "without any direct participation by the United States Government." Chennault happened to be in the U.S. at this time. His contract provided for a month's vacation in the year, and toward the end of 1939 he flew to San Francisco on the "Clipper" flying-boat service of Pan American Airways—a five-day, island-hopping voyage across the Pacific. He visited his family, hunted waterfowl, and with his son John (now an army pilot) toured the Curtiss-Wright factory in Buffalo, New York. He also went to Washington, where his only certain activities were to brief an army intelligence officer on the CAF and to ask about his chances for returning to active duty. He then joined Bill Pawley and Bruce Leighton for a tour of aircraft factories in Southern California, before flying back to Kunming.

In the spring of 1940, German divisions overran Denmark and Norway, then Holland, Belgium, and Luxembourg. The French army and a British expeditionary force rushed into the Low Countries to stop them, only to have German tanks burst through the supposedly impassable Ardennes forest behind them. Cut off, three hundred thousand British soldiers were rescued from the beach at Dunkirk, leaving France to swift and humiliating defeat. For all practical purposes, the war on the continent was lost in nineteen days, leaving Britain as the only country opposing Adolf Hitler's hegemony in Europe. With patience and guile, President Franklin Roosevelt began to maneuver the United States into the position of Britain's savior.

Chiang Kai-shek took advantage of the new thinking, sending his brother-in-law to Washington to speed the flow of American aid to China. T. V. Soong was the most endearing member of a large, clever, and unscrupulous family. Like Madame Chiang, his sister, he got along well with Americans. He was a Harvard man; he spoke English more readily than Mandarin Chinese; and he was as neat as a doll, hair cut short and combed straight back, ears tucked against his head, and thin-rimmed spectacles reflecting the light. On July 9, he met with Henry Morgenthau, Roosevelt's portly, balding treasury secretary. On the table, with luncheon, was a proposal that the United States lend China $140 million to stabilize her currency, improve the Burma Road, and buy military supplies, including three hundred fighter planes and one hundred light bombers. The Pawley-Leighton proposal had been doubled.

Soong also cultivated Thomas Corcoran, Lauchlin Currie, and Joseph Alsop. The first was a lawyer, lobbyist, and member of Roosevelt's informal "kitchen cabinet" of advisers. The second was a Canadian-born economist and White House aide. The third was a bright young writer whose columns were published in seventy-four newspapers. Alsop was also related to Eleanor Roosevelt, hence to the president—not an insignificant qualification in prewar Washington, where the work got done through a network of friendship, kinship, and talent. Morgenthau routinely made decisions that belonged to the War and State departments, and Corcoran sometimes overruled Morgenthau when it came to determining the size of the federal budget.

The United States had already loaned China $70 million, to be repaid with exports of tin, tungsten, and tung oil. The transactions were handled by the Universal Trading Corporation, its staff composed mostly of bureaucrats detached from the government for that purpose. Though forbidden to deal in war matériel, Universal was clearly the purchasing agent for a nation at war: 1,000 portable ten-watt radios, 48,000 scalpels, 72,000 forceps, 4 million blankets, 6 million yards of khaki cloth . . . To these supplies—bound for Rangoon, Lashio, and the Burma Road— T. V. Soong was determined to add military planes and the pilots to fly them.

Chapter 2

The Special Air Unit

Every day, Japanese navy bombers roared up the Yangtse to Chongqing. Each of the gray, twin-engine G3Ms was freighted with 1,100 pounds of explosives, and they were sometimes joined by army bombers—Mitsubishi Ki-21s—with double the bomb load. "This thing . . . is beyond all description in its brutality," the American ambassador reported. "These daily visits of a hundred or more bombers swinging back and forth over a city of helpless people who cower for hours in dugouts where many are overcome just by the bad air, [or flee] up over the hills, old and young, mothers carrying babies under the hot sun, up, up the hills. . . ." Yet the CAF managed to shoot down nine G3Ms and damage three hundred—nearly 10 percent of the raiders, a toll regarded as prohibitive in Japanese service.

The losses were staunched by the introduction of a long-range escort fighter. The Mitsubishi A6M was a slender, cigar-shaped monoplane with an enclosed cockpit and retractable landing gear. It was as nimble as the A5M but could fly faster and farther, and was armed with two 20-mm cannon in addition to the usual rifle-caliber machine guns. On September 13, 1940, thirteen A6Ms claimed twenty-seven CAF interceptors shot down over Chongqing, so easily that a navy pilot boasted: "When we chase the enemy, we must be very careful not to get in front of him!" (Actual Chinese losses were thirteen planes.) The triumphant A6M was dubbed *reisen*—"Zero Fighter"—with the cipher standing for the year 2600, as the Japanese reckoned 1940.

The Japanese took advantage of the European war to move into Vietnam, giving them control of the Michelin railroad, vast rubber plantations, immense stores of rice—and Gia Lam airport outside Hanoi. From there, on September 30, navy bombers raided Kunming for the first time. Next day they destroyed the intermediate flight school at Mengzi. Six days later, they came out of the overcast to hit Kunming again: twenty-seven G3Ms and seven of the new long-range fighters. This was Chennault's first sight of the Zero, which he noted was "far superior" to the fighters he'd studied in the Yangtse Valley.

That week, Chennault was ordered to Chongqing. He went out to Wujiaba on Sunday morning, only to have the warning net report another Japanese formation: twenty-seven G3Ms, nine single-engine bombers, and half a dozen Zeros. Chennault fled the field in a battered Plymouth, the property of the new flight-school commander, Colonel Wang Shu-ming. The raid lasted three hours, wrecking Chennault's house among others. No CAF fighters got into the air.

With General Chou again directing the Aeronautical Commission, the Generalissimo decided to send Mao Pang-chu to Washington as air adviser to T. V. Soong. And to advise General Mao—who but Chennault? The idea came from Soong, who'd cabled on September 27: "It would assist in convincing authorities here if program . . . were supported by Colonel Chennault."

The Generalissimo evidently pumped Chennault on the subject of American planes and pilots, for on October 18 he had a proposal for the U.S. ambassador. "Japanese bombing goes unchallenged," Chiang explained, "and the people are filled with disquiet." The United States must send China a Special Air Unit of 500 planes and pilots, to relieve the pressure upon Chongqing and enable China to carry the war to the enemy's home islands, thus effecting a "fundamental solution" to Japanese aggression.

In Washington, Bruce Leighton was working along the same line, to judge by a letter from the secretary of the navy to the secretary of state. "I am told," Frank Knox wrote Cordell Hull, "there are a considerable number of American aviators who would be glad to volunteer their services to China . . . if they could be absolved from any penalty for such action. Is it at all possible that we can handle this matter . . . as we have handled the same situation with respect to young men volunteering for service in Great Britain[?]" In other words: discharge them from U.S. service and let them travel as civilians to another country, to join the foreign air force without taking an oath of allegiance.

On October 19—the day Frank Knox dictated his letter to Cordell Hull—Chennault was again summoned to Chongqing, and two days later he dined with Chiang Kai-shek and General Mao. "Ordered back to U.S. for duty with Dr. T. V. Soong," he wrote in his diary. Late the following afternoon, a Douglas transport of China National Airways Corporation (CNAC) took him and Mao to Hong Kong, where he caught the Pan Am Clipper to the United States.

The Japanese Army Air Force replaced the navy at Gia Lam airport, its mission to bomb the "aid-to-Chiang route" from the Burma border to Kunming. On October 26, fifty-nine Mitsubishi Ki-21s virtually demolished the new CAMCO factory at Loiwing, along with dozens of half-completed planes. But Bill Pawley had a genius for turning adversity into opportunity. He salvaged the machinery and aircraft assemblies and shipped them to Bangalore in India, where he set up shop as Hindustan Aircraft Ltd., building Harlow trainers for the Indian Air Force. Loiwing was rebuilt as a maintenance and repair facility for the CAF.

Pawley was about Chennault's age, though he looked a decade younger. A photograph shows him togged out in pinstripe suit, boutonniere, folded handkerchief, and what might be a diamond tiepin—an impressive man, though a bit flashy. ("Shifty as the devil," Major McHugh once wrote of him.) The British took to him, in any event. They not only let him set up a factory in India, but gave him what they'd refused Harvey Greenlaw: permission to set up a plant to assemble sixty-six North American and Ryan trainers still in their crates on the Rangoon wharf.

Chennault and Mao joined the infant China lobby at the end of October, beginning with dinner at T. V. Soong's home in suburban Chevy Chase, Maryland. Then they went to work in the Washington apartment of Arthur Young, financial adviser to Chiang's government. They developed a proposal for an air unit consisting of 250 air-cooled fighters, which Chennault knew and trusted from his own experience; 100 fighters powered by the liquid-cooled engines favored in Europe; and 150 bombers, 10 transports, 190 training planes, and 350 flight instructors and ground crewmen . . . but no pilots, unless the instructors were meant to fill that role. (It is a curious feature of these dealings that the pilot Chennault concentrated on acquiring hardware, while the salesman Pawley seemed more interested in recruiting pilots.) T. V. Soong presented the revised shopping list to the President's Liaison Committee on November 25.

By the end of 1940, warplanes were pouring out of American factories at a prodigious rate—ten a day in the case of the Curtiss-Wright plant in Buffalo. (Mitsubishi, by contrast, was building only one A6M Zero a day.) Roosevelt's "arsenal of democracy" had set out to build six thousand military aircraft in 1940, eighteen thousand in 1941, and fifty thousand in 1942—more planes than all other countries of the world combined. They were destined in the first place for Britain, her production crippled by German bombing, labor strife, and outmoded factories. After the RAF came the U.S. military, which was in the enviable position of acquiring aircraft after they had been improved to British specifications and the price driven down by British orders. Any leftovers were allocated to colonial air forces in the Pacific or to Sweden, Greece, or Brazil. In this pecking order, China had no place. The Sino-Japanese War was a sideshow—"yellow man killing yellow man," as *Time* magazine put it—compared to the epic conflict among the white nations of Europe.

While his genial brother-in-law made the rounds in Washington, Chiang Kai-shek played the tough cop from Chongqing, warning Roosevelt of a Japanese puppet regime in Nanjing. In earlier years a left-wing contender for the leadership of China, Wang Ching-wei had defected to the Japanese, who set him up as head of the Reorganized National Government. If Wang attracted support in China, Chiang warned, he would free Japan to move south, seizing oil from the Dutch Indies and perhaps joining hands with Germany and Italy across the Indian subcontinent. Duly alarmed, Roosevelt told his advisers to work up a loan for China. He also sent Lauchlin Currie to see the clever and useful Tommy Corcoran in his office at 1511 K Street, four blocks from the White House.

Corcoran's profession was an honorable one at the time, though it later fell into disrepute: he was a fixer. Nobody else had so many and such useful friendships in government, or maintained them so well. He eagerly performed such favors as Currie now asked of him: "to check with my friends on Capitol Hill [about the likely consequences] if the president sent modest aid to China just to forestall Chiang's surrender. I reported back to Currie: there'd be very little trouble as things then stood and were likely to stand in the near future."

He also interviewed Chennault. "If he had left in the first ten minutes," Corcoran mused, "I would have written him off as a fanatic." By the end of an hour, however, the aviator convinced the fixer, and Corcoran sent word to Roosevelt that they had found a useful weapon against Japan. He warned, however, that Chennault must be allowed to run his own show. Their relationship, he said in an analogy that flattered both men, would be that of Sir Francis Drake to Queen Elizabeth I. The president was convinced. "Roosevelt," Corcoran recalled in later years, "sent back orders for me to take Chennault around town and introduce him to . . . influential men who could keep their mouths shut."

The pivotal man was General George Marshall. On December 12, Chennault briefed the army chief of staff about the Mitsubishi Zero. Marshall was impressed, and he duly warned the State Department and his own subordinates about the "new fast pursuit plane [that] has grounded all the Chinese Air Force." But the warning didn't penetrate peacetime inertia and national pride. If Chennault was right, the Zero was better than anything in U.S. service—but that couldn't be. Everyone knew that the Japanese only built inferior copies of western machines.

China couldn't export enough tung oil, tin, and tungsten to pay for the aid T. V. Soong was requesting. A cash loan was needed, so Henry Morgenthau called his staff together on November 29. "The president just called me," he told them. "He is worried about China and he is evidently worried about something going on between Wang and Chiang, and he wants me to make a . . . loan of $50 million to the Chinese in the next twenty-four hours."

On cue, T. V. Soong appeared next day, blinking through his round lenses: the nice cop. Morgenthau haggled valiantly for the U.S. Treasury. "Well now," he began, "let me ask you, how much money have you in mind?"

"General Chiang asked for between $200 million and $300 million, that is what he asked for."

"What will you take?"

"Well, we are not choosers, Mr. Secretary."

"But as to take care of the immediate situation, say for six months—"

"I should imagine $100 million," Soong said.

After some haggling, Morgenthau tried again: "What would you call a minimum that might be helpful?"

"I should say $100 million," Soong repeated.

"Okay," said Morgenthau.

So it was settled, except for finding the planes. Not even this was outside Morgenthau's jurisdiction, and a solution emerged at a meeting the following Sunday. Curtiss-Wright was building 630 liquid-cooled Tomahawk fighters for the Royal Air Force, and it had parts on hand for even more. The company was eager to build the extra planes, to use up its inventory and keep the Buffalo plant running at capacity. So China's needs could be met simply by extending the production run.

Morgenthau didn't mention this possibility to Soong when they met later that day, December 8. Instead they talked bombers: "After lunch at the White House," Morgenthau wrote in his diary, "T. V. Soong was with me going back in the car and . . . I said that I had read General Chiang Kai-shek's memorandum. . . . I said, 'Well, his asking for 500 planes is like asking for 500 stars.' I then said that we might get him planes by 1942, but what did he think of the idea of some long range bombers with the understanding that they were to be used to bomb Tokyo and other Japanese cities? Well, to say he was enthusiastic is putting it mildly."

Enthusiastic, indeed. Soong checked with Chongqing, and in a week was back with a higher bid. What China really needed was that marvel of American aeronautical engineering, the Boeing B-17 Flying Fortress, so jealously guarded that not even the British had acquired it. Thus armed, Chiang promised, he would not only bomb the Japanese homeland but move south to recapture Canton and Hankou, preventing a likely Japanese move against the British fortress at Singapore.

The B-17s came up at a December 19 meeting between Roosevelt and the secretaries most concerned—Morgenthau for the treasury, Hull for the State Department, Knox for the navy, and Henry Stimson for the army. (Mrs. Stimson called them the Plus Four.) They studied a map that purported to show 136 airfields in East China, including one only 600 miles from Nagasaki. "The President was delighted," Morgenthau told Soong next day. "I said, and I hope you will back me up, that if they could get [American pilots] who knew how to fly these four-engine bombers, that China would be glad to pay up to $1,000 a month in United States dollars. Was that too high?"

"No," said Soong. "Not at all." Money was no object, since like the planes and pilots it would come from the United States.

The China lobby gathered at Morgenthau's house Saturday evening. The treasury secretary directed his questions to Soong, who deferred to General Mao, who deferred to Chennault. In this fashion, it was agreed that American pilots would fly the B-17s to the Philippines, where they'd be released from active duty and paid $1,000 a month to take them to China . . . and eventually to Japan. Each B-17 would be accompanied by five American mechanics, with the CAF providing gunners and radiomen. Then Morgenthau, his pince-nez glasses sparkling, advanced an idea of his own: "inasmuch as the Japanese cities were all made of just wood and paper," perhaps they could carry incendiary bombs? A splendid idea, Chennault said, pointing out that this plan had the additional advantage (incendiaries being lighter than high explosives) of allowing the B-17s to carry more fuel and thus fly deeper into Japanese airspace.

That the scheme got no further was due to General Marshall. Tall, aristocratic, and everyone's candidate for Washington's most honorable man, he wasn't particularly troubled by the ethics of the proposal. Rather, he wanted the B-17s to go to Britain.

Stimson, too, was having second thoughts. The scheme was "half-baked," the army secretary decided, and he asked Marshall, Knox, and

Morgenthau to his home that Sunday—a beautiful afternoon, virtually a second Indian Summer—"to get some mature brains into it." The brains were Marshall's, and Morgenthau capitulated to the general's cool logic. By Monday morning, only fighter planes remained on the table.

Cordell Hull convened the next meeting at the State Department. It was attended by the Plus Four and assorted civilian and military advisers, including General Marshall and Admiral Stark. Morgenthau opened the discussion. Curtiss-Wright, he said, could build three hundred extra Tomahawks in the spring of 1941. How to spread them around? Like boys choosing sides in a baseball game, the great men haggled, their words recorded by a secretary who could scarcely follow the argument. In the end, it was decided that the British should divert to China one hundred Tomahawks out of current production, and in return get three hundred later-model aircraft.

Roosevelt approved the deal that afternoon, December 23, and at 5:30 PM Morgenthau met with the British to nail down such details as where the "GFE"—government-furnished equipment—would come from. Warplanes were customarily ordered without engines, guns, or electronics. In this case, the British had arranged to buy engines from the Allison division of General Motors, and large-caliber nose guns from U.S. Army stores, but had made no provision for wing guns, radios, or modern gunsights. Once the planes reached North Africa, these items would be supplied from British stocks or cannibalized from fighters no longer fit for combat.

Neither Morgenthau nor the British thought to raise the question of "GFE" for the planes to be diverted to China.

After Christmas, Chennault went to Buffalo "to see the Curtiss-Wright people and negotiate for the planes and see their performance." (He'd served with the company's president in the Army Air Corps.) This may have been his first view of the Tomahawk, though he knew the airframe as well as his face in the mirror: it was his old friend, the Curtiss H-75 (P-36, in U.S. service) fitted with a new engine, heavier guns, and protection for its pilot and fuel tanks. From the moment it went into service, the P-36 had been outclassed by the liquid-cooled fighters coming on line in Europe. Curtiss chief designer Donovan Berlin therefore replaced its air-cooled Pratt & Whitney engine with an Allison V-1710 from General Motors. The horsepower was the same, but the Allison's cylinders were arranged in two rows of six, allowing Berlin to streamline the fighter's nose and thereby increase its speed.

At the same time, its appearance changed radically. Where the earlier version had the stubby, no-nonsense look typical of air-cooled fighters, its replacement was slender as a fish, its lines broken only by an air scoop beneath and behind the propeller spinner. (Ultimately, all engines are cooled by air. In the Allison, the heat was first soaked up by a bath of ethylene glycol—trade name Prestone—then dissipated through a radiator.) Berlin's first drawings had the air scoop on the plane's belly, but he moved it forward after wind-tunnel tests showed that the new location would cause less drag. The result was a plane with a distinct face: the conical spinner suggested a nose, the air scoop a mouth. To the company, this was Curtiss model H-81. The U.S. Army adopted it as the P-40, and the Royal Air Force as the Tomahawk.

Chennault didn't like liquid-cooled engines, since a single bullet could cause a coolant leak that would disable the plane. But he appreciated the tradeoff between frontal area and speed, and he liked other features of the redesign. The original P-40 boasted two fifty-caliber (half-inch) machine guns in its nose and two thirty-caliber guns in the wings. The British bought several hundred, then asked for two more wing guns, bullet-resistant windshield, armor plate behind the pilot, and a wraparound rubber membrane to keep gasoline from spilling if a fuel tank were hit. This was the Tomahawk II, which the U.S. Army adopted as its P-40B. By the time Chennault reached Buffalo, another refinement had been made: an interior fuel-tank membrane, which did a better job of stopping leaks. This was the Tomahawk IIB.

Though they bought it by the hundreds, the British didn't like the Tomahawk. With a single-stage mechanical supercharger, its Allison engine was woefully inadequate above 20,000 feet, and high-altitude combat was the norm in Europe. The planes therefore went to North Africa, where fighting usually took place at lower altitudes.

As part of the deal for its Tomahawks, China agreed to take them just as they came off the assembly line. Their topsides were painted in standard RAF camouflage—alternating bands of brown and green, called "sand and spinach"—and their undersides light gray. There were even "holes" in the paint job, on the wings and fuselage, where the British roundels, or recognition disks, were to have been applied.

Unknown to the Chinese, Curtiss evidently took advantage of the one-hundred-plane order to use up its stock of outmoded parts. Most important, the China-bound fighters came off the assembly line with fuel tanks from the earlier run of Tomahawk IIs, with their less effective exterior membranes. There were other anomalies as well. Perhaps in recognition of these differences, Curtiss logged the China-bound fighters on its books with a new designation, H-81-A3.

The bill for the airframes came to $4.5 million. In violation of the China Trade Act, it was paid by Universal Trading Corp. in New York.

By this time, General Mao had flown back to China, accompanied by Lauchlin Currie. Roosevelt's aide, whose high starched collars, rimless spectacles, and thinning hair gave him the look of a clerk in a Dickens novel, was to tour Nationalist China on behalf of the president. Chennault was left to work out the details of acquiring the Tomahawks, equipping them, and finding people to fly and maintain them. His first step was to draft a table of organization calling for 100 pilots and 150 ground crewmen. "American pilots," he argued, "cannot operate efficiently and successfully in China unless supported by American technical and clerical personnel."

Bill Pawley knew about the Tomahawks, and as Curtiss-Wright representative in China he expected to receive a 10 percent commission on the deal. He also expected CAMCO or Intercontinent (he used the names interchangeably) to assemble the planes in Burma. Twelve miles north of Rangoon, his brother Ed had leased a plot of land near Mingaladon airport and brought ninety Chinese workers and their American foremen down from Loiwing to assemble the trainers left in Rangoon by Harvey Greenlaw. Mingaladon was Burma's largest airfield, guarded by the Royal Air Force, so it was the obvious place to assemble the China-bound Tomahawks.

Logically, too, CAMCO-Intercontinent would be hired to recruit

American military personnel. On February 18, Bill Pawley cabled his brother in Rangoon: "Negotiating extensive training program requiring employment by CAMCO of approximately . . . 100 pilots 150 technical including mechanics clerks radio operators doctors nurses. . . . [General Mao] possibly familiar with part of program. Diplomatically ascertain progress he is making in providing facilities such as quarters fields but do not disclose any information. One hundred P-40's purchased 35 being shipped immediately balance soon. Intercontinent signed contract covering assembly and flight test Rangoon. Special revolving fund being arranged New York payment of expenses this program." If a contract existed, no trace survives, and it is odd that Pawley's manpower figures were identical to Chennault's. Was he really negotiating, or was he catching up with events?

Each China-bound Tomahawk was fitted into two crates, the fuselage and engine in one and the wing assembly, tail, and propeller in the other. Railway flatcars took the crates to Weehawken, New Jersey, where they were loaded into the hold of a Norwegian freighter, which cleared Ambrose Lightship on February 19, bound for Rangoon via South Africa and the Indian Ocean.

At the Treasury Department, Henry Morgenthau learned that his obligations didn't end with the shipment. On February 21, a dreary Thursday in the capital, his telephone rang shortly after 9 AM, and Tommy Corcoran's voice came on the line, at once urgent, confidential, and soothing. After some banter, he got down to business: "Soong has asked . . . me to represent him in some things. . . . He said that this is not a trading business, this has to do with things after you get the planes." The best course, he thought, was to bypass Universal Trading Corp. with its restrictions on military aid. What they needed was a separate company, controlled by Corcoran instead of some wheeler-dealer who might "bring all kinds of influence to bear and who might not play ball."

"Well, all those things are true, Tom," Morgenthau replied, "but you don't know what the nature of it is?"

"Well, may I talk on this line?"

"Yes, you can."

"What Soong wants me to do," Corcoran said, "is to help him recruit pilots . . . to go over and wrangle for him with the army and the navy to have them practically order certain men to enlist in the Chinese Air Force."

The new company was China Defense Supplies, located in the Chinese embassy. T. V. Soong was chairman, and Roosevelt's elderly uncle, Frederic Delano, signed on as "honorary counselor." The work was done by youngsters from the Ivy League network. "My brother David took a leave of absence from Sterling Drug to become president," Corcoran recalled (Sterling was one of the companies that employed him as a fixer). "A friendly and influential congressman loaned me William Brennan to serve as our full time congressional liaison. . . . The Marine Corps supplied an intelligence officer and Harvard Law man, Major Quinn [Shaughnessy], to be our eyes and ears around the War Department. . . . Finally, there was Whitey Willauer, my brother Howie's roommate at Exeter, Princeton, and Harvard Law." Tommy Corcoran wasn't on the payroll. "By design I took no title," he recalled, "and only earned a modest $5,000 fee for putting the company together."

Returning from China at the end of March, Lauchlin Currie leaked details of the "Special Air Program" to Joe Alsop. China needed a few dozen bombers and two hundred fighter planes, wrote the columnist. "With this comparative handful of supplies, the Chinese think they could knock spots out of the Japanese invaders." Furthermore, the planes could "drop incendiary bombs on Japan's concentrated, almost undefended *paper and matchwood* industrial areas [my italics]." There was no mention of who'd fly them.

Currie took Chennault to see his old antagonist at the War Department. Even with a presidential assistant in the room, Hap Arnold wouldn't release pilots for China. It wasn't only that he preferred to have them flying for the U.S. Army; he needed them even more to train thirty thousand cadets in 1941, as the air force geared up for the war that was sure to come. Chennault and Currie fared no better with John Towers of the U.S. Navy.

Tommy Corcoran had better luck behind the scenes. One Harvard man to another, he sent the president a copy of A. E. Housman's "Epitaph on an Army of Mercenaries" who *saved the sum of things for pay.* As Corcoran recalled: "If Roosevelt was troubled by the soiled label that Chennault's irregulars might wear, he was moved by the poem's wisdom. It bolstered his determination to act as forcefully as political constraints allowed." With the president's blessing, Corcoran met with the army and navy secretaries and promised that Chennault wouldn't pillage either service but would take a few pilots from each. The agreement was never more formal than that. Knox wrote a letter allowing China's recruiters into navy facilities, and Stimson authorized them to visit army airfields.

At the Colt factory in Hartford, Connecticut, Morgenthau's scouts located some machine guns chambered for the 7.92-mm cartridge commonly used in Asia. Universal Trading Corp. bought them, and the British agreed to release some .303-caliber Brownings—altogether, enough wing guns for 50 Tomahawks. Universal ordered 100 two-way radios from RCA, of a type intended for civilian sports planes, and it bought 150 Allison engines from General Motors—those delivered with the Tomahawks, plus 50 spares that Allison apparently assembled from parts rejected for use in British and American aircraft. Universal also had to reimburse the U.S. Army for the large-caliber nose guns provided at the factory, and apparently it also bought a quantity of sophisticated gunsights from the army. With ammunition, the "GFE" seems to have doubled the price of the fighters: Universal spent $9.3 million for aircraft in the first half of 1941, and the Tomahawks were the only planes on order.

The wing guns reached Weehawken in time to sail with the second lot of Tomahawks. Then Bill Pawley threatened to stop the shipment unless Curtiss-Wright paid his $450,000 commission. Morgenthau called the principals to his office on April 1 and knocked heads together. Pawley settled for $250,000, to be paid by the Chinese, and he also got the contract to assemble the planes in Burma. All obstacles cleared, the Tomahawks sailed for the long voyage around South Africa.

On April 15, CAMCO was further employed as recruiter and fiscal agent for what would eventually be known as the 1st American Volunteer Group—not that any such organization was specified. Rather, Bill Pawley and T. V. Soong seemed to have joined hands in an educational enterprise: "The [Chinese] Government intends to establish three advanced instruction and training units . . . equipped substantially as follows: eighteen American active trainers [airplanes] plus

50 percent reserves, plus necessary complement of ground transport, field repair equipment, night landing floodlights, portable radio communication sets, clerical equipment, etc. The operation of these units in China shall be under the immediate direction of an American supervisor."

Gene Pawley, the youngest brother, advertised in the *Los Angeles Times* for "aviation people for work overseas." Among the respondents were Byron Glover, a burly test pilot, and Walter Pentecost, a balding Allison engine specialist. They signed up at Vail Field after an interview with two CAMCO foremen. (Pentecost's contract, when he received it, turned out to be with Intercontinent, indicating how porous were the boundaries between Pawley's holding company and the manufacturing enterprise he owned in partnership with the Chinese.) Then they met Gene and Bill Pawley, who treated them to a slide show of the Burmese countryside. "I didn't care what they showed me," Pentecost said. "It was something different, and I was ready." He sailed from Los Angeles on April 24.

Byron Glover went by Pan Am Clipper to Hong Kong, thence by CNAC to Chongqing and Rangoon, arriving before Pentecost. He found that CAMCO had no access to Mingaladon airport, requiring the planes to detour along the highway. A contractor was building an assembly hangar of brick and bamboo thatch; Glover asked for it to be trussed with steel, and for an outdoor U-frame hoist to be set up nearby, so assembly could start immediately.

Rangoon had several companies fabricating truck bodies for the Burma Road. (The trucks came to Rangoon in knockdown form, to be assembled as cab-and-chassis at a General Motors plant near the docks.) Glover went to one of these entrepreneurs and ordered a trailer big enough for a crate 35 feet long, 10 feet high, and 6 feet wide. More Chinese workers arrived, swelling the CAMCO crew to 130. Though passed through immigration as civilians, they were actually CAF mechanics from Kunming, where Colonel Wang believed that the Tomahawks were intended for him. They were bossed by the same American foremen who—at Hangzhou, Hankou, Loiwing, and Mingaladon—had assembled Hawk fighter bombers, Vultee attack planes, Curtiss H-75s, and North American and Ryan trainers for the CAF.

Following local custom, CAMCO hired Indians for the heavy work, muscling a four-ton fuselage crate onto a trailer at the docks and unloading it at Mingaladon. At the assembly area, forty or fifty Indians pried off the top and sides, slid 4-inch steel pipes under the floor, and rolled it to the outdoor hoist, which lifted the fuselage free. Next came the wing crate, weighing a ton and a half. The assembly was picked up by "as many coolies as could conveniently get a grip on the wing without getting in each other's way." They walked it to the fuselage, set it on padded wooden supports, and lowered the body onto it, to be mated with forty-four large bolts. Chinese mechanics hooked up the hydraulic system, cranked down the wheels, and rolled the Tomahawk away, making room at the hoist for another fuselage.

The AVG had already suffered its first losses. The first Tomahawk uncrated proved to be missing so many items it couldn't be made airworthy, so it was set aside as a "Christmas tree" of parts that had failed or were missing on other planes. The wing of another had been dropped into Rangoon harbor, salvaged, and stacked with the rest; by the time it was uncrated, saltwater corrosion had ruined the aluminum skin. That fuselage, too, was set aside for cannibalization.

The first Tomahawk uncrated at Mingaladon was also the last assembled there, hence the "99th" daubed on the fuselage of this plane. When flown up to Toungoo, it went on the AVG roster as P-8101. The mat sheds kept the metal from becoming too hot to touch. (Walter Pentecost photo, National Air and Space Museum)

After a fuselage and wing were mated, a truck towed the Tomahawk out to the highway on its own wheels, thence to the airport, where the British allowed CAMCO to do final assembly. Seen from the air, the gravel runways of Mingaladon formed the letter A, chalked upon a green slate, with the crosspiece extending beyond one leg. CAMCO was located at the south, near the apex of the A.

The monsoon arrived in May, bringing squalls so violent they could strip the paint from the leading edge of a wing. The Indians built a crushed-stone taxi strip from CAMCO's final assembly area to the runway, so the Tomahawks wouldn't bog down. The temperature dropped to a more tolerable 95 degrees, at the price of a humidity so high it rotted shoes, belts, and tires. "When it is not raining the sun is shining brilliantly and the air is both very hot and very humid," Glover recalled. "It was found necessary to drain the water from all fuel tanks and to drain the fuel strainers immediately prior to each flight. The sun shining on the unprotected airplanes caused the metal to get so hot that the workman could not touch them. This necessitated the construction of about eight mat sheds . . . under which the aircraft could be placed when it was necessary to work on them." On June 12, he test-flew the first of the Tomahawks. It was designated P-8113: pursuit plane, Curtiss model 81, from the thirteenth crate to be opened at Mingaladon.

Meanwhile, Chennault and Currie were searching for more planes. Their first coup was 144 air-cooled, steel-and-wood Vultee Vanguard fighters. They were built for Sweden, but the U.S. government canceled the contract, and the British agreed to take them, for fear they'd fall into German hands. Turning them over to China would save Britain several million dollars while costing the Chinese nothing, since the transaction could be handled under the "lend-lease" program recently authorized by Congress. To satisfy the letter of the law, the Vanguards were first adopted by the U.S. Army, which gave them the designation P-66.

Then the army—"ever helpful in steering Chinese demands away from its own prospective equipment"—let the China lobby know that Republic Aviation also had some fighters available. Republic had arisen from the ashes of the Seversky company, bankrupted when China's order for P-35s fell through. The new management updated Seversky's design as the P-43 Lancer, but the U.S. Army now required fighters with pilot armor and self-sealing fuel tanks. Republic sketched its redoubtable P-47 Thunderbolt to meet these requirements, but meanwhile it needed a customer for 125 unwanted Lancers. Who but China?

Chennault and Currie drafted a "Short-term Aircraft Program for China" to include the Vanguards, the Lancers, and 100 twin-engine bombers diverted from British orders. With the Tomahawks already shipped, Chiang would thus receive 469 aircraft, nearly fulfilling his request for a 500-plane Special Air Unit. "If this program were adopted," Chennault and Currie wrote, "China would possess . . . a respectable air force, judged by Far Eastern standards, which should be sufficient to (a) protect strategic points, (b) permit local army offensive action, (c) permit the bombing of Japanese air bases and supply dumps in China and Indochina [Vietnam] . . . and (d) *permit occasional incendiary bombing of Japan*. . . . Ships comprised in the above program would all be flown by American reserve officers and maintained by American technicians and mechanics. They would be under the command of an American reserve officer, Captain Chennault, directly under Chiang Kai-shek. To improve discipline and efficiency, 4 or 5 staff officers from the Army Air Corps are urgently desired. *The opportunity for our men to acquire actual combat experience appears to be a factor that should be given some weight.*"

My italics. Make no mistake: this was a proposal for U.S. airmen, flying U.S.-built planes, to go into combat against the Empire of the Sun, and even to carry out fire raids on the Japanese homeland.

Chapter 3

Too Good to Be True

To recruit pilots for the American Volunteer Group, Bill Pawley employed Richard Aldworth, widely but wrongly believed to have flown for France before the U.S. entered World War I. Aldworth was bedridden that spring at Walter Reed Army Hospital, so someone else was needed to do the legwork. Skip Adair from the flight school at Yunnan-yi was available: a flight of Zeros had strafed the airfield toward the end of 1940, destroying twenty training planes and persuading Adair it was time to go home. Chennault signed him on as an army recruiter. A retired U.S. Navy commander, Rutledge Irvine, was scouting naval bases even before CAMCO got the contract to recruit for China. Supposedly there were others, and Chennault claimed to have been threatened with arrest at Hamilton Field while looking for pilots. But no AVG veteran remembers being signed up by anyone except Irvine, Skip Adair, or (toward the end of the summer) Richard Aldworth with his aura of the Lafayette Escadrille.

In almost every case, potential volunteers were offered the rank of pilot officer, paying $600 a month and (they were told) equivalent to first lieutenant in the U.S. Army. For an especially qualified man, there was the possibility of appointment as flight leader, $675 a month and supposedly equivalent to captain.

These were heady offers. Most of the pilots approached by CAMCO were serving at the lowest commissioned level—second lieutenant or ensign—and at least one was an enlisted man. Signing up with CAMCO thus meant instant promotion and double or triple what they earned in U.S. service. The recruiters also promised a bounty for each Japanese plane they shot down, but in terms so vague that not everyone believed it.

Irvine's first prospects were a couple of dive-bomber pilots on *Ranger,* one of two U.S. Navy aircraft carriers on the Atlantic Coast. Twenty-two years old and fresh out of flight school, Eddie Rector had joined *Ranger* the previous summer to fly one of its monoplane Vought SB2U Vindicators, which did double duty as scout planes and dive bombers. Rector was a North Carolina native, medium height, handsome as a movie star. After his first tour with the fleet, supporting U.S. Marines practicing amphibious assaults on Cuba, *Ranger* brought him back to Norfolk, Virginia. There, on New Year's Day 1941, he met a new pilot. He was tall and lanky, with jug ears, a worried expression, and an unlikely background: born in Japanese-occupied Korea, the son of a missionary who later became chaplain to the Texas Rangers. This was David Hill, who of course was called Tex.

Ranger took them to the Caribbean for further landing exercises, then home again to Norfolk. "The word spread," Rector told me in 1986, "that there was this guy looking for people to go out and fly for China." He and Hill decided to look into it. In what would become a familiar script over the next four months, they went to a Norfolk hotel room to meet Rutledge Irvine. He promised them exciting work, fabulous pay, and all in a worthy cause. Pilots were needed, Irvine said, to stop the Japanese from bombing the Burma Road and enable China to continue to receive supplies from the west. As Rector recalled Irvine's pitch, he showed them a map that included Rangoon, Kunming, and Chongqing. "The only way the Chinese can keep fighting," Irvine told them, "is to maintain the supplies that come up the Burma Road, and you will go over there under the command of Colonel Chennault and you will defend the Burma Road all the way up to Kunming, the capital of Yunnan province."

"You will go over there under the command of Colonel Chennault and you will defend the Burma Road all the way up to Kunming." In the mile-deep gorges of the Mekong and Salween rivers, the road looped upon itself like Christmas candy, obliging trucks to back and fill at every turn. (National Archives)

"Well, hell," Rector recalls saying, "we're interested." But he had doubts—not about the job, but the likelihood that it would ever come to pass. Back at their billets, he mourned: "Tex, this is too good to be true. This will never happen; they'll never let us go."

Their next assignment was even more exciting than the Cuban landings. *Ranger* escorted British convoys out to a line drawn from Iceland to the Azores—the entire North Atlantic, for all practical purposes. Here, in what President Franklin Roosevelt, with astonishing panache, had defined as U.S. waters, the airmen swept out in front of the convoys, look-

ing for German submarines. If they saw anything threatening, they radioed the information to the carrier, which informed the Royal Navy
destroyers that made the actual attack. Officially, this duty was "neutrality patrol." American sailors called it "the secret war." Whenever *Ranger*
returned to Norfolk, Commander Irvine met his prospects with news of
the fighter group being readied for service in China.

S kip Adair was doing similar work at U.S. Army airfields. Adair was
thirty-two, tall, dark-haired, and sober. He made an especially rich
strike at Mitchel Field on Long Island, where he signed up nine pilots from
the 8th Pursuit Group, all with experience in the Curtiss P-40B, virtually
identical to the Tomahawks diverted to China. Among them was Parker
Dupouy, an engineering graduate from Brown University, who explained
that he volunteered because Asian duty seemed less dangerous than serving in Europe. "It seemed to me," he told me, "that sooner or later we
would be in the war, and I would rather be shooting Japanese than Germans. That was wrong, but I didn't know it at the time."

The same thought occurred to Albert Probst, a redheaded second
lieutenant at Maxwell Field in Alabama. Skip Adair turned up one day,
looking for a pilot named Baumler (also first-named Albert, but better
known as Ajax) who'd flown as a volunteer in the Spanish Civil War. Red
Probst explained that the former soldier of fortune was temporarily assigned to Eglin Field in Florida. "Adair then started talking to me," he told
an interviewer in the 1970s, "and the first thing I knew, he had recruited
me." Probst was in debt, and he figured that shooting down Japanese
bombers would be both safe and lucrative: "Let's see now," he mused. "I
am making $210 a month now, and you are going to pay me $600. I get a
free trip to China, and if we go to war with somebody, I won't be on the
first string, but the second string. I don't want to have anything to do with
them Germans, so I'm going to get over there and help those Chinese."

Ajax Baumler didn't wait to be recruited. According to Matthew
Kuykendall, then at Eglin, the combat veteran knew "most of the brass in
the Air Corps" because of his escapade in Spain. Hearing that pilots were
needed for the Chinese Air Force, Baumler commandeered a Seversky
P-35 and flew up to Washington to check out the rumor. He returned

with a contract and assured Kuykendall that he, too, could qualify for service in China. A cautious type, Kuykendall didn't commit himself until he returned to Maxwell Field and talked to his buddies. Then he signed up, along with Red Probst and two more.

Eddie Rector was perfectly willing to fly against Germans, given the chance. But that did not seem likely, and by the end of June he was ready to sign the contract Irvine was offering. "All I'd ever lived for since I was twelve years old," he told me, "was to fly airplanes, and I [thought] if I'm going to fly combat airplanes, I want to smell a little cordite, and this is my opportunity to do so. But more important than that was the fact that I'd read everything Kipling had ever written, and I was just fascinated with that part of the world—Burma, India, China—*the old Moulmein Pagoda, looking eastward to the sea.* I thought: This is my opportunity to see it, and I'll get paid for it. . . . And I thought: My God, I've come along in life at the proper time. And those two things are why I signed up."

Tex Hill signed, too. "I'd always wanted to go back to the Orient," he told an interviewer in 1962. "But the thing that motivated me to go to China was, more or less, adventure. I had no particular dedication to anything." Also joining from *Ranger* was Bert Christman, who as a civilian had worked as a comic-strip artist for Associated Press Feature Service, chronicling the adventures of Scorchy Smith, an American mercenary pilot who flew and fought in Latin America. As Rector told the story, when the three young men announced they were resigning their commissions, the base commander climbed aboard his personal seaplane and flew to Washington to complain to Admiral Stark himself. The commander flew back to Norfolk a chastened man, Rector recalled, his protest rebuffed with the words: "This is presidentially approved, and that is *it.*"

Across the continent in San Diego, the commander of *Saratoga* was similarly rebuffed when he tried to stop four dive-bomber pilots from resigning. One was Bob Neale. Tall and rugged, nervous and shy, Neale had three years of fleet duty behind him, and he expected to be discharged soon—not a happy prospect for a lad who'd joined the navy to escape the Great Depression, and who couldn't imagine an economy in which jobs were plentiful. "And as far as knowing what I was getting into," Neale said, "the country or the people [or] the living conditions, I didn't have the faintest idea. It was an adventure, not motivated by patriotism or anything like that. . . . Looking back on it, actually, I don't know why I went out there." The navy owed him almost $1,500 in pay and accrued leave. Neale took his discharge and used the money to finance his wedding on June 19.

Also on *Saratoga* was Bob Layher, who'd tried to volunteer for British, Dutch, and Canadian air forces, so as to escape the boredom of peacetime service. Each time, the navy refused to let him go. Layher's deliverance came in a telephone call from one of his shipmates, Henry Geselbracht, who told him in great excitement: "I've got a deal here!"

"What do you mean, a deal?"

"We can get out of the navy and go to China."

"Sign me up," Layher said.

But Irvine wanted experienced fighter pilots, as Layher recalled: "It cost us about three fifths of Scotch to get this nice guy [persuaded]. We wouldn't give up on him until he said he'd sign us up, about eight o'clock in the morning, and before he sobered up he had us signed up."

As a bonus, Irvine got a fighter pilot from *Saratoga*. This was James Howard, a gangling young man (in his wartime photographs, he bears a striking resemblance to the young Prince Charles) on temporary duty with the carrier. Like Tex Hill, Howard was born in Asia—in Canton, where his father had been a medical missionary—and wanted to see it again. "But the overriding reason," Howard said, in words that echoed Hill's, "was my yearning for adventure and action." Having flown the navy's new Grumman F4F Wildcat, he evidently impressed Irvine, who signed him on as a flight leader.

At Randolph Field in Texas, R. T. Smith and Paul Greene were sweating through the summer of 1941 as flight instructors. They were hostages to the great military expansion that President Roosevelt had ordered into effect: just out of flight school, they'd been kept at Randolph to teach new cadets, as the air force grew exponentially. R. T. especially had little hope of becoming a fighter pilot. A recent directive said that anyone taller than five-foot-ten couldn't be assigned to fighters, and he stood well over six feet. He read about the recruiting drive in *Time* magazine, which reported that one hundred Curtiss P-40s had been supplied to China, and that pilots were on the way. "For the past few months," the magazine reported, "tall, bronzed American airmen have been quietly slipping away from east- and west-coast ports, making their way to Asia." Actually, no pilots had left, but Smith and Greene were panicked that they might miss out on the great adventure. They asked around, got the recruiter's address, and sent him a telegram: "We each have a thousand hours flying time and are ready to go." Skip Adair met them a week later at the Gunter hotel in San Antonio, but turned them down when he learned that they'd never flown anything hotter than a North American BT-9 trainer. They returned next evening with a bottle of I.W. Harper. When Adair was mellow enough, they put the case to him again, and this time he signed them up.

A likelier prospect was Charlie Bond, whom the army had trained as a fighter pilot, then assigned to the Ferry Command. Movie-star handsome like Eddie Rector—like Smith and Greene, for that matter—the stocky young man would fly a Lockheed Hudson bomber from Long Beach to Montreal, turn it over to a Canadian pilot, and board a commercial airliner for the trip back to California. It was a boring routine for a man who'd set out to fly the hottest planes in the sky, so Bond was a ready listener when a friend called one night with the news that fighter pilots were needed in China. He asked around and got the number of a "Colonel Green" in Washington—probably Claire Chennault at China Defense Supplies.

"The next day I called Colonel Green's office," Bond recalled in a 1984 memoir, "giving name and duty station. In addition I told the secretary the names of two of my closest friends, who also were ferry pilots— George Burgard and James D. Cross. Within twenty-four hours a wire arrived at our headquarters, informing our commander that three of his pilots were resigning and were to be released immediately from active duty."

At Pensacola Naval Air Station in Florida, so many flight instructors wanted to sign up that the base commander tore the list in half. John (Gil) Bright and John Donovan made the cut, along with Hank Gilbert, fresh out of flight school, and a forty-three-year-old enlisted pilot named Louis Hoffman. Dick Rossi—in the wrong half of the alphabet—should have stayed behind with the training command. But Rossi went to the recruiter and signed up anyhow. "When you're young, you're looking for adventure, more than anything else," he explained. "Also I was put out because I'd been assigned as an instructor instead of to the fleet." Rossi was twenty-six, a former merchant sailor.

A prize catch, or so he seemed, was Greg Boyington, twenty-eight and a first lieutenant in the U.S. Marines. He was hired on the spot as a flight leader. Broad-shouldered, thin-hipped, with the moody face of a Cherokee setting out on the Trail of Tears, Boyington was a heavy drinker, through nights that would end with the challenge: "I'll wrestle anybody in the crowd!" He'd grown up believing his stepfather to be his natural parent, and he graduated from the University of Washington, married, and became a draftsman at Boeing Aircraft under the name of Hallenbeck. When he learned his birth name, he seized the chance to start anew as a bachelor and an aviation cadet. (Navy and marine pilots couldn't marry for two years after earning their gold wings.) The lie had since caught up with him, and he was required to report each month on how he'd distributed his salary among those with a claim on it, including his ex-wife and three children.

Boyington described his recruiter as a retired captain and a veteran of the Lafayette Escadrille. This was Richard Aldworth. The pitch was delivered in the usual downtown hotel room. "The Japs are flying antiquated junk over China," Aldworth assured him. "Many of your kills will be unarmed transports. I suppose you know that the Japanese are renowned for their inability to fly. And they all wear corrective glasses."

"Captain," said Boyington, "it's quite a setup, but how do you know the pilots wear glasses?"

"Our technical staff determines this from the remains after a shoot-down. . . . Best of all, there's good money in it—$675 per month. But the sky's the limit," Aldworth went on, "because they pay a bonus of $500 for each Japanese aircraft you knock down."

Boyington just sat there, as he recalled, calculating how rich this project was going to make him. (In his 1958 autobiography, Boyington played the story for laughs, but his account was true in its essentials, as Claire Chennault would discover to his sorrow: some recruits were indeed told they'd be going against unarmed transports.)

Of all the recruits, the strangest case was that of a navy pilot who'd begun life with the name of John Perry. After dropping out of San Diego State, he joined the army as an aviation cadet, but was washed out for buzzing his girlfriend's house. Perry then borrowed a friend's name and academic record and started again as a navy cadet. In time he earned his wings as a flying-boat pilot, skippering a stately Consolidated PBY Catalina off the coast of California. Under the *nom de guerre* of Edwin Conant, he offered to go to China, and was accepted, though he'd never flown a fighter. For more than a year, in fact, he hadn't landed on a hard-surface runway.

Altogether, one hundred combat pilots signed up, though only 99 would actually sail for Asia. (Missing from the final roster was the name Chennault would have most liked to see: that of Ajax Baumler, with his claim of four German and Italian planes shot down over Spain. Baumler was refused a passport on the inarguable, if somewhat foolish, ground that he'd violated his earlier passport by serving a foreign government.) Reflecting Commander Irvine's early start, and perhaps the more enthusiastic support of Secretary Knox, fifty-nine volunteers were navy men, and seven more came from the marines. The army supplied thirty-three, though CAMCO would later hire ten army instructors for the flight school at Yunnan-yi.

The contract they signed was a marvel of circumlocution. There was no mention of combat, bonus payments, or even of flying: "WHEREAS, the Employer . . . operates an aircraft manufacturing, operating and re-pair business in China, and

"WHEREAS, the Employer desires to employ the Employee in connection with its business and said Employee desires to enter into such employment,

"NOW THEREFORE. . . .

"ARTICLE 1. The Employer agrees to employ the Employee to ren-der such services and perform such duties as the Employer may direct and the Employee agrees to enter the service of the Employer who, in consideration of the Employee's faithfully and diligently performing said duties and rendering said services, will pay to the Employee a salary of _____ dollars United States currency. . . .

"ARTICLE 2. The said employment shall become effective . . . from the date of the Employee's reporting in person to the Employer's repre-sentative at the port of departure from the United States . . . and shall continue for one year after the date on which the Employee shall arrive at the port of entry to China . . . unless sooner terminated as hereinafter provided."

CAMCO was to provide travel documents, train ticket to California, food and lodging while there, $100 in walking-around money, transport to Asia, and $500 toward his return fare at the end of his tour. If he were disabled or killed, CAMCO would pay six months' salary to him or his estate. (He would also have a $10,000 life insurance policy, the premiums deducted from his pay.) There was no provision for him to resign, but he could be fired for insubordination, malingering, revealing confidential information, drug or alcohol abuse, or "illness or other disability incurred not in line of duty and as a result of Employee's own misconduct"—i.e., sexually transmitted disease.

To remedy such matters as that last, CAMCO hired a U.S. Army flight surgeon, Thomas Gentry, who in turn recruited two other doctors, a dentist, and a male nurse. Gentry wanted women nurses, too, so he inquired at the Yale School of Public Health, where he was told to look up red-haired Emma Jane Foster. As an undergraduate, Red Foster had spent her junior year in China and wanted to return. She could find no offers from China when she graduated, so she went to work in the Chicago slums. Doc Gentry telephoned her father, who relayed the offer, figuring that any job was better than the one she had. Foster signed up with CAMCO, along with an older nurse, Jo Stewart.

Then there were line chiefs, crew chiefs, mechanics, armorers, radiomen, propeller specialists, parachute riggers, photographers, weathermen, clerks, and orderlies—the men who'd keep the planes and pilots in the air. The air force table of organization called for 1,000 ground personnel in a fighter group. CAMCO's quota was 200, and only 186 would actually sail for Asia. Most were army men. Signing on for $300 a month was Sergeant Robert M. Smith, a twenty-six-old college graduate serving as a mechanic in the 20th Pursuit Group. Smith had caught the travel bug from *The Royal Road to Romance,* an immensely popular account of the around-the-world odyssey of Richard Halliburton, formerly of Princeton. Salary was less important: "I would have signed up for $100 a month," he wrote in his diary.

Frank Losonsky was just twenty—so young he had to get a sergeant to countersign the CAMCO agreement. But he was an Allison engine mechanic, and therefore a rich find for Skip Adair, who signed him on as a crew chief at $350 a month, the top salary offered to any enlisted man. "I wasn't motivated to save the world, or run away from anything," Losonsky explained long after. "The reason[s] were the money, a subsidized trip to the Orient, and the promise of adventure."

At Mitchel Field, Skip Adair found a thirty-nine-year-old technical sergeant named Joe Jordan, who remembered Claire Chennault from the 1st Pursuit Group in the 1920s. In the 1930s, as a finance clerk, he'd paid off some pilots who were going to teach at the Hangzhou flight school. He, too, volunteered for Asia, mostly to oblige a buddy who wanted to go, and who wanted Jordan to keep him company.

An especially good catch at Mitchel Field was a P-40 mechanic named Chuck Baisden. "I had just turned 21," he recalled long after. "I was making $72 a month as a staff sergeant, and these guys were offering $350 a month to do the same job. That was more money than the Group CO [commander] made! . . . There are guys who say they joined for patriotism, and I'm sure there were, since anyone who could read could see that things were getting worse with the Japanese; but the truth is, most of us were a bunch of adventurous kids who saw a chance to make good money and travel."

Among the navy men who signed up were Allen Fritzke, Don Whelpley, and Randall Richardson, three weathermen at Norfolk Naval Air Station. As Fritzke told me in 1985, it was a Saturday morning in July, and he was hanging around the office for lack of any better plan. When the phone rang, he picked it up. "This is Commander Irvine," said the voice on the other end of the line. "Does anybody there want to go to China?"

"Yes," said Fritzke. "You're talking to one."

"Is there anybody else there?"

"Oh, there's a couple fellas here." He turned to Whelpley and Richardson: "You guys interested in going to China?"

"Sure," they said. They were young, they were bored—why not China? Following Irvine's instructions, they went to the customary downtown hotel and were offered $300 a month to work for CAMCO. They went back to base, told the petty officer on duty they needed special-order discharges, and were sent over to see the base commander.

He was outraged. "What kind of nonsense is this?" he shouted, and telephoned Irvine to set him straight. To the delight of the sailors, the admiral ended by eating humble pie: "Yes, sir, Commander, those men will be released within fifteen minutes."

Also signing on at Norfolk was Tom Trumble, who as a seaman on *Augusta* had seen CAF bombs make a shambles of Shanghai. He went AWOL to find Commander Irvine, looking for him in every hotel in town. Of all the reasons for joining the AVG, Trumble's was the maddest: he'd left a Russian sweetheart in China, and after his tour with CAMCO he meant to find her again.

But there were no staff officers for the AVG. Even more than pilots, the services needed these uniformed bureaucrats to preside over the great expansion ahead. Chennault tried to hire his half-brother Joe, then a college student, who turned him down. He had better luck with Skip Adair, who agreed to become supply officer when his recruiting chores were done. Chennault next talked to the China hands at the State Department. They suggested Paul Frillmann—the missionary who'd played left field for him in 1938, and who was now unemployed and living with his family in Chicago.

Frillmann flew to Washington, reported to the Chinese embassy, and was appointed chaplain and officer in charge of recreation, physical training, and liaison with the local populace, $350 a month. Chennault promptly put him to work, buying everything needed by three hundred Americans for two years in China—coffee, ketchup, peanut butter, canned meat, canned butter, mustard, mayonnaise, flour, and sports equipment—omitting what could be purchased locally. Frillmann spent the morning drawing up lists and the afternoon in telephoning orders to Washington wholesalers. He returned to Chicago that same night, bewildered and a bit resentful at the way Chennault had taken him up, wrung him out, and sent him packing. Indeed, he was a paradigm of the Chennault technique, whose distinguishing characteristic was to grab what lay at hand and work a miracle with it. "He was a genius," Joe Alsop told me, "at doing things with string and chewing gum."

———

In June, the first contingent reported to Gene Pawley in Los Angeles. There were some epic transcontinental journeys. Joe Jordan and his buddy decided to fly, but got off the plane in Omaha so the finance clerk could visit his ex-wife in Sioux City. There being no other transport, they chartered a plane. Back in Omaha, they missed their scheduled flight and boarded a train, then abandoned that in Cheyenne to stretch their legs and buy a bottle of whiskey. They couldn't find any liquor, so they sought a taxi to take them to Utah. (Jordan's memory, or his knowledge of geography, may have been playing tricks by the time he told this story to a Columbia University interviewer in 1962.) Failing in that, they boarded a train with a club car. This saw them safely to the Jonathan Club in Los Angeles, where they arrived on June 6, only to be sent north by bus to San Francisco.

Paul Frillmann chaperoned the advance party on *President Pierce,* her name painted over and her staterooms converted to barracks. The ship was crammed with reinforcements for General Douglas MacArthur's army in the Philippines. The AVG contingent consisted of thirty men, all ground crewmen and clerks except Frillmann, whom they called "Holy Joe." The senior army officer was annoyed by the former enlisted men who bedded down in the first-class lounge: he wanted them to drill with his troops, stand for inspection, and snap to attention when he passed. "Go away, soldier," they told him. "We're free men." In Honolulu, they tried to smuggle women aboard the transport. In Singapore, off the southern tip of the Malay Peninsula, they whistled at British customs officials in tropical shorts. Quartered for sixteen days in the Raffles Hotel, they played golf in their rooms. Jim Regis, hired as a photographer, dunked the secretary of the English Club in the swimming pool. There was also a bogus beauty contest, for which prizes were promised but none awarded, and at which Regis, Jordan, and—yes—Frillmann served as judges. "Drove the Limeys wild down there," Paul Perry fondly recalled. "Bunch of crazy Americans, bringing all the native girls into the Class A dining room and drinking all their gin and tonic and everything."

Somebody was indiscreet enough to explain their mission to a United Press correspondent, who filed this dispatch on July 9: "Thirty United States airplane mechanics and maintenance men arrived here today from New York, and will go to Rangoon next week en route to [China], where they will aid the Chinese Air Force. It was understood that a number of American planes of various types already had arrived at Rangoon and that more were en route there." So much for the secrecy that was supposed to surround their mission. With the *Time* story earlier in the summer, the Japanese had ample warning of the American Volunteer Group's arrival.

The main contingent—thirty-seven pilots, eighty-four ground crewmen and clerks, and two nurses—were now gathering at hotels in San Francisco. They wore civilian clothes, and their passports described them as anything but what they were. Gil Bright, former flight instructor at Pensacola, put himself down as a hardware clerk as a wink to his father, a wholesaler in Reading, Pennsylvania. Robert M. Smith, the diary-keeping mechanic, went as a radio announcer, a profession he'd followed for two years at KFXJ in Grand Junction, Colorado. Robert (Moose) Moss, a stocky P-40 driver from the 1st Pursuit Group at Selfridge Field, put himself down as an acrobat. Lanky Bob Neale from *Saratoga* was a rancher.

As for their commander, Chennault's passport identified him as "executive"—close enough in the circumstances. Overnight on July 7, four years after the opening shots of the Sino-Japanese War, he flew to San Francisco. He paid a courtesy call on the Chinese consul and conferred at the Mark Hopkins with Richard Aldworth and Doc Gentry. Among other concerns, they debated the wisdom of sending two women on a ship full of lusty males. The nurses prevailed, but were given an above-decks cabin to keep them out of harm's way. The vessel was *Jagersfontein* of Dutch registry, belonging to the Java Pacific line.

Chennault then boarded the Pan Am Clipper for the overnight flight to Honolulu. The AVG contingent sailed next morning, July 8, which was foggy and cold in the tradition of San Francisco Bay. Charlie Mott, former dive-bomber pilot on *Saratoga,* was in charge. At twenty-six, he was older than most of the pilots, and a married man, in violation of navy regulations. "When I left my darling wife at ten [AM]," he wrote after *Jagersfontein* motored under the Golden Gate Bridge, "I was trying to be casual . . . but just about managed to do it without breaking down. Words can't tell of the void this parting has left in me." At sea, Mott did

his best to keep discipline, policing the below-decks crap game, offering
a bridge tournament as an alternative, and leading religious services on
Sunday in the ship's dining room.

After Honolulu, *Jagersfontein* was joined by the cruisers *Salt Lake
City* and *Northampton*. The escort was the work of Lauchlin Currie, who
feared that Japan might have the airmen kidnapped. The warships escorted *Jagersfontein* as she swung south of the equator to avoid the Marshall and Caroline islands, former German colonies seized by Japan
during World War I. Off Australia, they were replaced by a Dutch cruiser,
which escorted the liner through the Indies (now Indonesia) to Singapore. She docked on August 11, all her brandy drunk, along with five
thousand bottles of Coca-Cola.

Chennault spent three days in Hong Kong, ingratiating himself with
the RAF and recruiting staff officers. His likeliest prospect was
Harvey Greenlaw, former aircraft salesman, who was heading home to
the United States. He and Olga were packing their trunks when Chennault came to their hotel and offered Harvey the job of executive
officer—second in command—of the AVG. Chennault also signed up
William Davis, an Anglo-Irishman known as Daffy. Davis claimed to
have served with the Royal Flying Corps in World War I, but now
wanted to avoid military service. Also a salesman, and also at loose
ends, he was living in Hong Kong with a married woman named Doreen
Lonborg. She regarded herself as English, though born in China and
carrying a Danish passport, courtesy of her estranged husband.

Of this little band of expatriates, only Doreen survived into the
1980s. She remembered Olga Greenlaw with particular awe: "She was
a beautiful thing. She had green eyes and the longest lashes I've ever
seen—the most exotic creature!—and her eyes were *literally green.*" In
photographs, what is most striking about Greenlaw is her height. Wearing heels, she stands eye-to-eye with the men who cluster around her.
Her father was a mining engineer in Durango, Mexico, where Olga and
her sisters were born; in the 1920s, a tumultuous time in Mexico, the
girls and their mother relocated to Hollywood, California. Olga gradu-

Harvey and Olga Greenlaw at Wujiaba airport outside Kunming, at the top of their form in AVG uniforms, shoulder tabs, and Flying Tiger pins. He was forty-four when this photo was taken, in April 1942, while she was ten years younger. (Alicia Schweizer collection)

ated from Polytech High School, probably in 1929, ostensibly nineteen years old but actually a mature twenty-one—like Chennault's, her age was fudged, with two years subtracted to ease the transition to an American city high school. She was "friendly, attractive, and knowledgeable," her sister told me in 2001, then corrected herself: "She was *beautiful*. Whenever she entered a room, everybody looked. She *demanded* it."

Harvey was a West Point graduate, though on his second attempt and in a two-year program designed to speed the flow of officers for World War I. He ranked near the bottom of his class. Worse, his first marriage ended in scandal, forcing him to resign his commission in 1931. In Hollywood, he met and courted the young Olga Sowers, before setting out to China to become a flight instructor. Harvey had never served at a grade higher than first lieutenant, but he called himself *Major* Greenlaw. A portrait from the AVG era shows him in a uniform cap and a khaki shirt open at the throat—a handsome man, though with an uncertain mouth and washed-out eyes. Snapshots are less flattering, showing him as overweight, puffy, and tired. Olga looks half his age, though she was in fact only ten years younger.

Chennault told the Greenlaws and Daffy Davis to wrap up their affairs and follow him as soon as they could. (Lonborg, too, was to come to Kunming after divorcing her husband, the Dane.) On July 18, he flew up to Chongqing on a CNAC Douglas, arriving in concert with twenty-seven Mitsubishi bombers. The raiders were new to him, twin-engine G4Ms with nearly twice the bomb load of the older G3Ms.

So the American Volunteer Group had failed in its intended mission, defending Chongqing in the summer of 1941. Nor were there any Russian pilots to oppose the Japanese: in a masterstroke of deceit and folly, Hitler had turned on Stalin the month before, and Soviet air units were withdrawn to the western front. The G4Ms and their escorts came and went with no opposition except from antiaircraft guns. Very few were shot down—but they did include a Mitsubishi A6M. After inspecting the wrecked Zero and questioning prisoners, Chinese intelligence produced a remarkably accurate data sheet, along with a set of recognition sketches. Major McHugh at the U.S. embassy sent this information back to the United States, and he gave a copy to Chennault when he arrived.

As it happened, the side-view drawing had a significant flaw. The Zero's tail was drawn out to a point, giving it a cigar-shaped silhouette. Because the tail of the salvaged fighter was too damaged for reconstruction, the Chinese artist endowed it with the rounded rudder of the JAAF's fixed-gear Nakajima Ki-27. The composite bore a strong resemblance to a retractable-gear fighter then going into production at the Nakajima company, and no doubt contributed to the difficulty AVG pilots would have in identifying the planes they encountered in Burma and China.

The AVG's late start had another consequence. Its intended base, Wujiaba airport near Kunming, was sodden with the monsoon rains, making a training program there impossible. Ed Pawley had a solution—the Pawleys always had a solution! He got the British to lend him Kyedaw airfield in Toungoo, Burma, an arrangement that served everyone's purpose. It put the AVG base close to the Pawleys' Mingaladon assembly point. It enabled Chennault to train his squadrons without fear of attack. And it assured Chiang Kai-shek that AVG supplies wouldn't compete for cargo space on the crowded Burma Road.

As for the British, Air Marshal Robert Brooke-Popham thought he'd done a very fine thing to provide a base for the AVG. In truth, giving up Kyedaw was a scant loss for the RAF. Toungoo in summer was a petrie dish breeding malaria, dengue fever, and dysentery. The only planes stationed there were the Blenheim bombers of RAF 60 Squadron, which could be more conveniently and comfortably accommodated at Mingaladon airport near Rangoon. And there was a bonus: "an understanding, amounting practically to an agreement," as Brooke-Popham put it, that if Japan moved south, "part, or the whole, of this American Volunteer Group would be detailed for the defence of Burma." Chennault apparently knew nothing about this unwritten clause in his lease on Kyedaw airfield.

Toungoo was located in the broad valley of the Sittang River, 175 miles north of Rangoon. Its main street rumbled day and night with trucks bound for Lashio, while its railroad thundered with freight to the same destination, whence it would be pushed over the Burma Road to Kunming. The town lay a bit to the west, its narrow, twisting streets closely lined with bamboo shops and huts, including a liquor store and an establishment that purported to be a hotel but was in fact a brothel. The most notable building was the sprawling, redbrick railroad station, containing the town's only restaurant. The principal product was teak, hauled out of the rain forest by elephants and gangs of coolies under the supervision of young British "jungle wallahs." The population was

23,000, including a few thousand Indians, some half-wild Karen tribes-men, and a few hundred westerners.

Toungoo society was dominated by a dozen British families who lived on the outskirts. The men were army officers (Toungoo was headquarters for the recently formed 1st Burma Division) and managers for the Mac-Gregor teak company. Off hours, they gathered at the Gymkhana Club—golf, tennis, billiards, and whisky-soda—and at dinner parties given by the wives in rotation. Black tie was obligatory, and afterward the ladies left the gentlemen to smoke cigars and discuss world affairs with unquenchable optimism. Sundays, they met again at St. Luke's, Church of England, which had more headstones in its graveyard than communicants in its pews. Southeast Asia was not a gentle land for Europeans.

Six miles north of town—past the hulks of trucks broken down on the road to Mandalay; past a pagoda guarded by statues of *chintha,* the ferocious seated lion of Burmese mythology—was the side road to Kyedaw airfield. Its single runway ran north–south for 4,000 feet and was surfaced with asphalt. Eastward lay the Karen Hills, a sawtooth mountain wall, blue with haze and marking the Burma-Thailand border. Away from the squalor of Toungoo, the countryside had a wild tropical beauty, with gnarly trees and fantastic flowering shrubs.

The RAF had outfitted Kyedaw with a small control tower, hangars, and office buildings. A mile from the field were barracks built from teak and bamboo according to the architectural fashion of Southeast Asia: no interior partitions, and the exterior walls open from waist-height to the eaves, with the sunny side sheltered by a veranda. There were no screens. Instead, the occupants slept under mosquito netting, on slat-bottomed cots sternly labeled "On His Majesty's Service." Ceiling fans stirred the air, if the electric generator was running. The roofs were bamboo thatch, and the latrines were open pits with urine buckets on the side, attended by Indian "sweepers."

Chennault inspected Kyedaw on July 26 with Butch Carney, who'd accompanied him from Kunming; Group Captain E. R. Man-ning, the Australian who commanded the RAF in Burma; and Ed Pawley, who laid on CAMCO's twin-engine Beechcraft for the tour. Chennault wasn't impressed, but he had no better alternative, and he approved the arrangement.

Skip Adair was still on recruiting duty, and the Greenlaws and Daffy Davis were still in Hong Kong, waiting for visas. So Chennault left Butch Carney in charge. Carney lived with an enterprising Chinese woman, Rose Mok, who among other things was a freelance trader on the Burma Road—buying a truck in Rangoon, filling it with goods, and selling vehicle and cargo after a hired crew brought them to Kunming. She followed Carney to Toungoo, to keep track of her dealings on the Burma Road and to see what opportunities this new venture might pose.

In Washington, meanwhile, President Roosevelt approved the formation of the 2nd American Volunteer Group, to fly the twin-engine Lockheed and Douglas bombers that had been diverted from British orders. Their mission included "the incendiary bombing of Japan." Poor George Marshall. It was like keeping a cat off the couch: no matter how many times he put it down, it jumped up again.

Chapter 4

Looks Mean as Hell

*P*enang *Trader* took the AVG advance party from Singapore to
Burma. On July 28, she crept up the tortuous channel of the
Rangoon River, the greenery broken by the Burmah Oil refinery, the MacGregor teak mill, and clusters of drooping, lilac-like flowers. At Rangoon, the coastal steamer tied to a float below the concrete
docks and eleven acres of cranes, warehouses, and crates of war matériel bound for China. Stately white buildings—British embassy, customs
house, Strand Hotel—lined the waterfront. This was the beginning of
European Rangoon, five broad avenues with sidestreets at right angles.
Beyond lay suburban roads with names like Windsor and Athlone, and
the native maze where lived 250,000 Indians, 40,000 Chinese, and (a
minority in their own capital) 160,000 Burmans. Towering over all was
the golden dome of the Shwedagon Pagoda, holy symbol of Burmese
Buddhism.

Chennault had spent the night at the Strand. Hearing that the advance party was at the quay, he hurried across the street to greet them.

"Hello, Frillmann," he said, as if he'd planned the reunion just so. "I told you I'd be here first." Then he turned on his heel, as the chaplain recalled with his blend of admiration and resentment: "He was wearing some slapdash adventurous costume as usual—mosquito boots, officer's shirt with Chinese insignia, beat-up Air Force cap—which emphasized his gamecock look. . . . I don't think any of the men on our ship had ever seen him before, and as I looked down the rail where they were lined up, staring silently at him, I could see that [he] had them all in his pocket."

Chennault dispatched the mechanics to Mingaladon, to help CAMCO assemble Tomahawks. He settled the others at the Strand—not the Raffles, perhaps, but lavish enough with its high ceilings, parquet floors, brass-railed bar, and wicker furniture. To Frillmann he gave a new want-list: parts for planes and automobiles, electrical and telephone supplies, musical instruments, screens, typewriters, rifles, coffins. . . . "Get the money from the Pawleys," he said, "and bring the stuff up to Toungoo when you come."

Then he left for Singapore, 1,200 miles south at the tip of the Malay Peninsula, where Air Marshal Brooke-Popham and his staff weren't particularly interested in what the old China hand had to say about Japanese tactics and equipment. "Hope their confidence in themselves is justified," Chennault grumbled in his diary. He flew back to Rangoon, took the CNAC Douglas to Kunming, and hired John Williams (his former radio instructor, now free-lancing cargoes on the Burma Road) to transform the flight-school building into a hostel for the AVG. Then he flew to Chongqing, at a time of full moon and around-the-clock bombing. Between raids, he hammered out an agreement with the Aeronautical Commission, giving him command of the AVG and any Chinese squadrons working with it. Order Number 5987 was duly stamped with the Generalissimo's "chop" (signature block) on August 1, 1941: "1. The First American Volunteer Group is constituted this date. 2. Col. Chennault will organize this Group with the American Volunteers now arriving in China to participate in the War. Additional personnel required to complete the organization of this Group shall be supplied by this Commission."

He also found a staff officer: Joe Alsop, who'd joined the navy and been posted to India. Alsop set out for Delhi by way of Chongqing, where he caught up with Chennault at a tea party given by Madame Chiang. Was there a slot for him in the AVG? Certainly, the Old Man told him: get a special-order discharge and report to Toungoo.

The *Pierce* contingent had meanwhile boarded the Up Mail, a darling train with piping whistle, wood-fired boiler, and no aisles. Instead, each compartment had a door to the outside. (The men visited back and forth by climbing out the window and running along the roof.) It took all day for the 175-mile run to Toungoo, crossing and recrossing the muddy highway, stopping every hour to take on water and once for a box lunch provided by the Savoy company, caterers to the Burma railroad. The day was so hot, armorer Paul Perry recalled, that when he reached Toungoo, he was naked except for his shorts. A flatbed truck took them to Kyedaw airfield. "And that's how we got there," Perry said, "twenty-nine wild military men who didn't give a shit, out in the middle of nowhere."

In Singapore, British officials were anxious to avoid a fortnight of wreck and riot such as they'd suffered at the hands of the *Pierce* contingent, so they ordered the captain of *Jagersfontein* to take his passengers straight to Burma. This the Hollander did, in a bad humor and without an escort, mooring at Rangoon on Friday evening, August 15. Next morning, Butch Carney cleared the 123 passengers through immigration and took them for breakfast (ham, eggs, and "corn flakes like cardboard") at the Silver Grill, Rangoon's all-purpose restaurant, nightclub, and brothel. Then he put them aboard the Up Mail, himself staying behind to party with Charlie Mott, Jack Newkirk, Red Foster, and Jo Stewart.

The advance party "got us more or less assigned to quarters in large buildings about thirty feet long by twenty feet wide, with bunks in them and mosquito netting," as Bob Neale recalled his arrival at Kyedaw. "The latrines were around the back [and] there were a considerable number of bugs, from mosquitoes to things falling off the ceiling and dropping on top of the mosquito netting." It was so uninviting that the men drove into Toungoo, where they found that the only drinking establishment was the railroad station buffet (the Savoy, like all such establishments in Burma) and the only entertainment a cinema starring Gary Cooper in *Beau Geste*. The ground crewmen sat with the natives, feeling more comfortable in the pit stalls than in the boxes occupied by the British toffs in evening dress. Afterward, they inspected the hotel-brothel, where they found that their arrival had doubled the price of a "black wench" to five rupees ($1.50). Back at the airfield, they cursed the bugs, the heat, the rain, the springless cots, the "slumgullion" (beef stew) at the RAF mess, and the flavorless British cigarettes. Paul Frillmann went into a funk, sure that mutiny was in the air and that the Old Man would hold him responsible.

Butch Carney turned up next day with his gang of four, thoroughly hung over. On Monday he appointed three squadron leaders, apparently without looking at their personnel records. The equivalent of a U.S. Army major, or so they were told, the rank carried a salary of $750 a month. The 1st Squadron went to Robert (Sandy) Sandell, former flight instructor at Maxwell Field; the 2nd to Jack Newkirk, a homely and likable man who'd flown radial-engine fighters from the deck of *Yorktown*; and the 3rd to Arvid Olson, a P-40 veteran from Mitchel Field. The squadron leaders each chose a dozen pilots, like the captains of so many sandlot baseball teams. Newkirk filled the 2nd Squadron almost entirely with navy fliers, and Oley Olson picked army fliers exclusively, including his friends from Mitchel Field.

Byron Glover had delivered three Tomahawks to Kyedaw, and three more were ready at Mingaladon airport. Olson and two other P-40 drivers took the Down Mail to Rangoon to collect them. Just look for the railroad, Glover instructed them, and follow it to Toungoo. Henceforth this style of navigation would be known as IFR—not "Instrument Flight Rules," as at home, but "I Follow Railroads."

"There were no guns in the airplanes," armorer Don Rodewald wrote in his diary, "and no gunsights. . . . There wasn't even a bracket for the gunsight." When he'd signed up for the AVG, Rode asked if he should bring tools to Burma. "Oh, no," Skip Adair assured him. "All the tools will be furnished—the best tools that you can get." But there were no tools, so Rode stole a kit from a truck bound for China, and with it began to install the guns that were shipped with the second batch of Tomahawks.

Mysteriously, he had a surplus of large-caliber nose guns but only enough rifle-caliber guns for thirty-one planes. To simplify maintenance, the armorers outfitted two squadrons with 7.92-mm Colt wing guns, and the third with .303-caliber Brownings. These weapons were approximately the same caliber, but their cartridges were incompatible.

At Kyedaw airfield outside Toungoo, Noel Bacon poses in front of a Tomahawk before his first flight in a liquid-cooled fighter. He was one of the "water boys"—Jack Newkirk's Panda Bears, made up almost entirely of former navy pilots. (Noel Bacon collection)

They couldn't test the results: in theory, Burma was self-governing, and the British considered a ban on target practice a reasonable price to maintain the fiction of independence. (When 60 Squadron needed live-fire practice, it flew its Blenheims to Singapore, a practice that would have dire consequences for Burma when war fell upon it.) In time, a dispensation was received from London, and the armorers built a firing range. The Tomahawks were towed to a "gun butt," their tails jacked up level, and their nose guns aligned so the bullets converged on a target 300 yards out. The wing guns were harmonized at 250 yards. Each pilot was given a few practice runs against a target on the ground—but not in the air, for that would have offended Burmese sensibilities. In any event, the AVG had no tow targets.

The U.S. Army reflector sight was a primitive form of heads-up display. It was to be mounted below the instrument panel, close to the floor, from which location it projected a circle and "pipper" (bull's-eye) onto a half-silvered mirror; the mirror was positioned between the windshield and the pilot's face. The idea was to give him a luminous image of a gunsight reticle, hanging in the air between him and the enemy aircraft. But British "armourglass" had no holes to mount the mirror, and the armorers' attempts to drill them proved fruitless. The pilots would have to depend on old-fashioned ring-and-post sights, less sophisticated than those on an infantry rifle, until Charlie Mott came up with a work-around.

It was much the same with the radios. Radioman Bob Smith's first task was to rip the British radio harness out of the Tomahawks, working with a hammer and screwdriver through a small door in the tail of the aircraft. Then he began the chore of adapting the twelve-volt civilian radio to the Tomahawk's twenty-four-volt electrical system. It was a miserable job, and every day at midmorning, as the heat began to build, Smith had to stop work long enough to vomit up his breakfast.

In Kunming, meanwhile, Chennault inspected Williams's progress on the AVG hostel. Then he flew down to Burma in Bill Pawley's Beechcraft. "As Chennault stepped from the plane and looked around the airfield and the motley group of men standing nearby," Jim Howard recalled, "I knew instinctively that here was a man who was going to make a go of our organization. With his military bearing he radiated a feeling of confidence that everything was going to be all right now that he was here and in charge. . . . Here was a man who said what he believed and did not mince words—he offered no apologies or excuses. He touched all of us with his sincerity and singleness of purpose. Here was a man we could follow."

As Frillmann had feared, the Old Man wasn't pleased by the situation at Kyedaw. "Apparently agitators have stirred up resentment against mil. discipline and against volunteer combat service," Chennault noted in his diary. He talked to the men, soothing the discontented and bawling out the rebellious. In Rangoon on August 26, he conferred with Bill Pawley, discussing what to do with the men who wanted to go home. When he returned to Toungoo, he had Olga and Harvey Greenlaw in tow.

Harvey was certainly an improvement over Butch Carney, who went back to running the CAF flight school at Yunnan-yi, but the new executive officer didn't hit it off with the men. "While he had a sort of nebulous job," Jim Howard wrote of him, "many of us couldn't tell just what it was he was supposed to do. He was usually dressed smartly in a khaki bush jacket and spent much of his time sucking on his pipe observing others at work." For her part, Olga provided a fillip that had been lacking at Toungoo: "Startlingly attractive," Howard recalled. "Her tight slacks and alluring makeup gave her a provocative look that suggested she was on the make."

So Olga Greenlaw became, and would forever remain, a sex symbol in the rain forest. When Ken Jernstedt arrived at Kyedaw airfield that fall, his first question was about the woman situation. "The executive officer has a wife," Noel Bacon told him, puffing on his pipe, "that would make a dog strain on his leash."

Skip Adair reached Burma soon after the Greenlaws, and Joe Alsop came in from India, a civilian again. With this pickup staff, Chennault set out to whip the AVG into shape. He restricted the vehicles to business, obliging the men to bicycle into Toungoo if they wanted to see a movie, drink at the Savoy, or visit the hotel-brothel. On a heavy-duty Raleigh, the trip required half an hour each way, so for all practical purposes the town was off limits except on Sunday, which the Old Man did his best to fill with church services and softball games.

There were two mess halls—one for pilots and staff, the other for ground crewmen—which after hours served as drinking clubs on the same segregated basis. (Chennault liked to stress the democracy of the

AVG, but his diary regularly speaks of "officers" and "enlisted men.") The RAF supplied food, cooks, and servers for 120 rupees ($36) a month, deducted from each man's pay, but the men were so unhappy with the food that Chennault got them a rebate on the first bill. He put Bill Towery, former army mess sergeant, in charge of the Indian cooks and, when Alsop showed up, put him in charge of Towery. In the end, Chennault made a new contract with the Savoy company. The meals improved, but they never ceased to evoke complaints from men spoiled by the bountiful food and obliging mess boys on *Jagersfontein*.

Reveille was moved up to 5:30 AM. The ground crewmen were on the job before sunrise, worked five or six hours, took a siesta, and worked a second shift in the evening—an arrangement that cured radioman Bob Smith's morning sickness. For the pilots, the day began in a small teakwood classroom in the operations building, with a lecture by Chennault or a guest speaker. As with the *Pierce* contingent, the Old Man soon had them in his pocket. "The more I see of the old boy," Charlie Mott noted in his diary, "the better I like him and the more I admire his talents. . . . We are indeed fortunate in having such a man as head of the project."

They were especially attentive to what he said about Japanese fighter planes. He chalked the outline of a Mitsubishi A6M on the blackboard, marking its vulnerable spots and advising them on the angle of attack. "He showed us these things," Tex Hill recalled, "and I got the very distinct impression from his lectures that he had actually engaged the Japanese Zero. Everything that he told us in his tactical lectures happened exactly. He knew. When we made our first contact with those enemy Zeros, they behaved exactly as he said they would." In fact, Chennault had only glimpsed the A6M from the ground; his information was mostly based on the drawings and spec sheet given him by Major McHugh.

Using a training manual captured by the Chinese, Chennault explained the tactics used by Japanese pilots: attack from above; sow confusion; break up the enemy formation; destroy his planes one by one. He told them to forget what they'd learned in U.S. service and to use Royal Air Force combat rules, battle-tested over Britain. And he drew on his own theories and what he'd seen Russian pilots do in China: employ a two-plane flight against enemy fighters, for better maneuverability; but use a three-plane flight against bombers, for increased firepower. Always take the high perch: dive on the Japanese planes, open fire with your large-caliber nose guns, add the rifle-caliber wing guns as you close the distance—then dive away and do it again. Harry them when they turn for home, low on fuel and ammunition. Destroy 10 percent of a Japanese bomber formation, he promised, and they'll go home to think again; shoot down 25 percent and they'll quit—rules of thumb hard-learned at Nanjing, Hengyang, Hankou, Chongqing, and Kunming.

Alas, he didn't write out these lectures, nor did anybody think to transcribe them at the time. More than sixty years later, Tex Hill paraphrased Chennault's introduction to the enemy they'd be fighting: "The Japs are very disciplined flyers, and their training is good. . . . They hold formation as well as anyone you've seen. They bomb accurately, they shoot accurately, and they know how to handle their planes." But they could be beaten by hit-and-run tactics: "The way to attack their formations is by getting above them. Dive into the formation at high speed, pick your target, fire at it, then continue on through, breaking away in a dive until you're clear of the formation. Once you're well away from the fight, climb back up above them and do the same thing [again]. Above all . . . *never* turn with their fighters. The P-40 cannot do it; they'll be right behind you in one turn, maybe two. Don't even think about it! If you do, we'll be picking up pieces of you all over the jungle. They *will* shoot you down, gentlemen. Make no mistake."

Following the lecture, the pilots drove out to the runway for hands-on training. From cockpit checks they progressed to familiarization flights, aerobatics, and mock combat. For practice runs against a bomber formation, Group Captain Manning would send a few of his Blenheims up from Mingaladon airport. For fighter training, they used each other. Whenever two pilots met in the air, they were to go at one another—head-on if it came to that. In U.S. service, this practice was banned as too dangerous, but Chennault believed in the hard school of training. Better lose a few pilots, he reasoned, than teach them to be timid.

Gil Bright, the "hardware clerk" from Pennsylvania, was a striking young man, with luminous dark eyes and a thoughtful face. He'd prepped at exclusive Phillips Exeter and matriculated at Princeton. Off-campus flying lessons interested him more than his studies, and he left Princeton after two years to enroll as a cadet at Pensacola Naval Air Station. Like many of the pilots in Jack Newkirk's 2nd Squadron, he'd trained to fly dive-bombers from the deck of an aircraft carrier.

On September 8, Bright was cruising over Toungoo when he saw a Tomahawk in the distance. Following protocol, he rocked his wings to challenge the other pilot to a dogfight. This was John Armstrong, slight of stature and boyish in appearance, but with a thousand hours in his logbooks. A week earlier, Armstrong had nearly rammed Charlie Mott in a dogfight. Now he tried the same tactic on Bright, approaching head-on and forcing him to nose down. Armstrong nosed down also, so close that his propeller seemed about to slice through the canopy. Bright rolled to the right, expecting Armstrong to roll in the opposite direction, so they'd pass belly to belly—but Armstrong didn't roll. "The collision," Bright wrote his parents, "sounded like a very loud chop." His plane lost a wing and began to spin. Bright slid back his canopy, unsnapped his harness, and was flung out like a stone from a slingshot.

Armstrong wasn't so lucky. The "crash party" found him still strapped in his seat, and his body was prepared for burial by flight surgeon Sam Prevo: "I . . . do hereby certify that on Sept. 9, 1941, the remains of John D. Armstrong were fixed in 10 percent formalin and wrapped in a formalin saturated sheet and placed in an hermetically sealed metal container. The metal container was placed in a teakwood casket. I further certify that I was present at the preparation of the body and the sealing of the metal container, and that the casket contains only the remains of the deceased."

Paul Frillmann conducted the funeral in the pilots' mess, after which Armstrong was buried in the rain at St. Luke's graveyard, with most of the local British colony accompanying the AVG to the plot on the south side of the village. "A Burma frontier guard played the ['Last Post']," Bright wrote, "and we all went home."

Chennault missed the funeral. With Butch Carney and Doc Gentry, he'd flown to Kunming to certify fifty Chinese cadets for advanced training in the United States.

Eddie Rector and Tex Hill were among seventeen pilots who reached Singapore on *Bloemfontein,* sister ship of the Java Pacific liner that

The first to die was John Armstrong, in a midair collision on September 8, 1941. At St. Luke's cemetery in Toungoo, his teakwood casket was supported by planks while Paul Frillmann (in uniform) read a modified Lutheran burial service. (National Air and Space Museum)

brought the main contingent to Asia. Also aboard were R. T. Smith and Paul Greene of Randolph Field. Like the *Pierce* contingent, they spent a fortnight in Singapore before getting onward passage on *Penang Trader*, which delivered them to Rangoon on the morning of September 15. They went upcountry the same day, to be met at the Toungoo railroad station by a three-piece band playing "Stars and Stripes Forever." Driving up to Kyedaw airfield, they were welcomed at the turnoff by one of those cheerful signs that followed Americans wherever they went: "Los Angeles City Limits."

Next morning the "Bloom Gang" was assigned to squadrons. Jack Newkirk signed up most of the navy pilots, while Oley Olson took his pick of the army men. Few had ever flown a liquid-cooled fighter. "That damn engine stuck out there so far," Rector told me, "I thought, if I step on my brakes this thing is going to tip over!" He was also dismayed that he couldn't see over the nose: when taxiing he had to weave from side to side, like a pigeon turning its head to see what was in front of it. After a few takeoffs and landings, however, he realized that the length of its nose had little to do with a plane's flight characteristics.

It was the same with R. T. Smith, whom the army had barred from fighters because of the distance between his heels and his head. Neil Martin gave him a cockpit check on September 17. It was a tight fit, even with the seat bottomed out and the rudder pedals full forward. But from the moment he advanced the throttle, R. T. began to think of his Tomahawk in the first person plural: "I closed the canopy and turned onto the runway, got lined up, and firmly eased the throttle forward. The big prop began to bite into the humid air as eleven hundred horsepower thundered a message I'd never heard before. We began to accelerate rapidly, manifold pressure gauge showing 48 inches, 3,000 rpm on the tachometer, now holding lots of right rudder to counteract the powerful torque. . . . Now there was a clear view over the nose . . . and in a matter of seconds the airspeed indicator was showing 100 mph . . . and we broke free of the runway. . . .

"At this point," R.T. concluded, "I was grinning and chuckling to myself like a kid with a beautiful new toy." As Tomahawks were ferried up from Mingaladon, they were given fuselage numbers, painted two feet tall behind the cockpit. Numbers 1–33 were allocated to the 1st Squadron, 34–66 to the 2nd, and 67–99 to the 3rd. R. T. chose 77—Lucky Sevens—for the fighter assigned to him.

Not all the Bloom Gang did so well. Eight days after reaching Burma, Maax Hammer crashed to his death in the rain forest. Though an experienced pilot, Hammer apparently "got into an inverted spin and could not get out of it, probably because of faulty technique," as Charlie Mott noted in his diary. "He hit with tremendous force, so naturally the remains are just so much meat. We decided to sell such of his effects as would be more valuable [here] than they would be in the U.S. bearing in mind of course that all bargain sale methods are to be avoided."

Chennault was discouraged, and not just by the deaths. "Six pilots want to quit," he wrote in his diary. "Rains go on daily and nightly." Most of the unhappy pilots belonged to Oley Olson's 3rd Squadron. Olson later explained that they'd joined the AVG to "get off of Active Duty with the Army and get into the more lucrative and immeasurably safer occupation of civilian flying"—an opinion shared by others, though it doesn't explain why so many malcontents were his P-40 drivers from Mitchel Field.

Altogether, seven pilots and a crew chief left at the end of September. (Two of the Bloom Gang, both ground crewmen, had jumped ship in Singapore and were discharged without ever reaching Burma.) Not quite balancing the attrition, six pilots arrived on October 10. Three were marines from Quantico, whom Olson grabbed for the 3rd Squadron. Then, on October 25, he lost another P-40 veteran. Don Rodewald finished the guns on a Tomahawk that morning, and Pete Atkinson volunteered to test it out. He promised to buzz the field, so Rode (an acute observer, though his spelling was shaky) watched for him: "He started to pull out of a long dive at terrific speed about a mile away to the south when the plane seemed to disintagrate and fall about 1500 feet. The motor fell free and wound up at a high rate till it hit. I went in a car as Armorer and got there to see the wreckage over a mile area. . . . Pete, still strapped in his seat, fell free of the plane so was still in one piece. His head was bad. The fuselage was along the RR tracks. The two wings were out in the rice fields about 300 yrds apart. I [have salvaged] some of the ammunition and two wing guns so far. This is a sad occasion because Pete was so well liked."

By now, the AVG had a protocol for funerals. The staff officers were the "official mourners," while pilots from the dead man's squadron served as pallbearers. They wore khaki pants and shirt, black tie, and pith helmet, which they doffed during prayers; they saluted when the coffin passed by, and again when the bugler played "The Last Post." "After Pete's funeral we returned to the barracks," recalled crew chief Frank Losonsky. "The movie [*Flying High*, a 1931 romp starring Bert Lahr] took the edge off the day."

Shaken by so many deaths, Dave Harris—like Atkinson, a P-40 driver from Mitchel Field—announced that he'd had enough. "If these guys can't do it," he said, according to another pilot, "I'm sure not ready." Chennault, who despite his fierce appearance was a kind man, at least toward those who stuck by him, put Harris to work at headquarters at no cut in pay.

K unming hadn't been raided for a month. The quiet bothered Chennault: "Japanese tactics," as he wrote on October 13, "can usually be counted on to repeat until a severe check is met with." He guessed that the Japanese were repositioning their squadrons for an attack elsewhere—and what target more likely than Kyedaw airfield? Toungoo was only sixty miles from Thailand, a neutral kingdom no doubt infiltrated by the Japanese. On October 24, he sent his three squadron leaders to take a look. Officially, the British forbade such overflights, but RAF commanders knew about the patrols and even suggested where the Americans might look for Japanese activity.

Sandell, Newkirk, and Olson crossed the sawtooth Karen Hills at 20,000 feet and scouted as far east as Chiang Mai—Thailand's second city, the terminus of its railroad, and the logical base for a raid on Toungoo. Chennault told the squadron leaders to stay high, dropping down only if they saw anything suspicious. With the rice fields drained and the rainy season ending, a convoy couldn't move in Thailand without raising a plume of dust. The patrol saw nothing.

Two days later, "a strange silver ship" scouted Kyedaw from 6,000 feet. Five Tomahawks took off and clawed for altitude but couldn't catch the stranger. The same thing happened the following day, though a pilot got close enough to count five intruders. Friendly aircraft in Burma and Malaya were painted in camouflage colors, so Chennault assumed that the visitors were Japanese scouts from Thailand. He was half right: in an operation so secret it was kept from the Japanese high command, a reconnaissance flight was based at Hanoi, Vietnam. The Mitsubishi Ki-15s (later called "Babs" by Allied pilots) flew 1,200 miles round trip to photograph British bases in Burma.

As Chennault told the story, Group Captain Manning sent up a ship's bell to be rung in the event of a raid on Kyedaw. He also provided a guard of Gurkha mercenaries from Nepal, legendary for their exploits in British service. But he did nothing to improve the border watch, which consisted of Burmese civil servants with binoculars and field telephones, who reported over the easily tapped wires of Burma Post and Telegraph.

Ten more pilots arrived October 29. To fill the 3rd Squadron vacancies, Oley Olson got three navy pilots: Robert (Catfish) Raine, who'd logged ninety hours in fighters; young Hank Gilbert from Pensacola; and the flying-boat captain who'd had been born John Perry but now traveled under the *nom de guerre* of Edwin Conant. Raine and Gilbert made an easy transition, but Conant was too accustomed to settling onto a harbor while seated high in the cockpit of a PBY Catalina. He "leveled off at about twenty-five feet," as R. T. Smith recorded the disaster; "stalled, and dropped in. Bounced up, collapsed the landing gear, came down on one wing and the belly, and turned around 180 degrees on the runway."

Then came November 3—"Circus Day," as it would be known. Conant burst a tire and ran off the end of the runway. Raine followed him into the bushes, collapsing his landing gear and damaging the propeller and a wing—"a wash out," Frank Losonsky noted in his diary. Sandy Sandell made a ground loop while landing from a cross-country flight. The crew chiefs then dispersed the Tomahawks for the evening—whereupon John Overly taxied one plane into another, chewing up its aileron. Bill Blackburn followed suit, damaging the prop on his plane and on the one he hit. Gale McAllister braked so hard he stood a Tomahawk on its nose, with two scared mechanics clinging to the wings. "Worst day of all," Losonsky wrote.

Two days later, Conant struck again, and the pilots joked that if he disabled two more Tomahawks, he'd qualify as a Japanese ace. Chennault wasn't amused. He dictated a letter to CAMCO in New York, complaining about the men it was sending him: "Typical of these problems is the case of pilot-officer E. S. Conant, who reported at this station with nine other navy pilots on October 29. Conant has the rating of a four-engine flying boat captain, [and] he has cracked up three planes in the first week. . . . Two more [pilots] decided to go home within twenty-four hours after their arrival at this station. Their stated reason was that the conditions of service had been falsely described to them."

Chennault demanded a more honest recruiting policy: "In telling the AVG story to pilots who may think of volunteering, nothing should be omitted. Far from merely defending the Burma Road against unaccompanied Japanese bombers, the AVG will be called upon to combat Japanese pursuits; to fly at night; and to undertake offensive missions when planes suitable for this purpose [i.e., the Hudson and Douglas bombers of the 2nd AVG] are sent out to us. These points should be clearly explained.

"Then," he instructed, "after the timid have been weeded out, the incompetents should also be rejected. I prefer to have the employment quotas partly unfilled than to receive pilots hired on the principle of 'come one, come all.'"

The letter would have been typed by Joe Alsop, who served as "staff secretary" in addition to his duties as mess officer. "He is surely a great help in this work," Chennault wrote in his diary: the sigh of relief is almost audible. But to the pilots and ground crewmen, Alsop was a figure of fun with his spectacles, fussy manner, and elevated speech, honed at Groton, Harvard, and the Washington dinner circuit. Tom Trumble, the navy yeoman who'd left a sweetheart in Manchuria, and who was clerking in the headquarters building, remembered Alsop following the Old Man with an armload of papers: "Joe was always very much perturbed and anxious to get something signed."

Most of the papers involved supplies and spares. Cannibalization had become a way of life for the AVG mechanics, who scavenged pieces of wrecked planes and installed them on those that could be made airworthy. But recycling couldn't replace tires blistered by 100-mph landings on hot asphalt. Or props twisted by nose-overs, ground loops, and belly landings—or the E-1B solenoids that activated the Tomahawk nose guns, and that routinely failed after five hours' service.

Alsop's requisitions went in the first instance to the CAMCO-Intercontinent office at 42 Phayre Street in Rangoon, around the corner from the Strand Hotel: "We need six ounces of luminous paint for gun sights, which you should be able to get locally. We also need 100 Bausch and Lomb Ray-Ban sunglasses. The pilots were instructed to bring their own, but some failed to do so, and others have broken theirs. We find that the lack of good sunglasses appreciably lowers pilot efficiency, so I should like this order to be cabled to the United States and shipped by air express."

China Defense Supplies also had an office in Rangoon. Alsop visited it with a list of one thousand items, which required a day and a night to encrypt into cable code. The codebook author had failed to anticipate Ray-Bans, silver solder, solenoids, or the items on another wantlist—432 packages prophylactics, 19 cases rye whiskey, 21 cases bourbon,

10 cases Camels, 5 cases Lucky Strikes—all of which had to be spelled out in full.

And ammunition! At the Raritan Arsenal in New Jersey, Lauchlin Currie found 900,000 rounds of .303-caliber ammunition bound for Canada. He persuaded the Canadians to give them up, and he also wangled 600,000 rounds of .50-caliber ammunition from the U.S. Army in the Philippines. Pending their arrival, Alsop scrounged odd lots from the British Bush Warfare School at Maymyo, from the CAF, and from Chinese dealers in Rangoon. The Chinese bullets were so old that they sometimes "hung fire," causing pilots to shoot holes through their own propeller blades.

Chennault invited Major McHugh down from Chongqing to see how shabbily the AVG was being treated. With Alsop's help, McHugh drafted a lengthy protest to the Navy Department: "By its very nature, the war in China offers the United States a unique opportunity to strike

Air Vice Marshal Conway Pulford of the Royal Air Force inspects Kyedaw airfield in October 1941. From left: Harvey Greenlaw, Pulford, Chennault, Sandy Sandell, Oley Olson, and Olga Greenlaw—as always, the center of their attention. (Flying Tigers Association)

a blow in self-defense with more effect and less expenditure than would be remotely imaginable anywhere else in the world. . . . [But] without any staff officers competent to direct the enterprise; with less than a third of the material requested, and with less than half the pilots and men, the A.V.G. cannot be expected to attain the great objectives originally set for it." McHugh itemized what was needed to salvage the situation, from radio tubes to long-range bombers.

A similar message went to the War Department under the signature of Brigadier General John Magruder, head of the U.S. Military Mission to China. General Marshall had sent the clerkish Magruder to Chongqing to monitor the flow of lend-lease supplies and keep an eye on the AVG. When he visited Kyedaw airfield, he got the usual earful: with only forty-two airworthy Tomahawks, the AVG would be routed if it were thrown into combat, posing a "serious threat to American prestige in Far East and possible repercussions at home." To head off a debacle, the War Department should commandeer six tons of parts from the RAF in North Africa and U.S. Army squadrons in the Philippines.

T. V. Soong joined this campaign, in similar words, warning the White House that "if this air force tries to fight it may be destroyed with disastrous repercussions." Soong, however, didn't trifle with spare parts: he wanted the United States to ship eighty Douglas SBD dive-bombers to the Philippines, fly them to China, and turn them over to the AVG. "Would it be possible," he asked, "to direct the Army and the Navy to make these planes and ordnance available *now?*"

Bill Pawley had another idea. CAMCO owned three CW-21 "Demon" export fighters, acquired as prototypes for its factory at Loiwing. Pawley now offered them to the AVG "on the chance that some government authority could be found to pay for them" at the 1939 list price. This was a great bargain, as everyone agreed, and after much correspondence the U.S. allowed China to use lend-lease funds to buy the flimsy but fast-climbing CW-21s. Chennault didn't like the Demon— two years earlier, he'd likened it to a "sardine can"—but he thought it might be able to catch the mystery planes that were scouting Kyedaw airfield.

On November 12, *Boschfontein* brought twenty-six pilots to Rangoon. They were led by Curt Smith, thirty-three years old, who'd tried without success to enforce military discipline on the voyage. Smith had joined the military in 1928 and spent ten years jumping between the army and the Marine Corps; when CAMCO signed him up, he was a reserve pilot taking a refresher course at Pensacola. With two thousand hours in his logbooks, he was an impressive catch, though by the standards of the time he was too old for combat flying. Also on *Boschfontein* were Charlie Bond, Jim Cross, and George Burgard of the Ferry Command—and Greg Boyington, who immediately caught the green eyes of Olga Greenlaw.

"He was about five feet eight inches tall," she wrote not long after, "with tremendous shoulders and narrow hips; his head held on by a strong neck. He had coarse features, large eyes, wide, flat nose, and heavy jowls." The others, she thought, were afraid of him. If so, they had reason: drunk as a skunk one night, Boyington shook Noel Bacon awake and demanded the use of the AVG station wagon. Bacon, who doubled as transportation officer, handed over the keys when he found himself looking down the barrel of a .45 automatic.

The newcomers were given cockpit checks. Afterward, with some of the older hands, they drove into town for Saturday-night baked beans at the home of Chester Klein, a Baptist missionary who often invited members of the AVG to his house. On this particular evening, two Englishmen were present. (Klein's son told me that they may have been covert-warfare agents, recruiting guerrilla fighters in case of Japanese invasion.) After dessert, they moved to the living room, where they talked about the European war and wondered when it would spread to the Pacific. Bored with the talk, Charlie Bond thumbed through the *Illustrated Weekly of India* and spotted a photograph of a Tomahawk in North Africa, its air scoop painted to represent the mouth of a shark.

The shark motif was used by pilots on both sides in World War I, though usually with comic effect. The first sinister version was painted by the men of Luftwaffe 76th Group on their Messerschmitt Bf-110s in the spring of 1941. Over Greece and Crete, they sliced through the Gloster Gladiator biplanes of RAF 112 Squadron, causing the Commonwealth pilots to be withdrawn to Egypt and refitted with Tomahawks off the same assembly line as those sold to China. They adapted the shark face for their own use, and it was one of their Tomahawks that the AVG pilots now admired. Next day they asked permission to adopt it as a squadron emblem. "Chennault said no," Erik Shilling recalled, "but would rather use it as a group marking."

All that week, pilots and crew chiefs busied themselves with chalk and paint, transforming Tomahawks into man-eating fish. They were delighted with the results. "Looks mean as hell," R. T. Smith gloated over the shark face on No. 77. They painted the CAF's twelve-pointed white sun on the wings, and finally they added distinctive squadron emblems. Sandy Sandell's pilots chose a green apple, with a naked Eve chasing a uniformed Adam, representing mankind's "first pursuit." In the 2nd Squadron, Jack Newkirk's men chose a black-and-white panda, emblematic of China. Oley Olson's 3rd Squadron opted for a scarlet nude with a halo and wings: they'd be Hell's Angels, after a Howard Hughes film celebrating the air war on the Western Front in World War I.

Chennault asked the Royal Air Force to send up its best man for a joust with Shilling, a former army test pilot whom the Old Man evidently regarded as the hottest flier in the AVG. Mingaladon had recently been reinforced by RAF 67 Squadron from Singapore, equipped with the lend-lease Brewster Buffalo. Most of its fliers were sergeant-pilots from New Zealand, but there were a few RAF officers including Flight Lieutenant Jack Brandt, who flew up to Kyedaw on November 19. (Brandt was born in Shanghai, the son of a Sino-German Yangtse River captain; he was called Pancho because of his vaguely Mexican appearance. Vic Bargh of 67 Squadron regarded him as a senior pilot but not a particularly skilled one.) Wrote Bill Schaper in his diary: "Shilling had a dog fight with a Limey in a Brewster and licked the pants off of him, so it should increase the confidence in our pilots quite a bit."

Which was Chennault's intention, of course. Like the Sunday-afternoon softball games—like the shark face and the squadron emblems— the joust was another technique for molding his irregulars into a fighting team. Gradually, the AVG was becoming a combat force with its own heroes and heraldry.

The final contingent reached Burma on November 25, bringing four pilots for the squadrons at Kyedaw. They included Louis Hoffman, the middle-aged enlisted pilot, who'd joined the navy in 1915 and earned his wings in 1929, and who was nicknamed Cokey because of his fondness for the quintessential American soft drink. Also in this group were nine army flight instructors who'd signed contracts with the CAF flight school. They were sent to China, to teach at Yunnan-yi under Butch Carney.

Chennault prepared the AVG to follow them, sending surplus men and supplies up the road to Mandalay, Lashio, and Kunming. The first convoy consisted of ambulances under the command of CAF flight surgeon Joseph Lee. He was to assess the hazards of the Burma Road, including thieves, customs officials, and vendors of gasoline, food, and lodging; in Kunming, he was to set up a hospital on the grounds of Hostel Number One, formerly the CAF flight school.

John Williams seemed to be running a rather loose ship in Kunming. "For the past few weeks," wrote the AVG's Chinese liaison officer to Chennault, "I have found that some of the personnel . . . are always drunk in the hostel, and this is not the worst. On several occasions they were badly drunk in the city, so much so that one of them lost his head completely and caught hold of a cook's chopper intending to kill a woman with it, but fortunately he was prevented from doing any injury by another person. . . . It is not customary that a military organization permits the bringing of girls into the sleeping rooms of the hostel. This may entail some misunderstanding among the public and, at the same time, spoils our reputation. . . . Some of the Chinese here are planning to cooperate with a few Americans in the Volunteer Group in the hope that they could utilize the [AVG] trucks to smuggle goods into China from Burma and sell them here at market price. [This] is not only illegal, but profiteering at the country's expense, and as such, particular heed should be paid to nip it at the bud."

For bringing women into the hostel, Williams fined each man $25 "gold." (The Americans spoke of U.S. dollars as precious metal, while scorning Chinese currency as "Mex.") When the next convoy from Kyedaw contained quantities of coffee, soap, and cigarettes not mentioned on the manifest, Williams locked it inside the AVG compound until he could sort things out: cargo, trucks, drivers, and their Chinese commander, who complained of "cruel treatment from bad feeding and poor beddings during the time of detention." Williams had to apologize, no small concession in face-conscious China.

When not otherwise occupied, the Kunming detachment belted ammunition, built a softball diamond, set up a movie theater, and cared for two dogs. One was a dachshund named Joe, a Christmas present for Chennault. The other answered to the name of CAMCO—an inside joke, no doubt. The animals got along fine, Williams wrote toward the end of November. He added that the business of hardening the Wujiaba runway was going well, the Chinese having run a railroad spur to the airport to speed the delivery of crushed stone. On the other hand, a thief had made off with a clock from a parked Tomahawk, and Japanese planes were once again scouting Kunming from Vietnam, suggesting that bombers might soon follow.

In Washington, General Marshall warned reporters in a confidential briefing: "We are preparing for an offensive war against Japan." The weapon would be B-17 Flying Fortresses based in the Philippines. If war broke out, Marshall said, squadrons of these huge bombers would "be dispatched immediately to set the paper cities of Japan on fire." So Marshall had bought into the plan proposed a year before by Morgenthau, Soong, and Chennault—had even adopted their language—though not its covert nature. Marshall's B-17s would bear U.S. Army markings, the crews would wear American uniforms, and they'd go into combat only after a declaration of war.

Since it was preparing to bomb Japan on its own account, the army was loath to release men for the promised 2nd AVG. In the end, Lauchlin Currie drew up a directive for the president's signature, ordering Henry Stimson to release the bomber crews. "In the next few months," Roosevelt wrote, "we are delivering to China 269 pursuit planes and 66 bombers. . . . I suggest, therefore, that . . . you should accept the resignations of additional pilots and ground personnel as care to accept employment in China, up to a limit of 100 pilots and a proportional number of ground personnel." It has often been said—by Chennault among others—that Roosevelt created the AVG with a "secret executive order" on April 15, 1941. No such document has ever surfaced. Nor was any needed: Roosevelt preferred to give a wink and a nod, leaving it to underlings to fill in the details. This directive to Stimson is the only one I found, relating to the AVG and signed by the president.

With this authority, CAMCO hired 82 bomber pilots and 359 ground crewmen for the 2nd AVG. The planes had already been diverted from British orders. Thirty-three Douglas Bostons—called A-20s in U.S. service—would travel by sea to Africa, then fly the rest of the way. The same number of Lockheed Hudsons would travel in the other direction, carrying their own air crews across the Pacific, once the manufacturer installed additional fuel tanks. The same tanks would enable them to bomb Japan from airfields in East China. The group's ground crews left California on November 21 aboard *Noordam* and *Bloemfontein*.

To equip the 3rd AVG, a fighter group like the one already in Burma, a shipment of Vultee Vanguards was on its way to Rangoon. Under Tommy Corcoran's share-the-pain plan, the pilots would be navy men, but the navy insisted that none be released before January.

The British, too, came on board. Prodded by Washington, Prime Minister Winston Churchill told Brooke-Popham to do what he could for Chennault. The air marshal offered a Buffalo squadron from Singapore, with volunteer pilots and ground crews, with perhaps a bomber squadron to follow. Chennault was delighted. "Rush organization and equipment [Buffalo] unit fastest possible," he radioed Joe Alsop, whom he'd sent to Singapore on a scrounging mission, "and explore possibility Blenheim volunteer squadron early date."

Alsop wasn't there to receive the radiogram. The British had given him permission to requisition parts and supplies, but he found little in Singapore that could be used by the AVG. Then Bill Pawley flew in, saw the letter of authority, and realized it would be more useful in the Philippines. He took Alsop and the letter to Manila and used it to obtain some P-40 tires and parts, which the U.S. Navy loaded into three flying boats and delivered to Rangoon.

The logjam was broken. There wasn't a man of importance in Washington who didn't understand that war was about to break out in the Pacific. The only question, as Henry Stimson phrased it, was "how we should maneuver [Japan] into the position of firing the first shot without allowing too much danger to ourselves." As a result, Lauchlin Currie acquired 4,000 pounds of tires, ailerons, and spare parts for Chennault.

The ailerons and half the tires were put aboard *Silver Star,* which sailed November 25. Currie put the other tires and the emergency spares on the Pan Am Clipper flying to Hawaii on December 3. Six army officers were bumped from the Clipper to make room for the cargo and the man in charge of it: Lieutenant Ajax Baumler, who'd been denied a passport to join the AVG. Another 1,000 pounds would follow on the Clipper leaving San Francisco on Sunday, December 7.

At Mingaladon, the Pawley brothers closed their assembly line. The last Tomahawk off the line was P-8101—the first to be uncrated, but used as a Christmas tree because it lacked parts. It had since been made whole with pieces of the Tomahawks wrecked in training. Byron Glover delivered it to Kyedaw, bringing the AVG's strength to sixty-two planes, though two of them had no guns or radios. The Tomahawk whose wings were ruined by saltwater immersion was still at Mingaladon, so CAMCO workers loaded the fuselage onto a flatbed truck and sent it up the dusty road to Loiwing. The American supervisors and most of the Chinese workers soon followed. Bill Pawley kept his office in Rangoon and a skeleton crew at Mingaladon, since he expected to be given the contract to maintain China's "International Air Force," as he called it. If every bet came up a winner, this would involve fourteen squadrons—nine manned by American, three by Chinese, and two by British Commonwealth crews.

At Kyedaw, in these final days of peace, three more pilots left for home, leaving Chennault with eighty-two names on the pilot roster. But not all had checked out in a Tomahawk. By the most generous estimate, the American Volunteer Group in the first week of December had about as many combat-ready pilots as planes: sixty.

Chapter 5

Flaming Till Hell
Won't Have It

Sunday December 7 brought high winds and rain to Southeast Asia. On the Vietnamese island of Phu Quoc, a truck nosed up to a fighter that Chennault's pilots would have identified as a Mitsubishi Zero. In fact, it was an army plane, the Nakajima Ki-43 Hayabusa (Falcon), so new that only fifty were in service. This one had an olive green topside and a pale gray belly. Its wings and fuselage were painted with huge red disks—*hinomaru*—honoring the rising sun and Japan's imperial destiny. Its rudder was slashed by a white arrow, emblem of the 64th Sentai (Group). A white band around its fuselage, aft of the cockpit, identified it as the commander's plane.

If Japan had a Claire Chennault, he was Kato Tateo. They'd crossed paths in 1938, when Kato flew the fixed-gear Nakajima Ki-27 in its first combat mission and claimed three CAF biplanes near Hankou. A year later the 64th Sentai was in Manchuria, where Japan and the Soviet Union were fighting across the border in Siberia. Kato was credited with seven Russian planes, promoted to major, and hailed as the best of the "Wild Eagles" of the JAAF. His fame—unusual in Japan, which rarely celebrated a hero who hadn't died in the emperor's service—probably resulted from the army's desire to glorify a bloody and unproductive war. A photo from the time shows Kato as a full-faced, handsome man with a broad nose and a full-blown mustache. The similarities to

An idealized portrait of Kato Tateo graced the cover of this 1987 memoir by Hinoki Yohei, who served under him in Burma. The plane is a Nakajima Ki-43 Hayabusa bearing the 64th Sentai arrow on its tail fin and the commander's diagonal stripes on its wings. (From Hayabusa sentotai cho Kato *by permission of the publisher)*

the young Chennault are irresistible: his mustache, his sheepskin flying suit, his gamecock stance, and even (as we are assured by Kato's eulogizers) his flair for leadership and love of baseball, which he played in roughhouse fashion with his men.

The truck had an auxiliary engine in back and a rod-and-claw device extending over the cab. This spun the Hayabusa's propeller and thus cranked the engine. When all engines were ready, the fighters rolled along the sod runway, taking to the air between rows of mechanics and clerks who waved their caps in farewell.

At midafternoon, Major Kato sighted the gray troopships through the rain. In the leading vessel was General Yamashita Tomioka, commander of the 25th Army, a barrel-shaped officer with a piggish face and a genius for improvisation. The convoy had hugged the Vietnam coast all morning, to disguise its intentions, but now was steaming for Malaya. Kato and his men flew air cover until sunset. They couldn't communicate with the fleet: the Hayabusa radios were unreliable in the air, and the army and navy transmitted on different frequencies, just as they used different ammunition and controls. (For more power, Kato pulled the throttle toward him, a legacy of the French air force; a navy pilot, in the British or American fashion, pushed it forward.)

The major had a notebook strapped to his thigh. "All the planes under my command are working according to plan," he wrote. Then, in the glory of the moment, he cried out to the troops: "Please make a clean job of it!" Or so his posthumously published diary would have us believe.

In the fall of 1941, like two wheels turning, the Japanese air forces had undergone a massive transformation. Navy fighter squadrons boarded the aircraft carriers that would take them across the Pacific Ocean to Hawaii. Other JNAF units went to Taiwan and Vietnam to support the army's move into the "Southern Treasure Chest"—Malaya, the Philippines, and Indonesia. The navy had 1,300 planes, all committed to the breakout scheduled for the night of December 7/8. The army air force was nearly as large, but JAAF squadrons also had to defend the Japanese home islands, maintain the border watch in Manchuria, and pursue the war in China, leaving only 682 planes to support the landings in Malaya and the Philippines.

The breakout was an astonishing venture, across 4,000 miles of ocean, against the combined might of the British Commonwealth, a Dutch colonial army, and the United States. Everything depended upon the raids scheduled for the first hours of war. The defenders nearly matched them in aircraft, and the mood among the Japanese pilots was somber, as suggested by Kato's diary entry of December 6: "It occurred to me that this was one of the heaviest responsibilities ever thrown on my shoulders, but there is nothing to be done but to fulfill the task to the best of my ability and at all costs. . . . I saw [Lieutenant Colonel Onishi Hiroshi] in Saigon, who is detailed to lead the convoy fleet and to command a heavy bomber unit. I discussed details with him. Made up my mind to die with the heavy bombers, if need be."

No need. The only challenge came from a PBY Catalina flying boat that blundered across the convoy on the afternoon of December 7. Nakajima Ki-27 Nates from the 1st Sentai shot it down—first blood of the Pacific War.

Then night fell, a better escort than the fighters. At 7:30 PM Tokyo time, Kato led his squadrons back across the Gulf of Thailand, wingtip lights aglow. The nearer they came to Phu Quoc Island, the stronger the wind and the heavier the rain. Unlike navy fighter pilots, they had no radio-direction finders, and three Hayabusas were lost at sea—the 64th Sentai's worst hour in the four years it had been at war.

At midnight, shells exploded on Malaya's northeastern coast. The moment was brilliantly chosen. In Malaya, the troops had a high tide and a full moon to help them ashore. In Hawaii, it was daybreak on Sunday, lighting the target for the JNAF planes while American sailors and airmen slept late.

N obody thought to alert Kyedaw to the attacks on Malaya and Pearl Harbor. The men slumbered until reveille, got up, ate breakfast, and went to their stations. The news broke upon them at 7 AM. "Somebody ran in to the ready-room and said the U.S. was now at war with Japan," wrote R. T. Smith in his diary. "We could hardly believe it even though it was confirmed on the radio. Everybody stood around laughing and kidding about it, although it was easy to see there was really plenty of tension."

Harvey Greenlaw telephoned his wife in Toungoo. Olga wept, told her maid to make coffee, and tuned the radio to KGEI San Francisco. The Japanese, she concluded from the news bulletins, were "rushing up and down the globe like mad dogs, frothing at the mouth and biting everything in sight." So it seemed, with troops ashore in Malaya, U.S. forces devastated in Hawaii, and bombs crashing on Hong Kong and Wake Island.

Chennault had fallen into the habit of standing a dawn watch in the control tower, a bamboo box providing Kyedaw's best view of the mountains to the east. On December 8, sunrise came without incident: dark one moment, and then, as if a switch had been turned, blue sky and scattered clouds. Chennault climbed down and walked across the runway, to be intercepted by a radioman waving a piece of paper. He snatched the bulletin, read it, and hurried to the headquarters shack, where he put the AVG on a war footing.

The Hell's Angels (Oley Olson's 3rd Squadron) would be his "assault echelon," their Tomahawks gassed, armed, and parked at the south end of the runway. The support echelon was Jack Newkirk's Panda Bears, with Sandy Sandell and the Adam & Eves in reserve. Ground crews filled thirty-eight kerosene lanterns. If the Tomahawks had to take off at night, the lanterns would mark the runway; otherwise, Kyedaw would be blacked out, while decoy lights burned at the dispersal field to the north.

Chennault canceled leaves, ordered the hospital evacuated to Kunming, and dispatched Olson to Rangoon to borrow steel helmets from the British. Then he radioed Chongqing: "Suggest moving Group into Yunnan at once as we are not prepared for combat operations here."

Olga Greenlaw reached the airfield in time to see a CNAC Douglas taking off with the sick list and some of the medical staff. "Everyone was togged out in side arms," she recalled. "Gurkha guards with glinting bayonets walked their posts, and pilots and planes stood ready to take the air at a minute's warning. Our cars were being hurriedly camouflaged with green and yellow paint." She was refused a pistol, though she badly wanted one. She wandered over to the headquarters shack, where Chennault conscripted her to write the story of the AVG's first day at war. So Olga joined the staff. She closed the Toungoo house, moved into the Kyedaw infirmary, and became keeper of the AVG's War Diary for $150 a month.

The invaluable Joe Alsop was caught on Hong Kong island by the outbreak of war. He'd taken the last CNAC Douglas out of Manila but could go no farther. Chinese officials had evacuated their families to Hong Kong, to keep them from the bombing and deprivation of Chongqing; now they were grabbing every available seat to bring them home. CNAC flew only at night. Daytimes, Japanese planes roared over the colony, bombing and strafing, while Japanese troops attacked the land perimeter. Against them, Hong Kong had almost no defense, for its big guns—positioned by the Royal Navy—pointed out to sea.

Ajax Baumler made it as far as Wake Island, where he awoke to Japanese bombs, shells, and bullets. The Pan Am Clipper, a sitting duck at her mooring in the coral lagoon, escaped with twenty-seven bullet holes. Her cargo was dumped and she was filled with refugees, including Lieutenant Baumler, Pan Am staff, and a dozen civilian workers. At noon, the overloaded flying boat dragged herself clear of the lagoon and retraced her path to shattered Hawaii. Left on the wharf to be captured by the Japanese were 2,300 pounds of Tomahawk tires and spare parts.

Also in mid-Pacific was *Silver Star*, bound for Rangoon with tires and ailerons. She was diverted to Australia. So were *Noordam* and *Bloemfontein*, carrying the first contingents of Chennault's bomber group— ninety-nine ground crewmen and a pilot, by most accounts, though another shows only forty-nine on the roster. In Australia, they were inducted into the U.S. Army. The same fate befell their Lockheed Hudson bombers at Burbank, California. In Washington, Lauchlin Currie wanted to do the same with the AVG. There was no longer any reason to pretend that Chennault's airmen were volunteers in the service of China, he wrote in a memo to the president. If they were inducted, they'd be transformed into "an American task force" in the thick of the war.

On Wednesday, the Kyedaw alarm sounded at 3:30 AM. The 2nd Squadron had the duty, and four Panda Bears took off and circled the base for more than an hour before Chennault called them in. Guided by the faint light from the kerosene lanterns, Tex Hill overshot the runway and piled his Tomahawk in a heap at the far end. "He was knocked a little goofy," as a clerk told the story. "When we got there he was wandering around, his clothes soaked with gasoline. He had a cigarette in one hand and a match in the other. Luckily, he hadn't struck the match. Somebody took it out of his hand."

The ground crews lined up cars and trucks, aimed headlamps across the tarmac, and brought down the other Tomahawks without mishap. "This was a true alarm," Olga Greenlaw noted in the War Diary, "but evidently the Japanese mistook the location of the Kyedaw aerodrome and no bombs were dropped." More likely, thunder and lightning fooled the border watchers into reporting a raid, since Japanese accounts mention no foray into Burma that night.

At daylight, Chennault told Lacy Mangleburg to take another look at Chiang Mai airport. A Tomahawk had been fitted with a Fairchild camera, borrowed from the RAF and mounted in the baggage compartment over a hole in the bottom of the fuselage. The wing guns were removed, the gun ports taped over, and the fuselage otherwise slicked up, making the photo plane faster than any likely interceptor. Six Tomahawks escorted it to Chiang Mai, tucked among steep mountains 175 miles east of Toungoo.

The results were negative, so Chennault scheduled a more ambitious overflight for Thursday. With Eddie Rector and Bert Christman flying shotgun, Erik Shilling took the photo plane down to the RAF airfield at Tavoy on the Tenasserim panhandle, a sliver of Burmese territory bordering Thailand. They refueled, crossed the border, and flew to Bangkok.

When these photographs were developed, they showed an impressive number of planes on the tarmac at Don Muang airport. Eleven Nakajima Nates of the 77th Sentai had flown into Thailand on December 8, shooting down three Thai biplanes that challenged them. They were accompanied by nine Mitsubishi Ki-30 attack planes of the 31st Sentai. The squadron leaders set up headquarters at the Bangkok airport, and the remaining squadrons flew in to join them over the next few days—perhaps sixty planes altogether, plus whatever Thai aircraft remained at Don Muang. The AVG romances speak of five hundred planes seen on the ground at Bangkok, but Chennault wrote "80–100" in his report to Chongqing, a figure so worrisome that he wanted to move back to Kunming. "No aircraft reporting net here," he pointed out, "and position very dangerous because impossible to prevent surprise." As an interim measure, Ken Merritt took the train to Rangoon and brought back the first of Bill Pawley's fast-climbing CW-21 interceptors.

In Singapore, Air Marshal Brooke-Popham was also lobbying Chongqing. He urged Chiang Kai-shek to make good on their "under-standing, amounting practically to an agreement," that the AVG help defend Rangoon's airport, which the British needed as a staging base to resupply Singapore. Chiang shared Brooke-Popham's concern, though he was more interested in the harbor, through which the lend-lease cornucopia poured its bounty into China, and he agreed to send an AVG squadron to Mingaladon.

Chennault cut the orders on Thursday, December 12, and once again he gave the nod to Oley Olson's 3rd Squadron. Twenty crew chiefs, armorers, radiomen, and cooks went down to Rangoon on the overnight train. Four more ground crewmen and three pilots followed Friday morning, driving the trucks and sedans that the squadron would need in Rangoon, while eighteen Tomahawks lifted off from Kyedaw and flew to the south.

The pilots sent to Mingaladon included three from other squadrons, while nine Hell's Angels stayed behind. Chennault came out of the Pacific War with a reputation as a gambler—always attacking, taking risks—but he only gambled when he had a good hand. He wouldn't send a man into harm's way until he was ready for combat, even if that meant permanent reserve status for pilots like the former flying-boat captain, Ed Conant.

Among those thought worthy were R. T. Smith and Paul Greene, from Randolph Field. They were pleased by the billets at Mingaladon: two-man rooms in a barrack at the southern end of the airport. "After landing and dispersing our ships," R. T. wrote in his diary, "we went to our quarters in the officers' barracks. Nice quarters & good mess. A better setup than Toungoo."

Group Captain Manning assigned the Tomahawks to Mingaladon's east–west runway—the crosspiece of the letter A—while his Buffaloes used the one that ran north–south. Each squadron was split into flights, one at each end of its assigned runway. Thus, when the alarm went off, upward of thirty planes bounced across the gravel from four directions, blowing up a dust storm as they went. All pilots were supposed to keep to the right, and the Buffalo pilots to hold down and let the Tomahawks cross over them where the runways intersected.

The system was put to the test on Saturday, when Burma Observation Corps reported Japanese bombers flying into Tenasserim from Thailand. Fourteen Buffaloes and sixteen Tomahawks made the rush across the gravel, sweeping past each other with a flair that did credit to the Flying Trapeze—"the damnedest rat race you ever saw," Curt Smith recalled. One Hell's Angel had to stand on his brakes to avoid a Buffalo, but all thirty planes got airborne without damage, and faster than any other system would have permitted. They climbed to a chilly rendezvous, three miles above the chalk-white runways and green-brown rice fields.

The air force targeted on Malaya and Burma was the JAAF 3rd Hikoshidan, commanded by General Sugawara Michio. A clerkish-looking man with a forage cap planted squarely on his head, two broad patches for eyebrows, mournful eyes, and a mustache trimmed to the exact length of his mouth, Sugawara wanted to neutralize the Burmese panhandle so it couldn't be used to reinforce the British army in Malaya. Japanese commandos seized Victoria Point, Tenasserim's southernmost town, and Sugawara ordered the destruction of Mergui, the next town north. He gave the assignment to two heavy-bomber sentais, the 12th and 60th, with fifty-one Mitsubishi Ki-21s between them—the big army bomber that western pilots called "Sally."

The Allied interceptors never saw them. The Buffaloes returned to Mingaladon when the pilots realized that the raiders weren't bound for Rangoon. The Hell's Angels couldn't make radio contact with 67 Squadron or the airport, so they patrolled aimlessly until they were low on gasoline. Then they, too, went home.

On Sunday, the RAF issued passes to the Hell's Angels so they could drive the twelve miles into Rangoon. It was a drab city with half a dozen watering holes, from the raucous Silver Grill to the stately bar of the Swiss-run Strand Hotel. "Bad day for all men and lots of pilots," wrote Daniel Hoyle in the squadron log; "they went to Rangoon, Burma, on various amusement occasions, arriving back for duty at the aerodrome, in the wee hours of the morning." While the Americans had the day off, the Buffalo pilots strafed Japanese targets in Thailand and at Victoria Point.

L auchlin Currie's plan to induct Chennault's irregulars had been endorsed by the War Department and forwarded to AMISSCA in Chongqing. On December 12, General Magruder drafted a radiogram to Chennault, asking him to come back into the army and bring his pilots with him. The message had Chennault returning to active duty as "brigadier general or colonel," but before sending it, Magruder crossed out those words and inserted: "if so, what grade?" Not long after, he began a radiogram with an actual blank for the Old Man's rank: "If Chennault were commissioned immediately as _____," the AVG would benefit because it could be reinforced through normal channels.

Chennault would have been delighted to return to duty—but not as a colonel. He'd served in that capacity for four years, and now he wanted *stars* on his shoulder tabs. He composed a message for Madame Chiang, asking if the Generalissimo wanted the AVG to revert to U.S. control. Army pay would fall far short of what the men had been promised, but China could match their service income with local funds, as was done by South American countries hiring U.S. military personnel. Chennault scrupulously laid out the advantages: China would save money, reinforcements were more likely, and it would be easier to enforce discipline on the "enlisted men." As for disadvantages, he mentioned only one. The U.S. Army might assign an AVG commander who didn't understand China—i.e., somebody other than Claire Chennault.

Nervous as a cat at Kyedaw airfield, he ordered another patrol of Thailand. After touring Chiang Mai and nearby towns, the Tomahawks reported no aircraft on the ground in northern Thailand. Chennault wasn't reassured. He sent another radiogram to Chongqing, asking if he could move down to Rangoon—not the best disposition, perhaps, but better than gambling his people, planes, and supplies at this crazily exposed location on the Thai border. Getting no reply, he went back to plan one: could the AVG quit Burma altogether? This did evoke a response, dictated by Chiang Kai-shek, signed by Madame, and routed through General Chou. As always, it was a compromise: the Hell's Angels would stay at Mingaladon, but the rest of the group could fall back into China.

Kunming was 700 air miles from Toungoo, across one of the world's most inhospitable frontiers. The first step was for a CNAC transport to ferry a skeleton crew over the mountains to Kunming, which was done on Wednesday, December 17. Next day, three more transports picked up the headquarters staff and enough ammunition, oxygen, and supplies for two weeks of combat. Paul Frillmann was in the airlift of "combat personnel." Similarly privileged were Olga Greenlaw, her dog Lucy, and a monkey belonging to the 2nd Squadron ground crewmen.

As the Tomahawks rolled across Kyedaw's asphalt runway for the last time, Freeman Ricketts taxied into a Studebaker sedan and George Burgard went off the end of the runway, leaving thirty-four fighters to make the move into China. The Panda Bears made the flight in two stages, refueling at the brick-red airstrip at Lashio. The Adam & Eves flew nonstop, navigating IFR to Lashio, then northeast over the mountains, staying at 21,000 feet to clear the summits.

Kunming was easy to find, with smoke billowing into the thin, clear air. Hours before, the city had been struck by eight or ten medium bombers—twin-engine Kawasaki Ki-48s, code-named Lily by Allied pilots—from the 21st Hikotai in Vietnam. (A hikotai usually contained two squadrons with dissimilar aircraft.) The bombers were escorted by a like number of Nakajima Ki-27 Nates, equipped with auxiliary fuel tanks for the 750-mile round trip. "The streets were strewn with bodies," said Fritz Wolf of his first sight of Kunming. "The Chinese . . . walked about the streets and picked up their dead, placing them in neat piles."

The headquarters staff and the Panda Bears were billeted at Hostel Number One in the northern part of the city. Two men shared a room with bunks, chairs, table, bureau, desk, charcoal brazier—and "Number One Boy." (The charcoal was a mixed blessing. Without it the chill entered their bones; with it, they risked carbon monoxide poisoning.) The Adam & Eves were assigned to Hostel Number Two on the airport road, where the accommodations were more primitive. A cluster of sun-fired brick buildings, it was dubbed Adobe City by the men of the 1st Squadron.

The ground crews had a more difficult route to travel. On December 20, eight trucks and two sedans left Kyedaw on the road to Mandalay, and another convoy left next day. They carried most of the ground personnel, all the heavy supplies, and considerable contraband. They were two weeks on the tortuous mountain road, dealing with officious Britons, obsequious Anglo-Burmans, corrupt Chinese, and hill tribes with women whose necks were stretched to giraffe-like proportions. The trip delighted radioman Smith, that fan of *The Royal Road to Romance*: "We are driving on red roads through rolling, hilly forest. Great clumps of poinsettias grow wild at the side of the highway. . . . Red dust over green shrubs makes a purplish tinge; we ride over purple hills. There are no palm trees now; the people look more Chinese than Burmese. Their skins are lighter, and they wear trousers instead of skirts. . . .

"Yesterday we descended into a gorge and made 15 tight, steep hairpin curves to get out," Smith went on. "I stopped the car halfway up and watched the seven trucks below. Several could not make the curves at the first try, and the drivers had to back up to get around. If they had backed up an inch or so too far, they would have rolled hundreds of feet to the river below."

Twenty-seven men stayed in Toungoo—Point A, it was called— under Ed Goyette, a pilot now serving as a staff officer. They'd maintain Kyedaw as a backup field, repair facility, supply depot, and radio relay station between Kunming and Rangoon. Their first assignment was to overhaul twelve Tomahawks unable to make the flight into China.

In Kunming—Point X—Chennault picked up more volunteers. As if to make up for the loss of Alsop, the U.S. Navy lent him Lieutenant Commander Robert DeWolfe as a supply officer. Then there was Gerhard Neumann, a refugee German Jew whom Chennault had befriended in 1939, and who now joined the AVG as a mechanic. The ground crews, Neumann recalled, "were hard-drinking, poker-playing, rough and tough, [but they] went out of their way to teach me the American way of life. . . . Never before had I heard of Log Cabin syrup, hotcakes or waffles. . . . I had never seen—or even heard of—a baseball game. . . . When [we] walked behind an attractive Chinese girl in a tight silk dress, my Texan friend sighed[:] 'I'd like to bite her in the ass and let her drag me to death!' I couldn't imagine what this Texan had in mind: I knew neither the three-letter word for posterior nor why he wanted to be dragged to death." The Americans called him "Herman the German." Neumann repaid their friendship with concerts on his Hohner accordion, playing such 1941 favorites as "When the Lights Go on Again (All Over the World)."

Four pilots stood alert that first night in China: if the Japanese struck Kunming on Thursday, Chennault reasoned, they'd be back next day. But not until 9:30 AM Saturday, December 20, did the warning net report ten bombers crossing into Yunnan province from Vietnam. At Wujiaba airport, the yellow warning flag went up. Chennault hurried to his command bunker in a graveyard overlooking the field. Radioman Don Whelpley recalled the scene: "Inside the dank, dark dugout . . . were gathered Chennault, his Chinese interpreter, the usual radio operators and Chinese personnel. . . . I watched Chennault's face as reports from the Chinese air raid net came in, tracing the progress of the attackers. *Heavy engine noise at Kaiyuan.* The lines tightened about his mouth as he pulled a pipe from the pocket in his khaki jacket. I knew he was nervous by the way he crammed tobacco into it. *Unknown aircraft over Hwaning, headed northwest.*"

The red flare went up, and sixteen Tomahawks rolled down the gravel runway and rose into the air. These were the Adam & Eves, who climbed to 15,000 feet and flew southeast. As the assault echelon, Sandy Sandell's squadron was to prowl fifty miles of railroad track from Kunming to Iliang, intercepting the Japanese as they flew IFR to the target. "It's strange how big the sky really is, once you get up there," Jim Cross wrote of his first combat patrol. "No trick at all to completely miss a bomber formation, even though it may be only a couple of miles or so out of the path. . . . It was bitter cold and my [windshield] was already frosted."

Jack Newkirk's 2nd Squadron provided backup. Four Panda Bears circled the airfield and four others flew to the northwest, meanwhile climbing to 15,000 feet. Newkirk led this second flight. Ten minutes after takeoff, he was astonished to see a formation of twin-engine planes coming toward him, eight miles out and 2,000 feet below. The intruders were arranged in a "vee of vees," four bombers in a diamond followed by three more to starboard and another three to port. As on the earlier raid, this was the 21st Hikotai from Hanoi—this time without an escort. Long afterward, a survivor explained that the bombers were a *suteishi butai* (sacrifice squadron) intended to lure up enemy fighters and destroy them. The commander was Captain Fujii Tatsujiro.

In the command bunker, Don Whelpley heard the Panda Bears debating whether the formation was hostile:

"There they are."

"That can't be the Japs."

"The hell it can't. Look at those red balls!"

Indeed, Captain Fujii was following a favorite Japanese tactic, circling around the target and approaching from the far side. The four Panda Bears attacked from out of the sun, opening fire so soon that even their large-caliber nose guns couldn't bridge the distance. The Lilys tightened formation, turned east, and jettisoned their bombs. Thus lightened, they were almost as fast as the Tomahawks. Jack Newkirk led his flight back to Wujiaba, explaining that his electrical system had failed him and his guns wouldn't fire. "It turned out to work perfect on the ground," Don Rodewald noted, "so we all had our ideas."

Meanwhile Captain Fujii circled around Kunming to the south. Sandy Sandell spotted the Lilys coming toward him at 16,000 feet: "single tail, aluminum construction," he wrote in his combat report; "red sun on wingtips [and] fuselage, dull gray color." He ordered two Adam & Eves to prowl overhead as "weavers," guarding against enemy fighters, and divided the others into flights of four. Two flights would dive on the Japanese formation out of the sun while the third remained in reserve.

Sandell wasn't a popular leader—"a small fellow," Charlie Bond described him, "with a mustache and a very cold manner"—and in the excitement his instructions seem to have been ignored. So were the lessons Chennault had drilled into them at Kyedaw. Bob Little dove through the clouds to attack the Lilys from below, where their defensive armament seemed to be weakest; Charlie Bond, in the same flight, decided to attack from above. The Lilys were still in the porcupine cluster they'd assumed after Newkirk's attack. As the Tomahawks swept down, each plane lowered its "dustbin"—a hinged platform with a gunner lying prone upon it. The bombers could now put out directed fire to the rear, but paid for the protection with a considerable drop in speed.

Bond charged his machine guns. For the wing guns, this was done by yanking T-grips on each side of the seat, while the large-caliber nose guns had charging handles projecting from the instrument panel. Then he turned on his reflector sight—a "pipper" inside a circle, seemingly hanging in the air between him and the target. (The illusion came from a half-silvered mirror that Charlie Mott had rigged to a bracket on the left side of the cockpit. The lash-up was more accurate than the ring-and-post sight, but a pilot could easily knock the mirror out of alignment. "It only took a sneeze," armorer Chuck Baisden recalled in 1999.) Finally Bond flipped the toggles that readied the guns for firing.

The firing button was located on the control stick, which he held in both gloved hands. "I rolled and started down," Bond wrote in his diary. "As the nearest bomber eased within the gunsight ring, I squeezed the trigger on the stick. Damn it, nothing happened! I took a quick look at my gun switch. In my excitement, I had checked it so many times that I had turned it off. . . . I broke off violently—down and away, and then back up to my original position for another attack. . . . [All] guns were blazing this time. I saw my tracers enter the fuselage of the bomber. At the last second I broke off. . . . I attacked again and again. Two bombers began to lag behind, trailing smoke."

Also in the assault echelon was Fritz Wolf, who not long afterward recalled the engagement for a macho aviation magazine: "My man was the outside bomber of the right-hand V. I dived down below him and came up from underneath. . . . At 500 yards I let go with a quick burst of all guns. It was curtains for the rear gunner of the bomber. I could see my bullets rip into him and cut him to pieces. . . . At one hundred yards I let go with a long burst, and the bullets tore into the Jap plane's motor and gas tanks. A wing folded and a motor tore loose, then the bomber exploded in midair. I yanked back on the stick. . . .

"I shoved Old Bessie into a dive for another attack. This time it was the inside man of the outside V. I came out of the dive quickly and straightened out level with the bomber. . . . I could see the tail gunner blazing away at me, but none of the bullets was striking home. At fifty yards I let go with a long burst. . . . The bomber exploded, but this time I was too close and managed to pull up just inches away from the flaming coffin as it dipped earthward."

Flying on Wolf's wing through both attacks was Jim Cross of the Ferry Command, who also wrote about the battle for a wartime magazine: "There was the Jap plane, dead in front of me. I could see the sun glinting on the [dust-bin] gunner's goggles. . . . I saw my own tracer fire almost before I realized I'd pressed the button. The sky above me was ribboned with criss-cross fire. I waited a split second before letting go with another burst. Waited until I saw the engines of the bomber right in front of my ring sight. . . . Five hundred miles an hour is plenty fast. That's what I was doing as I passed the bomber. But I'd seen my tracers burying themselves in it. . . . The confusion, the screams and the roar of racing, diving Allisons. Even the sounds of the guns were lost in that."

The reserve pilots were led by Ed Leibolt, a former army fighter pilot. His wingman was Joe Rosbert, a stocky Italian-American from Philadelphia, to whom the combat seemed "like a bunch of swarming bees. I wondered why our planes did not collide with each other, they looked so close." Then Leibolt signaled the attack, as Rosbert recalled: "I tensed myself and followed him down, with my pucker string performing some strange gyrations. As the rear bomber loomed large in front of us, I pressed the gun button almost at the same time as Ed. Debris flew by as we dove down and away. As we started in for a second run, I saw only six bombers. Ed was in the midst of the other planes and I could not make him out; so I made the run alone. With a short burst, I knew the bomber had been hit, as I pulled away and down."

This free-for-all was joined by Eddie Rector of the Panda Bears. Off-duty that Sunday, he'd watched the two squadrons take off, then Jack Newkirk's flight return with its gun barrels whistling—audible proof they'd been in combat. (The muzzles were taped over for flight, to keep water and dust from entering.) A crew under Harry Fox was working on Rector's Tomahawk, but he sprinted out to the flight line and yelled: "Get that goddamned cowling back on!" While they did so, Rector buckled on his parachute and climbed into the cockpit. He taxied out onto the field, awed by the sight of the billowing clouds that awaited him. "I fired up that P-40 and got out and chased them," he told me years later, banking his hands to represent his plane, the Lilys, and the Tomahawks diving among them. "I saw eight damned airplanes out there engaging them. They were pulling up like this, and shooting, and it was bizarre beyond compare."

Rector remembered his navy gunnery practice and Chennault's lectures at Kyedaw airfield. He took the high perch and came down in a long, sweeping turn behind one of the Lilys: "I came on in, right behind the guy . . . and I drove up his ass. I got target fixation—I just saw my shots going into him, and I said, *Why doesn't he blow up?* At the last moment I realized what I was doing. I looked, and I'd shot away the jaw of the rear dust-bin gunner. I looked at him—right in the eye—and I'd shot away his whole jaw. And I can see him [now], and I can see the rivets and the camouflage pattern of that damned bomber. I know that I missed him by inches. . . . I pulled up and looked back, and he was on fire. I can see the flames. But he's still in formation, and I prepare myself for another run. And then I saw him do this: the formation goes ahead, and he gradually noses down . . . flaming till hell won't have it. All afire!

"And then I start my next pass. I go in, and I find out that there's only one thirty-caliber going putt-putt-putt. I pulled and I pulled [the charging handles]. I'd fired for three or four seconds, remember, going up the ass of that guy, and then I pulled out and they cooled, and the guns were so hot that they set."

As the story of the AVG's first combat is usually told, nine Lilys went down in flames, but only four victories were credited: two to Fritz Wolf, one to Eddie Rector, and one to Einar (Mickey) Mikelson. The point is important, because the December 20 firefight over Iliang was one of very few in which AVG claims were verified by the ground-observer network Chennault himself had established, as well as by Japanese accounts.

What happened is this: The starboard vee of bombers, led by Lieutenant Funamoto Shigeru, was hit again and again by the full force of the AVG. All three Lilys went down. For each engine that burst into flame, two or three Americans were pouring machine gun fire into it— adrenaline pumping, sphincters twitching, vision tunneled down to that eruption of scarlet flame and oily black smoke. Diving clear, each man was understandably convinced that he alone had killed the bomber.

Except for Bob Neale. He was that rarity among fighter pilots, a modest man. Asked in 1962 if he'd shot down any Lilys that day, Neale replied: "I didn't even know if I hit one. I could see them, all right, but you can see a lot better than you can shoot. . . . It was all new to me. I've never been a hero type, and I wasn't figuring on starting then, if ever."

A Chinese listening post reported seven bombers aloft at 11:25 AM, after the Tomahawks broke off, thus confirming the Japanese account. There was heavy damage to the survivors, however, as recalled by Suzuki Goichi in 1992: "We had the battle for about thirty minutes, and before it was over, the gunner sitting behind me died on [my] airplane. Then another gunner who sat on my left was also killed. . . . But since our airplanes had rubber covers over the fuel tanks to [seal them], they never had been set fire though they were carrying a lot of bombs. Therefore, seven of our airplanes could come back to the base though lots of us couldn't lower landing gear due to the damage from the shooting. So, some landed with only one gear, and others on their bodies. Everyone landed somehow, but all airplanes had bullets in their bodies. Even mine had about thirty shots."

A few days later, the Chinese reported that a fourth bomber had exploded in the air before landing at Hanoi. The pilots voted to share the kills among all those taking part: fourteen Adam & Eves plus Eddie Rector of the Panda Bears. For the record, then, each man was credited with four-fifteenths of a Ki-48.

Japanese histories agree that three Lilys were shot down in the fight, with others crash-landing afterward at Gia Lam airport outside Hanoi. (Perhaps a Chinese spy saw one such crash, accounting for the delayed fourth confirmation.) Three Lilys lost, seven damaged, and fourteen airmen dead—a disaster unprecedented since the first months of the Sino-Japanese War. In the teakwood classroom at Kyedaw, Chennault had assured his pilots that if the Japanese suffered 25 percent casualties, they wouldn't return. He was right: the 21st Hikotai never came back to Kunming.

The cost was one Tomahawk. Returning to Wujiaba, Eddie Rector ran out of fuel and made a belly landing in a vegetable field. He spent the afternoon stripping the machine guns and ammunition out of his Tomahawk, then found a bunk at an AVG listening post manned by Roger Shreffler. Next day, he hitched a ride to Kunming on a Chinese army truck, bringing his guns with him.

The people of Kunming, who'd endured Japanese bombing for more than a year, streamed out to the airport to show their appreciation. Joe Rosbert recalled the celebration: "Soon we heard a band coming towards the field and a long procession appeared at the entrance. Led by the mayor were hundreds of people, each one carrying something. He made a speech while we all stood in line listening. . . . Little girls, with pretty faces crowned by neatly cut bangs, stepped up and placed long pieces of purple silk around our necks and bouquets of flowers in our hands."

Chennault was less impressed. He dismissed Jack Newkirk's performance as "buck fever." He wasn't much happier with Sandy Sandell, whose assault echelons had scattered in the first pass, and whose reserves were drawn into the melee. "The Old Man looked crestfallen," radioman Don Whelpley recalled. "But . . . he didn't say so. Instead, he sat his boys down, and with the kindness of a fond parent, explained their mistakes. He ended the discussion with, 'Next time, fellows, get them all.' "

With the advantage of the international date line, American newspapers published the story on December 21—next morning, as it seemed. In a world resounding with gigantic clashes of arms, the Yunnan skirmish was a minor affair, and the *New York Times* relegated it to page 27. At *Time* magazine, however, Henry Luce saw more to the story. A genius of popular journalism, Luce had been born in China; and his belief in America's destiny there was reinforced by a visit in May 1941. His guide was Teddy White, Chennault's sometime messmate at the Methodist mission in Chongqing. When Luce returned to New York, he took White with him as *Time* editor for East Asia. It was the perfect melding of talents, motives, and events. White knew the background of the AVG's victory, Luce had the agenda to play the story large, and they had a catchy name to put on it.

The story was entitled "Blood for the Tigers," and it told how the Japanese had bombed hapless China for three years until "lean, hard-bitten, taciturn Colonel Claire L. Chennault" recruited American fliers and brought them to Asia: "Last week ten Japanese bombers came winging their carefree way up into Yunnan, heading directly for Kunming, the terminus of the Burma Road. Thirty miles south of Kunming, the Flying

Tigers swooped, let the Japanese have it. Of the ten bombers . . . four plummeted to earth in flames. The rest turned tail and fled. Tiger casualties: none."

Flying Tigers! It was the perfect conceit—but where had it come from? The credit went to the AVG "Washington Squadron," as David Corcoran, Quinn Shaughnessy, Bill Youngman, and Whitey Willauer had styled themselves. Months before, the men at China Defense Supplies had asked the Walt Disney studio to design a unit emblem. A dragon was the obvious choice—a *flying* dragon, with connotations of China and aerial combat. David Corcoran suggested a tiger instead, and that met with general agreement. (Another account has T. V. Soong making the substitution.) The request went to Hollywood, and in October two Disney employees—Roy Williams and Henry Porter—sketched a darling Bengal cat with wasplike wings and extended claws, leaping from a V-for-Victory sign.

So the name was ready when the news of the AVG's first combat reached New York, and *Time*'s Teddy White put it to good use. Over the years, journalists and historians have tried to find a source for the name in China, but its derivation is less exotic: the Tigers were christened by a well-paid suit in Washington.

Chapter 6

Such a Bright Red!

L ightly armed, moving fast, and living off "Churchill stores" (as they called captured British goods), the Japanese drove the Commonwealth army down through Malaya. They fared equally well against U.S. and Filipino troops in the Philippines. Meanwhile, Japanese bombers softened Indonesia for invasion—sparing the oil fields, however. Japan had hoarded enough fuel for six months of war. After that, like General Yamashita in Malaya, she'd depend on what she captured from the enemy.

Below this crumbling colonial barrier, Australia lay almost unguarded, her forces fighting for Britain on other fronts. To the west lay India—the jewel in Britain's crown, inexhaustible source of cannon fodder, and now the fulcrum of her war effort. Lose India, and Germany and Japan could join hands across the Middle East, turning their diplomatic Axis into geographical fact.

Before that final triumph, however, the Japanese had to pivot west through Burma—an impossibility, the British believed. The Royal Navy could stop a seaborne invasion, and nature guarded the overland route from Thailand. The geography of Southeast Asia has a north–south bias: mountains and rivers (and therefore roads, railways, and national boundaries) conspire to make east–west travel difficult. In 1940s Burma, the Irrawaddy and Sittang rivers provided cheap and easy transport upcountry while discouraging travel across it; the east–west roads were little more than mule tracks. This was part of Britain's strategy for defending, not just Burma, but India as well: the two colonies shared a 900-mile frontier, but no road led across it. The British intended Burma to be a cul-de-sac, never dreaming they'd be the ones caught in it.

The chiefs of staff were so convinced that Burma couldn't be invaded "across the grain of the country" that they left its defense to a scratch division under General Donald McLeod, headquartered at Toungoo. Olga Greenlaw remembered him as "a sweet old gentleman, tall, a bit heavy, with perfectly white hair and a ruddy complexion." Burma Division had 18,000 men on rations, but most were native conscripts, border police, and militia. The serious fighting would be done by 1,000 British and 3,000 Indian soldiers, trained for the desert rather than the rain forest of Southeast Asia.

McLeod reported to Brooke-Popham in Singapore, 1,200 miles southeast. This was a ludicrous arrangement. Two Japanese armies held the ground between them, and their radio link was so poor that messages had to be relayed through India. Late in December, therefore, the chiefs of staff took Burma away from Brooke-Popham and gave it to the new commander-in-chief for India: General the Right Honorable Sir Archibald Wavell, one-eyed veteran of World War I, the Boer War, and long-ago skirmishes in Afghanistan. Wavell flew to Rangoon on December 21. After a conference with Burma's commanders, McLeod for the army and Group Captain Manning for the air force, he decided to replace both of them. He ordered 17th Indian Division to Burma, and he told London that the colony must be reinforced by two squadrons of fighters, two of bombers, and a quantity of antiaircraft guns. That done, he flew to Chongqing to see what help he could wrest from Chiang Kai-shek. Accompanying him was his American deputy, General George Brett of the U.S. Army Air Forces. (It was Brett who'd signed the order authorizing AVG recruiters to visit army airfields the previous spring.) Chiang offered to send six divisions to Burma, but Wavell wasn't interested in soldiers. "Obviously," he wrote, "it was desirable that a country of the British Empire should be defended by Imperial troops rather than by foreign." Instead he wanted Chiang to pledge that "one of the AVG squadrons, which Colonel Chennault wanted to remove to China, remained in Burma for the defence of Rangoon." He also needed some of China's lend-lease supplies. "To neither of these requests," he glumly noted, "did I get a definite reply."

A t Mingaladon airport outside Rangoon, the Hell's Angels were calling themselves "the lost squadron." Except for Ed Goyette's detachment in Toungoo, there was no backup closer than Kunming, 900 miles away. RAF 67 Squadron had thirty-two Buffaloes on strength, but half were grounded with mechanical problems, and RAF 60 Squadron had only four Blenheims. The others had been sent to Singapore for bombing practice just before the Japanese attack, and they were promptly drafted into the defense of Malaya.

A Curtiss Tomahawk with full AVG war paint, probably at Mingaladon airport after the Hell's Angels moved to Rangoon—the men appear to be wearing British army helmets. Note the coolant flaps, which are open to increase the airflow across the Prestone radiator. (National Air and Space Museum)

The Hell's Angels had arrived without so much as a change of clothing, expecting the British to supply their needs. All they got was gasoline and three pallid meals a day. When they went to refill their oxygen tanks, they learned that the Tomahawk's coupling was different from a Buffalo's. British ammunition didn't fit their wing guns, which were chambered for 7.92-mm rounds. The Buffalo pilots agreed to use the AVG radio frequency when the squadrons patrolled together, but this arrangement hadn't yet been tested.

Enemy reconnaissance had counted forty-four planes at Mingaladon, Kyedaw, and the RAF fields in Tenasserim. To the Japanese, these numbers suggested that the British were preparing an airlift into Malaya. To prevent that, General Sugawara ordered the 77th Sentai to occupy Phitsanulok, on the Thai railroad 300 miles east of Rangoon. The 77th was a redoubtable force, credited with destroying eighteen Chinese and Russian aircraft in the Sino-Japanese War, but like most JAAF fighter groups it was still equipped with fixed-gear Nakajima Nates. They were painted an overall gray, armed only with two rifle-caliber machine guns, without self-sealing fuel tanks, and mostly without pilot armor; in combat, they'd prove much slower than Allied fighters, though much more maneuverable. The commander was Major Yoshioka Hiroshi, a cold-looking man with a thin mustache and narrow face. He was reinforced at Phitsanulok by the 31st Sentai, equipped with the Mitsubishi Ki-30 attack plane (Ann, to Allied pilots) with fixed landing gear, 600-pound bomb load, one fixed 7.7-mm machine gun, and a flexible gun at the rear of the greenhouse canopy. Major Yoshioka also established a forward airstrip at Raheng, just 200 miles from Rangoon.

Group Captain Manning asked the Hell's Angels to escort a troopship taking reinforcements to Mergui. Oley Olson calculated that his Tomahawks would have a gasoline reserve of forty-five minutes while over Tenasserim, so he refused the mission. The long-legged Buffaloes of 67 Squadron had no such problem: they returned in relays to Moulmein, refueled, and in this fashion were able to escort the ship until dusk. Meanwhile, two Buffaloes at Mergui nipped across the border into Thailand and strafed a train "travelling south with reinforcements" for the Japanese army in Malaya—the sort of interference Sugawara meant to prevent.

So it came to Tuesday, December 23, when sixty Mitsubishi heavy bombers lifted off from the airports at Bangkok and Phnom Penh. The Ki-21 Sally was a big-tailed monoplane with two huge radial engines and up to six defensive guns. Carrying a metric ton of bombs, it had devastated Chongqing, Kunming, Hong Kong, Manila, and Singapore. Now Rangoon was to be added to the list.

A true believer in the "battleplane" concept, Sugawara sent his heavy bombers to Burma without fighter escort. Worse, he assigned Mingaladon airport to the weakest group, the 62nd Sentai, mustering only fifteen early-model Sallys. They were commanded by the officer Major Kato had talked to on December 6: Colonel Onishi Hiroshi, a brutal-looking man with jug ears, wide nose, and lantern jaw. The Mingaladon attack would be bolstered by the 31st Sentai from Phitsanulok, with the Anns protected by Major Yoshioka's Nates. The three groups were supposed to rendezvous over Raheng, then fly as one great formation to Mingaladon. But the Sallys didn't wait for the single-engine aircraft, and when they crossed the border they were two miles out in front. The distance to the target was 125 miles. The day was beautiful, with a light southerly breeze and hardly a cloud in the sky.

Two other heavy-bomber groups were to rendezvous over Bangkok, fly north to Moulmein, then cross Martaban Bay to Rangoon. But the Bangkok-based Sallys left before those from Phnom Penh came over, so this formation too was split by the time it reached South Burma.

Sue Upfill was an American woman married to a New Zealand insurance agent; they lived on the airport access road, so convenient to the RAF operations building that the airport's commanding officer was billeted with them. "The morning of the twenty-third dawned cool and clear," she wrote long afterward. "The airport hummed with activity and lorries sped along the road." Still, it was nearly nine o'clock before they went off to their posts, Wing Commander Norman Rutter to the airport and the Upfills to the hospital where Sue was a volunteer with the St. John's Ambulance Brigade.

The operations room logged the news at 9:30 AM: "two large waves of enemy aircraft approaching Rangoon, one from east and other from southeast." It was another half hour before the Hell's Angels got the news.

Oley Olson had organized his pilots into four-man sections. From dawn to dusk, one section was on alert, while two more were on thirty-minute call; a "release" section was off duty for the day. Thus, of fourteen airworthy Tomahawks on December 23, only twelve had pilots assigned to them. They were to operate as six-plane flights under George McMillan and Parker Dupouy.

McMillan and R. T. Smith were apparently alone in the bamboo-and-canvas alert tent when the word arrived: "Clear the field!" They sprinted to the flight line, fired up their engines, and thereby alerted the standby pilots that they were needed. The first to arrive were Tom Haywood and Robert (Duke) Hedman, who scrambled into their cockpits and put on their earphones. "I heard McMillan over the radio saying we were taking off," Hedman reported a few days later. "I took it as a joke."

Circling over the airport, McMillan got further details on the radio: "Enemy bombers approaching from east." Two of his men were missing, but he decided not to wait. Instead, he took his four planes to the eastward and gained what altitude he could. At 10,000 feet, Tom Haywood yelled into his microphone: "Hey, Mac! I see the bastards!" Sure enough, to the east and high above, McMillan saw fifteen huge, twin-engine bombers. They were painted pale gray on their undersides, light brown with green splotches above, with red disks blazing on the fuselage and wings.

Since crossing into Burma, Colonel Onishi's air crews had the white A of Mingaladon's runways in view, and soon they saw the dust trails of the 67 Squadron Buffaloes, taking off to meet them. (Vic Bargh and Gordon Williams were on a standing patrol over Mingaladon, so were the first to spot the raiders. "Hell!" Vic shouted. "Showers of 'em, look Willie! Showers of 'em!") Spurred by the sight, the Japanese pilots opened their throttles, increasing the distance between them and the Nates that could have protected them.

Years later, Duke Hedman told me how the Sallys bore down on Mingaladon in vee formation, followed by an apparently aimless swarm of fighters: "There were hordes of fighters, going around in a kind of beehive formation—going around in circles, kind of looking out for each other, protecting each other, going up and down. It was a very peculiar formation." The swarm was actually two groups, the Nates hovering protectively around the slower, single-engine light bombers. "The [heavy] bombers by contrast were in very tight, perfect formations, based on three-three-three. . . . And they would not deviate at all. But the thing that amazed me was the *numbers* of them—and that perfect tight formation—and that bright red rising sun. Such a bright red!"

The 62nd Sentai settled into its bombing run, flying a course of 240 degrees toward Mingaladon. The Buffaloes hit them first, damaging the Sally flown by Lieutenant Niioka Akira, who dropped behind the formation with his port engine smoking. Then the Tomahawks swept down. If Hedman was awed by the quantity of enemy aircraft, and confused by their type, so were the Japanese. One survivor reported that he was set upon by "thirty Buffaloes and Hurricanes," while others identified the liquid-cooled fighters as Spitfires.

McMillan led the Hell's Angels, followed one at a time by his three wingmen. Crammed into the cockpit of No. 77, R. T. Smith experienced for the first time the cotton mouth, the pounding heart, and the bladder ready to burst: "And now it was my turn, diving and turning to line up my gunsight . . . squeezing the stick-trigger and hearing the crackling sound of my four .30 caliber wing guns and the slower, powerful thudding of the two .50s in the nose . . . the pungent smell of cordite filling the cockpit, a good smell . . . the bombers were firing back, tracers crisscrossing the sky in every direction, black smoke and flames streaming from the left engine of a bomber up ahead, and all the while that creepy-crawly feeling at the back of the neck, knowing their fighters must surely be about to pounce down on us."

R. T. quickly learned two things about going to war in a fighter plane. First, it was a lonely business: when he finished his run and porpoised back to fighting altitude, his companions had vanished. Then there was the exquisite difficulty of deflection shooting. It wasn't just a matter of leading his target, as a hunter aims in front of the duck, because in this case the hunter too was airborne. R. T. was traveling at 250 mph, trying to hit a Sally moving at 180 mph on a different heading—a problem in three dimensions. To help his aim, phosphorus-coated tracer bullets were mingled with the plane-killing rounds. (The usual mix was one tracer, one incendiary, and three armor-piercing rounds, though this varied between squadrons.) The tracers sailed out in front of him—

lazy red fireflies, they seemed—to show whether the lethal rounds were on a collision course with the Sally. If not, he could correct by jinking left or right, up or down. His feet worked the rudder pedals; his left hand the throttle and trim tabs; his right hand the elevator, ailerons, and firing button. If a gun jammed, he had to clear it by yanking the pistol grips on the instrument panel or the T-grips beside his seat. "And all this time," R. T. wrote, "if the pilot is to live, his head is constantly turning in every direction," looking for enemy fighters.

He decided to attack from behind and below, simplifying the problem of deflection shooting while reducing his chances of being hit by return fire. So he "got directly behind him and just under his prop-wash, and opened fire at about 200 yards. I could see my tracers converging on the fuselage and wing roots . . . until he blew up right in my face." The concussion, he recalled, tossed his Tomahawk upward. Then he came under attack by three fixed-gear fighters, who'd left the single-engine bombers to help the Sallys. R. T. turned into the Nates, fired a burst at the leader, then escaped by pointing No. 77 straight down.

Tom Haywood had a similar baptism, opening fire at 500 yards and pressing the attack until a Sally "fell off on one wing out of the formation." Then he, too, was bounced by a Nate. Haywood swung toward the fixed-gear fighter, got off a burst, and found that the Japanese pilot easily out-turned him, so he too left the scene. He landed with ten bullet holes in his Tomahawk and an aileron control wire shot away.

The Sallys dropped their bombs and turned south, directly over Rangoon and its recently installed antiaircraft guns. The lead pilot may have been too frightened to think straight. Lieutenant Hayashi Iwao, flying a Sally in the 3rd squadron, recalled the bombing run as a scene of "indescribable horror," as one friend after another was hit—Niioka, Shimada, Sabe, Ikura—each falling behind to be set upon by Allied fighters.

R. T. Smith was among them. He found a lone Sally under attack by George McMillan's Tomahawk and a Buffalo. This may have been the Sally piloted by Lieutenant Niioka, his left engine crippled by a Buffalo in the first encounter. McMillan reported that he shot one engine out of the laggard, and R. T. that he finished it off, the crippled plane diving away at a 30-degree angle, trailing smoke, to crash on the Rangoon waterfront. Another of R. T.'s targets evidently survived, because a Japanese historian relates that the pilot of No. 77 was "very eager" in his attack on a Sally. The Tomahawk's six guns, a crewman said, made "a sound so loud it filled the sky."

The battle had now been joined by two of Olson's off-duty pilots. When the alarm went off, Chuck Older and Ed Overend were bicycling into Rangoon; they wheeled about, pedaled back to Mingaladon, and saw two Tomahawks on the flight line. "Why don't we hop in and go flying?" Older said. He was a Californian with the face of an East Coast preppie, who'd joined the marines for a lark between UCLA and law school.

The two men took off and made their way to the eastward, reaching 8,000 feet before bringing McMillan's flight into view. Soon after, Older saw a "huge conglomeration of airplanes, more than I'd ever seen together at one time." He was still climbing when he opened fire. "I aimed at one of the wing planes on the left side of the formation," he told me in 1986, and "smoke began streaming from the port engine." (This, too, sounds like Niioka's plane.) Older rolled out and returned, this time closing to seventy-five yards. "I gave it a long burst, and the bomber suddenly nosed down out of the formation with smoke streaming behind. I saw it roll over into almost a vertical dive and disappear below. I continued making attacks from below, this time aiming at the leader of the formation. . . . I saw the bomber explode . . . and flame and smoke seemed to pour out from the bottom of the fuselage. I saw debris falling from this plane immediately after the explosion, and the bomber nosed straight down with flames and smoke pouring from it."

Meanwhile, Ed Overend worked ahead of the formation and made a frontal attack. His tracers went wide, so he turned with the Sallys and attacked from the side. He made three more passes to no effect, but saw two bombers go down, one with its port engine blazing and the other diving at a steep angle out of control—probably the planes flown by Niioka and Shimada. On his fourth and subsequent attacks, Overend concentrated on a Japanese straggler, at times joined by another Tomahawk. Finally the Sally's port engine caught fire, and it pitched over into a 70-degree dive—Lieutenant Sabe Keiji, in all likelihood. He followed it down to 4,000 feet before being driven off by three Nates.

McMillan's late-starting standbys, Paul Greene and young Hank

Gilbert, also joined the attack. Having closed their bomb-bay doors, the remaining Sallys assumed a porcupine cluster, so the gunners—especially those in the topside greenhouse—could support each other. Gilbert was caught in this crossfire. His Tomahawk blossomed into a ball of red and orange fire, hung suspended for a moment, then fell to the earth, trailing long fingers of flame and smoke. "I saw him go down," Paul Greene told me long after. "He was just on fire, and he was right in front of me." Gilbert was two months past his twenty-second birthday.

Greene worried the bombers for four or five passes, then broke off to defend himself from the Nates. On a climbing attack he poured machine gun fire into a Japanese fighter from 300 yards, saw the fixed-gear plane fall away, and immediately engaged another at close range. "Although I hit him plenty," Greene reported, "I did not see him fall, for about this time there were fighters firing at me and evidently hit [my] controls for the ship went completely out of control." He slid back the canopy and jumped, diving for the root of the wing so he wouldn't be hit by his own tail fin. A six-footer, Greene had clambered into the Tomahawk wearing boots, shorts, and the parachute belonging to the much shorter Bob Brouk. When the chute opened, the harness bit into his crotch and shoulders, lacerating his skin and tearing a neck muscle. Then he looked up and saw blue sky where white silk should have been: several of the panels were gone. (The parachutes were Chinese, and at Kyedaw the Americans had joked about the ideograms on the pack, said to mean "umbrella insurance" or to be instructions to return it to the factory if it failed to open.)

Greene's plane had been shot from under him; he was hanging from two-thirds of a parachute; and now a Nate turned to strafe him, its radial engine enormous behind the propeller blur. Yellow-white tracer bullets sailed toward him, then the Nate roared past, prop wash buffeting him. That plane didn't return—observers on the ground said it was driven off by a Buffalo—but other Japanese pilots took up the sport. Hand over hand, Greene climbed the shrouds, to collapse the chute and fall more quickly out of danger. At the best of times, a parachute landing is like jumping from a second-story window. Greene hit so hard he was knocked unconscious. When he awakened, he found a gun pressed up against his face. Greene convinced the British major holding the weapon that they were on the same team, whereupon the officer bundled him into a car and drove him to the hospital.

Greene was credited with shooting down a Nate—wrongly, it seems, for all Japanese fighters returned safely to Raheng. As for bombers, Chuck Older was credited with two Sallys, Ed Overend and Tom Haywood with one each, and R. T. Smith with one and a half, the other half going to George McMillan. The Buffalo pilots claimed three, for a total of nine. The 62nd Sentai's actual losses on Tuesday morning came to five Sallys and their crew of thirty—a third of its strength. A Japanese account has three of the big bombers destroyed by the AVG (Sabe's, Niioka's, and Lieutenant Shimada's), a fourth by the RAF (Lieutenant Shingansho's), and the fifth (Ikura's) by an antiaircraft shell after it was knocked out of the formation by Allied fighters. "One of the wings collapsed," a Tokyo newspaper reported of the Sally hit by ground fire. "Lieutenant Ikura threw up his hands again and shouted something"—a *banzai* cheer for the emperor, as any Japanese reader would infer. "In the back, Sergeant-Major Hiwatari . . . continued firing while their plane was being consumed in flames. Finally he shot down the last [Allied fighter] and was all smiles when his plane blew up." Of the surviving Sallys, all were damaged by gunfire, with one bomber bearing forty-seven bullet holes.

If the Allied fighter pilots overestimated their victories, the Japanese were even more optimistic. They claimed two Buffaloes and seven Tomahawks (which they called Spitfires) in this combat over Mingaladon, for a total of nine planes, when only Gilbert and Greene had been shot down.

The other Hell's Angels had taken off in better order, six Tomahawks climbing "in string." Parker Dupouy was a thoughtful, stolid man with an engineering degree from Brown University and a remarkable set of eyebrows: thick, black, and cocked like chevrons. Over the radio, fighter control told him to circle Syriam, site of an oil refinery southeast of Rangoon. Half an hour after takeoff, Dupouy spotted a "very tight" formation of twin-engine bombers approaching Rangoon at 17,000 feet, camouflaged in shades of green. This was the 98th Sentai with eighteen late-model Sallys, more powerful and more heavily armed than those raiding Mingaladon. They were commanded by Colonel Usui Shigeki, flying as copilot of the plane assigned to Major Atsumi Hikaru—the major having moved down to the bombardier's compartment in the nose while a younger officer flew the plane. There were four enlisted gunners in the back, doubling as radioman, navigator, crew chief, and mechanic.

Dupouy divided his Tomahawks into three-plane flights, as Chennault had told his men to do when faced with bombers. He led Bill Reed and Ralph Gunvordahl in a front-quarter attack on the Sallys, making no hits and agreeably surprised not to be hit in return. The other trio—Neil Martin leading, with Bob Brouk and Ken Jernstedt on his wing—didn't fare as well. "Martin broke away and scooted out in front," one American recalled. Boring into the 98th Sentai from the side, Martin was met by the massed fire of eighteen greenhouse guns. He pulled up, presenting his vulnerable underside to the storm of bullets. "I don't know if he had been hit," mused Ken Jernstedt years later, "or if he just made a terrible mistake." The Japanese airmen also recalled the Allied pilot who "turned away, showing his belly to our gunners." Martin went down in flames. He was one of Olson's P-40 drivers from Mitchel Field, a gifted athlete, graduate of the University of Arkansas, and not much older than Hank Gilbert.

Jernstedt dropped below the level of the greenhouse gunners. "I made a below side approach to the rear quarter," he reported. "I saw the plane . . . falter, so I switched my aim to the other wing man. I gave him a short burst and must have hit his [engine] or an incendiary bomb because the bomber burst into flames and left the formation in a blazing dive." This was the Sally flown by Captain Mitsui Iteya, which crashed near the waterfront after its fuel tank exploded. Probably double-counting on Mitsui, Bob Brouk claimed a bomber at about the same time.

Parker Dupouy made repeated head-on attacks but—cautious engineer—put in no claim. Bill Reed worried the bombers from the beam and from below. Afterward, he reported shooting the port engine out of a Sally and seeing the big plane fall out of formation. Using the same tactic, Gunvordahl also claimed a bomber. Again, the two Hell's Angels were probably double-counting on the Sally piloted by Lieutenant Nogami Ryohei. When his left engine burst into fire, Nogami made a choice unusual for a Japanese airman: he bailed out with two of his crew. At least one was taken prisoner, though Sue Upfill recalled a bizarre scene at the hospital, where one parachute came down: "Beneath its folds, silent in death, was the Japanese airman, a live bomb clutched tightly in his hand."

The commander's plane was also badly hit. Machine gun bullets tore into the Sally from above and behind, stitching the copilot's seat and hitting Colonel Usui in the back and left shoulder. Hearing the crash of bullets, Major Atsumi scrambled out of the bombardier's compartment and tried to help his commanding officer. But the gallant commander—as the Japanese told the story—waved the major back to his post, dying even as Atsumi loosed the Sally's bombs upon downtown Rangoon. Though the firefight continued for half an hour, the 98th Sentai returned to Thailand with no further casualties.

For the two bombers lost, four pilots were credited with a kill: Ken Jernstedt, Bill Reed, Bob Brouk, and Ralph Gunvordahl. For their part, the 98th Sentai gunners claimed no fewer than twelve Allied fighters destroyed, against the one actually shot down.

Ten minutes behind schedule, the 60th Sentai droned over Rangoon at 23,000 feet. Twenty-seven Sallys dropped their bombs on the city and headed back to Thailand with occasional interference from Allied fighters. A crewman was shot through the forehead, and one plane crashed on the way home, probably from battle damage; the fate of its crew isn't known. The gunners on the other planes were credited with ten enemy fighters, bringing the total for the day to forty-one planes—more than the AVG and the RAF had in Burma on December 23.

W hen the raid began, most of Rangoon's officials were in conference with General McLeod. Interrupted by the screech of the air-raid alarm, the genial, white-haired officer glanced at his watch. "Plenty of time, gentlemen," he said. "Let us go on with the next item." Not entirely convinced, his listeners fidgeted and glanced at the clock. At last McLeod went to the door, where he chatted with the officials as they left the room. When they finally managed to escape, they found

Rangoon in a carnival mood. Colonel Usui's 98th Sentai was approaching the city with fighter planes in hot pursuit. Few of the officials knew
that an AVG squadron was stationed at Mingaladon, so they assumed
the raiders were being chased by the Royal Air Force.

"Agleam in the sunlight," one of them recalled in 1956, "the enemy
bombers came on in arrow-head formation. Men climbed out of the
trenches to watch them; people stood on the roads with uplifted faces. . . .
Within a few moments they were clapping their hands and cheering. A
British fighter on the tail of a bomber had shot up the Jap, from which
streamed a trail of smoke. The bomber [Mitsui's plane] burst into flame,
crumpled, fell. Another [Nogami's] flared like a spent rocket and dropped.
Parachutes opened in the sky. We saw all this and cheered wildly; saw,
too, that deadly arrow-head almost above the centre of the city; our fighters had not turned it."

Of Rangoon's half-million residents, few had much love for the
British. An Indian shopkeeper recalled that people cried, "There comes
the enemy!" while pointing at the Tomahawks. Bombs, however, made
no distinction between those loyal to the Raj and those who favored the
Japanese. Blasted or strafed, torn by flying glass, crushed by falling
rubble, or trampled in the panic, more than a thousand died in the
streets of Rangoon. "It was a pitiable sight," the shopkeeper wrote, "to
see women with dishevelled hair and babes in arms crying and running
where their fear-laden whimsies took them. Children and teen-agers
having lost their parents were frantically searching for them. . . . More pa-
thetic were children who clung to running men and women, mistaking
them for their parents. The runners however discarded them as dangerous nuisances and fled the more vigorously to escape the bombs and save
their skins."

Sue Upfill saw the chaos from her ambulance. "The streets were
thronged with people, dazed and mad with fear," she wrote long after.
"Carrying a few tattered possessions, clutching wailing children, they
sought shelter from the bombs. Buildings were in flames, and the dead
and dying strewed the way. With siren screaming, [our] ambulance sped
along, the crowd parting to let us through. Overhead, bright planes flashed
in the sunlight."

Still some cheered the Japanese. "Oh, strike the rascal, boys!" cried a Ceylonese clerk, strolling up and down. "Bravo! Strike hard!" Then he panicked and ran down Phayre Street, to die in a burst of shrapnel outside the CAMCO office.

At Mingaladon, too, the first reaction was pleasurable excitement. "After the scramble," Chuck Baisden recalled, "we gathered around our barracks and stood looking up into the sky, just like a bunch of tourists. . . . We heard engines, and high in the sky we saw small silver specks flying in a V formation. Someone started counting, and when he reached twenty-seven, he yelled, 'They're not ours. We don't have that many.' I jumped into the nearest slit trench about the same time I heard the whoosh, whoosh of the bombs coming down. . . . I have never been so scared in my life."

"Suddenly bullets and bombs were hitting everywhere," crew chief Frank Losonsky wrote, "the operations building, the hangar, the runway. Japanese aircraft strafed the few aircraft that were on the ground. Stan Regis and I jumped into the trench alongside our ready shack." The shack was actually an open-sided tent. "During a pause in the bombing as we were trying to get off the field, Olson, the CO, drove by us in his jeep. He saw us but kept on going. Olson never mentioned the incident, nor did I, but I never forgot. Meanwhile the bombs kept coming. Finally, after what appeared to be an eternity of shelling and strafing, a British chap in a lorry stopped and picked us up."

Seventeen died at the airport, including three fliers of the Burmese Volunteer Air Force, the Indian crew of an antiaircraft gun, the RAF medical officer, and three enlisted men who were in the operations building when a bomb came through the ceiling. The same bomb destroyed the air-raid siren and wounded Squadron Leader Robert Milward. Others fell on the main hangar, wrecking two Buffaloes and wounding three mechanics. Fuel storage tanks were blazing, runways pocked, barrack windows smashed, and the mess hall damaged. Two Tomahawks were shot up in their protective pens, and another was wrecked when Bill Reed, landing from his running fight with the 98th Sentai, hit a bomb crater at 80 mph.

On Wednesday—Christmas Eve—Neil Martin and Hank Gilbert

were buried in the churchyard of Edward the Martyr at Insein Canton-ment, two miles south of Mingaladon. None of the Hell's Angels could afterward remember the funeral; perhaps they were too busy to attend. Mechanics tuned balky engines, patched control cables, and taped bul-let holes. Armorers refilled ammunition boxes, tending first to the nose guns that gave the Tomahawks such an advantage over the lightweight Japanese fighters. Other men topped off fuel, oil, and coolant tanks. As each plane was restored to fighting condition, it went up to relieve a Tomahawk on patrol over the airport, and that plane came down to take its turn in the maintenance pen.

By nightfall on December 24, the ground crews had brought the squadron's strength up to twelve Tomahawks, but they had no rifle-caliber ammunition beyond what was loaded in their wing guns. The RAF had fourteen airworthy Buffaloes. A substitute operations center was cobbled together, and the ground crews moved to the Rangoon Country Club. The mess hall had a lower priority, however, and the men dined that evening on cold bread and warm beer. (Rank had privileges, of course. Some of the British officers took their meals at the Upfill house, across from the wrecked operations building.)

Oley Olson sent a radiogram to Chennault, outlining his predica-ment and concluding: "Awaiting further orders." If he hoped they'd entail a retreat to Kunming, he was disappointed: Chennault told him to call on Kyedaw airfield for replacements. Mess supervisor Clayton Harpold drove a truck to Toungoo and loaded it with 70,000 rounds of 7.92-mm ammunition for the Tomahawk wing guns, return-ing Christmas morning. As replacements for the two dead pilots, Frank Adkins and Chauncy (Link) Laughlin came down to Mingaladon with the ammunition truck. "Hold on few more days," Chennault urged Olson. "Will move you soon if possible. Warmest Xmas greet-ings to all."

Photographs show Oley Olson as a good-looking man with black hair, narrow jaw, and sometimes fretful expression. Certainly he was fretting now. Squadron leaders in every air force are expected to fly in combat, but Olson didn't leave the ground on December 23. (Neither did his opposite number, Bob Milward of 67 Squadron.) The Hell's Angels don't remember Olson unkindly for this. "He was always over with the British," R. T. Smith told me, "making sure they knew what they were doing—which they didn't."

Bill Pawley's three CW-21 Demons were at Kyedaw airfield under the command of Erik Shilling, the wiry test pilot with his blond-white shock of hair. Shilling was fascinated by machines, whether modifying a Tomahawk for a photo plane or rocketing to 20,000 feet in the overpowered and undergunned CW-21. His boon companions were Ken Merritt and Lacy Mangleburg, whom he'd picked to fill out the Demon flight. Chennault wanted the planes in Kunming, as high-altitude scouts, so on Christmas Eve the three men left Toungoo and flew north along the railroad line to Lashio. Shilling's engine kept misfiring, and at Lashio he discussed the problem with Glen Blaylock, an AVG crew chief who was passing through. Blaylock guessed that the Wright Cyclone was running hot because of the 100-octane gasoline provided at Kyedaw. Try 87-octane, he advised.

Mangleburg's Demon was ready first, and he took off to wring it out, stunting over the field in a manner that convinced the British that an enemy fighter was strafing the airport. Not realizing that their buddy had caused the alarm, Shilling and Merritt hurried to get into the air, without waiting to be briefed about the route and the weather. They crossed into China at 5:30 PM, by which time Shilling's engine was sputtering again. Sixty miles from Kunming, it quit altogether, and he glided down to a belly landing on a rocky slope.

The Demons had no radios, and Merritt and Mangleburg had no maps. After wandering about for some time—an AVG radioman reported that they passed his station twenty times—Merritt made a belly landing on hard ground, which left him injured but able to walk. Mangleburg tried to make a wheels-down landing, but kept losing his nerve and powering off. His final attempt was in a river; when his wheels hit the water, he again tried to lift off, but slammed into a terraced slope. The fuel tanks ruptured, and the airplane boiled with flame.

Shilling knew nothing of these disasters. Chinese mountaineers thought he was Japanese and kept him prisoner that night. Next day he persuaded them to take him to an army post, where he composed a cheery message for Chennault: "I am all right; Mangleburg and Merritt arriving together."

A Chinese patrol recovered Mangleburg's body, so charred it had to be identified by the remnants of his passport. Chennault was furious. He launched a board of inquiry, which charged Shilling with an armload of mistakes: not providing maps for his companions, taking off for Kunming too late in the day, and not looking for an emergency field as soon as his engine faltered. He was fined and busted back to wingman, the AVG's new term for pilot officer.

Chapter 7

He Just Went
Spinning Away

Geneneral Sugawara reached Bangkok on Tuesday afternoon, just as his bombers were returning to Don Muang airport. He found his 62nd Sentai nearly wrecked as a fighting force: of its fifteen Sally-1s, only ten came home, and those riddled with bullet holes and carrying aircrew killed in the running battle. By Japanese reckoning, the 98th Sentai had suffered an even more grievous loss in the person of its commander, Colonel Usui. Altogether, Sugawara had lost eight heavy bombers and about fifty airmen in his effort to bomb Rangoon—this from a force that had fought over Malaya for two weeks without losing a single plane.

Follow-up raids were scheduled for the next two days. Some staff officers wanted to cancel them and send a fighter swarm to Mingaladon, to lure up and destroy the defenders. Others argued that Buffaloes and "Spitfires" were no match for the Nakajima Ki-27—the 77th Sentai hadn't lost a single Nate, after all, while claiming nine Allied fighters shot down. "Next time we will have a better result," they promised, "even against the Spitfire [Tomahawk]. It is faster and has more firepower than Japanese fighters, but its ability to maneuver is not so good. Also the Allied pilots' ability is not excellent. When fighting on the vertical side [dogfighting], the Japanese fighters are very good and will have a good chance to shoot them down." All that was needed was a fighter escort for the heavy bombers.

Sugawara split the difference, scrubbing Wednesday's raid while calling for reinforcements. From Phnom Penh came the heavy bombers of the 12th Sentai. From Saigon came the 47th Independent Chutai, equipped with the Nakajima Ki-44 Shoki (Demon), an experimental fighter cobbled together from a Hayabusa airframe and a 1,500-horsepower bomber engine. The squadron had only nine Shokis in service, and three of those crashed on the way to Bangkok. When the six planes reached Don Muang, their commander had to admit that they lacked the range to fly an escort mission from Bangkok, and were too heavy to stage out of the dirt fields closer to Rangoon.

With better success, Major Kato's 64th Sentai was dispatched from Malaya. In one of those displays of tactical agility that so bewildered the Allies at the beginning of the Pacific War, twenty-five Hayabusas left Malaya at noon on Christmas Eve, flew 450 miles to Bangkok, and were ready to leave for Rangoon next morning.

The 62nd Sentai ground crews had patched and repaired the bombers damaged over Burma, and had eight Sally-1s fit to make the return trip. Their orders were unchanged from Tuesday: fly north to Raheng, meet the 77th and 31st sentais, and fly with them to Mingaladon. In the bomb bays, along with the snout-nosed canisters of explosives, each crew placed a bouquet of flowers to be dropped upon Mingaladon, to honor the men who'd died on Tuesday.

The 60th Sentai had thirty-six airworthy bombers—more than it had sent on the earlier raid—and the newly arrived 12th Sentai had twenty-seven, all heavily-armed Sally-2s. General Yamamoto Kenji announced that he'd lead them in person. A plump desk officer, he'd commanded the 12th Sentai during the Sino-Japanese War, so he selected the lead bomber of that group as his personal plane. Colonel Kitajima Kumao, the current group commander, would also be aboard. The 98th Sentai, in mourning for its commander, was excused from Thursday's raid.

The Hayabusas met the Rangoon attack force over the Menam River, west of Bangkok. Major Kato led the formation with his headquarters flight and one squadron, while a second squadron provided top cover and the third brought up the rear. By JAAF standards, this was saturation coverage: twenty-five fighters protecting sixty-three bombers. It was another flawless day, and the air crews could see Rangoon and its shining lakes and rivers as soon as the armada crossed into Burma at 19,000 feet.

Then the formation came apart. The lead bomber, with General Yamamoto and Colonel Kitajima aboard, lost power in one engine and dropped out of the formation. The rest of the 12th Sentai followed it down to 18,000 feet, as did Major Kato and his ten Hayabusas. JAAF radios were almost useless for air-to-air communication, so it was a time-consuming business to get the formation reorganized. In the end, six bombers stayed with Yamamoto and Kitajima, as did Kato's fighters. The other planes climbed back to the assigned altitude, with Major Oura Yoshikuma in command. The 12th Sentai was now far behind the 60th, so Oura decided to fly directly to Rangoon instead of making the planned dogleg to Moulmein. The Rangoon armada was now split into three formations, and the 60th Sentai—thirty-six Sallys under the command of Colonel Ogawa Kojiro—had no fighter escort.

Meanwhile, the eight battered Sally-1s of the 62nd Sentai flew north to Raheng and linked up with twenty-seven Anns and thirty-two Nates. The bomber crews had been given box lunches for the flight, but they were too frightened to eat. After Tuesday's massacre, they didn't seriously expect to return alive from Mingaladon.

On Christmas morning, Oley Olson got the word when the first Japanese formation crossed into Burma, and he sent his Tomahawks into the air at 11:30 AM. Their stations were reversed as compared to Tuesday, with George McMillan circling the oil refinery at Syriam and Parker Dupouy patrolling over the airport. Pilots who'd been sweltering in tropical heat now shivered at Himalayan altitudes. Far below, they could see the white triangle of Mingaladon, the green-brown rice fields, and the shimmering lakes and rivers surrounding Rangoon. Also in the

This image from a Japanese movie shows a squadron of 12th Sentai Sallys under attack by a Tomahawk, suggesting that it was taken over Rangoon on Christmas Day. In fact, it was staged later, using a P-40 probably captured in the Philippines. Note the greenhouse gunner with his canopy raised like the visor of a helmet. (National Air and Space Museum)

air that noon was a Douglas DC-2 bearing Sir Archibald Wavell and General George Brett, returning from Chongqing. They landed at Mingaladon minutes before the bombs began to explode, and Oley Olson hustled them to safety in a split trench.

Major Oura's rump formation was the first to reach Rangoon. His Sallys dropped their bombs and flew southeast with fifteen Hayabusas pulling maximum manifold pressure to keep them in view. Soon after, General Yamamoto's smaller formation dropped its bombs from 14,000 feet and likewise headed for Martaban Bay.

George McMillan was over Syriam when he spotted the first group returning from Rangoon with its escort of retractable-gear fighters, which he took to be the Zeros that Chennault had chalked on the blackboard at Kyedaw airfield. The Tomahawks sailed into the Japanese formation, seven planes against thirty-five. The star of this clash was Duke Hedman, an unprepossessing young man who until Christmas Day had been admired mostly for his piano playing, a pastime he followed with great verve, little talent, and a cigarette dangling from the corner of his mouth.

"I came up from low rear on the left flank," Hedman wrote in his combat report for December 25. He fired until he was only 150 feet from the Sally, diving out when it seemed to explode in front of him. "I fell behind so came up from direct rear firing . . . at the last bomber until it began flaming from the underneath of the forward part of the fuselage and went towards the earth at a 45° angle. I stayed there, quickly charged my guns, and moved up and gave the next two in line good bursts . . . then half-rolled out. On my next attack, I noticed three of them [leave] the main formation. I came up from [below] and after short burst at 100 yards into the right wing plane, it began emitting heavy black smoke from the right motor and did a slow half roll to the right. I pulled up directly behind the leader and gave him a longer burst at 100 yards range. It went straight forward into a steep dive leaving a trail of heavy pitch black smoke behind. A bullet from the remaining bomber . . . broke my canopy and lodged to the left of my headrest. I half rolled sharply [and] saw a Navy Model '0' turning away from me on my right side at about 500 yards. I immediately turned inside him and at 300 yards range gave him a burst. He burst into flames and went straight down."

The Japanese fighter had been chasing Curt Smith, the thirty-three-year-old pilot who'd tried to enforce military discipline on *Boschfontein*. "I had thirteen pursuit ships on my tail at one time," he boasted a few days later. But his combat narrative consisted of only one word— "None"—an accurate assessment of his contribution to the battle of Rangoon. Smith returned to Mingaladon with his ammunition boxes nearly full, and everyone thereafter pretended there were only six Tomahawks in McMillan's flight.

After knocking the fighter off Smith's tail, Hedman himself was bounced. He half-rolled and went into a dive that dropped him from 20,000 to 5,000 feet, like falling down an elevator shaft. (The Japanese noted that "the enemy pilots used a technique of making one strike and then quickly escaping by diving away.") Taking sanctuary in a cloud bank, he flew on instruments to Highland Queen, an RAF dispersal field at Hmawbi, where he landed with his gas tanks almost dry. He was credited with shooting down four Sallys and a Hayabusa—an ace in a single combat!—but not all the victories went on his bonus account. In the alert tent that morning, Hedman himself had suggested that all members of the flight share credit for any planes shot down, so he missed the chance to become the first AVG ace.

The same was true of Chuck Older, credited with two Sallys and a "Model 0" to add to his bag of December 23. R. T. Smith was credited with two bombers and a fighter, George McMillan with three Sallys, and Tom Haywood and Eddie Overend with two Sallys each. On the record, however, each man came away with three victories and a fraction.

The cost was two Tomahawks. After attacking his second Sally, Overend "tried to pull away and found that my stick was jammed," he reported. "My right wing dropped and the engine was only just turning over. . . . I rolled full tab and held full left rudder and the wing came up." He made a belly landing in a dried-out rice field thirty miles east of Rangoon. The second victim was McMillan. With a flesh wound in his arm, and his right wing and his coolant tank blown open by the Sally gunners, the flight leader crashed in a field near Thongwa.

Parker Dupouy's flight went after Colonel Ogawa's 60th Sentai, which had circled around the target to approach Rangoon from the northwest. Meanwhile, the mixed formation that had gathered over Raheng was nearing Mingaladon from the east, and Major Yoshioka's fighters went to the aid of the 60th Sentai. In this the Nates were soon joined by some of Kato's Hayabusas. The combat thereafter generally involved one Tomahawk versus several Japanese fighters. "One tries to draw you into attack," Bill Reed reported, "and the other two [climb] to gain a position of advantage should you attack the decoy." Bob Brouk claimed a Nate and was bounced by four more, which he escaped by diving into the clouds. Ken Jernstedt claimed a "Zero fighter" and ran for home with two more on his tail. Fred Hodges (Fearless, he was called, in tribute to his dread of the bugs at Kyedaw airfield) was caught three times in these Tomahawk-traps before he called it quits. Dupouy had a similar experience when he made a head-on attack against a Japanese fighter "with square wing tips and an in-line engine." (He identified it as a Messerschmitt 109, and RAF pilot Peter Bingham-Wallis confirmed the sighting, though the JAAF had no such aircraft in service.) Dupouy watched his victim crash in the mudflats below Thongwa, then saw a Hayabusa coming down on him with its nose guns winking. Dupouy dove away. Three times he returned to altitude, tangled with an apparently isolated retractable-gear fighter, and was bounced by its companions.

Dupouy's persistent opponent may have been Major Kato. Flying to Rangoon, the major worried that the 60th Sentai had no escort: "anxiety grew in my mind," as he wrote in his diary. As soon as the 12th Sentai dropped its bombs, "I went back at top speed to meet the Ogawa bombing unit. On the way, I shot down two or three enemy planes." According to Hinoki Yohei, a 64th Sentai pilot, one of Kato's victims was Eddie Overend. Another may have been Dupouy, whose evasive tactics Kato interpreted as a knockdown. But the bushy-browed engineer was still in the fight, which had drawn him well out over Martaban Bay. Here Dupouy spotted the seven bombers that Kato had just abandoned, and he made a head-on run against the lead plane. What a coup if he'd shot it down! But he was driven off by the remaining Hayabusas, and Colonel Kitajima and General Yamamoto returned alive to Bangkok.

Bill Reed was working along the same lines, claiming a "Model '0'," engaging its companions, diving away, and chasing the Sallys offshore. There he came upon Dupouy dogfighting the escort. The skirmish continued for five minutes to no effect, and the Tomahawks turned for home. They were jogging along at 20,000 feet when they spotted two retractable-gear fighters below them and on the reciprocal course. With their altitude advantage, Dupouy and Reed simply turned 180 degrees and dove upon them from behind. "I opened fire on one from point blank range," Reed reported, "and he burst into flame immediately and went into [the water]." His victim was Sergeant Wakayama Shigekatsu, the first 64th Sentai pilot killed by enemy fire in the Pacific War.

Like his partner, Dupouy aimed first at Wakayama. When the enemy plane burst into flame, he kicked left rudder toward the other Hayabusa, only to realize that his speed was so great that he was overrunning his quarry. Dupouy went into a half-roll, intending to pass to the left and below the other plane. He almost succeeded. But the Tomahawk's right wingtip sliced into the Hayabusa at its weakest point, where the wing was bolted to the fuselage. Its left wing folded "like a butterfly," in the words of a Japanese writer.

The crippled falcon was piloted by Lieutenant Okuyuma Hiroshi, twenty-three years old, from the southern island of Kyushu. (Most accounts have Dupouy and Reed attacking three Hayabusas, with Reed shooting down two. But only Okuyuma and Wakayama were lost in this engagement, and the AVG record shows that one of Reed's victories took place over the airport.)

"He just went spinning away," Dupouy told me years later. "It was such an impact that I thought immediately that I had to get out." He watched Okuyuma fall seaward in a tight, crazy spiral, while the Tomahawk kept flying in the posture it had assumed before the crash, left wing pointing to the ocean, right wing to the sky.

Looking up, Dupouy saw that he was missing four feet off the tip of his wing, including part of the aileron. He felt out the controls and found that the half-aileron was still attached by its inside and middle hinges. Gingerly, he rolled the Tomahawk onto its belly. "When I found that the airplane would fly," he said, "I headed for the nearest shore." That was Tenasserim to the east, but after plugging along without incident for a few minutes, he decided to go home. "I turned, and in three-quarters of an hour I was over Rangoon. . . . I landed at 142 miles an hour. As far as I know, nobody ever landed [a Tomahawk] any faster. But I wasn't interested in that so much as dodging those bomb craters, because the airport at Mingaladon had been very heavily bombed. Well, I dodged those. And then—when I got out of the airplane and looked at it and started to think—then I started to shake." With Dupouy's unorthodox kill, the Hell's Angels ran their claims for Christmas Day to no fewer than twenty-four.

The RAF was notably less successful. Taking off after the Tomahawks, fourteen Buffaloes climbed toward Colonel Ogawa's formation as it droned toward Rangoon from the northwest; still climbing, they were bounced by the 77th Sentai Nates. Five Buffaloes were shot down and four pilots killed. The survivors were credited with three Japanese fighters and a bomber, bringing Allied claims to twenty-eight.

Actual Japanese losses were ten planes, including the Hayabusas knocked into Martaban Bay by Reed and Dupouy. The 77th Sentai lost four Nates, including those flown by Lieutenant Someya Masashi and a warrant officer named Aoki, both of whom were shot down and killed, and that of Sergeant Ri Kontetu, who bailed out and was taken prisoner. (Ri was Korean-born, as a Japanese historian points out, thus explaining his reluctance to choose an honorable death.) A fourth pilot crash-landed in Thailand. In the heavy bomber groups, Colonel Kitajima's divided 12th Sentai had three Sallys shot down—all, it would seem, by McMillan's flight—and a fourth damaged so badly that it crashed in a bamboo forest on the way home, with the crew surviving. One of the Sallys returned to Bangkok with eighty holes in the fuselage, the pilot and two gunners dead, and the interior looking "like a sea of blood."

The other bomber groups fared better. Several 60th Sentai Sallys were damaged, but the hard-luck 62nd escaped without a hit, to the incredulous joy of its crews. Having dropped their bouquet of bombs and flowers upon Mingaladon, they ate a belated lunch over the mountains of Thailand. The chocolate, wrote a survivor long after, tasted "very, very sweet."

If the Allied claims for December 25 seem exaggerated, the Japanese were far more fanciful, their fighter pilots credited with seventeen planes shot down and the bomber gunners with nineteen. (Actual losses: five Buffaloes and two Tomahawks, plus Dupouy's mangled airplane.) The apparent victory was little comfort to Major Kato. "I felt terribly chagrined," he wrote in his diary, "while at the same time I felt a strong sense of responsibility for not having trained my men more thoroughly. I offered my apologies to [Colonel] Kitajima. . . . Spent the whole day in mortification tortured by the sense of responsibility." Previously, against Chinese and Soviet air forces, Kato allowed his men to perform victory loops and otherwise strut their stuff, in the way of fighter pilots everywhere. No longer! Henceforth, he told them, they'd work as a team, with no more dashing off to individual combat. If his pilots smiled at that—Kato, of course, had done the same—they didn't mention it in their postwar recollections.

Mingaladon had again been damaged. Leo Clouthier and Paul Perry were nicked by shrapnel, and a bomb struck 40 feet from the trench in which generals Wavell and Brett were crouching—a near miss on the scale of what General Yamamoto had experienced over Martaban Bay.

Eight more Buffaloes were destroyed on the ground, several antiaircraft guns were blown up with their Indian crews, and every runway was cratered. Rangoon suffered worse damage, with estimates of civilian dead running as high as five thousand.

Legend has it that Bill Pawley brought Christmas dinner to the airport, loading a truck with groceries and driving out to Mingaladon for an impromptu feast. If so, the Buffalo pilots weren't invited. "On Xmas night we went to the mess which had the walls blown out," Vic Bargh wrote in a letter home, "and for Xmas dinner we had a bit of bully beef and a drink of pretty awful tea." The British officers who'd dined at the Upfill house were also out of luck: a bomb had destroyed it, and the Upfills had moved in with friends elsewhere in the city.

That Christmas dinner would have been Bill Pawley's last service for the AVG in Rangoon. Leaving a skeleton crew to work on Olson's Tomahawks, he closed the office on Phayre Street and joined the general exodus, which by now had swept up most of the population of Rangoon. By car and on foot, refugees streamed past the airport in an endless line—"the crocodile," it was dubbed by the men at Mingaladon. The privileged got out by boat to India.

At nightfall on December 25, having heard nothing from Eddie Overend and George McMillan, Oley Olson concluded that he'd lost two more pilots in addition to those killed and hospitalized on Tuesday—in all, a quarter of the men who'd flown down from Kyedaw airfield two weeks before. Some of the 3rd Squadron ground crews later claimed that they went to Olson, Curt Smith, and perhaps some other pilots, telling them to buck up and fight. If so, the advice wasn't taken. Before it closed for the day, Olson walked over to the RAF communications shack and sent the following appeal to Chennault: "Field hit badly. Two planes and pilots missing. Three more damaged. Have few ships left. Supplies short. Suggest move or reinforcements. Allied help in air doubtful. We doing work. Two ground crew slightly wounded. . . . Awaiting instructions."

Overend and McMillan turned up next day, inspiring Olson to send a jaunty postscript. The Christmas battle was "like shooting ducks," he boasted now—a phrase more often quoted by AVG historians than his appeal of December 25. Still, he hinted broadly for reinforcements: the Hell's Angels "would put entire Jap force out of commission with group

Oley Olson in the cockpit of his Tomahawk, showing the Curtiss-supplied ring sight on the cowling, British "armourglass" inside the windscreen, and the machine gun muzzles covered with tape to keep the barrels clean and dry. (Flying Tigers Association)

here"—i.e., if Chennault sent the Panda Bears and Adam & Eves to join him.

High-flying Japanese planes showered leaflets on South Burma, warning that an airborne invasion was imminent and spoiling the sleep of the Allied pilots. After all that had happened since December 8, even a night parachute drop didn't seem beyond the capabilities of the Japanese army, especially with the moon coming on to full. Nobody who hasn't seen a full moon in the tropics can imagine its brilliance, turning midnight into cool silver day. At Mingaladon, as Dan Hoyle wrote in the squadron log, the Hell's Angels were "somewhat on edge, nervous and in a rather frayed condition." The same was true of 67 Squadron. "A jumpier lot of lads I have seldom met," a British reporter said of the Commonwealth airmen at Mingaladon.

The AVG lost its staff secretary on Christmas Day, when the Commonwealth garrison surrendered Hong Kong. Having burned his AVG identity card and swapped his cash for sapphires, Joe Alsop was interned at Fort Stanley with the Anglo-American civilians. Doling out gems for food and a tutor, he not only kept himself alive but managed to read most of Confucius and Mencius in the original—"a quite useless but unusual accomplishment," as he put it, that "fills me with inordinate pride."

Also caught in the Hong Kong surrender was Doreen Lonborg, whose Danish passport and native wit convinced the Japanese that she was a neutral. They allowed her to book passage on a ferry taking refugees to Fort Baya (Zhanjiang) on the South China coast, from where she set out to reach Kunming and her sweetheart, Daffy Davis of the AVG staff.

Chiang Kai-shek had refused to share his lend-lease bounty with the British. But the man on the spot was Lieutenant Colonel Joseph Twitty of the U.S. Army, who could hardly refuse a Knight of the British Empire and a three-star general from his own service. Wavell siphoned off forty antiaircraft cannon and a hundred machine guns for the defense of Rangoon, and General Brett also dipped into the lend-lease hoard, to judge by his radiogram to Chennault: "Outfit at Rangoon doing superior work. . . . Have recommended to U.S. that they send you six planes per week, but feel that they should be used to defend Rangoon. Have asked Twitty to get spare parts on docks and help out Olson. Can't you send down six or ten planes and pilots to help out at this time? Feel that this area must be defended by AVG until British can get sqdn here."

Six planes a week! Seizing on this hope, Chennault composed a message for President Roosevelt. It was an extraordinary gesture. Picture him, a make-believe colonel in the badlands of China, writing to the president of a nation three weeks into the greatest peril of its history: "The American Volunteer Group which was authorized by you is happy to report to the Commander in Chief that in three combats it has shot down twenty-nine Japanese airplanes and has lost only two of its own pilots. If furnished with a very small number of aircraft of proper types and models and a few more men immediately we are confident that in cooperation with the Chinese *we can so damage and demoralize the Japanese air force that it will cease to be a factor in the China-Burma-Malaya theater of war* [my italics].

Any action taken must be immediate and must have the full support of the
Allied powers. Be assured that the Group desires to be of the greatest service to the general cause in this brutal unprovoked conflict."
    He wrote in similar terms to the U.S. Military Mission in Chong-
qing. "A study of these figures," he told General Magruder, "indicates
that our pilots and planes are distinctly superior to those of the Japanese, and that with some additional forces *we could quickly break the morale of the Japanese air force as well as destroy their aircraft and flying
personnel* [my italics]." To accomplish this feat, he needed an immediate
infusion of fifty fighters with extra props, radios, instruments, oxygen
tanks and masks, landing gear, windshields, canopies, generators, spark
plugs, and coolant tanks. They must be followed by twenty-five fighters
and fifteen pilots per month, along with regular shipments of bombs and
ammunition. Finally, he needed thirty-six twin-engine bombers (the
aborted 2nd AVG, in effect) with double crews of American pilots, gunners, and radiomen.
    He then returned to his immediate problem: the battered Hell's An-
gels at Mingaladon. On Saturday, December 27, he told Jack Newkirk
to get ready to replace Olson. Next day, CNAC transports flew the 2nd
Squadron ground crews and some pilots to Rangoon. "We were glad to
see them," wrote Dan Hoyle. "Everyone wishing or rather anxious to
leave and go to Kunming. . . . Today is Sunday and rather nice no activity something unusual I guess the Japanese feel they have had enough."
    Hoyle was about right. At Sugawara's headquarters in Bangkok, the
debate had continued without letup since Christmas Day. Where the Allied fighters had previously been reported as stodgy, JAAF officers now
described their speed as "incredible," a problem compounded by their
policy of "shooting and leaving" instead of sticking around to make
turns with the Nates and Hayabusas. In the end, Sugawara called off the
campaign against Rangoon. Henceforth, he'd concentrate on Malaya
and Singapore, where his heavy-bomber sentais could come and go as
they pleased.
    A rather different take on the December 25 battle was published in
Tokyo: "In large formations, the Japanese Army sky fighters swarmed
over Rangoon on Christmas in the third [sic] devastating air attack on
this British outpost, destroyed a power station and completely smashed

the airfield besides sending down 40 enemy planes in a dog-fight while eight machines on the ground were blasted to pieces."

Chennault's plea to Roosevelt hit its target. Lauchlin Currie responded with the president's "intense admiration and appreciation." More to the point, he told Chennault to pick up 7,000 pounds of spares in Calcutta and 500 pounds at Karachi. Best of all, more fighters were on the way: fifty P-40E Kittyhawks, the big-jawed Curtiss model that replaced the Tomahawks sold to China in the winter of 1940–1941. They'd be shipped on *Ferne Glen* to Africa, arriving before the end of February. U.S. Army personnel would assemble them and fly them to Kunming, and fifteen of the ferry pilots would remain in China—Chennault's first monthly allotment, in effect.

There was an ironic postscript to these transactions. On December 28, a freighter carrying thirty Vultee P-66 Vanguards—the wood-and-steel fighters built for Sweden, expropriated by the U.S., and allocated to the 3rd AVG—dropped anchor in the Rangoon River. But Chennault had no way to assemble them, since the Pawleys had closed down their Rangoon operation. The freighter had to weigh anchor and take the fighters to India.

Meanwhile, Lauchlin Currie proceeded with his plan to induct Chennault's irregulars. "Army would like to convert A.V.G. into regular U.S. Army units," he radioed General Magruder in Chongqing. "I am inclined to favor this as insuring steady and increased flow of planes, supplies and men. It is almost impossible to secure this result working outside the army." On the last day of 1941, therefore, Magruder composed a lengthy radiogram to the War Department, proposing that the AVG become the 23rd Fighter Group of the U.S. Army. Chennault's people would get lump-sum payments for the difference between their army salaries and what was due from their CAMCO contracts. Those who refused induction, or who didn't meet the army's physical, mental, or moral standards, would be replaced by Chinese pilots and ground crews, "thereby showing to the world a true spirit of mutual cooperation and consolidation of the democratic front." Having worked that out, Magruder still couldn't bring himself to grasp the nettle of Claire Chennault. He forwarded, without comment, the Generalissimo's recommendation "that Colonel C.L. Chennault, in view of his past services and

merits, be appointed commander" of all American air units in China—
no rank specified.

Magruder followed his upbeat radiogram with another on the same
subject. It stands as the most pessimistic assessment ever made of the
AVG's potential: "Despite Chennault's personal accomplishments and
the group's initial successes," he wrote, the AVG "has no staying powers
as now supplied and constituted." Its staff was "ineffective," its command "irregular," and its supply system "chaotic." Squadron leaders
from the U.S. Army should replace Oley Olson, Jack Newkirk, and
Sandy Sandell, and uniformed staff officers should take over from such
amateurs as Harvey Greenlaw and Skip Adair. Chennault also needed
a "complete enlisted staff" for his group headquarters and for each
squadron. Unless the AVG were reorganized in this fashion, Magruder
now believed, "its military value will deteriorate further."

Nor was he the only American officer to conclude—despite three
overwhelming victories in as many combats—that the AVG was no match
for the Japanese air force. A few days after General Brett radioed his congratulations to Chennault, he gave an interview to O'Dowd Gallagher, a
British war correspondent who'd rushed to Burma with two American
colleagues to cover the story developing there. How much more could
Rangoon withstand? "I give Burma three weeks," replied Brett—the senior American officer in Asia, and the man who'd oversee Chennault and
the AVG if they were inducted into the U.S. Army.

Chapter 8

Leaning Forward

Jack Newkirk was a lanky, coarse-featured man with a toothy grin, who at the age of twenty-eight was trying without much success to grow a fighter-pilot mustache. Women found him attractive—as he found them. The son of a lawyer in White Plains, New York, Newkirk had been an Eagle Scout, office boy for *Time* magazine, U.S. Army second lieutenant, and airline pilot before joining the navy, which trained him as a fighter pilot. "A tall, erect, handsome man," Jim Howard wrote of him. "While he had an easygoing, almost lackadaisical appearance, he was filled with nervous energy." He was also much frustrated to find that the Japanese had declared a truce in their campaign against Rangoon. For three days he waited for the enemy to come over. There was the occasional false alarm, but the vast blue sky remained empty of Japanese planes. So Newkirk called the Panda Bears together and said: "Let's take the war to the enemy!"

He was following the orders of Air Vice Marshal Donald Stevenson, who arrived on New Year's Day to replace Group Captain Manning as

Burma's air commander. Stevenson found that his air force consisted of two bombers and thirty fighters. Nothing daunted, as he boasted in his postwar account, "I therefore commenced to lean forward with a portion of my fighters [to] attack enemy aircraft wherever found. . . . I hoped to make him disperse his fighters by forcing protection for these widely separated points and so weaken him in the central sector opposite Rangoon. I gave instructions accordingly on January 2nd."

This account was in the grand tradition of British military dispatches, in which soldiers are brave, combat glorious, and the whole affair curiously bloodless. *Leaning forward.* Stevenson wanted the Commonwealth pilots and Panda Bears to fly into Thailand and attack the JAAF on the ground, against antiaircraft and small-arms fire, knowing that if anything went wrong, they'd be killed or captured. The New Zealand Buffalo pilots began to call him Killer Stevenson.

The first target was an airstrip near the village of Tak, fifty miles into Thailand, beyond the mountain ranges that guarded the frontier. The Japanese called this field Raheng, and its usual garrison was a three-plane detachment from the 77th Sentai. However, Captain Eto Toyoki had spent the night with nine Nates in order to mount a dawn attack on the RAF base at Moulmein. The raiders must have lifted off at about the same moment—Newkirk from Mingaladon, Eto from Tak/Raheng—just before sunrise on Saturday, January 3.

Unlike Oley Olson, Newkirk led the first mission. He set out with Bert Christman on his wing, but a balky engine forced the former comic-strip artist to turn back, leaving three Panda Bears in the raiding party. They flew east above the brown-and-green quilt of the South Burma delta, crossed the iridescent water of Martaban Bay, and reentered Burmese airspace north of Moulmein, its airfield now smoking from Captain Eto's attack. Four biplanes of the Indian Air Force had been destroyed on the ground before flying their first mission.

The Tomahawks crossed the Dawna Range at 10,000 feet and flew into Thailand against the rising sun. Newkirk led the flight beyond Tak, then circled back so the Panda Bears would have the sun at their backs. Dropping down at 250 mph toward the airstrip, they were elated to see Japanese fighters like sitting ducks on the gravel field, their propellers turning—about to take off, as the Americans assumed, but in fact just landed from their attack on Moulmein. There were spectators, too, in such quantity that Tak seemed to be holding an air show. As the Japanese told the story, three Nates were on the ground and three more just touching down when they were attacked by "Spitfires" out of the sun.

"I got so preoccupied with seeing the enemy planes on the ground," Tex Hill recalled, "that I didn't think about looking up. The three of us bent 'em over, and as we approached the field I looked up and there were three more planes in the traffic pattern with us. Like lightning, one Jap tacked onto Jim Howard's tail and was eating him up." This was Captain Eto's third flight, which had been about to land in its turn.

Since Tex was committed to the strafing run, that left Jack Newkirk to deal with the intruders. "I saw two enemy aircraft circling the field at 2,000 feet," he reported, "and attacked the nearest plane . . . from astern. After two twists it turned to the left streaming smoke, rolled over, and crashed into the jungle. Vice Squadron Leader J. H. Howard at this time strafed the field and I saw a large fire as the result."

One of the AVGs would dub Jim Howard "the automatic pilot" for his methodical way of carrying out his duties. As Howard told the story in a 1991 memoir, he knew the Japanese planes were in the air but chose to ignore them. "Our intended mission was to strafe the planes on the field," he wrote, "so I bore in to catch the prizes on the ground." He gave a five-second-burst to a fighter that seemed to be taxiing for takeoff. Glancing to the left, he witnessed a bizarre spectacle: "Crowds of people on a grandstand were scrambling over themselves in a kind of wave to get out of the line of fire." Meanwhile, the airborne Nate clung to his tail with both machine guns chattering—eating him up, in Tex Hill's phrase.

Tex now quit his own strafing run in favor of the live target: "I pulled around on him as quickly as I could and started firing as I did. I didn't even look through the gunsight—just watched the tracers like following a garden hose. With my diving speed built up, I came right up on him and he blew up. I flew through the debris and pulled up to come around and meet another Jap coming straight at me."

Having dispatched his first quarry, as he thought, Jack Newkirk went after another—evidently the Nate that was attacking Tex Hill. Newkirk got on its tail and fired several bursts, only to have it loop up and over "in the most quick and surprising manner." The Nate rolled up-right as it doubled back, so it was now flying straight at the Tomahawk—an Immelmann turn, developed during World War I and still a favorite of the Japanese. "Both of us were firing head on at each other," Newkirk wrote in his combat report, "and he pulled up over me. Several particles fell from his plane and he stalled and spun into the jungle."

Meanwhile Jim Howard finished his strafing run and returned for another: "I roared down the line of idling aircraft with my thumb on the firing button all the way. The machine guns left a wonderful line of de-struction the length of that array of fighters. I hauled back on the stick for the getaway. Nothing doing! As the nose came up, a dull thump shook my fighter. . . . Smoke poured from the cowling and the screaming Alli-son went dead. My prop idled to a windmill. I had been hit by ground fire." Howard circled back to land among the planes he'd just been straf-ing. Then a miracle: the Allison coughed to life. He brought the nose up and found himself flying in formation with two Nates, their pilots evi-dently focused on the flame and confusion on the ground.

Back at Mingaladon, the Panda Bears relived the combat as pilots have done since the days of Max Immelmann—laughing, boasting, and weaving hands and bodies like Balinese dancers. Tex Hill yarned about shooting a Nate off Howard's tail, only to have his partner deny that any-body had been eating him up in that fashion. To settle the argument, they went out to the flight line and counted eleven bullet holes in the tail and fuselage of Howard's plane. Then it was Tex's turn for second thoughts: his Tomahawk had thirty-three perforations in its wings. "I began learning fast from that time on," he afterward said, "and I think my neck size increased about an inch—you know, keeping your head on a swivel, looking around."

Jim Howard was credited with destroying four Japanese fighters on the ground, Hill with one in the air, and Newkirk with two. Japanese rec-ords show two Nates damaged on the field and one shot down: Warrant Of-ficer Yokoyama, who would need two months to recover from his wounds. Indeed, the other airborne Nates *must* have survived the battle. Newkirk, Hill, and the Japanese agreed that there were only three Nates in the air over the field, and Jim Howard saw two of them still flying when he left the scene, well after the others. They belonged to Lieutenant Beppu and Sergeant Matsunaga, the latter credited with shooting down a "Spitfire"—presumably Jim Howard's Tomahawk. Altogether, the Japanese were claiming three Spitfires destroyed and others damaged, a neat illustration of how combat can magnify the number of participants.

I n this first week of January, the JAAF had seventy-five planes targeted on Burma: Nate fighters from the 77th Sentai, Ann light bombers from the 31st Sentai, and Sally-1 heavy bombers from the 62nd Sentai. The rest of Sugawara's force had moved down for the kill at Singapore, leaving these three groups to soften Burma for the coming invasion. Thus the sunrise strafing of Moulmein . . . and thus the predawn bombings of the Rangoon airfields that began on Sunday, January 4.

The siren wailed at 5 AM. Under Stevenson's regimen, the AVG and RAF had dispersed their planes for the night. Half the fighters remained at Mingaladon, hidden in the mango trees or protected by dirt-walled revetments. The rest were flown off to Highland Queen, fifteen miles north—one of an arc of dispersal fields that Royal Air Force engineers were building beyond Mingaladon. Most would be named after brands of Scotch whisky.

The raiders were three of Colonel Onishi's older-model Sallys from Bangkok. They droned into Burma with wingtip lights gleaming and dropped their bombs after a burst of machine gun fire from the leader— signals made necessary by their lack of air-to-air radio communication. Their target was Highland Queen, where their bombs exploded without much effect. Meanwhile, the on-duty pilots took off from Mingaladon, while the standbys raced by sedan and truck to Highland Queen. By the time the Allied fighters were airborne, the raiders were on their way back to Thailand. The Tomahawks then landed at Mingaladon. They were refueled, and the Panda Bears retreated to the shade of their bamboo-and-canvas alert tent.

The alarm howled again at 12:30 PM. Each man ran to his plane, climbed the wing, slid into the cockpit, and buckled his seat belt and parachute harness. His fingers danced across the toggles and rotary dials: ignition switch on *battery*—fuel tank on *reserve*—generator *on*—propeller circuit breaker *on*—selector switch *automatic*—throttle *open*—mixture control *idle cutoff*—carburetor *cold*. Coolant flaps open, stroke the priming pump, and press the master switch to send current to the inertia starter. Hear the flywheel whine, faster, faster. Ignition switch from battery to *both* magnetos. Engage the starter. Hear the flywheel slow as it takes the load, followed by the coughing and spitting of the big Allison engine, belching smoke from twelve short exhaust pipes.

The clatter smoothed to a mellow roar, and the Tomahawk began its perilous roll, weaving past the soft spots where bomb craters had been filled by coolie labor, while other fighters competed for the same small bits of airspace, gray phantoms in the general storm of dust. At 100 mph the planes lifted off, wheels retracting and canopies closing as they broke free. . . . To an onlooker, the Tomahawks seemed both fragile and brave—little more than humming birds—bouncing and jittering in their eagerness to leave the earth.

Fourteen Panda Bears got off the ground, climbing through the clouds to 20,000 feet, where they found they'd lost radio contact with Mingaladon. Eight planes kept the high perch while the others spiraled down in hopes of regaining communications. The descending Tomahawks also divided. Frank Swartz led one three-plane element, with Gil Bright and Hank Geselbracht as wingmen; Bert Christman led the other, tailed by Pappy Paxton and Ken Merritt.

As Paxton recalled, they broke through the clouds at 11,000 feet, at which point the sky around them was clear and unmenacing. At thirty-nine, Paxton was the old man of the Panda Bears, with a face that seemed put together from slabs of clay. A Yale graduate, he'd worked as a banker before joining the navy, which trained him as a flying-boat captain. All of which was poor preparation for what happened next: thirty-one Nates swarmed in from the southeast, led by Major Yoshio Hirose, executive officer of the 77th Sentai. They were below the AVG top cover and invisible to them, but held the altitude advantage over the descending Tomahawks.

"The next second," Paxton said, as the story is told in a wartime account, "the air was full of little red and silver planes." The impression of red came from the rising-sun identification discs; the silver was the pale green body paint of the 77th Sentai Nates. "I reached for the gun switch and all hell broke loose in my cockpit—awful thud of bullets hitting everything, glass, armor seats, everything. It was deafening. My plane seemed to hang still in the air under the pounding." Paxton was shot through the left shoulder and right side. Another bullet hit a joint in his seat armor, shattered, and peppered his back with brass and lead. "Somehow I got over into a dive," his story continued. "Then I knew I was spinning. An awful smell of smoke filled the cockpit. I remembered wondering if I was going to burn. Then I was out of the spin and the pounding of the lead stopped. Thank God."

Ken Merritt had tacked onto the Japanese fighter, hosing it with machine gun fire until it "burst into flames and dived to the ground"—too late for Paxton, his Tomahawk spinning out of control, windshield covered with oil. Terrified that his plane would come apart, and believing the Nate was still behind him, he leveled off and circled back to Mingaladon. "The left side of the windshield fell out when I turned," Paxton recalled. "I could see enough to land then. Got the wheels down, but the plane veered off to the right as I went down the runway. Kicked left rudder and overcorrected. The rudder locked and the tail wheel seemed to fold." Then the main landing gear collapsed, and the Tomahawk screeched along on its belly until friction brought it to a stop. As the story is told, there were sixty-one bullet holes in the aircraft. Paxton vowed never to fly another combat mission, for which it's hard to blame him. A fighter pilot needs quick reflexes and a firm belief in his own immortality, qualities that are fading by the time a man reaches thirty-nine.

In the same element, Bert Christman also came under attack. "The wings, fuselage, tanks, and cockpit of my plane were riddled," he reported. "The engine stopped after five minutes of flying. Smoke came into cockpit and the controls were damaged." He opened the canopy and jumped into the airstream. Below his heels, the Tomahawk spun away and crashed with a great wallop of dust, while he floated down to a safe landing.

In the second element, Gil Bright counted twenty-seven Nates around him and "six or eight" bullet holes in the cowling of his plane. His engine on fire, he rode the Tomahawk down to a belly landing in a rice field, where his face was scorched when he opened the canopy. Then, when he scrambled out, he came under fire from his own guns, the bullets cooking off from the heat. Then a fuel tank exploded, knocking him to the ground. Bright got to his feet and staggered to the nearest building, which proved to be a station on the Toungoo railway line. He telephoned the duty officer at Mingaladon, explained his predicament, and asked for somebody to pick him up.

"Get on the train," he was told.

"But I don't have a ticket."

"Bugger the ticket, old boy," said the voice on the other end of the line. "Just get on the train."

Though Ken Merritt was credited with one fighter, the 77th Sentai lost no planes on January 4. And it had shot down three of the defenders, for a clear victory—Japan's first—over the AVG. Still, all the Americans were alive and able to fly again. That was the home-field advantage, such as the Royal Air Force had enjoyed in the Battle of Britain.

Bombers returned that night: half a dozen Anns of the 31st Sentai. At Mingaladon, they triggered the alarm at 2:20 AM. The Tomahawks didn't have exhaust shields or illuminated instruments, and their narrow landing gear made night landings treacherous. Nevertheless, three Panda Bears took off in the moonlight. They missed the raiders over the airport, though they saw the bombs explode in great lurid flashes, like sheet lightning against the clouds. The men on the ground took what cover they could find. "I jumped into a pit and crouched down," Noel Bacon wrote in his diary. "When the bombs started coming—wow! What a feeling! Each one felt like it hit me." Nine bombs exploded on the airport, one of them setting fire to General Wavell's DC-2.

The raids continued over the next few nights. Then, on January 7, the RAF commander got his chance to retaliate. After two weeks of traversing North Africa, the Middle East, and India, RAF 113 Squadron reached Mingaladon with fourteen twin-engine Blenheim bombers. Stevenson ordered them to Bangkok that very night. To prep them for the 700-mile round trip, they had the 60 Squadron ground crews, stranded at Mingaladon while their planes fought in Malaya. Still equipped with their ferry tanks and desert fuel filters, nine Blenheims took off at midnight, each carrying 1,000 pounds of fragmentation bombs and 160 pounds of incendiaries—half the load of Colonel Onishi's Sallys.

At Phitsanulok, meanwhile, a half-dozen Anns from the 31st Sentai lifted off for Mingaladon. The JAAF and RAF pilots were operating under the same imperatives: they wanted to bomb by moonlight, to make interception difficult, then return to base after sunrise, when the touchdown would be easier.

Jack Newkirk was now assigning one plane as his night interceptor. Pete Wright had the duty for January 7–8. He arranged his signals with crew chief John Hauser, then went to sleep in the alert tent. Profiting by the example of generals Wavell and Brett, the AVG ground crews had helped themselves to the treasures on the Rangoon docks, and high on their list were the little four-wheel-drive jeeps recently adopted by the U.S. Army. Hauser had so equipped himself, and in the event of a raid he planned to drive the jeep to the end of the runway, turn around, and aim the headlamps to guide Wright's takeoff. Then he'd put kerosene lanterns along the runway—white to starboard, red to port—to be lit when Wright signaled his intention to land.

The siren howled at 3:30 AM. Wright bounded off his cot, pulled on his flying clothes, and ran to his Tomahawk, which Hauser had warmed up hourly since sundown. The takeoff went perfectly, and Wright throttled back and leaned the fuel-air mixture, to lessen the glare of his exhaust; and he opened the canopy so he could hear and see better. RAF fighter control sent him conflicting messages: bombers to the east, bombers to the north. Then he saw large yellow flashes. The raid appeared to be over, so he returned to Mingaladon: "I let down to 2,000 feet and, flashing my running lights, I was rewarded a few minutes later by seeing the eight tiny pinpoints of light far below. . . . I was coming around the last turn now, concentrating on getting lined up with the runway. As I straightened up, I threw the flap handle to *down* and pushed the button on top of the stick to lower my flaps."

Wright was hit in the face by a jet of hydraulic fluid. He pushed up his goggles and leaned outside to escape the oil, which came from a ruptured gasket in the flap-control valve. Peering down, he saw Hauser's red lanterns vanishing beneath his left wing: "I waited a split second, and then pulled back the stick. I hit the ground in a left skid, and the landing gear gave way with a lurch . . . the plane skidded along its belly. Suddenly there was a terrific crash, and I violently cracked my head against the windshield." Wiping blood and oil from his face, Wright saw that his Tomahawk had rammed a Chevrolet sedan, tearing it apart. Much the same was true of the man inside: Ken Merritt, who'd driven up at the last moment and aimed his headlamps along the runway. He was buried beside Hank Gilbert, in the graveyard of Edward the Martyr at Insein Cantonment.

After sunrise, RAF 113 Squadron returned from Bangkok, and next day the Blenheims flew off to Lashio for the inspection and overhaul due them after their journey from North Africa. One bomber, damaged by taxiing into a bomb crater, stayed behind, to be destroyed by Japanese bombs.

The Panda Bears returned to Thailand that afternoon, January 8. Charlie Mott led the mission, accompanied by Robert (Moose) Moss, Gil Bright, and Percy Bartelt. Their target was Mae Sot, in the valley that marked the Thai-Burma frontier, where the Japanese were building

The Panda Bears. Kneeling, from left: Eddie Rector, Pappy Paxton, Pete Wright, Jack Newkirk, Tex Hill, Gil Bright, and the pilot known as Ed Conant. Standing, from left: Bus Keeton, Whitey Lawlor, Freeman Ricketts, Bob Layher, Hank Geselbracht, Tom Jones, and Frank Schiel. (National Archives)

a new airfield. Leaving Bright to fly top cover at 6,000 feet, Mott and the others "went down to do the business," as he told me years later. After his first screaming pass over the aircraft on the field, Mott spotted two planes hidden in the rain forest. He lifted his wing and swung back to strafe them. Then his world fell apart: "There was a big boom up in the engine, and the thing quit cold. I was [about] thirty feet off the ground. I had quite a bit of speed, naturally, and I pulled up and started to work on the engine, shifting fuel tanks and so on. But by that time I was out of airspeed. I rolled over—oh, I was 200 or 300 feet off the ground—and I kicked out." His parachute opened just before he hit, saving his life but leaving him with cracked ribs and a broken arm, leg, and pelvis. Japanese soldiers picked him up and took him to Raheng, where the 55th Division had set up headquarters in preparation for its invasion of Burma. His painful journey ended for the time being at Chulalongkorn University in Bangkok, which the Japanese had converted to a prison camp.

Moose Moss—the stocky pilot who'd traveled as an acrobat to Southeast Asia—kept strafing the Japanese aircraft. "I made three passes down the main line of the parked enemy aircraft," he reported. "The smoke and fire from burning aircraft was bad so I turned perpendicular to the line." He made six passes altogether, estimating that eight planes were burning when he left the scene.

The estimate was confirmed by Percy Bartelt. "My first run was made on an observation plane and carried on through the line of fighters," he reported. He next made two runs on the fighters, a fourth on the plane he thought was a scout, and a fifth on some tents bordering the field. By this time, Bartelt had only two rifle-caliber guns firing, so he broke off and followed Moss to the westward. "There were eight burning when we left," he concluded. The planes were divided among the pilots in the raid: one for Gil Bright, two each for Moss and Bartelt, and three for the missing Charlie Mott.

The 77th Sentai had indeed taken a serious hit. Four Nates were destroyed at Mae Sot, and three fighters and a transport (Bartelt's reconnaissance plane, no doubt) were damaged.

The next afternoon, four Tomahawks and six Buffaloes took off on a similar mission. They flew at 10,000 feet toward the Dawna Range, strung out in a loose line with weavers above to watch for enemy fighters.

"The first section dove straight into Tak Aerodrome out of the sun," Jack Newkirk reported. "The second dove from the south west, and the third from the north west in that order. On the first dive I was unable to distinguish any target, except the operations building. However, when reaching the field I saw four enemy aircraft, a few trucks and several ground personnel. On the next dive I attacked [a Nate] which was parked by the operations building. It was silver colored and had branches [camouflaging] it, and when I looked back it was in flames. On the same dive I fired on a truck which was driving across the field. The truck swerved and ran into the burning plane. On the next dive I fired on a plane across the field from the building, several pieces fell out of it and it collapsed on the ground. During this process I heard two *plunks* in my fuselage."

The plunks were rifle bullets. With the tenacity of samurai, Japanese riflemen stood beside the planes and emptied their weapons at the screaming Tomahawks. John Petach saw them as he roared across the field: "Fired on a compact group of ground riflemen," he reported, adding that he "dispersed" them and shot up several tents and a truck. Gil Bright had about the same luck: "Picked out a single enemy plane on the edge of the field and fired a long burst at it with no apparent results, although tracers were going into it. . . . Difficulty was experienced in distinguishing camouflaged planes from buildings, truck, etc." Noel Bacon, who "felt like hell" from a bout of diarrhea the night before, shot up a fighter and a truck, in turn collecting two bullet holes in his Tomahawk.

They returned to Mingaladon at 6:30 PM. Leland Stowe, a white-haired reporter for the Chicago *Daily News*, was among the spectators peering through the evening light to count the Tomahawks and Buffaloes approaching the field. "Across the airdrome," he wrote, "the umbrella-topped frames of trees suddenly stand inked out against the sky. Tropical twilight comes with a rush along the Irrawaddy Valley and the British–United States fliers are trying to beat it in. It is a pretty tight race but there are a succession of dust swirls off the lower end of the runway." A Buffalo pilot did a victory roll, all but scraping the treetops with his wingtip, Stowe wrote. That was followed by the usual chafing and boasting. "Pete" (John Petach, no doubt) kidded Newkirk about sending the truck into a plane that had already been hit: "You're a lousy billiards player. Why didn't you carom that truck into the plane that wasn't already on fire?" The RAF duty officer heard them out, slapped Newkirk on the shoulder, and gave him the ultimate British accolade: "Good show!"

Newkirk's flight agreed that they'd destroyed four Japanese fighters on the ground: two for Newkirk, one for Bright, and one shared by Bacon and Bob Layher. The Buffalo pilots claimed two planes, apparently light bombers. The actual toll: one Nate burned, a second disabled, and a starter truck destroyed—no small loss for a Japanese fighter group.

And so it went, the Japanese bombing Mingaladon at night, the Allied pilots strafing Japanese airfields in Thailand during the day, each side convinced that it was inflicting far more damage than was actually done.

In Kunming, Charlie Mott's personnel card now showed him as missing in action. "Tokio radio claims one American pilot, badly burned, in Jap hospital," the notation read. "This apparently is Mott. His wife has been so notified." Chennault arranged for Mott to be commissioned a captain in the Chinese Air Force, and for his paycheck to be sent to his wife in Alabama.* At the same time, Chennault arranged for pilots killed in action to be commissioned at one grade above their serving rank. So Hank Gilbert and Neil Martin likewise became captains on the rolls of the CAF.

Jack Newkirk felt that the 2nd Squadron was on a roll. "The more hardships, work, and fighting that the men have to do," he told Chennault in a radiogram, "the higher the morale goes. They seem to thrive on adversity." Perhaps, but the Panda Bears were as beat-up as the Hell's Angels at the end of the Christmas campaign: Ken Merritt dead, Charlie Mott captured, and five men hospitalized under the care of Sam Prevo, the AVG's chubby young flight surgeon. Four Tomahawks had been shot down and seven damaged on the ground. As a result, Newkirk could put only ten planes into the air, about what Oley Olson had mustered when he appealed for relief.

---

*In the prison compound at Chulalongkorn University, Mott set his broken bones, taught himself to walk again, and in September was sent to join the labor gangs building the "Death Railroad" into Burma—work that killed 16,000 Allied prisoners and 60,000 native conscripts. His wife was paid $675 a month until his CAMCO contract expired in July 1942, and after that a sum equal to what he'd have earned as a captain in the U.S. Army.

Chennault decided to reinforce him with eight Tomahawks from Kunming. In Adobe City on the airport road, the Adam & Eves drew slips of paper out of a hat to see who'd fly to Rangoon. Bob Neale led the flight. Plagued by headwinds, balky engines, and inadequate maps, the Adam & Eves reached Lashio so late that they had to spend the night. Indeed, they almost missed it altogether. "The maps were Chinese maps and I couldn't read them too well," Bob Neale recalled, in the best aw-shucks tradition of pilot stories, "and they were very small scale. The main physical aspects of the country were the Mekong and the Salween. . . . I called one fellow up on the radio and said, 'That was the Mekong River we just went over, wasn't it?' He said, 'No, that was the Salween . . .' [As] I was getting into a little panic, why, the little old field of Lashio showed up about ten miles to the north."

Dick Rossi did miss Lashio, putting down at an emergency field at Heho in the Shan Highlands. It was defended by a British airman who'd set up wooden antiaircraft guns to discourage the Japanese. He gassed Rossi's Tomahawk and pointed him toward Kyedaw, where he spent the night.

When the Adam & Eves straggled into Mingaladon next day, they found that the Allied airmen had mostly left the airport. The RAF servicing flight operated out of the Rangoon Country Club, as did the mess. (The noon meal was prepared at the club, trucked to the airport, and served chuck-wagon style at the alert tents. Bully beef was the usual fare, served with bread, dried fruit, and tea whitened and sweetened with condensed milk.) The RAF bomber crews also lived at the country club. The 67 Squadron ground crews had a hostel at Insein Cantonment, while the pilots moved in with British families. "Prior to that," Vic Bargh recalled, "they wouldn't look sideways at you in their cars, if you were going down the road. The next minute we're in their houses. Bloody great."

Similarly, the AVG ground crews were assigned to a hostel north of the airport, which they named Eighteen Mile Ranch for its distance from Rangoon, and the pilots were billeted in private homes.

The scattered accommodations, along with Stevenson's dispersal system, made for a long day. For an on-duty pilot, morning came at 5. If he was lucky, wake-up came in the person of a manservant with a pot of

tea, followed by a hearty English breakfast. Then he climbed into a pur-
loined jeep and drove to the dispersal field through the cool and misty
darkness—fifteen miles on a dusty gravel road that was sometimes no
more than the dike between two rice fields. He picked out his Tomahawk in the glow of the headlamps, climbed into the cockpit, warmed
the engine, and took off as soon as he could see the end of the runway.
That brought him down to Mingaladon by 7 AM, giving his crew chief
time to top off the fuel tanks and finish the preflight check before the first
alarm of the day.

In the evening, the ritual was reversed. Just before sundown, the pilot flew north to Johnnie Walker, the new AVG dispersal field. He se-
cured his Tomahawk and drove home, where he arrived about 8 PM.
Dinner was served by a houseboy who saluted him as "master," and afterward his host might provide whisky-sodas on the veranda. "If you have to
fight a war," Eddie Rector said of his billet in the Burmah Oil compound,
at the home of Basil and Joan Rigg, "that's the way to do it."

But there was exhaustion, too, and tension, and the debilitating ail-
ments that afflict westerners in Asia. Years later, Bob Neale remembered
those dark tropical nights at Rangoon: "A houseboy would serve me a
quart of Mandalay beer with some cheese sandwiches. That was just
heaven. We went into town a few times, but mostly we were too tired or
too upset. I can remember times where I'd be sick to my stomach before
combat, just from nervous tension."

British families received a "feedback" of money or rations for lodging the pilots, but for most that was a minor consideration. The Tomahawks were their best hope against the fate that had overtaken Hong
Kong and was now advancing upon Singapore. Dorothea Wilkins was
among the young Englishwomen swept up in the general adoration of
the AVG. Nineteen years old, the daughter of a colonial bureaucrat, she
hadn't yet been out without a chaperone, and in the ordinary course of
events wouldn't have done so for another two years. "Oh, we used to
have wonderful balls in the Jubilee Hall," she told me years later, "but
always our parents would take us, and after the function they would take
us home." Then the Americans performed their miracles in the sky over
Rangoon, and conventions began to fade.

Looking for girls one day, Bert Christman and Eddie Rector

knocked on the door of the Sacred Heart Convent and asked if they
might look around. The Mother Superior—guileless woman—gave them
a guide named Estre Healey, who taught at the convent school. As soon
as the nun was out of sight, Christman asked Estre if she had a friend,
and could they all go out to dinner? She telephoned the Wilkins house,
whispering: "Dorothea, Dorothea, there are two pilots here—the AVG is
here!"

"Where is here?" Dorothea asked.

"Here in the convent."

"What!"

"Yes, we're using the phone in Reverend Mother's study." She explained the plan, which Dorothea put to her father, who after some huff-
ing agreed that she could make a fourth at dinner. Dorothea relayed this
incredible news to Estre, begging her not to reveal that she was a child of
nineteen, on her first date.

"Estre came at about seven with the two young men, and I knew
from the way she took Bert Christman to my parents first, that he was
her date for the evening. Eddie [Rector] was at the back. And that beautiful person—I'll never forget—came up and shook my hand and said,
'Sure glad to meet you!' We'd never heard that, you see."

Every genteel girl of the time had an autograph book, and Dorothea
produced hers for the pilots to sign. Christman sketched a Tomahawk,
dated it—January 18, 1942—and wrote this caption: "Dorothea, may the
American Sharks of the air keep you safe."

With his infusion of Adam & Eves, Jack Newkirk now had more
pilots than he could use, so the newcomers once again drew lots,
this time to see who'd remain. John Croft and Greg Boyington lost the
draw and rode the CNAC Douglas back to China.

In Burma, the AVG was fighting on a front never imagined by its
creators. Kunming—expected to be the group's main combat base—had
turned out to be a pleasant backwater of the war. That thoughtful observer, radioman Smith, wrote in his diary: "The valley of Kunming is
an entrancing sight from the hills. One sees neat, small plots of ground,
green with winter wheat and vegetables. There are clumps of pines, vil-

lages of adobe and tile. The lake is fifty miles long and the water is a deep blue. The cliff of the mountain of Si San rises about 2,000 feet above the valley floor. The winter climate is perfect—better in some ways than that of California or Florida. There is an occasional frost. The noonday sun is always warm and the air clear and pure. There is a scent of pine on the air."

The headquarters section and the Hell's Angels were housed at Hostel Number One, a virtual fraternity house near Green Lake in the northern part of the city. In the rear courtyard was a softball diamond, tennis courts, and a basketball hoop. Inside was a recreation room with Ping-Pong table, hand-cranked record player, books—and a bar, of course. There was even a barbershop, where they discovered one of the luxuries long enjoyed by white men in Asia. "I could go down and get a haircut and a shave and a shampoo," Ken Jernstedt told me, "for the equivalent of eight cents American, when a Gillette blade would have cost ten cents. That was the life of Riley, to have somebody shave you every day." Peter Shih, graduate of George Peabody College in Nashville, offered Chinese lessons. Paul Frillmann screened movies in the dining room. "Also," John Donovan wrote his parents, "nicest thing of all, we have hot running water."

A few days earlier, Colonel Wang Shu-ming had made a tardy appearance as Santa Claus, bearing presents from Chiang Kai-shek. Don Rodewald described the festivities: "Worked all day then the Chinese threw us a swell Xmas party tonight. The Col. was presented with a Air Force sword from the General Issimo. [Chennault] made an inspiring speech. We all got a silk scarf with the General Issimo's personal chop on it. We had wonderful entertainment by the Chinese."

John Donovan, a former navy pilot from Alabama, regularly wrote his parents about life behind the combat zone, on subjects ranging from China's inflation to Chennault's bronchitis, both of which had taken an alarming turn. Donovan was almost bald, and Link Laughlin remembered him as "an abrasive, taciturn character always looking for action." Yet his letters reveal a temperament unusually sweet: the Generalissimo's gift and the invigorating climate made him "feel good all over and every day seems like Xmas and I keep waiting for something good to happen. . . . We have wonderful food served in excellent style for which we pay $1,500 per month." Those were Chinese dollars, of course, worth about two cents on the black market.

Donovan's major complaint was that he couldn't fly combat patrols because he had no single-engine experience, and he couldn't get the experience without going on patrol. Thanks to this Catch-22, he'd logged only fifteen hours in a Tomahawk. Another, smaller regret was that he'd neglected to bring a uniform to Asia: "We wear flight clothing like that issued in the Navy. However, since we have no uniforms, we wear any combination of articles of clothing that simulates a uniform. I certainly wish that I had brought my Navy greens, as some of the Army guys brought their uniforms and with the Chinese insignia on them they look real 'snazzy.' "

On the back of his flight jacket, Donovan wore a silk panel containing the twelve-pointed Nationalist sun and a message identifying him as a friendly airman who, if forced down, should be taken to the nearest army post. This was the "blood chit," iconic decoration of American airmen in China. It was first issued to AVG pilots after Erik Shilling's misadventure with Chinese mountaineers (who'd thought he was Japanese) on December 23.

Alas, the Kunming idyll was due for interruption. The JAAF, too, was realigning its forces in the first weeks of January, and on a grander scale. In the Philippines, where U.S. and Filipino troops were making their last stand on the Bataan Peninsula, General Obata Eiryo's 5th Hikoshidan was declared surplus and ordered to Bangkok. There, Obata was to command the 77th, 31st, and 62nd sentais in addition to the units he brought from the Philippines. These included two Nate-equipped squadrons of the 50th Sentai, commanded by Major Makino Yasuo; the 8th Sentai under Major Honda Mitsuo, equipped with Mitsubishi Anns and Kawasaki Lilys like those the AVG had battled at Rangoon and Kunming; and a heavy-bomber group, the 14th Sentai under Colonel Hironaka Magoroku. With about seventy-five planes, the three groups flew to Canton on the Chinese mainland.

It wasn't lost on General Obata that his route gave him an opportunity to inflict some pain on the old enemy, Chiang Kai-shek. Reconnaissance planes reported cloudy weather over Kunming, so Mengzi would be targeted instead. Three Sallys were assigned to the mission, with an escort of Nates from the 50th Sentai. They flew down to Hanoi on January 16, while the rest of the air force remained in China to mount a raid on Chennault's old stamping ground, the CAF airfield at Nanchang.

In one of those coincidences that seem commonplace in wartime, Chennault was planning a similar strike. The Hell's Angels had recovered from their Christmas ordeal, and most of the Adam & Eves were still in Kunming, with nothing to occupy them but the occasional Japanese reconnaissance plane. Why not send them against enemy installations in Vietnam? They'd stage through Mengzi—more important to the AVG than the pilots realized. As the main source of tungsten for the U.S. war effort, the Mengzi mines stood behind the $100 million loan that paid their salaries. Furthermore, it had a gravel airfield (formerly the CAF intermediate flight school) 75 miles from the Vietnam border. John Williams had established a radio station there and staffed it with Richard Ernst, two Chinese radio operators, a cook, and a squad of soldiers to fend off thieves. A ground crewman later recalled that the station had a live-in Chinese prostitute as well.

Chennault and Obata picked the same day—Saturday, January 17—for their raids. The AVG patrol consisted of George McMillan, Chuck Older, and Tom Haywood, all veterans of the Christmas campaign at Rangoon, plus Erik Shilling, now restored to his former rank of flight leader.

For ten years Chennault had argued that a radio-equipped spotter network could guide fighter planes to an incoming bomber formation, destroying the intruders before they reached the target. In China, the CAF had never been strong enough to prove this argument, while Burma Observation Corps was expected only to warn that raiders were on their way, after which its job was done. But at Mengzi it all came together. On Saturday morning, Ernst reported heavy engine noise near his station. The report was duly plotted on the map in the AVG command bunker, in the graveyard near Wujiaba airport. "Reports came in that loud noises were heard over Mengzi field," Olga Greenlaw wrote in the War Diary. "Reports also came in of noise heard overhead northeast of Yunnan Indo-Chinese border at Lao Kay. . . . McMillan took off at 0950. About 1005 a report came that enemy aircraft was in the vicinity

Cigarette break at Wujiaba airport. From left: Harvey Greenlaw, John Williams, and Chennault. Their uniforms are U.S. Army issue, but the insignia—and the wings over Chennault's left pocket—are Chinese. (Flying Tigers Association)

of [radio station] V-28. McMillan was given orders to proceed to P-27. At 1017 news came over the Plotting Room radio that McMillan's [flight] had contacted the enemy."

The intruders were the 14th Sentai Sallys that had spent Friday night at Gia Lam airport outside Hanoi. Incredibly, they'd arranged to meet their escort over the target, a nonchalance probably explained by the fact that their raids in the Philippines were never opposed by enemy fighters. The rendezvous failed to come off, though from Hanoi to the border was a straight run, northwest along the Michelin railroad and the Red River Valley (Song Hong Ha). In China, the terrain was more rugged, but still they had the gleaming river and the tracks of the Michelin to guide them. Nevertheless, the Nates got lost. It was probably their comings and goings that caused the traffic on the AVG net.

George McMillan also followed the Michelin, southbound from Kunming. After half an hour, the Hell's Angels spotted the big-tailed Sallys, twenty-five miles east of Mengzi at 16,000 feet. The Japanese bombers, Erik Shilling reported, wore a "fairly light colored camouflage" and were in the usual vee formation. But unlike the planes that had held such a steady course over Rangoon, they turned tail when the Tomahawks came into view. The Sallys were so fast that Shilling's manifold pressure gauge was showing forty inches of mercury by the time he caught up with them—at this altitude, for the early-model Tomahawk, a bit more than the "maximum boost" permitted by U.S. Army regulations, though in a pinch a pilot could push the manifold pressure to fifty inches or more. (In peacetime, a thin wire across the throttle quadrant stopped it from moving past the setting needed for takeoff. The wire was missing in most or all of the AVG Tomahawks.)

In a test pilot's clinical prose, Shilling described what happened next: "We made two runs on them as they were heading north. Then they turned and went south. I made about two runs when I saw a thin stream of smoke coming out of the leader's plane but who shot it down I couldn't say. A little later it went down in flames. Then I saw thin smoke coming out of the second ship." Shilling attacked from below and behind, while tracer bullets drifted toward him from the remotely controlled machine gun in the tail, "almost like they were dropping pieces of paper on fire out of the back."

Chuck Older reported that the Sallys were light gray on their undersides and "greenish tan" above, with red and white stripes on the rudder, "like the American Flag"—the tail marking for the 14th Sentai. "After one or two passes, two of enemy aircraft were trailing smoke, and I made attack on leader and he blew up in the air. . . . [The second bomber] glided down to overcast and dipped in and out. The [third] was trailing smoke and I ran out of ammunition except for a few in one .30-caliber

gun. . . . Two enemy aircraft were shot down and one was pursued beyond border."

As the combat was recorded in the War Diary, the first Sally exploded when it hit the ground, killing all aboard; the second skidded in
on its belly, with at least one crewman scrambling out; and the third was
found by Chinese ground searchers later the same day, the pilot dead
and the big plane half-buried in the ground. So it appeared to be a clean
sweep, with the three Sallys credited to McMillan (one), Older (one and
a half), and Haywood (half). Added to his Rangoon victories, that made
Chuck Older the first official ace in the AVG.

But Older's combat report had it right: only two Sallys went down
over Yunnan province. The first to fall was piloted by Lieutenant Hironaka (no relation to the group commander), and so quickly did it drop
out of the sky that a survivor in another plane didn't fully understand
that the formation was under attack. Next to go down was the Sally
flown by Captain Miki. The remaining bomber, flown by a pilot named
Fujiyoshi, was badly shot up, with gasoline pouring out of the main fuselage tank and two crewmen badly wounded, but it stayed airborne long
enough to cross the border and crash-land at a small field belonging to
the French colonial air force. Here Fujiyoshi commandeered a French
transport to fly his casualties to Hanoi, where one of them died in the
hospital.

The debacle left Colonel Hironaka with sixteen Sallys. They
bombed Nanchang next day, then flew southwest across the rolling green
mountains of Vietnam and the rain forest of Thailand, to reinforce the
62nd Sentai in its campaign of attrition against the Allied airfields in
Burma.

Chapter 9

They Fell in a
Straight Line

General Brett had expected Burma to fall in three weeks, but the port of Rangoon was still pushing lend-lease supplies up the Burma Road to China. Lieutenant General Thomas Hutton had taken charge of Burma's defenses, and 17th Indian Division was arriving to bolster the battalions on the Thai frontier. More dispersal fields were ready, in a layout suggesting a baseball diamond: Running the bases from Mingaladon, one came first to Zayatkwin, where the Blenheims and some Buffaloes spent the night. Second base was Johnnie Walker, used to disperse the Tomahawks; third was Highland Queen, used by Buffaloes; and back to home plate again. And on January 16, HMT *Neuralia* reached Rangoon with an even more important reinforcement: the ground crews and headquarters staff for three Hurricane squadrons, though the fighters were still en route. Two squadrons were also on their way with a dozen high-wing, fixed-gear Westland Lysander utility planes.

So Rangoon seemed secure enough. The situation was different on

Tenasserim, that sliver of Burmese territory running 500 miles down the Malay Peninsula, with airfields at 150-mile intervals. To secure General Yamashita's flank in Malaya, Japanese commandos had seized the southernmost of these fields, at Victoria Point, then set out to cut the panhandle at Tavoy, two-thirds of the way to Moulmein. "Wild elephants, leopards and venomous snakes roamed this section of thick jungle," a Japanese officer recalled of his trek across the mountains. Cutting their way through the rain forest, and living on precooked rice, dried fish, and pickled plums, Oki Detachment averaged eight miles a day. On the evening of January 16, on a mule track outside Tavoy, it ran into two companies of Burma Rifles. Native levies under the command of young British jungle wallahs, they were easily brushed aside, and Oki Detachment attacked Tavoy on Monday morning, January 19.

The airfield was defended by Indian border police. They fared no better than the Burma Rifles, and six Blenheims were sent down from Mingaladon "in an endeavour to evacuate 30 R.A.F. personnel . . . cut off by Japanese troops." A few Tomahawks and Buffaloes flew shotgun. The day was murky, the planes scattered, and when the bombers reached Tavoy they were bounced by seven fixed-gear Nakajima Nates. The Ki-27s, from the 77th Sentai, were there to escort some 31st Sentai light bombers in a raid on Tavoy.

Thus, when Dick Rossi arrived, he was amazed to see a daisy chain in the air over Tavoy. A Blenheim was under attack by a Nate, which was being chased by a Buffalo pilot—Sergeant Ted Sadler, who'd gone to the rescue of the Blenheim, only to have the Nate tack around and get on his tail. The New Zealander escaped by flying into a cloud. This was Rossi's first combat, and he roared into it with more zest than wisdom. As he told the story in later years, he made four head-on passes against the Japanese fighter before realizing that another Nate was on *his* tail. Rossi, too, escaped by diving into the clouds. Low on fuel, he flew along the coast to Moulmein airfield, thence to Mingaladon.

Frank Lawlor reached Tavoy after Rossi had left. He saw no Allied aircraft, nor the white cross that was to show that the airfield was in friendly hands. After a running scrap with the Japanese fighters, he, too, turned for home. (Ever optimistic, the 77th Sentai pilots claimed three Allied aircraft shot down.) By this time, Tavoy's defenders had faded into the rain forest, leaving the RAF garrison to be captured by the Japanese.

Four other Tomahawks were meanwhile strafing the Japanese forward field at Mae Sot in Thailand. On their first pass, they saw no aircraft and satisfied themselves with shooting up a hangar. On the next go-around they met a single-engine plane attempting to land. Jim Howard, Bob Layher, and John Petach shared credit for the kill, which isn't mentioned in Japanese accounts, perhaps because it was a Ki-51 Sonia attached to the ground forces.

Unseen by the three Americans, 35,000 troops were trudging through the mountains on either side of Mae Sot. "As the war had progressed far more favorably than had at first been anticipated," a Japanese officer recalled, the high command decided "to proceed with the Burma Operation without waiting for the completion of the other Southern Operations"—i.e., without waiting for Malaya and Indonesia to fold. The 55th Division under General Takeuchi Yutaka would take Moulmein, while the 33rd Division under General Sakurai Shozo swung around Martaban Bay into Burma proper. The terrain proved more difficult than expected, though not as difficult as the British had hoped. Unable to bring motorized vehicles across the Dawna Range, Takeuchi reorganized the 55th into pack-horse units, which crossed the frontier on January 20.

The Allied air force returned to Thailand that morning: six Tomahawks shepherding a like number of Blenheims. Jack Newkirk led the escort, consisting of "self & Moss & Neale & Bartling & Christman & Gesel[bracht]." In the misty valley that marked the border, they ran into eight Nates from the 77th Sentai. Newkirk claimed two, to become the Panda Bears' first ace. Bob Neale of the Adam & Eves also tore into the Nates, though with less effect. Neale needed a moment to realize that he was involved in mortal combat: "I was quite incensed," he admitted in a 1962 interview. "It seems a little strange for [another man] to be shooting at you, and the first time you get shot at. . . ." His voice trailed away—this large and gentle man—unable after twenty years to express his wonder that the Japanese pilot actually meant to kill him.

Moose Moss also claimed a Nate before he was bounced by two more. His engine caught fire, but he kept the Allison ticking over until he was back across the Dawna Range. Then, 1,500 feet above the tree-tops, he opened his canopy and kicked out. The parachute fall left him knocked about but cheerful enough to persuade a Burman to give him a lift in a buffalo cart. Bert Christman—lucky in love, unlucky in war—was also shot up, returning to Mingaladon with a shattered windshield and twenty-seven bullet holes in his Tomahawk.

The 77th Sentai lost one plane in this engagement, piloted by Lieu-tenant Suzuki Shigeru, while claiming four Tomahawks. The Nates had just returned from strafing Moulmein, where they'd killed two Buffalo pilots—John Finn and Paul Brewer—who took off to challenge them. Moulmein, it seemed, was as risky as Tavoy. So when Moose Moss reached the airfield next morning, asking if he could hitch a ride to Ran-goon, the Commonwealth airmen greeted him as an apparition. Didn't he know that the Japanese were across the border, and that he'd passed through their lines during the night? "Well, I sure am surprised to hear that," Moss drawled. "I sure am." The British, who appreciated under-statement, never tired of repeating that line.

General Wavell now understood that "the grain of the country" wouldn't protect Burma, and that he must accept Chinese reinforce-ments. Hordes of sandal-shod infantry—without tanks or artillery, with-out trucks or field kitchens, without ambulances or even such homely prophylactics as mosquito nets and quinine—began the thousand-mile march down the Burma Road to Toungoo, to guard against any effort to flank South Burma. No exploit now seemed too daring for the Japanese, and the British feared that Burma might be cut in half, trapping the Com-monwealth army with its back to the sea.

This threat seemed all the more likely when spies reported that 1,500 troops had been airlifted to Mae Sariang in northern Thailand. On January 22, Air Vice Marshal Stevenson sent six Blenheims and eleven Tomahawks to destroy the mythical invasion force. Seven other Tomahawks were dispatched to support 17th Indian Division, retreating through the rain forest toward Moulmein. This was the Americans' first experience with "ground cooperation," and they didn't care for it. Skim-ming the rain forest at 250 mph, there wasn't much chance of hitting anything on the ground, and a real danger of being knocked down by rifle fire. And what would they accomplish? The Indians probably thought the Tomahawks were attacking *them,* for Japanese light bombers were also busy between Moulmein and the frontier, bombing and strafing in support of Takeuchi's 55th Division. For this line of work, the Mitsubishi Ki-30 Ann—stodgy and slow, with two machine guns and 600 pounds of bombs—was a more effective tool than the high-powered Tomahawk.

Next day, however, the AVG was back in business at the old location, on the terms it understood best. The newly arrived JAAF 8th Sentai sent a twin-engine Kawasaki Ki-48 Lily to have a look at Mingaladon. The scout counted four bombers and twelve fighters on the ground. At his headquarters in Bangkok, General Obata concluded that he had a golden opportunity to destroy the Allied air force, worth risking the heavy bombers on their first daylight raid since Christmas. On Friday morning, January 23, six Sallys from the 14th Sentai would fly to Raheng and rendezvous with the Nates of the 50th Sentai, which had moved into quarters at Nakhon Sawan, on the railroad line 80 miles south of Phitsanulok. The heavy bombers would be followed in the afternoon by the Anns of the 31st Sentai, escorted by their usual companions from the 77th.

Obata was a chunky man with round-rimmed spectacles, pith helmet, and open-collared shirt, more informal than the neatly turned out Sugawara. But he was no better at coordinating his raids. Major Makino's Nates flew up to Raheng, refueled, and took off to meet the heavy bombers. But the Sallys couldn't find the airfield and turned back to Bangkok. Makino went ahead without them, so when the Japanese formation passed over Moulmein at 10 AM, it seemed to be a repetition of the fighter sweep of January 4. Mingaladon that Friday was defended by a mixed bag of fighters. Most of the Tomahawks were escorting the Blenheims on their commute to Thailand, leaving only a handful at the airport, plus half a dozen Buffaloes. They were reinforced at 9:15 AM by three Hurricanes, just finishing their nine-day, 4,000-mile journey from North Africa.

The Blenheims encountered a squall and turned back to Zayatkwin. Most of the escorting Tomahawks also landed at the dispersal field, to

take on fuel, while three Adam & Eves provided top cover. When his radio crackled the news of a Japanese formation crossing the border, Bob
Neale steamed south with Bill Bartling and Bob Little. They brought
Mingaladon and the Nates into view at the same moment. As the Americans watched, twenty-four Japanese fighters dropped their auxiliary
fuel tanks—"like a bunch of confetti," Neale recalled.

Meanwhile, pilots scrambled into the newly arrived Hurricanes.
Ferry tanks still bolted beneath their wings, they climbed to 9,000 feet
and there were bounced by six of Major Makino's Nates. *"Quelle bêt-
ise,"* wrote Squadron Leader Bunny Stone in his combat report. He
managed to escape, but not before his Hurricane was shot through the
tail, fuselage, and starboard ferry tank. "Couldn't do a damned thing
with the tanks on," he reported; "never got a shot while the little bug-
gers queued up on my tail and filled me full of holes." The Hurricane
never flew again.

Three Buffaloes got off the ground, claiming one Nate for the loss of
Flight Lieutenant Colin Pinckney. Twenty-three years old, graduate of
Eton and Cambridge, Pinckney was one of the few Allied pilots credited
with victories over each of the Axis air forces—two German fighters, one
Italian, and a Japanese transport, destroyed on the ground at Mae Sot
nine days earlier. "The squadron is doing well," he wrote his parents at
the time, "though we don't get the publicity given to the Americans."

Five Tomahawks also joined the combat, and to better effect. Frank
Lawlor made his attacks from out of a friendly cloud bank: "I would spot
an enemy from above, dive in on his tail and shoot and pull up again into
the clouds for protection from the greatly superior numbers always present. I repeated this procedure in all of my attacks on fighters and succeeded in catching several completely unawares. I never experienced
any difficulty in getting rid of attacking enemy aircraft as the Japanese
seemed to be afraid to fly in clouds." Twenty-seven, good-looking, with
pale Nordic features—he was nicknamed Whitey—Lawlor had graduated from the University of North Carolina. As a navy fighter pilot on
Saratoga, he'd served with Bob Neale and other future AVG volunteers,
but was in the last contingent to reach Burma. He claimed two Nates
shot down. So did Tex Hill, flying Jim Howard's Tomahawk and wearing Howard's helmet, which proved too large for him. Bill Bartling

claimed one, for a total of six Japanese fighters supposedly destroyed that Friday morning.

Major Makino's actual losses were two Nates shot down, flown by Lieutenant Niino Minoru and Sergeant Kimizuka Sadao. Their squadron mates put in claims for two Tomahawks (probably including Bartling, forced down when his control wires were shot away), a Buffalo (Pinckney), a "Spitfire" (Bunny Stone, no doubt), and one unidentified aircraft.

George Rodger of *Life* magazine was at Mingaladon that week, another journalist drawn to Burma by the dash and daring of Chennault's pilots. When the Americans landed, he posed them in front of a Tomahawk. The result was a marvelously evocative photograph, one of a series that did much to establish the legend of the Flying Tigers, jaunty and invincible. Its centerpiece is the rudder panel from a Nakajima Ki-27 of the 77th Sentai, shot down in an earlier raid. Hunkering on the gravel, Tex Hill and Eddie Rector pretend to examine the rudder, while Tom Cole and Whitey Lawlor look on. They're togged out in helmets and goggles, and—despite the 95-degree heat—Rector and Lawlor are wearing leather flight jackets. Behind them, a shark-faced Tomahawk stares off-camera with its baleful painted eye, as if standing sentinel for these clowning, vulnerable young men.

The photo session was interrupted by the mournful wail of the air-raid siren. This time, nine Tomahawks and three Buffaloes took off, while the Hurricanes stayed put. The Japanese formation consisted of twelve Ki-30 light bombers. They'd missed their escort in heavy rain over Raheng, so once again the Nates were far behind when Jack Newkirk spotted the Anns at 10,000 feet: "We singled out the bombers and made an attack on them from three directions, dead ahead and the port and starboard beams. After several repetitions of this, the lefthand plane which I was following fell out of the formation about seventy-five feet, but joined up again. Then the formation turned, one plane gave several large puffs of smoke and flame and finally went down near the satellite field"—probably Johnnie Walker, second base on the diamond of dispersal fields. (The Americans and British sometimes used different names, and the Japanese identified a field by the name of the nearest village, so I can't always tell which is meant in a given reference.) Newkirk,

Gil Bright, and John Petach each claimed an "army type 98 bomber" in this encounter, and Percy Bartelt claimed three. Only one Ann actually went down, though ten were damaged.

Noel Bacon came on the scene just as the Anns were jettisoning their load. Fearing he'd be hit by a falling bomb—for a fighter pilot, a peculiarly distasteful way to die—Bacon turned away and found himself in the path of Major Yoshioka's Nates. "Down they came," he wrote in his diary, "and I got one head-on. He spun in aflame. It was most encouraging to me. I dove out of the fighting maneuver and came back up, firing on the bomber formation, bow to stern. The other three [fighters] jumped me again, and the sky looked like it was full of them. Got another one head-on and dove out with one on my tail. He put twelve slugs in me: one across the top of the engine, one through the cockpit at my right heel, and the rest in my gas tanks and wings."

Jack Newkirk also ran into the 77th Sentai, which drove him down 3,000 feet before breaking off. One Nate lagged behind, and Newkirk went after it with war-emergency power. "I caught him just past satellite," he wrote in his combat report, "and after one burst his wing came off and he went down. Another bunch of fighters had been shooting at me while I fired on that one. My engine cut out and heated up and lost power, so I returned to the field where I crashed due to the fact that my flaps would not come down." Newkirk was credited with a Nate to go with his light bomber. Whitey Lawlor claimed two Japanese fighters—running his first day's score up to four—and Noel Bacon was also credited with two.

There was one American loss, and that a hard one: Bert Christman had his Tomahawk shot full of holes. As he'd done on January 4, he cranked open his canopy and jumped free. But his luck had run out, and he was shot through the neck, apparently while swinging from his parachute.

Despite the expansive AVG claims, all of Major Yoshioka's fighters returned to base that afternoon. The Japanese pilots claimed eight Tomahawks shot down. "The enemy had a great will to fight," they conceded, but "their technique in the air was not superior." Hedged though it was, this was a considerable compliment. Japanese fighting men, in every service and on every front, had been assured that westerners were effete, more interested in dancing than in fighting. The events of the past seven weeks had done little to change their thinking—except in the air over Burma.

For the three Japanese planes that were lost, the Americans claimed seventeen kills on January 23, and another was credited to Sergeant Bill Christiansen of 67 Squadron. The tally escalated from there: the *New York Times* reported twenty-one Japanese planes destroyed in "two terrific battles over Rangoon," and a Chinese observer, Captain C. P. Huang, radioed Chongqing that the Allied pilots shot down no less than thirty-two planes. A more sober view was advanced by Major Frank Merrill of the U.S. Military Mission, who set up shop in Rangoon about this time, his assignment to send daily reports to General Magruder in Chongqing. Merrill's estimate of Japanese losses was more conservative, and he pointed out—as no one else did at the time—that the British seemed ready to abandon South Burma: "Jap casualties nine fighters three bombers. . . . Our loss one Buffalo one P-40. Govt leaving Rangoon and military stores being shipped north. . . . Situation not critical yet as [we] have local air superiority but main danger is attack in force on north and gradual attrition small air and ground forces available for defense Burma."

Colonel Hironaka's 14th Sentai set out again next day, January 24. Saturday's formation consisted of six Sallys under Captain Motomura Ryosuke, to be escorted by the 50th Sentai. The Nates flew to Raheng and refueled. Taking off from the rough dirt field, Major Makino lost power and crashed, leaving twenty of his fighters to continue the mission under Captain Sakaguchi Fujio. Then, when the formation came in sight of Mingaladon, the bomber pilots made the usual fatal mistake, speeding up and leaving the fighters behind.

To intercept them, Jack Newkirk got seven Tomahawks into the air, while the British put up four Buffaloes and two Hurricanes. The Commonwealth pilots went after the bombers, as did Tex Hill, Eddie Rector, Ray Hastey, and Bob Neale. The ten fighters swept down on the Sallys, which for the first time in the Burma campaign they actually outnumbered. The results were awesome, as Hill reported: "On first attack they released some bombs which fell short of the field. . . . They then re-versed course and we continued to make passes at the bombers with en-emy fighters making passes at us. I saw the bombers crash one by one until there were three left. . . . I made a run on the one on right side and he blew up. Pieces of his plane blew against belly of my plane causing slight damage. One of the AVG shot down the remaining two bombers." As he left that great hole in the sky, which moments before had been filled by a squadron of heavy bombers, Hill met a Nate coming toward him. "I attacked him and he went down in flames," he concluded.

Hill claimed a bomber and a fighter shot down. So did Eddie Rec-tor. Ray Hastey claimed one Sally, and Bob Neale claimed two, which he attacked with his customary deliberation: "Closed on one to about 100 feet from the rear and blew up his starboard engine. Only two left by now, so took after the leader. Closed on him although I was getting a hell of a lot of return fire. I didn't seem to be getting hit, so I closed to fifty feet and gave him a burst, and the whole damn plane blew up, part of it coming back and tearing up my right wing and aileron." His Tomahawk flipped upside down, then plunged toward the ground. Neale felt out the controls, leveled off, and headed back for Mingaladon. A Nate dove past his gunsight, and Neale hosed him but didn't shoot him down. Then he was bounced by two Nates that disappeared almost as fast as they'd come, leaving two bullet holes through his cockpit and his microphone shot away. "Too damn close," Neale wrote in his diary.

The Commonwealth pilots, meanwhile, were convinced that they were scything the bombers out of the air. Bunny Stone and Thomas (Jimmy) Elsdon made their first attack from out of the sun. "Petrol streamed from one enemy aircraft after this attack and large pieces were seen falling from another," according to the 17 Squadron log. "S/Ldr. Elsdon's engine cut out but he succeeded in landing at Base safely. S/Ldr Stone carried out two more attacks. The starboard machine of the for-mation had large pieces falling from the engine and fuselage and bril-liant flashes from the starboard motor. It was later seen to go down on its back." The flashes—better than tracer bullets when it came to confirm-ing a pilot's aim—were Stone's incendiary rounds, flaring when they hit the big radial engine.

The Buffalo pilots also attacked the Sallys, running the RAF's claims up to at least four. However the credit was spread around, the Allied pilots did, in fact, make a clean sweep of the Japanese formation. Pappy Paxton—making good on his vow to sit out combat on the ground—recalled how the huge bombers had dropped out of the sky, like a flaming arrow pointing back to Thailand. "They all fell in a straight line," he marveled, "as though somebody was dropping smoke pots." Forty Japanese airmen died, Captain Motomura among them. In a month of combat over the Philippines and Hong Kong, the 14th Sentai hadn't lost a single plane in combat. Just ten days before, it had left Taiwan in good spirits and with nineteen Sallys, of which ten now remained—an attrition rate of nearly 50 percent in two encounters with the AVG and RAF. Henceforth, Colonel Hironaka would follow the example of Onishi's 62nd Sentai and send his bombers to Mingaladon under cover of darkness.

Jim Howard, Tom Cole, and Frank Schiel were each credited with a Nate shot down, and Percy Bartelt with two, bringing the AVG fighter claims to seven. Three Nates actually went down, including the plane flown by Captain Sakaguchi. For once the Japanese pilots put in no claims of their own, though in fact they'd disabled another Hurricane, again flown by Bunny Stone.

Saturday ended with a low-level fighter and bomber sweep. Major Yoshioka's Nates and some 31st Sentai Anns "sneaked in and made poor job of strafing field," as Newkirk reported, while the Tomahawks patrolled unaware at 20,000 feet. Also in the air was Derek Fuge of RAF 136 Squadron, flying the only Hurricane still airworthy. He landed at Mingaladon in the middle of the raid, not only escaping injury but apparently frightening off the Japanese pilots. Though they claimed four Allied planes destroyed on the ground and one in the air—Fuge's Hurricane, no doubt—the only actual damage was six bullets through an unserviceable Blenheim.

Bert Christman was buried at dusk in plot C-93 at the church of Edward the Martyr, making three in a row with Hank Gilbert and Ken Merritt. Estre Healey and Dorothea Wilkins were among the mourners. "It was the fourth row on the aisle, going into the cemetery," Dorothea told me half a century later. "I could take you there today." As she remembered the funeral, Christman had to wait while the British buried a

Japanese airman who'd fallen to his death near Mingaladon. The enemy pilot received full honors, including an RAF bugler playing "The Last Post."

Chennault never visited his squadrons in Rangoon, a curious lapse in a leader so devoted to his men. Health was a factor: influenza, aggravated by Camel cigarettes and chronic bronchitis, put him in bed at Christmas, and he was sick for the rest of the winter. "I alternated between brief spells in my airfield office," he wrote of this period, "and longer sieges in my sickbed" at Hostel Number One.

Dealing with the Chiangs was also debilitating. The Nationalist government combined aspects of a civil bureaucracy, a military command, a personal despotism, and a marriage in which the wife was smarter than the husband. Most Americans were soon lost in the labyrinth. Chennault thrived in it, but not without penalty. Among the trivia that filled his days was the case of eight Chinese cadets sent from Chengdu to be checked out in Tomahawks, with the Generalissimo specifying how much flight time they should get: two hours each. Chennault had forty-eight airworthy fighters to defend western China, the Burma Road, and Rangoon, and to go on the offensive in Vietnam. In such circumstances, it required an act of faith to give cockpit time to his own men. (John Blackburn, one of Butch Carney's flight instructors at Yunnan-yi, qualified in a Tomahawk on January 24 and was assigned to the Adam & Eves. John Donovan and Catfish Raine, flying-boat captains attached to the Hell's Angels, also got some Tomahawk time.) As tactfully as he could, Chennault explained the problem to General Chou at the Aeronautical Commission. Back came the order: Do it anyhow. Seven Chinese cadets were duly checked out, and only one Tomahawk was damaged.

Chiang also fine-tuned the AVG in Burma. When Chennault suggested bringing his pilots back to Kunming, he was told to leave them in Burma "until British Air Force has arrived." A week later, Chiang ordered him to keep eighteen Tomahawks at Mingaladon, then that the squadron remain "until next Wednesday." All the World War II leaders—Churchill, Roosevelt, Stalin, and especially Hitler—meddled in military affairs, but here was the Generalissimo of 400 million people, deciding the size and location of a single squadron.

Then there was the question of induction. In a January 20 message to Madame, Chennault warned that the "combat effectiveness of AVG will be greatly lessened for months" if it became part of the U.S. Army. A week later he went further: The group "cannot be inducted as majority of personnel prefer terminating contracts and returning home, but it can be destroyed." In milder terms, he made the same argument to his friend at the White House. After thanking Lauchlin Currie for sending him thirty props, Chennault returned to the main irritant, as to a broken tooth: "Induction AVG into army will have bad effect." Only then did he list his current needs, which included 100 solenoids, 200 gunsight lamps; 4,000 spark plugs, 400 radio crystals, 20 oil coolers, 25 propeller switches, 32 tires—and three staff officers.

In a radiogram to the War Department, marked "personal" for George Marshall and Hap Arnold, General Magruder explained the situation with commendable frankness: "Chennault is an extraordinary leader who has proved his worth. . . . He is probably the only man with qualities and experience who can effectively take operational command of both American and Chinese air forces. His fear of being superseded in this position by an officer inexperienced in China I believe arises from mixture of personal ambition and loyalty to Generalissimo. He has suggested to me that he be made a general officer in order to be assured of command of air forces in China. . . . To what extent this view has politically been advanced by the sub-surface Chinese government in Washington I am not aware." Magruder then grasped the nettle he'd been avoiding so long: Chennault, he suggested, should be recalled to active duty as a colonel, then immediately given his first star.

Chennault was certainly thinking like a general. Two of Butch Carney's instructors at Yunnan-yi had handed in their resignations, prompting the Old Man to order their names "stricken from the rolls." (Carney lost another instructor when Marion Baugh was killed in the crash of his Ryan trainer between Kunming and Yunnan-yi.) Chennault also issued a set of quasi-military regulations for the AVG and ordered each man to turn in a summary of his military experience. This sent the Kunming rumor mill into high gear, as Dan Hoyle noted in the 3rd Squadron log:

"Personnel very upset about the possibility of joining the Army. Most of the Pilots and Technicians have already showed their dislike at the prospects by some of them tendering their resignations, but the resignations were refused acceptance by the Group Commanding Officer." Not everyone felt this way, but there was enough mutiny in the ranks that Chennault decided to clean house. In a gloomy and reflective letter to Lauchlin Currie, he noted that the AVG still had "a few members who are trouble makers or who lack the fiber to stay with us." These bad cases, he added, would be invited "to terminate their contracts before January 20."

Four pilots accepted Chennault's invitation to leave. Leo Houle, Don Bernsdorf, and Don Knapp hadn't been sent down to Rangoon with their squadrons because Chennault didn't think them ready to fly in combat. Perhaps they were troublesome; perhaps they were only discouraged by the Catch-22 that prevented them from getting Tomahawk time because they had no experience in Tomahawks. The fourth pilot was Ralph Gunvordahl of the Hell's Angels. The "Gunner" didn't lack fiber—he'd taken part in the Christmas combat over Rangoon and had one Japanese bomber to his credit—and there's no evidence that he was any more troublesome than anyone else. Five ground crewmen also agreed to quit at the same time. (They included two clerks, Larry Moore and Kenneth Sanger, who were believed to be romantically involved, at a time and in a profession that did not regard homosexual liaisons with favor. "Good riddance," was the reaction reported by Olga Greenlaw. "We don't want that kind of guy here with us.") These men—two flight instructors, four pilots, and five ground crewmen—were given dishonorable discharges, though how that term could apply to civilians was never made clear.

Also consuming Chennault's energies was a plan to raid Hanoi. General Mao Pang-chu visited Kunming in mid-January. He and Chennault went hunting and afterward shared their bounty with Olga and Harvey Greenlaw. Dinner began with oysters flown in from Calcutta by Billy McDonald, now a CNAC pilot; the oysters were followed by roast goose, washed down by French wine. Afterward, Chennault and Mao huddled with a group of pilots to plan the raid on Hanoi, the Tomahawks escorting Soviet-built bombers of the CAF. The Tupelov SB was

a midwing monoplane with two liquid-cooled engines, retractable landing gear, large tail assembly, and Plexiglas nose for the bombardier and
machine gunner. It had been a formidable weapon when introduced into
China in 1937, but the specimens remaining in Chinese service were little more than relicts.

On January 22, eighteen SBs flew down to Mengzi, where they were
met by an escort of Adam & Eves. After refueling, the raiders took off for
Hanoi, flying a compass course with dogged fidelity, as Sandy Sandell
reported: "The bombers headed on a course of 135°, failing to make any
corrections for wind. I dove down to the leader of the formation and indicated the direction of flight to be 150° because a very strong wind was
blowing from the southwest. . . . After flying for 1:35 hours on a haphaz-
ard course varying from 150° to 120° over a solid overcast without finding a single hole in the clouds, the bombing formation turned to a course
of 240° and flew this course for several minutes, then they dropped their
bombs through the clouds. I estimate the position to be about twenty
miles east of Haiphong because I saw one hole in the clouds that was
near the Gulf of Tonkin. This hole was over the mouth of a wide river or
a very marshy back bay region."

The Tomahawks were near the outside limit of their combat radius,
so when the bombers took up their course for the return to China, Sandell wasted no fuel shepherding them. He flew direct to Mengzi, where
the Adam & Eves landed safely after three hours and five minutes in the
air. One SB was not so lucky. Apparently hit by antiaircraft fire over
Haiphong, the bomber fell back from the formation, lost altitude, and
disappeared into the clouds, half an hour into the homeward flight.

Two days later, ten Hell's Angels under Oley Olson escorted a similar mission, with similar results, except that all the bombers returned
safely to Chinese territory.

The JAAF retaliated by sending six Anns of the 21st Hikotai to
bomb the airfield at Mengzi, which in turn brought down a flight of
Tomahawks from Wujiaba. Hearing the English-language radio traffic,
the Japanese scrambled their fighters to head off what they believed
to be another raid on Vietnam. The French colonial air force also scrambled, sending up three Morane-Saulnier 406 fighters. From a distance,
the liquid-cooled French fighter was a twin of the Curtiss Tomahawk,

and when the two flights met in the air, the Japanese pilots promptly shot the Frenchmen down. They were the only certain casualties of the Sino-American campaign against Vietnam.

But Chennault had proved his point—that even with antiquated bombers and Chinese crews, he could take the war to the enemy. This was part of his long-standing campaign for a bomber force, as he made clear in a January 26 radiogram to the White House: "Can begin attacks on Japan's industries at once if you can send regular or volunteer bombardment group equipped with Lockheed Hudson as specified by me in June 1941 and American key personnel to operate under my command and control of the Generalissimo only." Lauchlin Currie went into action, and in just five days he sent Chennault the good news: "Hudsons will be ready by February 20. Probably accompanied by combat crews though no final decision yet."

Really, the man was a miracle worker. The thirty-six Lockheeds would come from U.S. Army stocks, and at least some were the same planes commandeered from the 2nd AVG on December 8. Now they were bound in the other direction—Florida to Brazil, across the Atlantic, north to Egypt, and through the Middle East to India, Burma, and China—nearly 18,000 miles from the Lockheed factory in Burbank, California.

Chapter 10

Hoffman Down and Dead

Newkirk's planes were being chewed up at an alarming rate, so Chennault told Sandy Sandell to reinforce him with twelve more Tomahawks. The Adam & Eves again drew lots in the squadron leader's room at Adobe City, and the winners flew into Burma on Sunday, January 25, refueling at Lashio and landing at Mingaladon just before dusk. They filled their tanks again, dispersed the planes to Johnnie Walker, and repaired to the RAF club for drinks.

Sandell was a narrow-featured man who was cultivating a small English mustache. The face behind the mustache was shuttered—suspicious—or perhaps only shy. ("Gentle, sweet, serious Sandy," Olga Greenlaw wrote of him, in the fond language she reserved for pilots fated to die.) The army had trained him as a flight instructor, but he'd fared well in the December 20 battle near Kunming—better than Newkirk, as a matter of fact. The victory, however, had done nothing to endear him to his men.

The Adam & Eves naturally wanted to know what awaited them at

Mingaladon. The RAF club was a partial answer, strafed as it had been on several occasions: drinking at the bar, Greg Boyington found that he had to be careful where he put his elbows, not to get a splinter. Six more Hurricanes had also arrived, so there were several groups of newcomers to take each other's measure. "We stood there," an RAF pilot wrote of his meeting with Chennault's irregulars, "and frankly eyed one another, and in our association felt the pride of manhood—like members of friendly bandit gangs meeting." The Americans were put off by the speech and manner of the Commonwealth pilots, who struck them as dandies. (They made a mistake in assuming they were English: 67 Squadron was dominated by New Zealanders, while 17 Squadron had Irish, Scottish, South African, Rhodesian, Canadian, and American pilots on its roster.) Some of the Adam & Eves drove into Rangoon to eat at the Savoy and find beds at the Minto Mansions hotel. Boyington drank his dinner at the RAF club and slept in a derelict barrack.

Monday morning, Newkirk and Sandell sorted their planes into four flights. The Panda Bears were designated "blue" and "green" flights and assigned to one end of Mingaladon's east–west runway. The Adam & Eves would be "red" and "yellow," stationed at the opposite end of the same strip. The RAF used a similar system on the north–south runway, Buffaloes at one end and Hurricanes at the other. "The takeoff procedure is a hell of a mess," fretted Charlie Bond. "If we get our timing screwed up, there are going to be a lot of fighters in a tangled mess at the intersection." Wind direction was ignored—and in an emergency, so was the rule that the Tomahawks passed overhead when they crossed the Hurricanes' path. "Time was more than money," a British pilot recalled. Burma Observation Corps had retreated with the army to Moulmein, and the radar station was brought back to Mingaladon to keep it from capture, so the warning time was down to fifteen minutes. If a man got off the ground thirty seconds before his mates, he might grab an extra 500 feet of altitude before the Japanese arrived.

There were three false alarms that morning, January 26. Each time, the pilots sprinted for their planes and took off in a lunatic race against the other Tomahawks and the RAF. From the torpor of Mingaladon to the thin, cold air of 20,000 feet—up and down, up and down—a routine that could leave a man weeping from sinus pain. Between scrambles, they tried to relax in the alert tent, while the sun climbed toward noon and RAF armorers put wet cloths on the ammunition boxes of the Hurricanes, for fear they'd explode. (You could fry an egg on the aluminum surface of a wing, as a mechanic demonstrated one day.) They talked, read, and played acey-deucey, a variant of backgammon popular in the U.S. Navy. And they waited for the siren to howl, which it did for the fourth time at 10:45 AM. This time the alarm was real: a low-altitude sweep by twenty-three Nates of the 50th Sentai.

The Panda Bears got three planes into the air, flown by Jack Newkirk, Gil Bright, and Moose Moss. Climbing away from Mingaladon, Newkirk picked up four of the newly arrived Adam & Eves. Then his radio went dead, so he signaled the other flight leader to take charge, while he flew off to the northward. Bright and Moss likewise went off on their own. That left the interception to Red Probst, the plump young man from Maxwell Field who'd joined the AVG so he wouldn't have to fly against the German air force. This was Probst's first day at Mingaladon; he'd never been in combat; and his AVG career had been one damn-fool adventure after another. Followed by Cokey Hoffman, Greg Boyington, and Bob Prescott, he climbed toward the incoming swarm of Nates.

Boyington assumed he was being led into combat by a veteran, until he saw that Probst was attacking from below and into the sun. Prescott, flying on Boyington's wing, was untroubled by this unorthodox approach. "You don't see anything except your leader when you fly in formation," he explained years later. When he did spot the radial-engine fighters overhead, Prescott took them for Buffaloes: "They were diving, looping, and just going nuts. I thought, *Silly bastards. . . . Hell, let's get these people out of here and we'll fight this war.* Then I looked again. . . . *Hell, that's no Buffalo—that's a Jap. He's diving at us!* . . . I was on Greg's left wing, and this Jap was diving over my left shoulder. I couldn't leave the formation, but nobody said I couldn't move over and get on Greg's right wing, so he'd shoot Greg first."

Red Probst quit the scene. "The enemy jumped us while [we were] climbing up to attack," he explained. "When they came within range I led my flight into a dive." He neglected to communicate his change of heart to Cokey Hoffman, who was his wingman if anyone was. In his AVG identification photo, Hoffman has the look of an Apache warrior, dark and scowling. On December 20 outside Kunming, he'd earned a commendation for the way he raked the Japanese bombers at close range. He was no less aggressive when it came to the Japanese fighters at Mingaladon, and watchers on the ground thought he collided with a Nate. "Out of the whirling center of the battle," wrote the British reporter O'Dowd Gallagher, "came one in a spin. . . . A wing came off as it sped to the ground. The rest of the plane left it far behind. It raised a great cloud of dust as it hit the ground. I saw it bounce. Many seconds afterward the severed wing came switching down like a piece of paper and also raised dust as it lit in a paddy field." Hoffman's Tomahawk crashed near the railroad tracks, upside down, with his mutilated body half out of the cockpit. Forty-four years old, husband and father, he'd spent more than half his life in the U.S. Navy, including thirteen years as an enlisted pilot.

By this time, Bob Prescott had repositioned himself. "Once I moved over, Greg saw [the Nate]," he recalled. "He rolled over with a split-S and said *foosh* and went down." Prescott followed, but in his excitement pushed the stick forward without first rolling onto his back, so that inertia pulled him out of his seat instead of pushing him into it. The safety belt nearly sawed him in half. "They said we could outdive these guys, but you never believe this stuff. I look around, and there he was, right on my tail. . . . At the last minute, I [pulled out]. And I forgot to take the throttle off. So by the time I pulled up, I was back up 13,000 feet. I looked over, and there's a P-40 diving down and a Jap shooting at him, going *boom boom boom. I gotta go over and help him.* You know, you can turn those sticks with your finger, but with all the strength I had, I couldn't turn that airplane around."

Boyington likewise climbed back to altitude and began making turns with a Nate—like everything else the Adam & Eves had done this morning, a flat violation of Chennault's teachings. As a college wrestler, Boyington knew to tighten his neck to keep from blacking out, and at Kyedaw he'd used the trick while dogfighting his squadron mates. But tensing his muscles did him no good against the nimble Japanese: he couldn't see where his incendiaries were going. "I had pulled myself plumb woozy," he wrote in his autobiography. "All the time I was pulling this terrific 'g' load, tracers were getting closer to my plane, until finally I was looking back down someone's gun barrels. 'Frig this racket,' I thought, and dove away."

Prescott, too, was driven to the deck again. He decided that fate hadn't intended him to be a fighter pilot, and that he should just get out of the way. So he skulked around until he heard "free beer!" (the recall signal) in his earphones. Then he flew back to Mingaladon, intending to take Boyington aside, apologize, and promise to quit the AVG if the flight leader kept the fiasco to himself. "So I just sat in the radio shack and waited, and Greg didn't come back and he didn't come back, and I thought, *Oh-oh, that Jap got him.* . . . Well, thank God, he finally did land. Boy, I ran across that field. He whipped the airplane around and threw dust all over me. . . . I jumped up on his wing and pulled his canopy [open], and he looked at me with a big grin, and he said, 'We sure screwed that one, didn't we?' "

While this was going on, Gil Bright and Moose Moss had sought the high perch. "My wing man and I dove through a light cloud on two of them," Bright wrote in a letter home, "but they saw us and looped up, firing at us on their backs."

Moss thought there were seven Nates. "I was on a Jap's tail, firing," he told a reporter, "when my plane flopped over, out of control, probably from an attack from someone I never saw." He rode the Tomahawk down for nearly a mile, so the Japanese couldn't strafe him in his parachute as they'd done to Paul Greene and Bert Christman; then he opened the canopy, unsnapped his harness, and kicked out. To his horror, a plane did come down to look him over, but it was only Gil Bright, who convoyed him to a safe landing near a water hole. Moss skinned his forehead, blackened an eye, and broke some teeth. He was soon surrounded by Burmans. One spewed a mouthful of water on Moss's forehead, to wash off the blood; another stuffed his pockets with crackers to provision him for the trek back to Mingaladon.

Bob Neale had led the second flight of Adam & Eves into combat. "Picked up about 20 Jap fighters," he wrote in his diary. "Looked like a bunch of buzzards milling around." When the Tomahawks approached, the Nates split up, with one group taking the high perch. Whenever

Neale tried to get at a Japanese fighter, others tacked onto his tail, forcing him to dive out. He lost contact for a time, but picked up the Japanese again as they headed for Martaban Bay, paying more attention to their gauges than to the air above them. With an altitude advantage of 2,000 feet, Neale dove on the rearmost plane and opened fire at 100 yards. As he watched, the Nate burst into flame and spun into the water. William McGarry—Black Mac, he was called, a dark-haired, frowning P-40 driver from Selfridge Field—was also credited with downing a Nate in this engagement.

After escorting Moss to the ground, Gil Bright likewise chased the 50th Sentai eastward. He overhauled a Nate, fired a long burst, and later saw the same plane (as he believed) burning on a sandbank. The victory made him an ace.

Three Hurricanes joined the combat over Mingaladon but didn't stay long. One of the RAF pilots fired "a short burst" at the enemy fighters but fled when he discovered that only three of his guns were working. Another Hurricane was hit by enemy fire and came down with its starboard aileron cable shot away.

Jack Newkirk's report to Kunming on Monday's action set a new standard for terseness: "Combat with twenty enemy pursuit at 1100. Shot down three enemy planes. Hoffman shot down and dead." The laurels for January 26 went to the 50th Sentai, which actually lost one Ki-27 while claiming four Allied fighters.

That afternoon, the Blenheims trundled off to bomb Takeuchi's 55th Division near Kawkareik—on the near side of the Dawna Range, meaning that nothing now protected Moulmein but the bayonets of Indian Division. Two Hurricanes and six Tomahawks escorted the bombers and did "a little strafing." Upon their return to Mingaladon, the Allied planes were flown off to the dispersal fields, except for two Hurricanes that Bunny Stone assigned to himself and Jimmy Elsdon. A bandy-legged Englishman of the upper class—his full name was Cedric Arthur Cuthbert Stone—the squadron leader may have struck the Americans as a dandy, but he'd been credited with three German planes in Europe and a Sally on January 24. For his part, Elsdon was an ace with seven German warplanes to his credit. As for their mount, the Hawker Hurricane was a reasonably good night fighter, thanks to good cockpit vision, shielded exhaust pipes, and wide-track undercarriage.

Under the glow of a three-quarter moon, six bombers made the long journey from Bangkok and rained high explosives and incendiaries upon Mingaladon. The night fighters were caught on the ground, with one Hurricane damaged beyond repair. The Japanese were back the following night, January 27–28. Colonel Onishi's crews had been pushed out of Don Muang by the bomber groups arriving from the Philippines, and had spent two weeks finding new quarters at Nakhon Sawan and familiarizing themselves with the Sally-2s that had arrived to make good their losses. Four of the new bombers made the long trip to Mingaladon, and this time Stone and Elsdon got their Hurricanes off the ground.

There was a scrim of clouds above the airport. The moon and stars shone through, but the watchers on the ground—including Leland Stowe of the *Chicago Daily News*—could distinguish the planes only by the sound of their engines, a booming noise for the bombers and a shriller sound for the liquid-cooled fighters. "Now we stood alongside the sombrero-shaped kokobin trees, staring and staring," Stowe wrote. "The buzzing Hurricane still remained invisible although a million stars winked at it. . . . Then we were yelling all at once, 'The Hurricane's on her. . . .' Hundreds of crimson dashes chased each other madly in a straight line up and up. . . . Then, well under the darkened sky where the machine gun bursts extinguished themselves, a great flame suddenly lights the sky. It hovers momentarily, then plunges straight down. Across the flat land, a mile and a half north of us, the horizon is illuminated with one huge flash."

The triumphant night fighter was Bunny Stone, who thereby became an ace. The fireball was the newly arrived Sally piloted by Lieutenant Hirabayashi Akio—himself new to the 62nd Sentai, having reached Thailand as a replacement sixteen days earlier.

The JAAF was baffled by the resistance in Burma, so unlike its experience in Malaya, the Philippines, Hong Kong, and the Dutch Indies. "Crushing the enemy was like killing flies," complained a Japanese officer—probably Colonel Hironaka of the 14th Sentai—when the campaign was over. "We thought we had . . . disposed of [the Allied air force] for once and all, only to find to our dismay 10 days or so later that the enemy was as strong as before in numbers of planes." It didn't occur to the Japanese, any more than it did to the Allied pilots, that the enemy's seeming resilience was a result of their own inflated claims of damage inflicted.

On Wednesday, the Adam & Eves buried Cokey Hoffman in plot C-97 at the church of Edward the Martyr. The corpse was two days old, as Greg Boyington recalled, and the pallbearers gagged on the smell. To make matters worse, the native diggers had made the grave too short, and the coffin jammed halfway down. Afterward the pallbearers drove into Rangoon to eat strawberries and cream at the Silver Grill, buy gems at Coombes's jewelry store, and make an unsuccessful pass at two young Englishwomen.

The on-duty pilots had scrambled once already, and now were sprinting for their Tomahawks again. The siren foretold a massive fighter sweep: twenty-seven Nates from the 77th Sentai, plus ten from the 50th. To intercept them, the Panda Bears put seven fighters into the air, the Adam & Eves nine, and the RAF two. This was Sandy Sandell's first combat in Rangoon. "I, leading red-yellow squadron, engaged enemy fighters about twenty miles east of the field," he reported, "and continued fighting to about twenty miles west of the field. On my first attack, one fighter caught fire and dived toward the ground from 17,000 feet, disappearing from sight still in a dive. After two more unsuccessful head-on runs, I hit one more ship that similarly went down. About twenty minutes later, I made a head-on run to very close range and could see parts of the plane coming off. The ship rolled away smoking, but it did not go down." He was credited with two kills.

Also claiming victories were three Adam & Eves who'd arrived earlier in the month. As the Japanese told the story, the Allied pilots—Bill Bartling, Dick Rossi, and Frank Schiel—boxed in Captain Matsuda Mitsuhiro. Seeing his squadron leader trapped, Lieutenant Yamamoto Kanekichi dove to the rescue. Matsuda was shot down and Yamamoto's plane mortally hit. When his engine began to burn, the young lieutenant looked about for a target to take out with him. What he saw was the chalk-white A of Mingaladon's runways.

Meanwhile the yellow warning light came on in Sandy Sandell's Tomahawk: his engine overheating. With smoke pouring into the cockpit, he glided down to a dead-stick landing at Mingaladon. He burst a tire but managed to stop the Tomahawk without wrecking it. Then he looked up and saw that his problems had only begun. Diving down on Mingaladon to strike a last blow for the emperor, Lieutenant Yamamoto saw the Tomahawk and jinked toward it, his propeller windmilling. Sandell sprinted for a ditch. Seconds later, Yamamoto crashed just behind the Tomahawk, tearing off its rudder and sending a piece of Nakajima engine across the ditch in which Sandell was crouching. Greg Boyington was among those who ran over to help Sandell and gawk at the suicide pilot. "The largest part of the pilot I could recognize," Boyington wrote, "was a tiny left hand with the severed tendons sticking out." Yamamoto, he guessed, had thrown up his arm in an instinctive attempt to shield his face from the impact.

In flight school, Japanese cadets practiced suicide dives as routinely as gunnery or formation flying. "It was taken for granted," one of them explained after the war, "that any pilot with a disabled plane would die in the samurai tradition. . . . He would dive into an enemy ship or plane, taking as many of his adversaries with him as possible." This was *ji-baku*. Japanese is rich in words denoting death in combat: a pilot could turn himself into a missile, join a scheduled suicide flight, disembowel himself, or otherwise commit suicide—each with its own descriptive name—and there are words as well for dying from enemy fire, in an explosion, and from wounds. Even a generation later, Yamamoto's death was limned as beautiful in a Japan that had forsaken war but not its adoration of dead warriors: "The English general was impressed by this," declares a 1977 history of JAAF fighter operations; "and Yamamoto's ashes remained there, buried carefully." (The elegy was omitted from the English-language edition of the book.)

The RAF apparently made no claims for January 28, while the Americans claimed six—Sandell's two, plus one each for Rossi, Schiel, Bartling, and John Petach. The 77th Sentai had indeed been bloodied, losing a warrant officer named Kitasaka in addition to Captain Matsuda and Lieutenant Yamamoto. Between them, the two Japanese fighter groups claimed fifteen Allied aircraft shot down, a considerable overestimate: in addition to Sandell, Ray Hastey was forced down and Pilot Officer Brown of 136 Squadron had his starboard aileron shot away.

After dinner, some of the AVG pilots sat on the veranda of the RAF club and watched the British bombers take off for their long, lonely journey to Bangkok. As the Americans looked on, a Blenheim lost power and crashed at the end of the runway. Jack Newkirk, meanwhile, was composing a situation report for Chennault. "The planes that we have here now are beginning to look like patchwork quilts for the holes in them," he wrote. "The engines are also getting tired. . . . There are not sufficient ground crews for the job, and there is not enough time for them to teach the Chinese or other helpers which they steal from our neighbors [the RAF]. . . . There are four of my men who need a rest, they are [Jack] Jones, who is getting over another bad attack of fever, [Pete] Wright, who is recuperating from appendicitis, [Moose] Moss who had some teeth knocked out when he was shot down and bailed out and [Alex] Mihalko who has piles." In an apparent reference to rumors of induction, he concluded on a defiant note: "I am firmly convinced that . . . the A.V.G. does not need anything except cooperation from the army or any other organization, as far as we are concerned."

The 77th Sentai returned next day, January 29, with twenty Nates. To oppose them, Jack Newkirk took off with a five-plane flight of Panda Bears. Three Adam & Eves were also in the air, along with two Hurricanes—ten Allied fighters altogether. Newkirk spotted the enemy swarm above him and to the east, and he turned west to gain altitude before closing. "When the Japs dived on our planes," Noel Bacon wrote in his diary, "Jack Newkirk and a wingman climbed and dove on them. The dives brought the Japs . . . under us, so my wingman and I jumped the Japs. I made a pass, went into a cloud, turned while in it [an RAF tactic Chennault had taught his pilots at Toungoo] and climbed again and attacked. One Jap turned up at me, and I got a 45-degree shot in his bow. His prop immediately began to windmill and he started to spiral down. I dove through the clouds and met him beneath them. He was still in a slow spiral. I dove on his tail and opened all guns, setting fire to his left tank. I went on past and saw the pilot was dead. I watched him crash and burn 10 miles northeast of the base, then I followed another little old devil out over the bay. He was running for home, and I got too eager and lost him."

Charlie Bond of the Adam & Eves had followed Newkirk to the west. He didn't see the Japanese fighters until he was above them; then he charged his guns, flipped the switch to illuminate his reflector sight, and went down in an almost vertical dive. "I missed him by a mile," he wrote in his diary. "I continued my dive on down a few thousand feet further. As I started pulling up I partially blacked out. I realized then that I had the throttle full up against the firewall and I was getting detonation in my engine. No one on my tail, so I stole a peek at the air speed indicator— over 400 mph. Using this speed I climbed back up to 18,000 feet." He missed again on a second pass, circled back, fired at a Nate, then found himself in a killing position behind another. When he fired, the Japanese pilot dove into a cloud. Bond stayed above, confident that the Nate would emerge—which it did, climbing out of the cloud and squaring off for a head-on run against the Tomahawk: "He must have been within two or three hundred yards as I closed in and opened fire with all six guns. He made no effort to turn; it was probably too late. My tracers tore into his cockpit and engine. Suddenly I was right on him. I had to raise my left wing to get over him as I zoomed past. His cockpit was flaming. I squealed in delight, laughing aloud. Enough for him. 'Got one! There you are, Hoffman, old boy!'"

Greg Boyington also followed Newkirk's flight. As he remembered the day, he hit his first Nate "just right," setting it afire, then heard someone yell over the radio: "This is for Cokey, you son of a bitch!" That would have been Charlie Bond: the words were different, but the music was the same.

After his first pass through the Nates, Jack Newkirk had a head-on encounter with what he thought was a retractable-gear fighter, though there were no "Zero types" over Mingaladon in January. "I held my fire and put a short burst in his engine at 300 yards," he reported. "A cylinder came off and the plane went down smoking. I fired three more bursts into him from above and behind him. Then he went into a cloud and I followed him through and saw him hit somewhere east of Dabein."

Meanwhile Sandy Sandell tangled with a group of Nates above a skim of clouds. He followed one down through the clouds, firing as he went, then turned away and watched it crash. He climbed back up and set another Nate aflame, then shot the engine out of a third. The second

Nate was a likely kill, he wrote, and the third was "undoubtedly badly damaged but due to stress at the moment from other aircraft I could not follow them down to observe results."

The main swarm was now heading for home. Charlie Bond "fire-walled everything" and charged after it, but each time he framed a Nate in his sights, the Japanese pilot doubled back and met him head-on. After sparring for a time, Bond realized the clouds were filling in, so he called it quits. He flew back to Mingaladon and executed "the first victory roll in my life"—first radioing the control tower for permission. When he landed, Bond saw a crowd of airmen near one of the revetments that protected planes from being destroyed by a near-miss explosion. Another Japanese pilot—probably a sergeant named Nagashima—had made a suicide dive on Mingaladon, trying to destroy a parked Blenheim. Bond taxied past the wreckage. "An RAF airman held up a leather helmet with the pilot's head still in it," Bond wrote, "and with parts of his throat hanging down in a bloody mess. With his other hand the airman pointed two fingers skyward in the usual V-for-victory sign. I returned the V-sign and taxied on. I could not, however, return his broad grin."

The Allied pilots put in fourteen claims on January 29. Sandy Sandell was credited with three Nates, to become the first ace among the Adam & Eves—and newly popular among his men. ("Sandell seemed to be a changed man," Dick Rossi recalled. "After his first combat encounters with real bullets and a couple of victories, he became downright likeable.") Charlie Bond was credited with two Nates, and John Dean, Tex Hill, Bob Little, Jack Newkirk, Bob Prescott, Noel Bacon, and Whitey Lawlor with one apiece. Squadron Leader Frank Carey and Pilot Officer Jack Storey were also credited with kills. The 77th Sentai actually lost four planes on January 29—bad enough, from the Japanese perspective. Major Yoshioka had lost a third of the pilots and half the planes he'd led into Thailand on December 8.

The combat over South Burma that Thursday was witnessed by a wire-service reporter, who filed this breathless account: "Paced by three resolute Texans, the unbeaten American Volunteer Group's squadron and its Royal Air Force colleagues tore thirteen and possibly seventeen Japanese planes out of a mass enemy fighter sweep over Rangoon

A jibaku dive upon Blenheim bombers parked at Mingaladon airport, as rendered by a postwar Japanese artist. The Nakajima Ki-27 Nate was the fighter most often encountered by the AVG, and the 77th Sentai was its most persistent opponent. (From Hein tai Guramen by permission of the publisher)

today. . . . It was truly Texas day over the rice paddies of the Kipling country. Sandy [Sandell] of San Antonio got three Japanese for sure, a total of five in the two days since he was transferred here from China. Bill [Tex Hill], also from San Antonio, got one for certain, increasing his bag to seven. Kirk [Matt Kuykendall] of San Saba came down safely, drenched with oil from a broken fuel line and creased across his forehead by a bullet. 'Now I'm really mad,' he drawled."

The pressure eased on Friday, so Jim Howard led Tom Cole and Eddie Rector to the killing ground beyond Moulmein, to provide what relief they could to Indian Division. "We were low over the ground when we arrived at the area of Kawkareik," Howard wrote in his combat report. "Pilot Cole and I spiraled down to see if there was any troop concentrations to strafe. I saw a number of lorries in the road about 2 miles north of Kawkareik and went down and made a pass at them but did not fire. I made another pass and still did not fire, because I did not see anything of special importance nor did I know for certain that the particular lorries were ours or the enemies. I started to climb and headed for home, but looked back and saw Cole headed in a glide for the trucks presumably to strafe. The next thing I saw was an explosion and a flame shot up 100 feet into the air. Black smoke ensued. At first I thought that Cole had hit an ammunition truck but as I passed over the target I realized the pilot had crashed because there was a path cut thru the tall trees which bordered the road and bits of plane were visible scattered all over."

A former PBY pilot, Cole was the first of the flying-boat captains to transition to fighters. In his AVG identification photo, he is a glum, heavy-set man, well on the way to baldness. He had one Nate to his credit, and Jim Howard remembered him as the "spark plug" of the Panda Bears' softball team. His death made a great impression upon the pilots. "Group wanted us for two other crazy missions," Noel Bacon wrote. "I told them to go to hell."

Howard and Bacon were right in their reluctance to attack the truck traffic, for the Japanese had no vehicles west of the Dawna range: Tom Cole had plunged to his death while attacking friendly troops.

General Takeuchi's 55th Division was moving into position around Moulmein. Like the one at Tavoy, Moulmein's airfield was defended by paramilitary border police, who pulled out when night fell. That was bad enough, but John Smyth, commanding Indian Division, got word that the Japanese were also operating "in strength" near Paan to his north, threatening his line of retreat. (This was General Sakurai's 33rd Division, advancing into Burma proper.) Smyth appealed to Rangoon for permission to withdraw, which was granted by General Hutton. During the night on Saturday, the Commonwealth troops commandeered all the boats they could find, and early next morning they rowed to the northern shore. Tenasserim province now belonged to the Japanese, two weeks after Oki Detachment had fired the opening shots outside Tavoy.

At midnight, while Smyth was abandoning Moulmein, three Sallys came from Bangkok to bomb Mingaladon. Unable to find the airport, they jettisoned their bombs on Rangoon. Two hours later, six Lilys made the same journey with better success, not only finding the airport but putting its radar out of operation. Finally, before dawn on Sunday morning, four Sallys bombed the dispersal fields to the north, hitting a Tomahawk at Johnnie Walker.

General Obata had also targeted Kyedaw airfield for destruction. On Tuesday, February 3, six Anns of the 31st Sentai flew up from Phitsanulok to bomb the old AVG training base at Toungoo, with an escort of twenty-four Nates of the 77th Sentai. Robert Keeton (called Buster in honor of the cinema comic) was stationed at Kyedaw to check out Tomahawks as they were repaired. When the Anns came over, Keeton and two ground crewmen jumped into a car, which they promptly careened into a ditch. "I, being in the back seat, the door jammed, and I couldn't get out," Keeton wrote in his diary. "The bombs were whistling and then hitting making a tremendous noise. I knew they were dropping awfully close from the impact and the car was being filled with dirt. I could hear the scharpnel falling and wizzing by sounding like machine gun bullets." Thirty bombs hit the runway, by his count, but the only casualties were two Burmese soldiers injured and one killed.

Also sheltering in a ditch were Bunny Stone and another Hurricane pilot, who had stopped to refuel. Stone's Hurricane was apparently damaged, a 113 Squadron Blenheim was riddled with shrapnel, and a Tiger Moth biplane nosed over when its pilot tried to take off with the wheel chocks still in place. Vic Bargh and Ted Sadler did manage to get their Buffaloes into the air, but without oxygen they couldn't intercept the raiders. "I never fired the guns," said Bargh of his days protecting Kyedaw.

Bus Keeton had better luck. "At 3:30 p.m.," his diary continued, "the siren went off and having a plane ready I jumped in and took off. Had reached about 300 feet altitude when they dropped their bombs. Circled field climbing until reaching 20,000 feet." He, too, was flying without oxygen. "After circling for about 30 minutes and I began to feel dizzy and the lack of oxygen my head was hurting like the devil and I was breathing hard. I decided to come on back and land. I just nosed the plane over and started down when I saw a twin motored Jap plane practically flying formation about 1,000 feet below me and to my right. I switched on guns, and dove on him from above and the left side with all 6 guns going full blast. Passing under him and looking back I thought he was smoking but not certain." The plane must have been an 8th Sentai Lily returning from a raid upcountry, though there's no mention of the loss in Japanese accounts. An AVG ground crewman saw the bomber crash, and Keeton was duly credited with a victory.

Kyedaw was bombed again next day by six Sallys from the 62nd Sentai. Chennault's nightmare of the previous autumn had become reality: so close to Thailand, with no warning except observers with heliograph mirrors, Toungoo couldn't be defended against enemy raids. Bus Keeton pronounced two of the Tomahawks airworthy but not fit to fight, so Noel Bacon and Frank Swartz drove up from Mingaladon and flew them to Kunming—the first of the Panda Bears to move back to China. John Hennessy came down in the AVG Beechcraft and picked up some of the ground crewmen, and the rest headed up the Burma Road in a four-truck convoy.

A fter more than a month in the pipeline, Hurricanes from North Africa were moving into Burma in such numbers that RAF 135 Squadron was activated at Mingaladon under Frank Carey. There was even talk of lending fighters to the Americans, "to tide them over until their own reinforcing aircraft arrived." Jack Newkirk did check out in a Hurricane, but a disaster on February 3 put an end to the reverse lend-lease. Eighteen Hurricanes left Calcutta's Dum Dum airport in the afternoon, and night overtook them above the mountainous Shan Highlands. The fighters lost sight of the "mother Blenheim" that was navigating for them, and one by one they crashed.

A dozen Westland Lysanders made a more successful flight into Burma. These high-wing, fixed-gear planes were intended as artillery spotters, but Group Captain Seton Broughall—Mingaladon's new commander—pressed them into service as bombers. The Lysanders had a rack on each wheel spat, intended for a 25-pound bomb, and these were adapted to carry 250-pound bombs, posing a serious risk of self-destruction whenever they took off. Nothing daunted, Squadron Leader Karun (Jumbo) Majumdar flew his first mission on February 3, bombing a Thai airfield under the protection of Vic Bargh and Ted Sadler of 67 Squadron. Like them, the Lysander pilots were based at Toungoo, but operated as needed out of the Rangoon airfields.

Those airfields, meanwhile, were bombed almost every night that week, though not to great effect. Early Friday morning, February 6, four Sallys raided Mingaladon, missing by such a margin that they nearly hit the Burmah Oil compound four miles south. The sound of the unsynchronized Mitsubishi radials was almost as bad as the bombs themselves; to a listener on the ground, the engines seemed to beat out a personal threat: *"DOOM-ba-boom-ba-DOOM."* They were followed an hour later by six more Sallys, and an hour after that by fifteen Anns. The RAF night fighters claimed two of the 31st Sentai light bombers shot down, double-claiming on the one that was actually lost.

The siren howled again at 10:30 AM. Six Tomahawks and six Hurricanes scrambled to intercept the enemy formation: twenty-five Nates from the 77th Sentai plus a flight from the 50th. Bob Neale led the interception. "I was in a good position," he wrote in his diary, "with eight planes [including two Hurricanes] about 2,000 ft. above and behind" the incoming swarm.

One of the Tomahawks was flown by Charlie Bond, who caught a Nate "in my sights at about five hundred yards and let go with all guns. My firing engulfed him. As I closed in, I misjudged my speed and had to pull up and away drastically to keep from hitting him. [Then] I had to dive out when a Jap got too close on my rear, and when I leveled off and climbed back up, I lost the enemy fighters." Turning east, he searched the horizon for the retreating enemy. He spotted a lone fighter, went after it, and dove on it from behind. But only one of his guns was firing, so he rolled out and charged them. "In I went again, and in my concentration I did not see another Jap who had come down on me but overshot me. He pulled around to get on my tail; I dove away. Just as I did, I got a glimpse of another P-40 whizzing past me—No. 23."

That was Bob Neale. Together, they cornered the Nate. "Bob and I fought that little devil some five to ten minutes," Bond wrote. "He must have known he was done for, but he was a game little guy." At one point, the Japanese pilot doubled back and attacked Bond head-on: "All my guns were firing as we barreled on at each other. He started pulling up and I followed as long as I dared, then broke off in a screaming dive out. He flipped around in an amazing turn and followed me down. . . . I was in a vertical power dive and skidding like mad, since I did not bother [with] the rudder trim."

Neale was credited with the Nate, to become the second ace in the Adam & Eves. Also scoring were Greg Boyington and Bob Little, each credited with two Japanese fighters; and Bob Prescott and Mac Mc-Garry with one apiece. In addition, Jack Storey and Guy Underwood of 135 Squadron claimed three Nates shot down, for a grand total of ten that morning.

Japanese accounts show just one plane lost over South Burma on February 6. The dead pilot was Lieutenant Kitamura of 77th Sentai. In addition, Major Hirose, the group's executive officer, was hit over Min-galadon and made a forced landing at Moulmein, returning to his unit the next day. For their part, the Japanese fighter pilots claimed five Tom-ahawks and Hurricanes shot down, when there were no Allied losses. "Obviously, on both sides," wrote the British aviation historian Christo-pher Shores of this battle, "enthusiasm had run riot."

Chapter 11

Get the Heck Out of Here

O n Saturday morning, February 7, line chief Harry Fox pronounced Tomahawk No. 11 restored from the effects of Lieutenant Yamamoto's *jibaku* dive. Sandy Sandell took it up for a
test flight, concluding with a barrel roll over the airport; he stalled the
plane and augered in. All that could be salvaged from the wreck were the
tail wheel and a main wheel assembly. "The boys had to dig Sandy out,"
Fritz Wolf recalled, "and it wasn't pleasant."

Unlike many Adam & Eves, Bob Neale liked and respected his
squadron leader. When Chennault appointed him to take over, he tried
to pass the job along to Greg Boyington, on the theory that the marine
aviator could "out-fly or out-fight" anyone in the AVG. Boyington refused, so Neale took the job.

Lanky, big-featured, and curly-haired, Neale might have posed for a
recruiting poster as the all-American fighting man. A British pilot saw
him as "a well-built fellow of medium height, dressed in shirt and trousers and having a revolver slung in an unorthodox, finely-worked leather

holster. He looked dusty and tired, but his eyes were of a merry, friendly shade." But Neale's diary doesn't suggest a merry-hearted man. "No one will ever know the mental anxiety I am going thru," he wrote, "for on top of losing a very close friend I have shouldered the responsibility of running the Squadron and assuring its safety. . . . Chennault places full confidence in my decisions. I only pray that I will be deserving." Jack Newkirk seemed to enjoy the combat that surged back and forth across Martaban Bay, but Neale was a more typical warrior: the man who fights because he must.

To compound his problems, he was also taking Newkirk's place. The Panda Bears were leaving South Burma, by train, truck, and war-weary Tomahawk. Among those who flew to Kunming was John Petach, who immediately proposed to Red Foster, his sweetheart almost since *Jagersfontein* had cleared the Golden Gate Bridge. They were married February 17 at Hostel Number One, the bride with a black eye sustained in an arm-wrestling contest with Claire Chennault.

Fortunately for Bob Neale, General Obata decided to shift his fighters and light bombers to the Salween front, and he sent the battered 62nd Sentai home to refit. That left only twelve Sallys targeted on South Burma: Colonel Hironaka's 14th Sentai, which moved from Bangkok to Nakhon Sawan to be closer to the action. Like the Panda Bears in the first week of January, the Adam & Eves were therefore granted a lull before battle. They buried Sandy Sandell in plot C-99 at the church of Edward the Martyr. In the week that followed, this was a typical radiogram to Kunming, detailing planes on hand, reinforcements trickling in, and missions flown: "Sixteen planes. Four pilots arrived. No enemy action. Six sharks combat patrol over Paan. Six sharks bomber escort to Paan."

Neale had twenty-two pilots on the roster, some without combat experience and others worn down by combat. To keep sixteen planes on alert, he had to use almost every available flier. The others got staff assignments: Charlie Sawyer as RAF liaison; Ray Hastey as transportation officer; and Ed Goyette (who'd moved down from Kyedaw) as supply-and-maintenance officer. Neale also had an all-purpose aide in Paul Frillmann, the AVG chaplain, whom Chennault sent down from Kunming for a taste of war.

The Adam & Eves enjoyed the interlude. They played golf at the

Rangoon Country Club—four caddies per pilot. They swam at the Ko-
kine Swimming Club "and acted like rich kids." They bought sapphires.
They caroused through Rangoon, brawling with the RAF and each
other in squabbles that were potentially lethal since everyone went
armed. One donnybrook began when the Silver Grill's proprietor tried
to evict the Americans, whereupon they shot out his chandeliers, causing a panic among the prostitutes and their clients on the second floor.
Another time, the Adam & Eves drank so hard and late at the brass-
railed bar of the Strand (the bar stayed open though the hotel was
closed) that seven pilots missed roll-call next morning. One latecomer
was Robert H. Smith, who showed up too drunk to fly. (Not to be confused with R. T. Smith of the Hell's Angels, Robert H. was shorter and
known by the nickname Snuffy, after a comic-strip character.) Greg Boyington was another casualty of the battle of the Strand. Still drunk
when he reported for duty, he got into an argument with Bob Neale, who
never afterward placed much confidence in him.

Then there was crew chief George Reynolds, who wrecked an AVG
vehicle and shot some Burmans who crowded around, killing one and
wounding two. Reynolds spent the night in jail, but the British released
him into Neale's custody next day, and no more was said about it. The
feeling was general, among westerners in Rangoon, that the natives
would murder any white man they caught alone.

Another popular activity was to borrow a truck, drive down to the
waterfront, and have the dock workers load it with whatever took one's
fancy. "I spent every day," Paul Frillmann wrote, "with whatever ground
crewmen could be spared from the airfield, smashing open crates and
barrels, loading our trucks with spare parts for planes and vehicles, tires,
tools, radio equipment, guns and ammunition." The freebooting must
have struck the laborers—many of them convicts working at gunpoint—
as something of a double standard. Looters were being shot in Rangoon
at the rate of twenty-four per day.

Much of the booty was converted to personal use. The ground
crewmen (including some who'd quit the AVG in the fall of 1941 and remained in Rangoon) built up huge stores of contraband they hoped to
smuggle into China. The pilots had less opportunity to play this game,
but they helped themselves to the possessions in the houses where they

slept, and which were now being abandoned by their owners. George Burgard and Ed McClure, pilot and crew chief, filled a truck with contraband—"so much stuff it would not be believed if I listed it," Burgard wrote—and consigned it to the convoy taking surplus AVG supplies and personnel to Kunming. They hoped to sell the cargo for $1,500. Ray Hastey was generally believed to be making a good thing out of his job as transportation officer. Even Charlie Bond, the quintessential square shooter, accepted a shortwave radio, knowing it was stolen from China's lend-lease stores.

An Australian journalist at the Burma-China frontier admired the style with which the Americans bullied their cargoes past Chinese customs guards: "With 'AVG' in huge letters plastered across their windscreens, they drove straight through, every man bristling with [weapons]. . . . Their prestige and Tommy guns allowed their smuggled goods to pass through without hindrance."

For the past month, the pilots had luxuriated in private homes while the ground crewmen clubbed together at Eighteen Mile Ranch. Don Rodewald described the routine at the hostel: "[Harry] Fox calls us at 5:30. We have breakfast prepared by [Clayton] Harpold a former Army mess sgt. He usually has eggs and flapjacks, jam, syrup, coffee and bacon. We go to the field immediately. It usually gets light about a half hour after we get there. We preflight all ships right away then continue with our work on individual ships. At 8 A.M. Harpold brings us coffee, bread & jam. At noon Harpold brings us dinner. We usually have cold slaw, potato salad, cold meat bread & jam and Iced tea. We stay at the airdrome till 6:30 P.M. and then go like hell to the ranch to get a shower before dark. . . . We pay the native boy an anna to pump water for the shower. We then have chow and usually to bed by 9 P.M."

Now, however, as the pilots found themselves returning to empty houses, with no whisky-soda or dinner in prospect, they began to take the evening meal at Eighteen Mile Ranch. With most of Rangoon's white women having taken passage to India, they also paid court to the Anglo-Burmans and Anglo-Indians they'd earlier left to the ground crewmen. The British didn't approve. "We don't mind you sleeping with them," they told the Americans, "but don't for God's sake drag them around in our hotels and restaurants."

The Japanese bombed Bassein, starting a rumor that their paratroops had landed there—to the west of Rangoon. The Adam & Eves joked that some day they'd drive out to Johnnie Walker and find Japanese pilots grinning at them from the cockpits of the Tomahawks. At night in the abandoned house where he was billeted, Charlie Bond dreamed of combat in the sky. Daytimes, too, had a nightmarish quality, as a British pilot recalled: "We sipped at another mug of tea, and lay supine under the wings, eyeing with suspicion every speck of a bird soaring on high, and sweating—and sweating." Whenever the siren wailed, they scrambled into their cockpits, roared down the runway in dust and confusion, and clawed for the altitude that could save their lives. On one such alarm, they climbed to 22,000 feet and promptly heard "snapper" in their earphones—radio code for a recall—so they pointed their noses back to Mingaladon, cursing the fools in the operations room. The debacle was the work of Sergeant John (Tex) Barrick, an American in 17 Squadron. In North Africa, "snapper" had meant enemy aircraft approaching; seeing what looked like a Japanese fighter, Barrick shouted the warning and was astonished when the defenders (including the Buffalo he'd taken for Japanese) dropped out of the sky.

The Commonwealth troops were in an unenviable position, holding a slab of land between two great rivers. The Salween served as their defensive barrier, but the Sittang was a mile-wide estuary blocking their line of retreat. Only a planked-over railway trestle connected them with Burma proper. The divisional commander wanted to move behind this bottleneck, but was ordered to hold as far east as possible, buying space and time for reinforcements to come up.

Indian Division had only eight thousand men on rations, about half the strength of a textbook division. Fully trained, they'd have ranked among the finest soldiers in the world, as they'd often proved in Britain's wars, whether fighting for the crown or against it. On the Salween front, however, the newcomers hadn't finished their training, while the early arrivals were demoralized by their defeats in Tenasserim. In addition to his Indian and Gurkha battalions, John Smyth had two battalions of British troops, the Duke of Wellingtons and the King's Own Yorkshires, plus four on loan from Burma Division. (With about five hundred men, a battalion was the basic unit of maneuver in the Commonwealth army.) Their morale wasn't improved when—on Sunday, February 15—the one-hundred-thousand-man garrison at Singapore surrendered to a much smaller Japanese army.

In India, the high command fretted that Indian Division wasn't "fighting with proper relish," so they did what comes naturally to desk officers: they fired General Hutton. Burma's new field commander—the third in as many months—would be Sir Harold Alexander, who in May 1940 had presided over the evacuation of the British Expeditionary Force at Dunkirk. Perhaps there was a portent in that.

For the Adam & Eves, the string of eventless days came to an end over the village of Belin on Saturday, February 21. Escorting a flight of Blenheims to the Salween front, six Tomahawks ran into the full strength of the 77th Sentai. The Japanese fighters were on a similar mission: twenty-three Nates escorting light bombers of the 31st Sentai, off to silence a Commonwealth machine gun position. "They were on our tails in a split second," Jim Cross wrote. "Everywhere the sky seemed suddenly filled with orange suns. They kept no formation but came in like a flock of sparrows."

"We were below them," George Burgard recalled, "and I had to dive out the first time without getting a shot. There were, it seemed, more than a million Jap planes all over the sky. I tried to shoot them all down myself, but got only two in a full hour of fighting. It was a wild scramble. They had no rhyme or reason to their method of fighting. [John] Farrell got a bullet through his canopy and I got one thru my wing that shot out my right tire. Some fun." In his excitement, trying to brighten the illumination on his jury-rigged reflector sight, Burgard tore the rheostat off its mount. Both his claims were recognized, and Farrell and Snuffy Smith were each credited with a Nate. Japanese records show just one Nate damaged in this engagement, while the Japanese pilots claimed one Tomahawk shot down.

No sooner did they land at Mingaladon than the Adam & Eves were sent off to attack a Japanese column of three hundred vehicles on a track to the north of Kyaikto. Since Indian Division was falling back on this village, the Commonwealth troops seemed to be heading into an ambush.

"For the first time in the campaign," Air Vice Marshal Stevenson exulted, "the enemy provided a satisfactory bombing target. . . . The total fighter effort of the Rangoon defence and what bombers were at readiness were ordered to attack at 1625 hours."

When he got the word to scramble, Charlie Bond was still writing up his combat report from the previous action. "I was eager as hell," he wrote in his diary, "and was hoping we would see [the Nates] again, since I didn't fare too well before. The Blenheims bombed the area, and then Bob [Neale] went down with his flight to strafe the Japanese columns on the road. I counted over fifty trucks in the column heading northwest toward Kyaikto, which is the British Army headquarters."

But the Japanese column was supposed to be heading south: it was Indian Division that was moving north. Six Blenheims and an undetermined number of Tomahawks and Hurricanes did their best to destroy it. "Straffed a Jap motorized column," Bob Neale noted in his diary. "Did a lot of damage." After an hour of flying top cover, Charlie Bond took his flight back to Mingaladon. He was sent out again with Snuffy Smith to find and destroy a Blenheim that had crashed in the rain forest after being hit by ground fire. They searched for the bomber in vain; then Bond decided to go back to the killing field: "I headed north to the main road on which I had seen so many trucks in my previous mission. This time I was at treetop level, and then I found the Jap motorized column. I strafed it from one end to the other. Some vehicles already were on fire and bombed out. . . . I circled back to come back down the column again, and Smitty was right behind me. I came close to the treetops in my porpoising and jinking to get in bursts at choice targets."

Snuffy Smith's combat report was equally upbeat, and equally sure that this was the main Belin-Kyaikto track. "Falling into single file," he wrote, "we strafed up and down the road, until our ammunition was exhausted, paying particular attention to trucks and cavalry groups."

There was no enemy motorized column—not on the side road above Kyaikto, and not on the Belin-Kyaikto track. What the Blenheims bombed, and what the Hurricanes and Tomahawks strafed, was Indian Division. Road-bound by their vehicles, the Commonwealth troops were strung out for fifteen miles on either side of Kyaikto, while the Japanese filtered through the rain forest and rubber plantations to the north, trying to beat them to the Sittang Bridge. The day was astonishingly hot, and red dust choked the marching troops. In the morning they were attacked by the Japanese, in the afternoon by the RAF and the AVG. According to the scuttlebutt at Mingaladon, 160 Commonwealth troops died under friendly fire; officially, the losses were described as "numerous." Even more disheartening to a western-trained army was the loss of its transport and supplies. Vehicles—including ambulances full of wounded men—were blown up, machine-gunned, and run off the road. Pack mules broke loose and stampeded, taking weapons, ammunition, and radios into the rain forest. (Next day, the Indians would take revenge of a sort by shooting down the Hurricane flown by Pilot Officer Dunsford-Wood of 28 Squadron. They may also have downed two Blenheims on February 21.)

The tragedy was one bad moment in a ruinous three days. A Frontier Force battalion and a company of engineers managed to beat the Japanese to the Sittang Bridge, where the military police set up a defensive position while the engineers prepared to blow the trestle. At nightfall, the column's rear guard was still southeast of Kyaikto, and the twenty miles between were choked with an army that was exhausted, demoralized, and crazed with thirst. No one who hasn't made a forced march in the tropics can imagine what these men suffered, retreating for twelve hours without water, under a sun burning like an open furnace door. Night brought relief from the heat, but not from the drought: even if he found water, a man couldn't swallow enough to quench his thirst.

All through the night, Indian Division straggled across the decked-over railroad trestle. At daybreak, the Japanese seized the bridgehead—lost it—seized it again—lost it a second time. The engineers finished their work at nightfall on February 22, but lacked the wire to put the blasting station on the western shore. The troops now coming down the road were stragglers, who told wild stories of being "ambushed, cut up and scattered" by Japanese commandos, and of jungle paths marked with paper arrows by Burmese collaborators.

The brigadier in charge—Hugh-Jones by name—tried to contact the main column, but its radios had been lost in the stampede set off by the Allied air attack. He concluded that the division had been destroyed. At 4:30 AM, a junior officer reported the situation to division headquarters over a bad telephone line. The question came back: Was "Jonah" safely across? This referred to another brigadier, named Jones, who at that moment was fighting his way to the river through a Gurkha position he believed to be Japanese. To this question, the officer at the bridge answered yes, in the belief that they were talking about his own brigadier. Jonah, Jones, and Hugh-Jones: upon this muddle of names, half a division would be lost. The conversation was reported to General Smyth, who concluded that his division was safe on the western shore. The explosives were accordingly detonated at 5:30 AM on February 23. The division's third brigadier (who had the refreshingly distinct name of Ekin) described the scene when he reached the river: "Here there was chaos and confusion; hundreds of men throwing down their arms, equipment and clothing and taking to the water. . . . As we crossed, the river was a mass of bobbing heads. We were attacked from the air and sniped at continuously from the east bank."

Next day, Indian Division mustered only 3,335 men, less than half its force. Most were barefoot, and many had thrown away their rifles. They were little more than a rabble, as their commander described them: "ready to defend themselves doggedly but otherwise unfit for any of the normal operations of war."

In Rangoon, the evacuation was now becoming total. On February 20, in an emergency meeting at Government House, the RAF commander had proposed that he withdraw his headquarters to India. He'd keep two operational wings in Burma, at Magwe in the Irrawaddy Valley and at Akyab on the coast, each about 250 miles north of Rangoon. His proposal was accepted without argument. Next day the authorities hoisted the "E" signal, telling nonessential personnel to leave the city. The telephone exchange shut down. Army engineers prepared the oil refinery at Syriam for demolition; the navy mined the river and prepared freighters for scuttling. When General John Magruder came down from Chongqing on February 22, he found the police gone, the city burning, dogs running wild, and looters operating with impunity. "Remembering previous British failure to effect destructions," as he put it, Magruder ordered Frank Merrill to destroy what he could. The major and his staff torched the General Motors assembly plant, destroying 972 trucks, 5,000 tires, 1,000 bales of blankets, and a ton of jacks, chains, paint, and other stuff.

Rangoon had two jails, a lunatic asylum, and a leper hospital. With
their Indian warders fleeing to the north, these unfortunates seemed
likely to starve to death, so a junior officer ordered the doors opened and
(in the case of the asylum) the inmates driven into the streets. Many
joined the "crocodile" crawling past Mingaladon airport day and night,
but others became looters or firebugs, or roamed witlessly around the
city. Driving through Rangoon one day, Bob Neale was hailed by what he
thought was a Caucasian woman; when he braked to a stop, he saw that
her seemingly fair complexion was actually the silvery scales of leprosy.

The Shwedagon Pagoda was guarded by cadres of orange-robed
monks, but all else was fire and chaos. The principal blaze was at the
docks—a great column of black smoke and red flame—but smaller fires
burned everywhere in the dying city. Sidewalks glittered with glass from
broken windows and smashed bottles. On his last foray to the docks,
Paul Frillmann saw typewriters in the streets, along with clocks, cameras, clothing, and jewels; the looters who'd dropped them were being
chased down the alleys by rifle-bearing soldiers. This being the case,
the chaplain felt justified in broadening his definition of war matériel.
When they passed an abandoned automobile dealership, Frillmann and
his crew stepped inside, took the keys to three new Buicks, topped their
tanks with gasoline, and drove them back to Mingaladon.

On February 22, coastwise vessels began shuttling RAF ground
personnel and heavy supplies around the west coast to Akyab. An operational group called "Burwing" was activated at Magwe the same day.
The half-dozen Blenheims of 113 Squadron moved back to this dusty,
brick-red landing field, along with the four surviving Buffaloes of 67
Squadron, joined a day later by four Hurricanes. (The New Zealanders
checked out in the Hurricanes and flew several missions in them. "An
awful aeroplane to fly," Vic Bargh wrote in his logbook.) Six Tomahawks
also moved to Magwe, to provide air cover for the AVG convoy that
would soon leave Mingaladon by truck, jeep, and Buick sedan.

What the Adam & Eves found at Magwe was a base more interested
in evacuation than combat. Most of the multi-engine planes in Burma—
Douglas transports, ancient biplane bombers, and six Lockheed Hudsons that had escaped from Singapore—were engaged in a daylong
shuttle, flying desk officers and high-priority civilians to India. Fritz Wolf

was bound for Kunming, but when he asked for fuel he was told to wait: the evacuation took precedence. Trying again next morning, Wolf cooled his heels until 8:30 AM, when the RAF arrived for work. Even then, nobody seemed to know whether the gasoline being pumped into his Tomahawk was 80 or 100 octane. It sufficed, in any event, because Wolf made it to Kunming and informed Chennault that the Tomahawks in Burma "are in an almost unflyable condition." His report was a litany of horrors: "The tires are baked and hard, and blow out on us continually . . . the battery plates are thin . . . and need recharging in a short time. There is no Prestone available down there at all. And there is no oxygen whatever. . . . The dust at Magwe and Rangoon fouls up the ship's engines considerably. It clogs the [carburetors] to such an extent that it is dangerous to increase the manifold pressure of the [aircraft] as the engine quits cold. . . . This tendency of the engines to quit makes it impossible to dogfight or strafe, especially at low altitude."

Wolf also talked to an American reporter, telling lurid stories of the death of Rangoon. Indian shopkeepers, he said, gave their keys to the Americans and told them to take what they wanted, rather than let the stuff fall into Japanese hands. Not to end his story on a downbeat note, the reporter had Wolf climbing back into his Tomahawk for the return to Burma. "It's hot in Rangoon," he supposedly said, "but all the fun is there."

At this perilous moment, 7th Armoured Brigade reached Rangoon with 114 lend-lease M-3 Stuart tanks from North Africa, still bearing the symbol of the Desert Rat. To the north, the leading divisions of the Chinese expeditionary force moved into the Shan Highlands. "All day long," wrote Leland Stowe, "you see them plodding the roads and bypaths, moving up and up toward the front, boyish little figures clad in worn, faded denim. With their visored hats of the same material, they look like coal miners in a child-labor district but they are carrying heavy packs and rifles and all sorts of equipment."

The Japanese, for their part, finished a 250-mile truck road from Phitsanulok to Moulmein, enabling them to bring supplies and bridging materials to the troops on the east bank of the Sittang. They mended the broken span, mounted bicycles, and pedaled into Burma proper, like Boy Scouts on summer holiday. Their only opposition was from the air. On February 24, the Adam & Eves escorted a flight of Blenheims to the

infamous Belin-Kyaikto road, where they attacked a Japanese supply column that included artillery pieces drawn by oxen. The Japanese, according to press reports, were "thick as ants" on the road.

Strafing was a gruesome business. No American left a record of his
thoughts, but a British pilot had this memory of it: "There were horses,
mules, dead and wounded Japs slumped on the road in all manner of
grotesque attitudes, just as if they had been shoveled there by a giant
spade. . . . I saw a number of them in their greeny-grey uniform scam-
pering like mice for the cover of the trees. Squat bodies they appeared to
have, and putteed bow-legs. . . . By the time I had wheeled on them they
were almost under cover, but I caught the last dozen and with my fire
jerked them to the ground where they sagged still. I'd never killed a man
like that before."

The air strikes troubled the Japanese out of all proportion to the
damage actually done, and General Obata drew up plans for a
knockout blow on Mingaladon. It would be an air superiority battle on
the scale of those that had raged through the Burma sky during the first
week of February. To direct the campaign, he moved his headquarters
to Lampang near the head of the Thai railroad, closer to the frontier. The
77th Sentai moved with him to the new location. Feeling the need for
retractable-gear fighters that could match the speed of Tomahawks and
Hurricanes, Obata also called up the 47th Independent Chutai, whose
Shokis had failed to get into action at Rangoon on Christmas Day. By this
time, Major Sakagawa Toshio had only four Ki-44s still airworthy. On
February 24, they flew to Moulmein, where Sakagawa and his pilots filled
their tanks with aviation fuel left behind by the British. They were joined
by a 14th Sentai Sally, forced down by a leaky fuel tank.

At noon, the Adam & Eves apparently swooped down on the airfield. Curiously, there's no mention of this raid in the War Diary or in Bob
Neale's journal, yet AVG records show that Neale, Mac McGarry, Bob
Prescott, and Snuffy Smith shared credit for destroying two bombers
on the ground that day, while Bill Bartling and George Burgard were credited with a fighter—though at Raheng, not Moulmein. To make matters more
confusing, four Hurricanes "accompanied by a pair of P-40s" supposedly

attacked Moulmein that afternoon, with the RAF pilots credited with shooting down a transport and destroying a bomber and a fighter on the ground. Whoever the attackers, there was indeed a strafe of Moulmein airport on February 24, leaving the Sally and a Shoki in flames.

The air superiority battle began next day, February 25, with a fighter sweep consisting of twenty-three Nates from the 77th Sentai, twenty-one from the 50th, and the three remaining Shokis.

The Adam & Eves nearly missed the encounter. Smoke from the burning city had combined with morning fog to reduce visibility to half the length of John Haig, their new dispersal field. (On the baseball diamond of airfields behind Rangoon, John Haig was the pitcher's mound.) When the alarm went off at 10:30 AM, the Adam & Eves put up six Tomahawks, led by Bob Neale and Bob Little. As was the rule in Burma, they took off from both ends of the sod strip, the pilots keeping as far right as they dared, and holding right rudder as their wheels left the ground. "A hazy day made a will-o'-the wisp game out of it," Greg Boyington recalled. "Here they are. No, they aren't." Boyington, Little, and Charlie Bond charged after a phantom formation and missed the combat altogether. That left Bob Neale's flight to deal with the raiders. He claimed two Nates, and Mac McGarry and Bob Prescott claimed one apiece.

Though none of the Adam & Eves reported "Zero types" that day, Lieutenant Kuroe Yasuhiko recalled that the Shokis had indeed tangled with the Tomahawks. The big-engined interceptors were flying in string, Major Sakagawa in the lead, followed by Lieutenant Mitsumoto, with Kuroe as tail-end Charlie. The major jinked to avoid a Tomahawk boring in from the left, then went after another Allied fighter. Mitsumoto chased a third—and was himself pursued by a fourth, while Kuroe looked on: "This was the most dangerous enemy, because Sakagawa and Mitsumoto were attacking and could not look around, so they did not see the enemy fighter, which was positioned outside of the battle area and now came to attack. . . . I went after him, but I was not fast enough. The enemy . . . fired at Mitsumoto, then turned upside down and got out of the battlefield by diving fast." One of the pilots in the daisy chain was Tex Barrick of 17 Squadron: "I attacked and shot down one [Nate] and was then jumped from above by a 'Zero' "—the day's only mention of combat with a retractable-gear fighter.

Though wounded in the skirmish, Lieutenant Mitsumoto was able to fly back to Moulmein with his comrades. The Japanese pilots reported that they'd been in combat against no less than twenty Allied planes, of which they'd shot down sixteen! That made a total of twenty-one planes supposedly downed that morning. In fact, none was lost on either side.

In the afternoon, some Blenheims flew down from Magwe, circled Mingaladon while the Tomahawks came up to join them, then flew across Martaban Bay and blasted the docks at Moulmein. The bombers returned to Mingaladon, and in a fatal error of judgment, their pilots decided to stay put for the afternoon. They belonged to 45 Squadron, which was replacing 113 Squadron in Burma.

The siren wailed again at 4 PM. Again the Tomahawks and Hurricanes scrambled to intercept the Japanese formation. Soon after takeoff, Ed Leibolt's engine began to falter. At 6,000 feet he opened his canopy, whether to bail out or to improve his vision for a forced landing. Dick Rossi took over Leibolt's flight, and didn't see him again.

Bob Neale estimated that the Japanese formation contained twelve twin-engine bombers and upward of thirty fighters. The bombers were Kawasaki Ki-48 Lilys of the 8th Sentai, escorted by the same Nates and Shokis that had swept Mingaladon that morning. The bombers were "damn well protected," Neale grumbled in his diary.

But the Allied fighters managed to get through, as reported by a Japanese war correspondent aboard the Lily piloted by Lieutenant Onodera Choji: "About sixty enemy planes were proceeding toward our direction in a mass formation, their machine guns spitting blue flames menacingly. . . . I pictured the proud expressions of . . . my friends in the fighter craft as I saw the enemy planes being sent crushing toward the earth. . . . One of the enemy fighters . . . challenged the plane on which I was aboard. Blue flames spitting endlessly from eight machine guns . . . reminded me that we were in the midst of a hail of bullets. Fortunately none of them found their mark. As the enemy plane started to loop in order to get into a better attacking position, our gunner let fly and a second later it was commencing its death-descent, leaving a trail of black smoke in the air."

Bob Neale was credited with two Nates that afternoon, putting him ahead of Jack Newkirk as the AVG's top scorer. Mac McGarry, Charlie

Bond, Bob Little, Snuffy Smith, and George Burgard were each credited with three kills, including a bomber for Burgard. Bob Prescott
claimed two fighters, and Dick Rossi, Joe Rosbert, and John Blackburn
(the former flight instructor) claimed one apiece. The Hurricane pilots
claimed six kills, making a grand total of twenty-eight. Alas for legend,
the Japanese lost only two aircraft that Thursday afternoon, both from
the 50th Sentai, while claiming one victory. Allied losses came to one
Hurricane shot down and Ed Leibolt's Tomahawk missing.

The greater damage took place on the ground. With line chief John
Carter and some others, Don Rodewald was working on Tomahawk No.
33 that day, on a low hill half a mile from the runway. When the siren
went off, the ground crewmen kept working. Then Carter yelled: "Look
at that formation of bombers!" The men ran for shelter on the lee side of
the hill, as Rode related in his diary: "I went right thru briers and everything without stopping to put on a shirt. . . . About that time we saw all
twelve bombers cut loose. . . . There must have been about 30 or 40
bombs at once. When they get close you can hear the wind whistle then
the earth shakes and it's all over. We were about ten feet below the terrain so just stood and watched. Heard a little schapnel drop around us.
We then came out of hiding and saw the airdrome ablaze. Those Japs hit
direct." Indeed they had, destroying an Indian Air Force Lysander,
damaging five Blenheims, and killing an Australian sergeant-pilot.

The Tomahawks and Hurricanes were scheduled to make a joint
strafe of Moulmein next morning, February 26, but a false alarm sent
the Adam & Eves aloft at 8 AM. "Since we are already airborne," Bob
Neale said, "let's go to Moulmein." He led the scratch flight across
Martaban Bay. They first hit the former RAF dispersal at Mudon, a
field south of Moulmein that now served as forward base for the 77th
Sentai and 47th Chutai. The Nates and Shokis had just returned from
strafing Zayatkwin—the attack that had caused the alarm at Mingaladon.

As Joe Rosbert told the story, there were two planes on the airstrip,
and the Adam & Eves needed only one pass to put them out of action.
"We left the two planes in ruins as we quickly headed north," he wrote
years later. "The east side of Moulmein was ridged with hills, so we
made our initial approach [to the main Moulmein airfield] directly out of
the rising sun. As we came down from the ridge and neared the field, a

wonderful sight met our eyes. The Japs had a little warning from the auxiliary field. Some of them were just getting into their planes and others were already making their takeoff runs." This was the 50th Sentai, which likewise had just returned from Zayatkwin.

What seems to have happened is this: the Moulmein airfield had moments before been attacked by six Hurricanes from 135 Squadron. The RAF pilots reported that they'd surprised the Japanese fighters in the act of landing, shooting down five Nates but losing Guy Underwood to antiaircraft fire. That's why planes were airborne when the Tomahawks arrived: they'd taken off to chase the Hurricanes. With flak bursting around them—the Japanese gunners "did not seem to have any regard for the safety of their own planes," Rosbert marveled—three Nates got into the air. The first flight of Tomahawks swept down in a diving turn and hit them at an altitude of 400 feet. Two Nates then glued themselves to Bob Neale's tail. Flying fifty feet above the water, he couldn't dive out, so he made himself small in front of his armor plate and waited for the big Allison to haul him out of danger, which it eventually did. "Japs can't hit the side of a barn door," he said upon landing. Paul Perry surveyed the damage. "Maybe not," the armorer said, "but they can sure hit a P-40." Neale's Tomahawk had seventeen bullet holes in the fuselage and tail, plus a fist-sized one that was probably the result of flak.

For the strafe at the Mudon dispersal, the seven Americans—Bob Neale, Joe Rosbert, Dick Rossi, Bob Prescott, Mac McGarry, George Burgard, and Bob Little—divided the credit for two Nates destroyed on the ground. Close enough: the 77th Sentai reported one plane burned up and another badly damaged at Mudon. But at Moulmein airfield, the claims were less credible. Neale and Little were each credited with three Nates, and McGarry with two. With the British claims, that brought the total at Moulmein to *thirteen* Ki-27s destroyed. There's no evidence of any Japanese planes destroyed at Moulmein, though Major Makino, the 50th Sentai commander, seems to have been wounded in one of these attacks. (He'd been flying a 77th Sentai fighter back to its base.) It was Makino's second set of injuries in as many months, sufficient for him to be replaced as group commander.

Later that morning, Dick Rossi and Charlie Bond went out to look for Ed Leibolt, who hadn't reported in from yesterday's mishap. They flew a grid over the rice fields west of the airport, but saw no wreckage, so they flew back to Mingaladon. Meanwhile the alert crews had scrambled. The Adam & Eves managed to put 18,000 feet of airspace below them before the raiders came into view. The Japanese formation was almost the same as yesterday's—twelve Lilys escorted by about forty Nates—and again the Tomahawks found it almost impossible to break through. The only one to claim a bomber was Snuffy Smith, and a Ki-48 was also credited to Flight Leader Bush Cotton, an Australian in 17 Squadron. Both seem likely: the Japanese reported seeing one Lily go down over Mingaladon, and another failed to return to base.

When it came to the escort, the Adam & Eves claimed seven Nates shot down. Dick Rossi and Joe Rosbert were each credited with two, and Charlie Bond, John Blackburn, and George Burgard with one apiece. According to Japanese accounts, the toll over Mingaladon was one Nate, from the 77th Sentai.

Altogether, the claims that arose from the February 25–26 combats were stupendous, and they were further exaggerated in press accounts. The Japanese pilots were every bit as optimistic, claiming no less than forty-three Allied aircraft destroyed during the two-day air superiority battle.

The Moulmein raids so puzzled British aviation writer Christopher Shores that he finally resolved the mystery of the duplicated claims by speculating that the RAF pilots had swept through, shot up the Japanese airfields, then "sold" their victories to the AVG, so that the two air forces could divide the bounty money between them. "There was subsequently much rumour about AVG pilots 'buying' RAF claims due to their system of payment by the Chinese authorities for aircraft confirmed shot down," he wrote in *Bloody Shambles,* his meticulous history of the air war in Southeast Asia. "Had both Allied formations attacked at the same time, or had the Americans 'acquired' this attack from the RAF? Certainly, Japanese records note only the one strafe, and identify the attackers as Hurricanes. Or had Carey's formation struck the main airfield and the AVG the satellite strip at Mudon? Much here remains unanswered."

I phoned the author in London and asked him who among the

Burma veterans had told him of these rumors, and he obliged with three names. But when I wrote and telephoned these men, they either backed off the allegations or explained that they'd only been repeating stories they'd heard postwar.

About the same time, I phoned Vic Bargh of 67 Squadron, at his home in New Zealand. Speaking of the bomber squadron wiped out over Rangoon on January 24—a battle that likewise saw parallel claims by AVG and RAF pilots—he told me that he and Ted Sadler afterward "walked over to the American Volunteer Group chappies, and we said to them, 'Look, there are four aeroplanes here; we can tell you exactly where they are. . . .' I said, 'Well, you chappies are getting five hundred dollars paid by the Chinese. You can have 'em. You can say they're yours. It don't worry us.' They put in a report saying they'd shot them down."

Perhaps it was Vic's story that inspired the postwar rumors among RAF veterans, who naturally would have been open to any explanation for the disparity between their victory claims and the Americans'. However that may be, there's a fundamental flaw in his account. The two New Zealanders may indeed have walked over to the American encampment, and they may even have discussed the Sally bombers they'd supposedly shot down. But they didn't transfer those victories, because both Vic and Ted Sadler were duly credited with their Sallys on January 24.

Finally, there's a privately printed memoir by Hedley Everard, a Canadian pilot in 17 Squadron. In his book, *A Mouse in My Pocket,* Everard claimed that on two occasions he'd shot down a retractable-gear Nakajima fighter in the spring of 1942, then "sold" the victory to two Americans. Unlike the New Zealanders, Everard came away from the Burma campaign with no victories to his credit. Instead, as he told the story, he earned $400 from bootlegging the Hayabusas to an unnamed pilot at Magwe (who could only have been Parker Dupouy, though Parker's victim crashed nowhere near the place Everard described) and to R. T. Smith at Loiwing. What happened to the money? Alas, he lost it during his evacuation to India, along with the logbook that would have confirmed his combat activities.

Perhaps it's significant that Everard's only certain "victory" in the Burma campaign was at Magwe, where he shot down "a dark blue . . . Navy Zero" that turned out to be the photo-reconnaissance Hurricane flown by Ken Perkin. "Not a bad day's work, Everard," Bunny Stone supposedly said on that occasion. "One of theirs and one of ours!"

Apart from the utter implausibility of Everard's story, there's another flaw in these accounts. When the AVG was stationed at Rangoon, the Americans didn't know for sure that combat bonuses would be paid to them, so they'd have been very unlikely to "buy" the victories at Moulmein. Later, after the recruiters' promises were confirmed by Madame Chiang, they still didn't have hundreds of dollars on hand. They were indeed affluent as compared to the RAF pilots, especially the sergeant-pilots from the colonies, but nobody received a combat bonus before April, which rules out Everard's "sale" at Magwe. And even after that date, the payouts weren't handled by Pappy Paxton, the AVG paymaster, but by the CAMCO office in New York City, which deposited the money directly into a pilot's bank account.

A t sundown on February 26, the Adam & Eves dispersed their Tomahawks to John Haig. They stopped at Eighteen Mile Ranch on their way home, to wolf Clayton Harpold's chow and listen to the 14th Sentai blasting Mingaladon for the second night in a row. The rumor for the evening was that the Japanese had cut the road to Prome and Magwe—a serious matter, if true, for it was the escape route for anyone without a plane to fly.

Most of the men went to bed after dinner, but Bob Neale returned to the airport for his nightly conference with Group Captain Broughall. He learned that the radar set had been sent up to Magwe. As the story was told, the information was dropped ever so casually at the end of the meeting: "I say, Neale, you'll have a bit shorter warning tomorrow." Indeed, since Burma Observation Corps was also pulling out, the Allied pilots could now count on no warning whatever.

Chennault had given Neale permission to leave Mingaladon on March 1—Sunday. Tomorrow was Friday, and it didn't seem worth risking the squadron by a foolish regard for forty-eight hours. Shortly after midnight, Neale made the rounds of the billets and shook the pilots awake. "Let's get the heck out of here, fellows," he remembered telling them. "We don't have any air raid warning at all. There's no sense keeping a fighter bunch around here to get caught on the ground." The pilots then routed the ground crew, as Don Rodewald recalled: "About 2:30 A.M. today I was woke up and told we were moving out, that the Japs were in dangerous position to us and the British had taken out their [radar]. I rolled my bed and threw it on my truck with my one traveling bag (always packed). That took all of 15 minutes then I drove to the airdrome and loaded the remaining armament equipment. By 5 A.M. was ready to leave. [Mingaladon] was completely evacuated. . . . The Limeys sure do give up before they know they are licked."

Several damaged Tomahawks had been left at Mingaladon, and the ground crews worked through the night to put them in flying condition. At daybreak, all but two were flown up to John Haig. Another group of pilots drove through the morning mist for the last time and mounted the Tomahawks that had spent the night in dispersal. While they waited for the takeoff order, they heard antiaircraft guns barking to the northeast. The 14th Sentai was blasting Johnnie Walker, which the AVG had stopped using the week before.

The first to leave was Bob Little, leading a flight of six Tomahawks bound for China. The ground crews assembled at milepost forty-nine on the Prome road, their convoy scheduled to depart at noon. After a lunch of canned pork and beans, Charlie Bond and three other Adam & Eves took off for Magwe. They buzzed the convoy in a gesture of goodwill that sent the men scrambling for the ditch; then they flew up to their new base. George Burgard and Mac McGarry refueled and went back south to patrol the convoy route. At 5 PM, the AVG trucks and cars reached Prome, safely above any Japanese cross-country thrust. From there to Magwe was a distance of seventy miles. They figured it would take them two hours, but the road turned out to be a cart track, and they didn't reach their new post until midnight. When they asked the RAF duty officer where to bunk, he told them to camp on the polo field.

The pilots also got to bed late, having checked out the American Club at Yenangyaung, an oilfield settlement offering iced drinks and a swimming pool. Returning to Magwe in the early hours, they found bunks in the hostel belonging to 67 Squadron. The Adam & Eves were pleased to discover, after all these months, that most of the Buffalo pilots came from New Zealand, and that they were willing and eager to master the AVG pastime of acey-deucey.

Bob Neale and Snuffy Smith spent a nervous night at Mingaladon, hoping that Ed Leibolt would walk in as so many pilots had done over the past three months. They took the radio out of the baggage compartment behind Neale's seat, figuring that Leibolt could squeeze in there if he had to. But Leibolt didn't walk in. Neale and Smith finally voiced aloud what in their hearts they already believed—that he'd been murdered by Burmese partisans. Twenty-five years old, a graduate of Miami University, Leibolt had been an army bomber pilot before coming to Burma with the Bloom Gang.

Late in the day, the two pilots took off for Magwe, only to miss the airport in the smoke haze blanketing South Burma to an altitude of 15,000 feet. Smith bent a prop, putting down in a riverbed at Myingyan, 100 miles beyond Magwe. Neale made a flawless landing in a peanut field at Singu, closer in, but didn't have enough gas to take off again.

That was Saturday, February 28. On the same day, the British hoisted the "H" signal in Rangoon, leaving only demolition teams in the city. Remaining to cover them were half a dozen Hurricanes operating out of Highland Queen. One of the last-ditch pilots was Sergeant C.E. (Tex) Wisrodt of 17 Squadron, who disappeared on a solo mission on March 3—the last American to lose his life in the defense of Rangoon.

On Thursday, March 5, Burma's new field commander finally reached Rangoon. General Alexander canceled Indian Division's withdrawal and ordered Burma Division down from Toungoo, but the time for such resolution had passed. On the west bank of the Sittang, the Japanese columns had crossed paths, the 55th Division driving north against Toungoo, the 33rd moving west to cut the Prome road. As Japanese bomber squadrons had so often done, General Sakurai intended to attack Rangoon from the far side.

On Saturday, the last charges were blown in the city. Toward midnight, launches took the demolition teams out to steamers waiting in the river, while Rangoon burned luridly behind them. Indeed, the river itself was ablaze, as thousands of gallons of tung oil from China spilled from the docks and caught fire.

In one of those great coincidences of war, Indian Division found its retreat blocked by a Japanese force not far from Eighteen Mile Ranch. The Commonwealth column had met the advance element of Sakurai's 33rd Division. Rather than reveal his intention to attack Rangoon from the northwest, however, the Japanese commander ordered the roadblock out of the way, and the Commonwealth troops went by, mystified but relieved.

On Sunday morning, 33rd Division drove into Rangoon, to find it empty and burning. The hour was 10 AM, March 8, 1942—the first time in 118 years that nonwhites controlled the capital and major port of Burma. Despite the demolition work, the fires, and the looting, the Japanese would recover 19,000 tons of China's lend-lease supplies from the Rangoon docks.

Next day the Dutch colonial army surrendered in Java. Except for U.S. and Filipino troops holding out on the Bataan Peninsula, the Pacific Rim was entirely Japanese, south to Australia and west to India.

Among the RAF units that quit Rangoon toward the end of February were the scavenger teams that inspected Japanese wrecks and gathered intelligence on the planes opposing the Allied air forces. (As a result of their work, the Commonwealth airmen knew the difference between the Nakajima Hayabusa and the Mitsubishi Zero, and they didn't confuse the fixed-gear army and navy fighters, as the Americans sometimes did.) In his post-campaign dispatch, Air Vice Marshal Stevenson summed up the results of the scavenger hunt: "Although air fighting frequently took place over scrub or jungle country, 32 crashed enemy fighters and bombers were located on the ground up to the fall of Rangoon. Technical examination of these—although many were burnt or otherwise destroyed beyond recognition—established the quality of equipment about which little was previously known."

Thirty-two! To be sure, some Japanese aircraft were destroyed over Thailand and behind enemy lines in Burma, and others lay undiscovered in the rain forest and beneath the waters of Martaban Bay. Nevertheless, a mammoth gap exists between the British count and the scores popularly attributed to Chennault's pilots. (The AVG romances sometimes have the British locating thirty or more aircraft after a single raid.) At most, the pilots at Mingaladon seem to have destroyed fifty Japanese planes in the air and on the ground, up to the fall of Rangoon. Many were bombers, so the JAAF probably lost upward of 150 airmen in its effort to subdue the Allied air force in South Burma. By every account, the vast majority fell to the guns of the AVG.

For their part, five AVG pilots were killed in action: Neil Martin, Hank Gilbert, Bert Christman, Cokey Hoffman, and Tom Cole. Two were missing: Charlie Mott and Ed Leibolt. And three were accidentally killed at Mingaladon or en route to Kunming: Lacy Mangleburg, Ken Merritt, and Sandy Sandell. About twenty Tomahawks were shot down or otherwise destroyed. Even allowing for the RAF's contribution, therefore, the AVG gave the JAAF better than it got: perhaps two-to-one in aircraft and twelve-to-one in personnel. It was a magnificent victory, though it seems small in comparison to the reports that were current in the winter of 1941–1942, and that were magnified at intervals over the half-century that followed.

Chapter 12

Did You Have
Any Warning?

By the end of January, all the pieces of the grand compromise were in place: Chennault would be commissioned in the U.S. Army, to become a one-star general commanding all American air units in China, while continuing to lead the AVG by virtue of his ambiguous rank in Chinese service. In July, his irregulars would be inducted into the U.S. Army and the two roles merged.

Then came the wrecking ball. General Marshall had never trusted Chennault, and when the AVG was approved over his objections, he immediately set out to bring it under his control. His campaign now intersected Chennault's. Marshall needed someone to take command of the U.S. effort in China, Burma, and India, and he picked Major General Joseph Stilwell, who as a colonel had served as U.S. military attaché in Beijing and Chongqing. Like Marshall, Stilwell was upright to a fault, but unlike him had no understanding of the role of politics in war. He was Vinegar Joe, the quintessential infantryman, with a foot soldier's tough body, narrow mind, and salty tongue. To Stilwell, the wheelchair-bound

American president was "Old Rubberlegs." His British allies were "bastardly hypocrites." Chiang Kai-shek was a "peanut dictator," the "little dummy," a "grasping, bigoted, ungrateful little rattlesnake," and a "stubborn, ignorant, prejudiced, conceited despot who has never heard the truth except from me." Altogether, to read Stilwell's diary is to be first amused, then sickened, by the venom of the man chosen to command U.S. forces in Asia.

A more immediate annoyance was Colonel Clayton Bissell, who at the Air Corps Tactical School had maddened Chennault with his views on fighter tactics. Chennault learned of Bissell's elevation in a good-news–bad-news radiogram from Lauchlin Currie. Yes, Chennault would have authority over American fighter and light-bomber groups—but not the heavy bombers. Another officer would get that job, with "Bissell over all."

Not if Chennault could help it! "Personally am willing make any sacrifice for sake of China and Allied cause," he replied "but cannot understand how either will be benefited by superseding me as senior air officer China. Particularly when officer selected, Bissell, was junior to me until my retirement. In addition he has no knowledge of conditions in China. . . . Am most discouraged by attitude War Department and quite willing resume private life as health continues poor."

Currie did his best, pleading Chennault's case in a February 9 meeting in Washington. "I spoke for Bissell," Stilwell noted in his diary, "and insisted that he rank Chennault." Currie backed down and promised to tell Chennault "to get in the game and play ball"—Stilwell's phrase, and one that occurs again and again in his diary. The good soldier did what he was told; the good soldier played ball. "They are acting like a couple of kids," he grumbled of Currie and Chennault, "and they'll both have to behave."

Currie put it more tactfully in his radiogram to Chennault, which he routed through T. V. Soong: "[Hap] Arnold is of opinion that you are A-1 as combat man and has fullest praise for AVG, but he wants member of his own staff to head larger show. . . . Bissell has now changed to your views on tactics and Stilwell adds you will have free hand regarding tactics." Currie also asked John Magruder to intercede with "Groco," as Chennault was code-named in radio traffic: "Arnold and Stillwell [sic]

insist on Bissell. . . . I wired Groco through T. V. informing him of decision and asking him to be content with full and free pursuit command.
You could help in easing this difficult situation. . . . His services must
not be lost. Bissell can get equipment and in operation he will be under
Stillwell and Generalissimo."

Magruder did his best, but the result wasn't encouraging. On February 13, passing through Kunming on his way to India, he radioed Currie: "Groco told me confidentially . . . that if he had to work under
Bissell he would resign."

Of course, there was no possibility that Chennault would let go of
the AVG, with parts, planes, and even pilots finally moving toward
China. Thirty Hamilton-Standard props and fourteen Allison engines
reached the CAMCO factory at Loiwing, and *Silver Star* was due at Calcutta with solenoids and tires—the same tires, presumably, that the ship
had tried to deliver in December. To expedite the shipments, Chennault
sent Commander Robert DeWolfe—his latter-day Joe Alsop—to open an
AVG supply office in the Calcutta Grand Hotel. As his secretary, De-
Wolfe hired Sue Upfill, the American who'd lived on the Mingaladon access road, and who had since fled Rangoon. (Her husband stayed behind
as one of the Last Ditchers, only to drown when he fell off the boat taking
him out of the abandoned city.) "Our office was mostly concerned with
military equipment and parts replacement for airplanes," she recalled
years later. "Always the office was crowded with men of the Flying Tigers coming in from sorties over Assam, awaiting transportation over
the hump or to the United States."

More likely they were headed for Africa: the first of Lauchlin Currie's replacement fighters had reached Accra on the continent's west
coast. U.S. Army mechanics assembled them, but Chennault had to
provide six pilots to pick them up. They flew to Calcutta on CNAC, to
Cairo by British Overseas Airways, and finally to Accra on an army
Douglas under contract to Pan American Airways—7,500 miles in
twelve days. "Our new ships are here on the field, ready to go," wrote
R. T. Smith. "They look pretty good to us too." The P-40E was the jut-
jawed fighter that had replaced the Tomahawk on the Curtiss assembly
line, so desired by the RAF that it gave up one hundred of the earlier
model to China. "The ships are quite a little nicer than the Tomahawks,"

R.T. went on. "These are called Kittyhawks, and have better cockpit arrangement, six 50 cal. m.g.'s, more power, speed, etc." Trying them out, he and Paul Greene "put on a little show for the Pan Am boys." Then they set out to the eastward, the Kittyhawks still emblazoned with the five-pointed star of the U.S. Army Air Forces.

Before R.T. reached Kunming, six more Hell's Angels set out for Accra. Altogether, to fetch twelve replacement fighters, Chennault tied up the 3rd Squadron for most of a month. Two other pilots went home, including Noel Bacon of the Panda Bears with 3.5 enemy aircraft to his credit.

A ttended by a lieutenant, three colonels, and a brigadier general, Stilwell flew to Africa on a Pan Am Clipper. He crossed paths with the AVG ferry pilots over Saudi Arabia, and in Calcutta had an interview with the Allied commander for Asia. Sir Archibald Wavell impressed him as "a tired, depressed man, pretty well beaten down" from the Allied defeat in the Dutch Indies. In Stilwell's lexicon of contempt, the general thereafter became "Bumble Wavell." Also in Calcutta was Major General Lewis Brereton, "slapping his fanny with his riding crop and darting around importantly." As commander of the U.S. 10th Air Force, with the world's largest theater of operations and a grand total of seven aircraft, Brereton could give orders to Bissell and Chennault—but not to Stilwell, as the latter took pains to inform him. Wavell didn't seem to get the message. When he set out for a conference with Chiang Kai-shek in Burma, he took Brereton along but left Stilwell and his entourage to follow as best they could.

On their way to the inter-Allied conference, the Generalissimo and Madame stopped at Kunming. The occasion was memorialized by Dan Hoyle in the 3rd Squadron log: "General Issimo Chiang Kai Shek and the Madame were at the Hostel and at 7:00 P.M. a Banquet was given in honour of the Generals visit and the achievements of the A.V.G. . . . There was a play done in the Chinese custom, we could not very well understand it as it was all in Chinese. The master of ceremonies gave us a synopsis of the story which helped. Some Chinese lady who had a music degree from Smith College . . . sang three songs for us. The General, Madame and Colonel

Chennault were the main speakers." Chennault had preemptively closed the bar, but Greg Boyington had his own supply, and with Percy Bartelt caroused in the hall during the speeches. The two pilots then made a drunken entry, falling over their chairs and loudly applauding the Chinese singer.

Madame called the Americans "my boys" and "angels with or without wings"—words that might have sent those tough young men into fits of laughter. But they were enchanted, many of them. "She absolutely captured our hearts," John Donovan wrote. "We cheered her to the rafters time and again." Gil Bright, late of the Ivy League, was more skeptical: "Madame gushed a bit. She thinks airplanes are just too-o-o romantic. One of the pilots from New England said she was just an old Wellesley girl that was on fire with the cause."

Accompanied by Chennault and an escort of Tomahawks, the Chiangs flew to Lashio next day to meet General Wavell. They saw Stilwell, too, but only in passing. Suspecting a snub, Stilwell ordered his chartered plane to Kunming, where he spent the night in

Three Hell's Angels strike a Wild West pose at Wujiaba airport near Kunming in January 1942. From left: Ken Jernstedt, Chuck Older, and Tom Haywood, doing their pistol-packing routine in front of R. T. Smith's Tomahawk, fuselage No. 77. (R. T. Smith photo by permission of Brad Smith)

Chennault's bed at Hostel Number One. Next morning he left Brigadier General Franklin Sibert to keep an eye on the AVG, and himself
went to Wujiaba airport to wait for Chennault to return from Lashio.
"Had a talk," Stilwell wrote. "He'll be O.K. Met a group of the pilots,
they look damn good." Much relieved by the encounter, he left for
Chongqing and a briefing by "Magruder's stooges" at the U.S. Military Mission.

The Chiangs also stopped at Kunming on their way home, to attend
another fete in their honor. This time Madame gave the pilots something
solid to cheer: the $500 combat bonus promised by CAMCO recruiters
would indeed be paid, not only for aerial victories but also for aircraft
destroyed on the ground. Harvey Greenlaw then detailed six pilots to
put on an air show. They dove to near-ground level, rolled, and screamed
across the field upside down. Bringing up the rear, Bob Lahyer became
confused when the plane in front of him disappeared from sight, and he
nearly flew into the ground. As the story is told, Layher's Tomahawk
came so close to Chennault and the Chiangs that they threw themselves
face-first onto the gravel.

The honor guard accompanied Chiang's "flying palace" as far as
Chanyi, with Greg Boyington leading. Alas, his compass was defective,
and when he left the DC-2, he led the Tomahawks south instead of
west. They ran out of gas near the Yunnan-Vietnam border, and one by
one bellied in. "The Colonel," Bus Keeton noted in his diary, in the
understatement of the month, "gave us a talk about the terrain . . . and
a little bit on how to navigate in China." In time, Boyington managed to
fly two of the Tomahawks to Mengzi, but the others had to be cannibalized for parts.

In Chongqing, Stilwell had his first formal meeting with the Chiangs.
It went well, apparently. On March 7, even as the Last Ditchers were
leaving Rangoon, he composed this optimistic assessment for Marshall:
"Believe Chennault matter can be handled satisfactorily and AVG inducted within reasonable time. A short message of appreciation to Chennault from the Sec[retary of] War for his excellent work would help
greatly."

On March 11, the Chinese gave posthumous commissions to four
Americans killed in Burma since the beginning of the year: Sandy Sandell

as lieutenant colonel, Bert Christman and Louis Hoffman as majors, Tom Cole as captain. But the really juicy promotions went to the U.S. Army officers in Chongqing. All through March, there was a blizzard of radiograms to the War Department on this pleasant subject. Stilwell was first, of course. No sooner did he reach Chongqing than he was promoted to lieutenant general—three stars. He then arranged for Frank Sibert to be bumped up to two-star rank, and promotions followed for most of the officers on his staff, though not for John Magruder. A high-strung officer with a file clerk's temperament, Magruder was held in contempt by the newcomers.

By the time the promotion fever had run its course, the U.S. Army in China consisted of seventeen enlisted men commanded by *sixty-seven* officers. On March 19, three more colonels reached China, including Chennault's nemesis from the Tactical School. Bissell was a prim, frail officer who dressed for Asia in the British fashion, in pith helmet and khaki bush jacket. ("A nasty, little man who always went around with a notebook," in the words of Major James McHugh at the U.S. embassy.) Stilwell immediately cranked the promotion engine to life on his behalf: "Strongly recommend Colonel Clayton L. Bissell . . . be appointed temporary brigadier general according to my conversation with Arnold prior to my departure. Recommendation on Chennault will be submitted later."

Later. That was the rub. In military service, officers of the same rank fall into a pecking order determined by their "time in grade." Bissell would be Chennault's superior if he ranked him by a single day.

With the new colonels in place, Stilwell's headquarters asked for four majors and four captains—a requisition followed by an "urgent request" for four typewriter ribbons. And when a colonel died in the crash of a CNAC Douglas near Kunming, the overriding concern was to replace him with more of the same. Bissell radioed Washington that the tragedy had left him as the "only air officer in China-Burma area." To plug this terrible gap, he asked for three air force colleagues by name.

Chennault, to be sure, was not entirely uninterested in the trappings of command. Unable to requisition personnel, he picked them up where he could, as when Doreen Lonborg walked into the AVG radio station at Chanyi, having trekked a thousand miles from Fort Baya by foot, sedan chair, train, and truck. On March 17 she married Daffy Davis—China hand turned AVG staff officer—in a ceremony at Hostel Number One. Next day she went to work in Chennault's office at the airport, where one of her first tasks was to type up a dress code for the AVG. Henceforth, on formal occasions, a wingman must wear a garrison cap with CAF sun, an olive drab uniform jacket with Sam Browne belt and two blue shoulder stripes, a white shirt with black tie, uniform trousers, and brown shoes. There were less elaborate costumes for "undress" and "service" duty. Paul Frillmann, too, was militarized: one silver stripe, consistent with the chaplain's status as lowest-ranking staff officer. By contrast, a pilot on headquarters duty rated two and a half stripes, putting him half a stripe ahead of a wingman flying combat.

The best that could be said of Magwe was that the evenings were lovely. The sun went down in a rosy glow over the Arakan Hills that marked the Burma-India border, while the mountains seemed to float like clouds in the dusk. The spectacular sunsets resulted from the dust and flame attending the collapse of the British Empire.

The Adam & Eves operated out of a small dirt airfield three miles south of town, surrounded by cactus, thorn bushes, scrubby trees, and a few rough buildings. The field had no revetments or dispersal pens, and the mountains made it easy for aircraft to approach unseen. To improve security, RAF engineers built a secondary field north of Magwe, on the road to Yenangyaung. They set up the peripatetic radar station at a third location. This tired old device could scan an arc of only 45 degrees, so it pointed southeast, to detect planes coming up the Irrawaddy Valley from Rangoon or traveling cross-lots from Chiang Mai in Thailand. The ground observer corps was similarly biased, with watchers assigned to the Commonwealth troops in South Burma and the Chinese at Toungoo, but none to the north or west.

RAF 17 Squadron stuck it out at Rangoon for a week after the AVG left. On March 6, the 77th Sentai caught it on the ground at Highland Queen, destroying two Hurricanes. The squadron hid out at Mingaladon next day, among the wrecks and dummy aircraft. Then it retreated to Zigon, a field so rough that it tore the tail wheels from the Hurricanes;

to Prome; and finally to Magwe. By this time, the last Buffalo had flown off to India, leaving the Hurricanes as the only RAF fighter presence in the Irrawaddy Valley. There were some Lysanders at Magwe, too, along with a dozen Blenheims and eight Tomahawks. At Akyab on the coast, Group Captain Neal Singer commanded six Hurricanes and some Lockheed Hudson bombers. Altogether, the Allied air force in Burma now amounted to fifty aircraft, most of them long past their useful lives.

The only reinforcement in view was Lewis Brereton's 10th Air Force, consisting of six newly arrived Boeing B-17s, plus the Consolidated B-24 that had flown Brereton and Wavell out of the Indies. They were based at Dum Dum airport in Calcutta, from which they might have supported the Commonwealth army in Burma. Instead, the big bombers moved a battalion of Royal Inniskilling Fusiliers into Magwe, bringing in 470 troops and taking out a like number of RAF personnel and high-priority refugees.

Despairing of finding a place in the airlift, hundreds of European and mixed-blood civilians drove on to Mandalay. The Indian refugees did not aspire so high. They'd walked most of the way from Rangoon, and they kept on walking, by their thousands, over the Arakan Hills that looked so gentle in the twilight but were so brutal in reality.

Bob Neale's Tomahawks were war weary, and Charlie Bond and John Blackburn flew two of the worst cases to Kunming and swapped them for better aircraft. They brought back the news that the Hell's Angels would soon replace the 1st Squadron. The Adam & Eves were sorry to hear it: they'd begun to enjoy life at Magwe, especially the nightly round-trip to the Yenangyaung oilfields, where the American Club offered the only iced drinks in Burma. Bond and Blackburn also brought word of the $500 combat bonus, which put a whole new light on the task of fighting the JAAF.

The correspondents who'd celebrated AVG victories at Mingaladon had followed the Adam & Eves to Magwe, and were on hand to greet the Hell's Angels. Locating the airfield "Somewhere in Burma," one reporter wrote: "Guns loaded and motors tuned for combat, another American Volunteer Group squadron roared from out of the China skies today to take over their share of the Battle for Burma from the little band of Yankee aces who smashed the last big Japanese air offensive in

Rangoon. . . . On a dusty, camouflaged field somewhere north of the actual front, tall, curly-haired Robert A. Neale of Seattle, with confirmed destruction of twelve enemy aircraft to his personal credit, relinquished command of the A.V.G.'s forces in Burma to Arvid Olson of Chicago and Los Angeles. . . . The group's new Curtiss P-40 fighter planes bear as fuselage insignia a nude winged damsel painted in rollicking red."

Olson's "squadron" actually consisted of four beat-up Tomahawks. A fifth, flown by Duke Hedman, had turned back with its engine on fire. Hedman set out again on March 10 with four more Hell's Angels, but they were waved away when they tried to refuel at Lashio, a false alarm having stirred up the field. They flew back toward Loiwing but ran out of gas before reaching the CAMCO airfield. Two bellied in with superficial damage, but three hit so hard that they could only be salvaged for parts. (The instruments and radio from these wrecks would go into Tomahawk No. 100, the only P-40 to be assembled at Loiwing. The CAMCO workers created it from the fuselage trucked up from Rangoon, plus the wings of a belly-landed Tomahawk.) Mac McGarry flew down from Loiwing to drop supplies to the stranded pilots—and he, too, ran out of gas and bellied in. With Boyington's farcical mission to Chanyi, that made eleven Tomahawks on the ground in a week, and none the result of enemy action.

The day after this disaster, Oley Olson led three more Tomahawks into Burma, losing one along the way. That gave him eleven pilots at Magwe. They lived in an abandoned house that also served as AVG communications center. The ground crews were billeted in another house, and Clayton Harpold stayed to cook for them, so it was Eighteen Mile Ranch all over again. Dan Hoyle found the setup better than expected: "We go swimming in the Irrawaddy River to get clean and some of us wash our clothes there. The food is good and we sleep well getting up early in the morning. Its so hot in the afternoon that one can hardly work. There was a dance at the American Club at Yenangyaung, Burma, about 30 miles from the field, last night, a number of our members attended but not much dancing due to lack of girls for partners."

At Magwe, the Hell's Angels found themselves pawns in a four-way power struggle. Chennault was trying to preserve them for the future, the British wanted them to cover the retreat of the Commonwealth army, and Chiang Kai-shek thought they should provide ground support for the Chinese army at Toungoo. As for Stilwell, he had little use for them: "AVG equipment now reduced to point where operations must soon cease," he told the War Department. At best, the good soldier thought, the Tomahawks might be used for reconnaissance. Stilwell won out, and the Hell's Angels went to work for the Chinese, carrying messages and scouting Japanese dispositions along the Sittang River. This work began on Friday, March 13.

On Monday, the 14th Sentai laced Toungoo with incendiaries and high explosives, turning the town into an inferno and wrecking the redbrick railroad station where the AVG had been wont to eat strawberries and drink Mandalay beer. The raid was Colonel Hironaka's farewell to Burma: he left his six remaining Sallys at Nakhon Sawan to serve as transports, with their crews going home to refit. Time and the Flying Tigers had worn the 14th Sentai out.

Ken Jernstedt and Bill Reed told the squadron leader they were tired of flying up and down the Sittang like bicycle messengers. Okay, Olson told them: go down to Moulmein and see what the Japanese are up to. So on Tuesday they flew over to Kyedaw, deserted except for an RAF detachment with a single officer, who gave them a meal and took them on a tour of yesterday's damage. Among other sights, they saw the bombed-out railroad station and the piles of bodies outside the Toungoo Pagoda. Then they drove back to the airfield and went to bed.

Kyedaw had no takeoff lights, but they knew the runway of old. At 5 AM on Wednesday, March 18, they climbed into their Tomahawks and aimed them at the Little Dipper. "It was sitting right smack over the end of the runway," Jernstedt told me years later. "So I just gunned it and kept my eye right on the North Star, and when it felt like taking off, why, I pulled it back." He laughed at the young fool of 1942, rolling a narrow-gaited Tomahawk down an asphalt runway in the dark of night. "The only time I've ever done anything like that," he marveled.

The two men flew south at 20,000 feet until they were abreast of Rangoon. The city was easy to spot, with Victoria Lake to the north and two rivers meeting to the south—so much water to catch the starlight. They turned east across Martaban Bay, heading first for the auxiliary field at Mudon. They reached it just as the tropical darkness lifted like a curtain, revealing fighter planes, transports, and bombers parked on either side of the gravel field. "Those doggone planes were just lined up wingtip to wingtip," Jernstedt said. They split up to strafe, one screaming north while the other screamed south; then they changed direction, back and forth for a total of six runs.

Then they flew up to Moulmein, its airstrip boiling with pilots and planes. Spotting a fighter in the act of taking off, Jernstedt hammered it with machine gun fire. "I was never too proud of that poor guy," he admitted. Then a hangar loomed in front of him. The Tomahawk had a tube for dropping flares; armorer Chuck Baisden had fitted three British incendiaries into the tube of Jernstedt's plane, taping them so that each bomb depressed the arming pin on its neighbor. Jernstedt now reached down with his right hand and yanked the flare-release lever. When the bundle dropped free, a wire stripped off the tape and the bombs separated, ready to explode when they hit the ground. "I missed the hangar," Jernstedt wrote in his combat report, "and hit [a Sally bomber] parked in front of the hangar. This ship was soon ablaze." Antiaircraft guns began to fire, the black clouds of flak bursting at low level over the field, so he decided to call it a day.

Jernstedt and Reed claimed fifteen planes between them—an astonishing total, but not a huge exaggeration of the damage actually inflicted on the JAAF. The 31st Sentai had left six of its light bombers at Mudon, of which three were destroyed and two badly damaged. A Mitsubishi Ki-51 Sonia—a long-range, single-engine plane of the sort that had scouted Kyedaw in the last weeks of peace—was also destroyed. Damage was severe at Moulmein, too, with two Sallys going up in flames and heavy damage to a Lily medium bomber and a Babs reconnaissance plane (Jernstedt's fighter, no doubt). The immediate loss to the JAAF was therefore ten aircraft, though some may eventually have returned to service.

Dan Hoyle, posting the squadron log next day, noted that Group Captain Broughall had signed off on the claims. "These pilots will probably get paid for same since they are confirmed," Hoyle wrote—the first mention of a combat bonus in any AVG document. It was also the most lucrative mission ever flown by Chennault's pilots: $4,000 for Bill Reed, $3,500 for Ken Jernstedt.

Retreating to Prome, the Commonwealth army was strung out for forty miles, but was never attacked from the air. For this respite, General Alexander could thank the commando mentality that so unnerved his men in the field. The Japanese took their objectives in a rush, then sat on their haunches until supplies and reinforcements caught up with them. General Obata's fighter sentais had used up all their drop-tanks in the campaign for Rangoon, and they couldn't engage the Allied air force until more arrived.

Over the course of two weeks, the Japanese rebuilt Mingaladon as Obata's headquarters and a base for the Nates of the 50th Sentai. (Major Ishikawa Tadashi had replaced the group's twice-injured commander, the unlucky Major Makino.) Two reconnaissance squadrons also moved into Mingaladon. At Hmawbi, fifteen miles northwest, Highland Queen was refurbished for the 77th Sentai under Yoshioka Hiroshi, who now wore the pips of a lieutenant colonel. At Hlegu to the northeast, the Japanese were delighted with Zayatkwin's long runway and the eight hundred barrels of aviation gasoline abandoned by the RAF; they modified the field for the 47th Independent Chutai and the Nate-equipped 1st and 11th Sentais, newly arrived in Burma. Mingaladon and its two major satellites were thus transformed into a defensive triangle against Allied air attack from the north.

In addition, Obata stationed two heavy-bomber groups in Thailand: the 98th Sentai at Nakhon Sawan and the 12th at Lampang. (The Hell's Angels had fought these same outfits over South Burma at Christmas.) A long-range reconnaissance squadron was also based at Lampang. To protect the Thai fields, Kato Tateo's 64th Sentai moved to the ancient walled city of Chiang Mai, due east of Toungoo. Kato, too, had been promoted to lieutenant colonel, and the group had left its early-model Hayabusas in the Indies, to be replaced with production-model Ki-43s with larger guns and more powerful engines. The group also brought along a Hurricane captured in the Indies, which Kato meant to employ as a werwolf when attacking RAF fields.

Finally, across Martaban Bay from Rangoon, the former RAF fields at Moulmein served as home for the twin-engine Ki-48 Lilys of the 8th

Nakajima Hayabusa fighters warm their engines for takeoff from a grass field. To save weight, Japanese army fighters weren't equipped with starters; instead a truck drove up to each in turn, and an auxiliary engine in the truck bed spun the propeller by means of a rod-and-claw device. (Robert Mikesh collection)

Sentai and the single-engine Ki-30 Anns of the 31st, another familiar antagonist for the Hell's Angels.

For three months, Allied pilots and war correspondents had wildly overestimated the number of Japanese planes ranged against Burma. But now the wolf was at the door. On March 20, when General Obata drew up his Central Burma Attack Mission, he had a magnificent air force to carry it out: 115 fighters, 66 heavy bombers, 67 light bombers, and 23 scouts and ground-cooperation aircraft. To fend him off, Seton Broughall at Magwe had only 38 planes: 15 Hurricanes, 8 Tomahawks, 9 Blenheims, and 6 Lysanders.

Yet Broughall nearly spoiled Obata's plan. A scout reported an "extraordinary concentration" of warplanes in the Rangoon area. "We are prepared to be attacked tomorrow morning or at early dawn," Dan Hoyle noted in the squadron log. But on Saturday, March 21, it was Broughall who went on the offensive, dispatching his Blenheims to blast the JAAF before it could launch an attack. As the Commonwealth pilots told the story, they were intercepted forty miles north of Rangoon and fought all the way in. The Japanese planes were identified as Zeros—i.e., the Shokis at Hlegu. Every Blenheim was damaged, but the turret gunners claimed two Japanese fighters shot down. The escorting Hurricanes claimed nine "Zeros" in the running battle plus sixteen planes destroyed on the ground. It was, concluded Air Vice Marshal Stevenson, "a magnificent air action."

The JAAF had sixty aircraft on the ground when the raiders came over. In addition to the fighters and reconnaissance planes based at Mingaladon, two light-bomber groups were to have staged through for the planned attack on Magwe, and at least one of these—the 31st Sentai with its Mitsubishi Anns—had already arrived. (Lieutenant Colonel Hayashi Junji had evidently moved two squadrons forward, leaving the third at Mudon to be savaged by Jernstedt and Reed.) As the Japanese told the story, the Blenheims came in from the northeast at 13,000 feet and destroyed a Nate on the ground. Then several "Tomahawks" made a low-level strafing run from the south, and after that a swarm of Hurricanes strafed the field. Altogether, four planes were destroyed and eleven damaged, with the light bombers taking most of the hits.

The British reported a mirror image of the raid, with the Hurricanes making the first assault. "Descending in a dive at about 400 mph," Bunny Stone recalled, "we were met by light flak. The aerodrome appeared packed with aircraft, mainly fighters and recce [reconnaissance] aircraft. I took on a fuel tanker and some recces parked wing-tip to wing-tip. Looking back as I broke to the north, there appeared to be a nice little fire starting." The main flight of Hurricanes was followed by a pair (the so-called Tomahawks) flown by Tex Barrick and Jack Gibson, another of the American sergeant-pilots in 17 Squadron. Last came the Blenheims.

However the raiders arrived, they dealt a setback to General Obata, but not so severe that he canceled his Central Burma Attack Mission. Or perhaps, given the fabulous detail with which he'd planned it—nine combat sentais converging upon Magwe from six airfields in two countries— he found it simpler to go ahead than to call it off.

The 98th Sentai was the first to set out, since its Sallys had to cover a 500-mile dogleg from Nakhon Sawan to Chiang Mai to Magwe. Soon after takeoff, the lead bomber fell out of the formation and crashed.

Among the dead was Lieutenant Colonel Osaka Junji, the second group commander lost by the 98th in its campaign against the Allied air force in Burma. There was the usual confusion before Captain Kodam Masato took over, causing the Sallys to miss their rendezvous at Chiang Mai.

The first plane over Magwe was a Mitsubishi Ki-46 Dinah, a fast, twin-engine reconnaissance plane. It carried Yamamoto Kenji, the plump general who'd nearly crashed going to Rangoon on December 25. Again his bravado nearly cost his life: the Dinah's oxygen system failed, the pilot passed out, and the Dinah plunged 7,000 feet before the pilot regained control. Meanwhile, the noise of its engines was heard at Magwe. Two Hurricanes took off, missed the Dinah, and returned to the airport, where the Blenheim crews were in the briefing tent, getting instructions for a follow-up raid on Mingaladon. The time was 1:23 PM.

By now, the main Japanese formation had swung around Magwe to strike from the northwest: twenty-six Sallys from the 12th Sentai, escorted by fourteen of Colonel Kato's Hayabusas. They'd passed north of the observers with the Chinese army and now were blind-siding the radar station. But the trap was prematurely sprung: in his rush to catch up, Captain Kodam took his 98th Sentai to Magwe by the most direct route. This formation was spotted from the ground, and the word was radioed to fighter control: "Bandits from the southeast at angels fifteen." Six Hurricanes and five Tomahawks took off to intercept them.

Parker Dupouy and Ken Jernstedt climbed to 13,000 feet before they broke out of the clouds and saw Sallys bearing down on them from the other direction—northwest—with Hayabusas following at the usual inexplicable distance, an armada very like the ones they'd fought at Rangoon on Christmas Day. Small wonder that the Hell's Angels came away from Burma convinced that the Japanese had limitless formations of heavy bombers and "Zero" fighters to throw against them. Dupouy and Jernstedt climbed to the high perch and made a rear-quarter attack on the Sallys. Jernstedt took a bullet through his windshield, a Plexiglas shard cutting his eye and putting him out of the fight.

Dupouy meanwhile was caught in a classic Tomahawk-trap: "After the third similar attack I saw a lone fighter Model 0 circling in behind me. I headed for him and then saw seven more Model 0 slightly above me starting down. I turned toward the nearest one and fired at him head on.

His engine caught fire before he passed me and one 30 calibre from his guns entered my cockpit directly below the wind shield on the left side. I dove straight for the ground and the other 6 followed for a few thousand feet. I saw the Model 0 on fire crash in the trees about 30 miles Northwest of Toungoo." Dupouy, too, was wounded in this exchange, his hand laid open by shrapnel. As for his victim, a Hayabusa did indeed crash on the way home, its unnamed pilot showing up at Chiang Mai a day or so later. (This is the only possible candidate for the retractable-gear fighter "sold" to the AVG by Hedley Everard, and it came down nowhere near the place described in his book.)

The 12th Sentai Sallys now reached their target, but found it hidden by clouds. Dropping 367 bombs by hunch, the bombardiers succeeded in hitting the airport dead-on.

The second AVG flight included Bob Prescott, Fred Hodges, and Cliff Groh. They climbed away from the airport toward the southeast, so the first planes they saw were the Sallys of the 98th Sentai under Captain Kodam, flying a compass course from Chiang Mai. Prescott chased the big-tailed bombers and damaged one. It moved inside the formation, another took its place, and the twenty-five pilots continued their approach. By now, the clouds had cleared out and the airport was marked as if by beacon fires from the 12th Sentai's bombs.

Thirty-one Nates—the 1st and 11th sentais from Zayatkwin plus the headquarters flight from Mingaladon—blundered onto the scene at about this time. The Hurricanes also joined the action, including one flown by Pilot Officer Kenneth Hemingway, who in two months at Rangoon had never seen a Japanese air armada. "Wherever I looked," he marveled, "I could pick out bunches of weaving Jap fighters protecting formation after formation of bombers." Hemingway dove away as the second salvo began to burst on Magwe airport. "I saw a sudden storm of dust clouds and a thousand flashes erupt," he recalled, after which "black smoke gushed forth from a blitzed oil and petrol dump." Then he was bounced by a Nate—like a fly on his windshield, as he described it. He laced the Japanese fighter with machine gun fire but was himself hit badly enough to be forced down near the airport. Another Hurricane crashed near Prome, shot down by friendly fire.

Cliff Groh also scored in the brawl. After chasing the Sallys almost to Toungoo, the former navy pilot was heading home when he spotted a lone Nate at 4,000 feet: "I got behind it without being seen and saw the [Japanese] markings on the wings. I turned on my gun switch and when in position pulled my trigger but the guns didn't fire. . . . I dived underneath the Jap and turned towards the left. I charged my guns and made an approach from his port side. I gave a deflection shot and fired several bursts before he turned towards me. . . . I kept firing burst after burst until just before I passed him. I saw the plane lurch but dived down in case he was all right. As I pulled out of my dive I turned and saw the Jap plane crash in the vicinity of the fires (forest) that is SE of the Magwe airport about 15 or 20 miles." Groh's victim was probably Major Okabe Tadashi, the 11th Sentai commander, shot down and killed on his way home from Magwe. His service with the group went back to the Russo-Japanese border conflict of 1939.

The Japanese fighters had concentrated on strafing the airport. For this work, JAAF pilots employed a figure-eight technique, diving almost vertically, climbing up, executing a wingover, and diving for another attack. His engine on fire, Hurricane pilot Neville Brooks tried to land in the middle of one such attack. Fritz Wolf watched from a slit trench: "He came in fast and skidded, throwing flame and smoke in every direction. . . . The pilot looked trapped for sure. But Crew Chiefs Johnny Fauth and [Henry] Olson jumped out of their shelters and rushed to the wreckage, breaking through and rescuing the RAF pilot from the burning mass."

They put Brooks into a jeep, which Olson (he was called Little Olson to distinguish him from the squadron leader) drove off the field. Johnny Fauth was hit in the shoulder by a machine gun bullet. Crazed with pain, he began to run across the field. Frank Swartz—one of the Panda Bears who'd volunteered to fill out Oley Olson's roster at Magwe—left his trench to sprint after him. "One big bomb fell within fifteen feet of them," Wolf recalled, "and both were wounded badly." Each man lost part of his jaw, Fauth's arm was nearly torn off, and Swartz's throat was laid open. Crew chief Wilfred Seiple was also injured.

Obata's final wave now reached Magwe. The 8th Sentai came over with seventeen twin-engine Lilys, followed by the 31st Sentai with the ten Anns that remained to it. They were escorted by twenty-eight Nates from the AVG's old antagonists, the 77th and 50th sentais. Altogether, Obata

put 151 bombers and fighters over Magwe that Saturday. It was the largest air armada ever mounted in Southeast Asia, and Tokyo newspapers
assured their readers that it was the largest the world had ever seen.

The last bomber left the scene at 2:30 PM. Explosions rocked the
airport for some time thereafter, making rescue and salvage impossible.
The Americans concluded that the Japanese had seeded the field with
delayed-action bombs, but the explosions had a simpler cause: 45 Squadron had gassed and armed its planes for a second strike on Mingaladon.
Set afire by fragmentation bombs and incendiary bullets, the Blenheims
were being blown apart by their own bombs.

When the AVG mechanics finished work, they pronounced four
Tomahawks fit for combat. The number increased to six when Oley Olson and Duke Hedman flew in from Lashio at dusk. Olson was handed a
radiogram from Chennault that in two sentences distilled the Old Man's
approach to war, always trying to outguess the enemy, and always trying
to ensure that his planes were not caught on the ground: "Look out for
follow up raid tomorrow. Did you have any warning of raid today?"

Somewhat unfairly, Olson replied that the AVG had received only one
minute's notice. He added that the raiders were mostly "Model Zeros,"
and that they'd flown back to Thailand in the direction of Chiang Mai.

Chapter 13

Like a Movie, Only Better

Johnny Fauth died at 4:30 AM. Sunday morning, March 22, the first AVG ground crewman to lose his life in the service of China. An agreeable young man with a mop of dark hair, he was posthumously commissioned second lieutenant in the CAF.

Within hours, General Obata's formations returned to Magwe. The radar station made the first plot at 8:04 AM, but the radio link to the airfield had gone dead, and Magwe was reduced to the information it could garner by ear. Hearing radial engines overhead at 8:30 AM, Hedley Everard and Al McDonald of 17 Squadron took off to intercept what they believed to be a Japanese scout. Instead, they met the armada from Mingaladon and its satellites: twenty-three Anns and Lilys, escorted by sixty-one Nates. The two Canadians gallantly attacked, claimed damage to two planes, and were themselves shot up, though not fatally. Some other Hurricanes got off the ground but failed to engage.

The first bombers droned over the airport at 8:47 AM. "Considerable damage was sustained," Air Vice Marshal Stevenson reported. "The runways were rendered unserviceable, communications were broken down and a number of aircraft, both bombers and fighters, were destroyed on the ground." The Americans sustained no casualties: when they heard engines overheard, they scrambled into vehicles and left the field. Afterward, Oley Olson returned to the airport and radioed the bad news to Chennault: "Absolutely no warning. . . . One shark burned up four hit badly. Three planes left now. Repairing and possibly have two others to fly away."

The Old Man ordered him, in effect, to get out. The ground crewmen worked on the damaged Tomahawks while Olson organized the retreat. For one thing, there was Johnny Fauth to bury. This was done without ceremony at the local Catholic church or (accounts differ) in a mass grave at the British cantonment. Early that afternoon, a CNAC Douglas flew in from Lashio to pick up Frank Swartz and Wilfred Seiple, whom Doc Richards wanted to send to India for surgery.

No sooner did the ambulance plane take off than Obata's second wave reached Magwe: fifty-three Sallys and eighteen Hayabusas from Thailand, plus twenty-three Nates from Rangoon. Again two Hurricanes took off, to no effect except to save themselves from destruction, and again the Tomahawks were caught on the ground. Olson's next radiogram was even more bleak: "All sharks hit possibly fly three. . . . Proceeding with convoy to Loiwing. Radio will operate until 10 p.m. tonight." The ground crewmen did better than that. Working all night, they patched and tuned and coaxed four Tomahawks into condition to fly. Frank Van Timmeran and Joey Poshefko waved them off the cratered airstrip early in the morning of Monday, March 23, then climbed into a truck and followed the squadron up the road to Mandalay.

The RAF also pulled out. Eight Hurricanes flew to Akyab, to be cannibalized for 135 Squadron, and the mechanics and headquarters staff set off in a sixty-truck convoy to Mandalay. They left twenty burned-out hulks at Magwe, including three AVG Tomahawks.

The Japanese, in their exultation, put the count much higher. After the war, one of Obata's officers assured Allied interrogators that no fewer than 120 planes were destroyed in the two-day blitz, and this fantasy number still appears in Japanese accounts of the air war in Southeast Asia. (The semiofficial Japanese Defense Agency history makes the more modest claim of 34 planes destroyed and 50 damaged—still more than double the number of Allied aircraft at Magwe.) Still, the JAAF had succeeded in its campaign to destroy the Allied air force in Burma. Obata's triumph was only mildly tarnished by the fact that his advantage in aircraft was seven-to-one.

W hen he got the first bulletin from Magwe, Chennault was choking with bronchitis in his bedroom at Hostel Number One. From Toungoo, in the opening weeks of the war, he'd sent patrols to scout the airports in northern Thailand; more recently, British intelligence had reported a base-building effort at Lampang. And Olson's after-action report had fingered Chiang Mai as the "Zero" base. On Sunday morning, not knowing that the Japanese were even then returning to Magwe, the Old Man rose from his sickbed to plan the AVG's revenge.

Compared to the aerial armadas Obata was sending across Burma, the AVG counterstrike was a puny affair. Five Adam & Eves—Bob Neale, Greg Boyington, Charlie Bond, Mac McGarry, and Bill Bartling—would fly to Chiang Mai and strafe the "Jap Air Force headquarters in Southeast Asia." Meanwhile, five Panda Bears—Jack Newkirk, Eddie Rector, Whitey Lawlor, Hank Geselbracht, and Bus Keeton—would attack Lamphun to the south.

In truth, Chiang Mai wasn't a headquarters but a forward base for a single fighter group, and Lamphun was a flat mistake. The westerners spelled local names any which way, and the Panda Bears variously recorded their target as *Lambhun, Lambhan, Lambhung, Lampong*—the last a fair approximation of Lampang, General Obata's headquarters and home for the 12th Sentai heavy bombers. This was the base Chennault actually meant his men to strafe.

Their ammunition boxes heavily laden with incendiary rounds, the Tomahawks took off from Wujiaba on Sunday afternoon. Two hours later they touched down at Loiwing, on a runway carved out of a hillside. Though China had paid for its construction, this was Bill Pawley's domain. So unprepared was he to support combat operations that there was no one at the field to gas and tune the Tomahawks: the AVG flights would have to wait until Monday morning, delaying their attack by twenty-four hours. The delay didn't affect the drama at Magwe, which was even then in its final act, but it was otherwise for Group Captain Neal Singer at Akyab. On Monday, he was blasted by the Sallys from Lampang and strafed by the Hayabusas from Chiang Mai, destroying at least four RAF aircraft and damaging many more. That raid might have been spoiled if the Adam & Eves and Panda Bears had flown into Thailand on schedule.

The CAMCO factory was eight miles from the airstrip: a neat little compound of whitewashed buildings with camouflaged metal roofs. There was a nine-hole golf course and a clubhouse outfitted with electric lights, polished floors, fireplace, jukebox, pool table, movie projector, refrigerated beer, and plate-glass windows overlooking the pretty valley in which Bill Pawley had set out for the fourth time to assemble warplanes for China. The guestrooms had thick Chinese rugs and tiled baths. There was even a housemother-cook named Davidson, who told the pilots to call her "Ma."

Paul Frillmann's convoy from Rangoon had reached Loiwing a few days earlier, and line chief Harry Fox had taken the opportunity to check out the CAMCO factory. He told Bob Neale that the Pawleys had accumulated thirty wrecked Tomahawks at Loiwing—nearly a third of the planes ever delivered to the AVG. Eighteen planes, Fox thought, could be put into combat condition, yet no effective work was being done at the factory.

Monday, March 23, dawned foggy and wet. Their Tomahawks serviced, the pilots sat around for the rest of the day, not wanting to fly to their next staging field—Namsang, an RAF airstrip in the Shan Highlands—until just before dark. So they were on hand when the four pilots from Magwe flew in with harrowing accounts of the Japanese raids. Moose Moss told a wild tale of jumping into a trench with Fred Hodges, whereupon Fearless tried to dig still deeper into the red earth, pushing the dirt under Moss and raising him to the surface again.

"They almost scared us out of going on our mission," Bus Keeton wrote in his diary, "which to my way of thinking is the most dangerous undertaking the A.V.G. has done, going 120 miles into enemy territory where if you have to force land and the Japs don't get you the jungle will." With such thoughts to keep them company, the raiders flew down to Namsang. They arranged for trucks and lanterns to light the runway in the morning, ate a tense meal at the pilots' mess, and washed up in the officers' billet.

Combat literature is filled with omens, and the Chiang Mai mission is no exception. Years later, Tex Hill recalled going into Newkirk's room at Hostel Number One before the mission began, to find him in a gloomy mood. The squadron leader wrote a note to Chennault, asking him to name Tex as his replacement if he failed to return. And Greg Boyington recalled that when the RAF told them not to use the Namsang tap water for brushing their teeth, because it was polluted, Newkirk scoffed: "After tomorrow, I don't think it'll make any difference." Certainly the mood was heavy. "Here goes *nothing*," Bob Neale wrote in his diary, underlining the final word twice.

A barrack-boy shook them awake at 4 AM, and they were dressing when the duty officer bounded in with the cry: "All right, you curly-headed fellows, it's time!" Joking and gabbing to keep their spirits up, they wolfed breakfast and went to their planes. Takeoff was 5:45 AM—black night in Burma, broken only by truck headlamps, kerosene lanterns, and the blue flames washing along the cowlings of their Tomahawks.

For some reason, Eddie Rector was now attached to Bob Neale's flight. (Did he have a premonition, too?) Jack Newkirk and the other three Panda Bears set off for Thailand without waiting for the planned form-up over Namsang. As they gained altitude, daylight came down to greet them, though the ground was still hidden in darkness and the smoke haze from the fall of Rangoon. They flew on instruments until they reached Chiang Mai about 7 AM, by which time they could make out objects on the ground. Newkirk tarried long enough to strafe the Chiang Mai railroad station—an astonishing breach of discipline, like poking a stick into a hornet's nest before your friends come along. Flying on, he found Lamphun but not the bombers he'd been sent to strafe, just some buildings that might have been warehouses or barracks. He laced them with incendiary bullets, then scouted some auxiliary airfields. At the third and largest field, the Panda Bears strafed more buildings, after which Newkirk turned north with the apparent intention of joining the Adam & Eves at Chiang Mai.

In his combat report, Hank Geselbracht told what happened

then: "The next target we dove on were two vehicles on the road south of [Chiang Mai]. Newkirk dove and fired and as he cleared the target I began to fire. I saw a flash of flames beyond the target and looked for Newkirk after my run. I realized he had crashed causing the flash. I pulled up and continued to the north on the way home." Bus Keeton saw the same explosion, and like Geselbracht failed at first to understand its cause. "As I pulled up to the right," he wrote, "I noticed a large flame of fire burst up on a field to the right of me. The fire spread along the field for a 100 or 150 yards. Thinking Jack and Gesel had set fire to some oil dumps and not seeing anything to shoot at I proceeded to follow Lawlor."

Newkirk was one of the immortals, the "Scarsdale Jack" of so many upbeat dispatches from Rangoon. He died in a fireball that skittered and bounced and smeared itself along the ground—a napalm canister with a man inside. Then the Allison engine broke loose and rolled 300 yards farther. Whitey Lawlor guessed that the squadron leader had fired on a Japanese armored car, which then shot him down.

Bob Neale's flight meanwhile reached Chiang Mai. Charlie Bond recognized a towering mountain he'd seen on a December reconnaissance, so he took the lead. If he remembered correctly, the airfield was a mile or so southeast of this landmark: "I nosed downward in a gentle left turn and hoped I was right. At about six thousand feet, and as the haze thinned, I saw the field and the outlines of the hangars. I flipped on my gun switch, and another thousand feet lower I fired my guns in a short burst to check them and let the other guys know this was it—the main Japanese Air Force of Southeast Asia!"

The plan called for Eddie Rector and Mac McGarry to stay high as top cover. Bond led the other three pilots onto the field: "I made my first strafing run firing everything into the [Fighters]. At the end I remained low and turned sharply to the left. . . . After turning 270 degrees I was in a position to strafe another line of parked aircraft. These were sitting practically wingtip to wingtip. Hell, I hadn't seen this many aircraft in years. Seemed like the whole Japanese Air Force had tried to crowd into this one little field." Bond made four runs with Japanese tracers streaking the air beside him and flak exploding overhead. Once he was so low that he thought he might decapitate the Japanese pilots scrambling into

their cockpits. (They were shouting *"Mawase, mawase!"*—Turn, turn!—
to the mechanics trying to start engines by swinging the propellers.) On
his last go-round, Bond concentrated on a larger plane that "seemed to
shake itself to pieces" under his machine guns.

Greg Boyington made just two passes. "The aircraft on the field were
parked mainly in two long lines," he reported. "All enemy planes were
turning up and the pilots and crews were running about." After his first
pass, he saw three transports burning in one great bonfire, the flames
shooting a thousand feet into the air; after his second, he counted ten fires
on the ground.

Bob Neale made three runs, estimating that forty planes were on the
field, and that half were destroyed by the time he veered away in the face
of antiaircraft fire, the "heaviest I have ever seen." He thought there were
eight or nine fires on the field, "two of them being very large." Signaling
the others to join up, Neale headed for the Burma border.

Boyington followed the squadron leader, but Charlie Bond joined
up with Bill Bartling, Eddie Rector, and Mac McGarry. The top cover
had taken the worst of the flak, and McGarry's engine was spluttering. "I
circled back & tried to rendezvous on his wing," Rector wrote in his
combat report, "but his speed was too slow & I overshot. . . . I saw
smoke coming from his engine intermittently & he seemed to be losing
altitude. After continuing on this condition for five or ten minutes & losing more altitude, McGarry turned left over a canyon, turned the plane
over & fell out. His 'chute opened instantly & he landed about 200
yards from his plane." McGarry waved to his buddies, who dropped a
candy bar and a map showing his location and the time: thirty miles
south of the Salween River at 7:41 AM, March 24, 1942.*

As they'd flown into Thailand, so they returned, refueling at Namsang before landing at Loiwing. At the American Club, Ma Davidson
made lunch while the CAMCO foreman fixed drinks. "Soon we were in
the bar," Charlie Bond wrote in his diary. "Everybody was laughing and
enjoying the moment. Yet Jack was gone and we weren't sure of Black
Mac."

---

*In 1991, McGarry's Tomahawk was found in the rain forest, and its propeller, canopy,
and other parts put on display at Chiang Mai Air Force Base.

American newspapers played down the disaster at Magwe while hailing Chiang Mai as a magnificent victory. Next morning, the *New York Times* gave the Flying Tigers top billing: U.S. FLIERS IN BURMA SMASH 40 PLANES. (In the end, Chennault settled on fifteen planes as a more reasonable score at Chiang Mai, the credit shared by the top cover and the four who went down to strafe.) The *Times* took special notice of Jack Newkirk, whose portrait in navy uniform accompanied the story. He was described as a Tom Sawyerish lad who'd impaled a sheriff with an arrow and who'd received his Eagle Scout badge from the Antarctic explorer Richard Byrd. In Burma, the story continued, the British had awarded Newkirk the Distinguished Service Order for destroying twenty-five enemy aircraft—a bit more than twice his actual tally.

In truth, the 64th Sentai lost only three Hayabusas that morning, plus the werwolf Hurricane brought from the Indies. Ten more Hayabusas were damaged, but Japanese mechanics were as industrious as their AVG counterparts, and by noon they had eleven planes fit to fly—only five fewer than the group had sent to Magwe on Saturday. Kato led this force 350 miles to the west coast of Burma, to support fifty-three heavy bombers while they blitzed Akyab airport and a "secret runway" to the north.

Nor was the ground campaign delayed in the slightest. Even as the Adam & Eves and Panda Bears were downing whisky-sodas at the American Club, the Japanese captured their old training base at Kyedaw airfield. The battle for Toungoo continued through the week, with two divisions—Takeuchi's 55th, plus the newly arrived 56th under Lieutenant General Watanabe Masao—pitted against a small and lightly armed Chinese army. In the Irrawaddy Valley, Sakurai's 33rd Division rolled up the Commonwealth army at Prome. Despite what western historians have written about the lack of spirit in Chiang's army, Japanese accounts of the Burma campaign leave no doubt that they considered the Chinese the tougher foe.

Obata's attack planes and fighters worked with the army during this climactic week, but he diverted his heavy-bomber groups to an operation that was a direct result of the Chiang Mai raid. Day after day, the Sallys bombed Allied airstrips at Heho, Loilem, Lashio, Mandalay, and (as they wrongly supposed) Loiwing. Following each raid, an observation plane inspected the target, hoping to see Allied engineers repairing it, and thus to discover the base responsible for the attack on Chiang Mai.

This diversion was inspired by Mac McGarry. Thai policemen captured him and took him to Chiang Mai, where Colonel Kato questioned him. The interrogation took place over two or three days, with McGarry kept between times in a cage he had to enter by crawling under a fence, and into which the guards tossed food as to an animal. Kato's questions were translated into Thai and put to McGarry in English, with the answers coming back in reverse order. In this roundabout fashion, Kato learned that the Tomahawks were based in China, but because of their short combat radius had staged out of fields in Burma. (McGarry apparently didn't name the fields.) Kato also picked up some insights into the mentality of American pilots—for example, that they painted small Japanese flags on their planes to represent enemy aircraft destroyed.

The most important result of the interviews was to persuade Kato that the "American air force" in Southeast Asia was a shadow of its former self, having lost most of its pilots since Christmas. Perhaps McGarry lied, or perhaps he told the truth about AVG losses and the facts were twisted in translation. However it happened, Kato concluded that he had little to fear from the Americans. He then handed the prisoner back to the Thai police. Instead of suffering the horrors of a Japanese prison compound, therefore, McGarry entered upon a lonely but tolerable existence in a Bangkok jail.

Chennault realized that his Chiang Mai raid had put Loiwing in jeopardy, and he so warned Dave Harris at the CAMCO compound: "Suggest repaired P-40's be flown here promptly. . . . Suggest all work be dispersed widely." (Harris was the pilot who'd gone off flight status after Pete Atkinson's death, and who'd since functioned as a staff officer.) Chennault then told Oley Olson to transform the Loiwing airstrip into a fighting field, from which the Hell's Angels could continue their reconnaissance and courier missions for the Chinese army. They'd also fly "special missions on call"—a somewhat ominous provision—and defend

The alert shack at Loiwing. From left: Herb Cavanah, Tex Hill, John Petach (in back, facing to the right), Bill Reed, Oley Olson, Moose Moss, Parker Dupouy, Bob Prescott, and Cliff Groh, who went missing soon after. (Flying Tigers Association)

Loiwing from attack. The Hell's Angels commandeered a bamboo-and-thatch building for their alert shack, mounting a sign over the door: OLSON & CO., EXTERMINATORS—24 HR. SERVICE.

To support this boast, Olson conscripted the ground crewmen straggling up the road from Magwe, RAF as well as AVG. They hadn't entirely recovered from their trauma. "All of the technical personnel are rather jittery about a raid," Dan Hoyle wrote. "It seems to be this Squadrons misfortune to be in every raid thiere is."

The first four Kittyhawks from Africa had now reached Kunming. The planes needed work before they were ready for combat—U.S. Army insignia replaced by the twelve-pointed Chinese sun, jaws decorated by the AVG shark face, machine guns harmonized at 300 yards—but the pilots were more flexible. Chennault sent them down to Loiwing in Tomahawks, bringing the number of fighters there to an even dozen.

The "special missions" called for the Hell's Angels to fly down to Toungoo and show the CAF insignia over the lines. The idea was to boost the morale of the Chinese soldiers, who were fighting a desperately mismatched battle against two Japanese divisions supported by the light bombers of the 8th Sentai and the Nates of the 50th. It was the longest set-piece battle in the Burma campaign, and would be remembered by the Japanese as the bitterest fighting in their conquest of Southeast Asia. With Jack Newkirk's death vivid in their minds, the Hell's Angels were not happy about the assignment. "We're all against it," R. T. Smith wrote in his diary. "It seems senseless, with a good possibility of nobody coming back. This is to be just for one day, but it's mighty low grade, Lord, mighty low!" The mission was scheduled for Sunday morning, March 29. Oley Olson took off with eight Tomahawks but brought them back within the hour because the weather was bad. It was a lucky call: the Hell's Angels were to have refueled at Heho airstrip, which was even then being bombed out of existence.

Hardly were they back at Loiwing than an AVG listening post reported a scout flying in their direction. Paul Greene and Chuck Older took off to intercept the intruder, and Older was credited with shooting it down—a bomber, as Japanese records show.

The Japanese were getting their range. On Tuesday, March 31, the Hell's Angels scrambled at 9 AM to intercept a formation heading for Loiwing. Finding nothing, they returned to the field. Most of the pilots went to lunch, but Oley Olson and Moose Moss stayed aloft to cover the field. Then the alarm went off again. R. T. Smith led a flight of four to 28,000 feet, where he heard over the radio that the Japanese were bombing Lashio, 90 miles south. R. T.'s diary gives the outline of what happened next, and some of the rest can be read between the lines, including the mutinous feeling of the pilots at Loiwing: "Oley sighted 27 bombers and 9 fighters. He was alone so didn't attack. We went down to Lashio & joined him but they had left. Moss landed at Lashio, we think, but not sure. Message from Chennault [who] wants the Toungoo job done still, but we're all agin' it. Think we'll go down & strafe Jap fields instead."

Volunteers from other squadrons had come down to Loiwing to help the Hell's Angels, including Greg Boyington of the Adam & Eves. On Tuesday, he crashed while trying to take off, because his engine quit (the story as Boyington told it) or because he was too drunk to fly (the recollection of Leo Schramm, the Tomahawk's crew chief). Plane and pilot were both damaged, but apparently not seriously.

Between alerts, the Hell's Angels planned their Thailand strafe, but that mission, too, was canceled by bad weather. The pilots had a blow-out night instead, and on Thursday they went one better and had a wedding.

The principals were Fred Hodges and Helen Anderson. She was about twenty, an Anglo-Burman woman with a splendid body, oval face, high forehead and cheekbones, long hair drawn back, and a smile calculated to break a pilot's heart, especially a skinny specimen like Fearless Fred. The pilots held a meeting, "incorporated" Loiwing as a town, and elected M.D. (Doc) Walsh of the CAMCO staff as mayor, on the theory that this would give him authority to perform a marriage. They converted the American Club into a chapel and appointed Duke Hedman to play the piano. As Boyington told the story, the pilots substituted a genuine minister at the last moment, transforming charade into sacrament, but a version written closer to the time had the wedding solemnized a day or two later by a British army chaplain. Whatever the sequence of events, they left Anderson confused as to whether she was married or not. "Full of whiskey" afterward, Boyington wandered off a cliff in the dark, gashing his head and laming both knees. He was flown to Kunming and put to bed in the little hospital at Hostel Number One.

The scrambles of March 31 and April 1 were caused by Colonel Kato, looking for the Tomahawks that had blistered his Hayabusas at Chiang Mai. But the sky was huge, Loiwing had no radar station, and the two sides didn't meet in the air. And since the Tomahawks had already scrambled, there were no planes on the ground when the 64th Sentai came over the airfield, prompting Kato to write Loiwing off his list of suspects. On April 3, he scouted Mandalay, causing another scramble at Loiwing, but again the two sides missed connections. Kato went home convinced that the American air force had indeed retreated into the interior of China, as McGarry had promised.

To the contrary, the CAMCO airstrip was beginning to look like a military base. Eight Hurricanes arrived from India on Easter Sunday, flown by some of the 17 Squadron pilots who'd recently fled Magwe. Not to offend Chinese sensibilities, they were billeted just across the border at Namhkam, on Burmese soil. They were impressed by the setup at Loiwing, especially "the excellent warning system provided by the wireless and telephone communications with Chinese lookouts on the surrounding hills." Five Blenheims also flew in. The RAF would base their planes at Loiwing and use Lashio as an advance field, from which to support the Commonwealth army in the Irrawaddy Valley.

At 9:30 AM on Wednesday, April 8, a high-flying Dinah passed over the CAMCO airstrip, spotting "fifteen small planes" on the runway. That was roughly correct: there were nine Tomahawks, four Hurricanes, and a Blenheim at Loiwing that morning, plus two U.S. Army P-40Es on their way to Kunming with civilian ferry pilots.

Colonel Kato had been scheduled to escort bombers that morning, but he felt it more important to hit the Allied air force before it vanished again. He cut the escort to a single squadron, leaving two squadrons and his headquarters flight to attack Loiwing. Japanese accounts are vague on how many Hayabusas were involved; AVG combat reports put the number of attackers at thirteen, but it's unlikely there were so many. Where the Tomahawks had refueled twice at Namsang, on the way down and on the way back, the Hayabusas would cover the 375-mile outbound leg on their external drop-tanks, then fight and fly home on their internal fuel supply.

For once, however, the 64th Sentai was operating at a disadvantage. For the first time, it was attacking an airfield protected by Chennault's early warning system. Worse, some of Kato's pilots were without combat experience. In what would become an increasingly common expedient for the JAAF, three of the group's veterans had been called away to form the nucleus of a new fighter group, and the empty slots filled by men fresh from flight school. This was a serious matter for an air force accustomed to overpowering its foes with the dash and skill of its pilots.

The Hayabusas crossed the China border at 20,000 feet, triggering warnings from Lashio onward. Meanwhile, three Kittyhawks flew into Loiwing from Kunming, newly decorated in AVG warpaint. They'd scarcely landed when, at 12:30 PM, word came into the bamboo alert shack: "Many ships headed this way." The Tomahawks and Hurricanes scrambled, as did the three Kittyhawks from Kunming. The Blenheim stayed on the ground. So did the eastbound U.S. Army fighters: one was being repaired, and in any event their civilian pilots had left the field.

Just before intruding the Loiwing airspace, Kato dropped down to 2,000 feet. He'd instructed Captain Maruo Haruyasu to stay high with a top-cover flight, but Maruo couldn't resist the temptation to join the strafing party. Since the Hayabusas had no air-to-air radio communication, Kato didn't know that his rear was now exposed. The Japanese pilots dove upon the field, twin nose guns spewing a hail of incendiaries into the Blenheim and the two U.S. Army Kittyhawks, whose unpreparedness seemed proof that the AVG was a sitting duck.

Word of the attack was flashed to the Hell's Angels at 22,000 feet: "Japs strafing the field." They wheeled about and screamed down on the Hayabusas, just as the Japanese pilots were climbing up for another strafe. Flying one of the new Kittyhawks, Oley Olson may have been the first on the scene. He fired at a Hayabusa near the top of its climb. "He rolled over and I passed my fire to another climbing," Olson reported; "passed him and fired a long burst into a third at about 3000 feet [that] turned over shedding a few pieces of airplane and dived straight down into the ground and exploded" west of the field. First blood for the squadron leader—first combat, for that matter.

Then the Tomahawks arrived. "It was the most thrilling experience I've ever had," wrote R. T. Smith, credited with shooting down two Japanese planes in the melee. "The guys on the ground saw it all & are still raving. They say it looked just like a movie only better. Ha!"

Not everyone was so jubilant. John Donovan, his radio dead, followed Fritz Wolf back to the field in the belief that the scramble had been a false alarm. Suddenly, two planes turned toward him with their guns winking. "Never have I been more scared," he confessed in a letter to his sister. "I felt more helpless than a baby and wouldn't have bet ten cents on my chance of getting out." Donovan was credited with his first kill in the fifteen-minute battle. The Japanese plane fell, he reported, on the north edge of the field.

Cliff Groh tangled with several of the nimble fighters before catching one unaware, southeast of the field. "I kept firing burst after burst into him until I was about 10 to 20 yards behind him," he reported. The Hayabusa dove toward the ground, recovered momentarily, then augered in.

Fred Hodges met a Japanese plane climbing toward him. "I opened all guns on him with a head on shot," he wrote in his combat report. "Without returning fire, the Hayabusa began to smoke, then dove to earth southwest of the field. First score for the bridegroom, too.

Link Laughlin's combat report is notable for its clear-eyed description of the Japanese fighters. He even noticed that their armament consisted of two machine guns firing through the propeller arc—information that ought to have told Chennault that the AVG wasn't facing the cannon-equipped Mitsubishi Zero. (Laughlin identified both guns as large caliber, which was true in some cases but not all. As compared to the early-model Hayabusas the AVG had met at Rangoon, Nakajima had taken a few inches off the plane's wings, slightly increased its power, weight, and speed, and armed it with two 12.7-mm "machine cannon"—equivalent to the Tomahawk's half-inch nose guns. However, the larger gun fired slowly as a result of a sychronization problem, and some ground crews replaced the port-side weapon with a faster 7.7-mm gun, like the first Ki-43s in service.) Laughlin shot one Hayabusa off a Tomahawk's tail, south of the field. He flamed another to the west, but lost sight of it between the shooting and the crash. They were the first and second kills of his combat career.

Fritz Wolf tangled with a Japanese plane and saw it crash west of the field. Then he shot another off a Kittyhawk's tail: "It started smoking in a glide. . . . I went down again and the Japanese did nothing to avoid me." Wolf was credited with both kills, though he saw only one Hayabusa go in.

Eddie Overend came on the scene later than his comrades. He skirmished with four Hayabusas without result, then caught a loner southeast of the field: "I fired from 150 yards until I was almost up on him, at which time he turned violently and I saw the canopy and upper part of the fuselage at this point tear away." The Hayabusa crashed without burning.

Bob Little was also credited with a Japanese fighter, meaning that the Hell's Angels were claiming twelve Hayabusas shot down. A close reading of the combat reports shows that most of the Japanese supposedly crashed in four locations: three in the vicinity of the CAMCO airstrip, and one a few miles southeast by the river. That's significant because only three wrecks were actually found near the airport—and because the 64th Sentai lost only four Hayabusas that day.

Four was plenty, representing a third or more of the planes that had

set out for Loiwing. Among the dead was one of Kato's squadron leaders, Captain Anma Katsumi, credited with destroying upward of twelve
enemy planes in China, Manchuria, Malaya, and the Indies. Anma was
the first of the great Japanese army pilots to die in World War II. It was
his Hayabusa that crashed in a paddy field two miles south of Loiwing,
with four Hell's Angels (Wolf, Overend, Smith, and Groh) each claiming it for his own. Another veteran to die that Wednesday was Sergeant
Wada Haruto, whose first kill had been an I-15 biplane over Luoyang in
1938. Wada crashed at the Loiwing airstrip, as did a replacement pilot
named Kuroki Tadao. The other man to go down near the field was
Lieutenant Okumura Muneyuki, thirty years old and a sergeant-pilot
who'd been commissioned at the outbreak of war.

Back at Chiang Mai, the mood was somber. Never before had the 64th
Sentai lost so many pilots in a single day's fighting, and Lieutenant Hinoki
Yohei so far forgot his manners as to attempt to console his commander.
"There was nothing you could have done," he blurted. But it wasn't in
Kato's nature to admit that a situation was past mending. "No," he told the
presumptuous young pilot. "I will go back there and attack again. What-
ever the hardship, we must not yield. There is always a way."

Chennault's reaction to the Loiwing fight was also perfectly in character. Olson's after-action report assured him that twelve "Zeros" were
shot down at the cost of a Kittyhawk destroyed on the ground, plus light
damage to a Blenheim and the other grounded Kittyhawk. Note the priorities in the Old Man's response, which read in full: "Why were two
P40Es left on ground during raid? Congratulations on fine work beating
Model 0."

Chapter 14

The Pilots' Revolt

Chennault replaced Jack Newkirk with his designated successor, the tall, jug-eared Tex Hill. For his debut as squadron leader, Tex hoped to shoot up Japanese airfields across the border in Vietnam. While they prepared for this raid, the Panda Bears took turns flying the AVG's new Kittyhawks as they reached Kunming and were prepped for combat. With three fifty-caliber guns on each wing, the big-jawed fighter actually slewed off course if a pilot fired the guns on one side but not the other. Less lovable was the plane's tendency to "mush" in a power dive: it kept dropping even after the pilot brought the nose up.

Walt Disney's darling Bengal cat, leaping through a V-for-Victory sign, had meanwhile reached Kunming. "My God, do we have to wear those things?" a clerk is supposed to have said. On Skip Adair's orders, the men at Wujiaba pinned the symbol of their fame over the right pocket of their uniform jackets, and before long they took pride in it. Perhaps it wasn't so bad, after all, to be a Flying Tiger. With more enthusiasm, they added the Bengal cat to the flanks of their Tomahawks and Kittyhawks. The decals shipped by China Defense Supplies came in two pieces; most pilots didn't bother with the V sign.

When not otherwise occupied, the Tigers brawled with the local populace and each other. A crew chief assaulted a French doctor who refused to perform an abortion on the woman who'd accompanied him from Rangoon. Others beat up the AVG police officer, Melvin Ceder, when he searched Adobe City for contraband. George McMillan was punched in the same quarrel. So was Skip Adair, whom the ground crewmen held responsible for the search: "Frank Metasavage . . . and I had just returned from the field and found our bunk area ransacked," one man recalled. "We asked the house boy who did it. He said some guy from HQ [headquarters] looking for stuff. Frank was angry. He went over to HQ, got into an argument with Skip Adair . . . and punched

Chennault conducts a briefing on the hood of an AVG jeep—no doubt one of those "liberated" from the Rangoon docks. The pilots (including Bob Neale and George McMillan, in leather-brimmed garrison caps) are wearing CAF insignia. (Wide World photo, National Archives)

him out." That was a mistake: Chennault had gone to Chongqing, Harvey Greenlaw was in Burma, and Adair was serving as the AVG's executive officer. He put Metasavage under house arrest, along with another crew chief, Glen Yarbery, presumably for attacking Ceder.

Then someone broke into the recreation room to get a drink, with Greg Boyington the leading suspect. "The man who did it twisted the lock off the door with his bare hands," Skip Adair reasoned. "Only one guy in the group is strong enough to do that, and that's Boyington." He also fined Matt Kuykendall $100 "for firing his gun in a reckless manner while intoxicated and off duty." The bullet ricocheted and struck an Allison engine specialist, fortunately without inflicting serious injury.

Chennault was in Chongqing to settle the matter of the AVG's return to the U.S. military. He presented Flying Tiger pins to Madame and the Generalissimo; and later, in a private conference with Madame, he agreed to accept induction for himself and his men, asking only that he be present when the decision was made. This was a face-saving request in the Chinese tradition, but it added another black mark to the Old Man's reputation at the War Department. Bissell forwarded Chennault's condition with the stinging comment: "His value to China and the U S is recognized but the conclusion that he is playing personal politics is unescapable." For an army man, there was no worse sin than playing politics (or to be *seen* playing politics, because they all did it, all the time).

The principals—including Chennault and Madame—met with Chiang Kai-shek that same afternoon. After long discussion, they settled on a day three months in the future, which would allow time for uniformed officers of the 23rd Fighter Group to reach China and settle in. The day was also wonderfully symbolic: America's birthday, with all its symbolism of fireworks and the flag. Madame radioed the good news to Lauchlin Currie: "After hour's conference with Stillwell [sic], Bissell, Groco, Magruder, final decision reached induct A.V.G's. Formal induction July 4. Meanwhile, every effort maintain efficiency unit. Thank Heavens. Inform T. V."

If Stilwell was equally pleased, he managed to conceal it. His radiogram to the War Department laid out the proposal in businesslike fashion, concluding: "Cardinal principal should be to maintain maximum effectiveness of AVG during induction. Approval requested." Then he turned to the matter of Chennault's place in the new scheme of things: "It is recommended that Col Clayton L Bissell O-10474 be promoted to brigadier general Army of the US and that Col Claire L Chennault be promoted to brigadier general Army of the US, effective date of Chennaults rank to be one day subsequent to the appointment of Col Bissell." The Army of the United States (AUS) was the huge and temporary force that prosecuted the war; a man's rank in it was often a grade or two higher than his permanent grade in the regular army. Stilwell was suggesting that Chennault and Bissell become brigadier generals in the AUS, though they'd remain as colonels in the regular army. (In fact, the Old Man was still a civilian when Stilwell sent this radiogram.)

Having ensured that his own man would outrank Chennault in the new scheme of things, if only by one day, Stilwell then turned to the problem of the Chinese ground forces in Burma. He wanted to bring them under his command, and to accomplish this he was willing to trump Chiang Kai-shek with his own air force: "Told him," Stilwell wrote in his diary, "I couldn't put American air units in support of troops in whose commanders I had no confidence." In other words, unless he directed them, the Chinese army in Burma would get no support from the American Volunteer Group of the Chinese Air Force. The Generalissmo gave in, flying to Lashio and telling his generals that (in Stilwell's words) "I was the boss—that they would take orders without question—that I would handle the British, that I had full power to promote, relieve, and punish any officer in the Chinese Expeditionary Force. (Jesus.)"

Watching the brass come and go, the American pilots guessed that their lives were about to change. "There is something in the air about to happen," Bus Keeton worried in his diary. Sure enough, Chennault called the pilots and ground crews together at Hostel Number One, chewed them out for their brawling ways, and told them that a new policy in Washington meant that there would be no further resignations from the AVG. (They were left wondering whether it was President Roosevelt or the U.S. Congress that had issued this fictional edict.) He didn't add that he himself was returning to active duty, though he must have known that he'd be commissioned next day. Bissell had sent him a radiogram to that effect, Magruder had sent two follow-up messages, and (when the messages evoked no response) Madame Chiang was asked to pass the word "through private channels."

In any event, Chennault was back on the team, and the AVG was committed to supporting Stilwell's priorities in Burma. Six of Tex Hill's Panda Bears were at Mengzi, ready to strafe the Japanese airfields across the border in Vietnam, so they missed Chennault's lecture at Hostel Number One. He called them back to Wujiaba and told them that the Vietnam offensive was canceled. Instead, Tex was to move to Loiwing with seven Kittyhawks and three Tomahawks. ("There is definately something in the air," fretted Keeton.) Using Lashio as an advance field, they'd fly three missions a day over the Chinese lines at Pyinmana, on the railroad north of Toungoo. Thus did Stilwell make his payoff to Chiang Kai-shek, tit for tat.

For his part, Chennault flew to Loiwing on a CNAC Douglas with the 2nd Squadron ground crewmen. In four months of war, this was his first visit to his pilots on the front line.

At Chiang Mai in Thailand, Colonel Kato gathered pilots and planes for a predawn return to Loiwing. His mechanics managed to put eleven Hayabusas into condition to make the 750-mile round trip, only to have three of them disabled when the pilots taxied into one another in the darkness. That left eight fighters to lift off at 3:45 AM, April 10—and three of those promptly turned back with engine trouble. The five remaining Hayabusas droned across the desolate Shan Highlands of Burma on their flight into China, wingtip lights glowing so they could keep formation and receive visual signals from the commander. At 6:10 AM, Kato waggled his wings, turned off his lights, and dove to the attack.

He rejoiced to see dozens of planes on the ground, lined up in neat rows—a perfect reversal of the situation at Chiang Mai two weeks before. Like the Adam & Eves on that occasion, the Japanese actually saw the enemy airmen as they ran across the field. ("Some one hollered bombers," as Dan Hoyle wrote, "and everyone took to the best available cover.") The Hayabusas strafed the airfield again and again, but failed to set any of the parked fighters afire. Finally Kato turned on his outside lights and waggled his wings for the flight home. To the astonishment of his pilots, he then fired a burst from his machine guns. Back at Chiang Mai, Lieutenant Hinoki asked the colonel about this unusual signal, and

Kato had to admit he'd been strafing Loiwing with dead guns. Reaching to turn off his lights, he'd hit a primary switch instead, and didn't realize his mistake until he went to turn them on again. He'd fired his guns to see if he had really done this stupid thing.

The Japanese were convinced they'd torn a great swath through the enemy air force, though puzzled why the planes didn't burn; they finally concluded that the Americans drained the gasoline from their planes overnight. But the damage at Loiwing was trivial compared to what the 64th Sentai had suffered at Chiang Mai. Of twenty-three fighters on the field—thirteen Tomahawks, seven Kittyhawks, three Hurricanes—only half were hit, and just one so badly that it was written off. With only an hour's delay, three Panda Bears left for Friday's morale mission, scouting Kyedaw airfield and showing the twelve-pointed sun over the Chinese lines.

Meanwhile, the 64th Sentai mechanics worked on the Hayabusas at Chiang Mai, and they had nine planes ready for a follow-up strike. At Loiwing, the alarm shrilled at 2:45 PM. Seven Tomahawks took off, but one had to turn back with a loose oil cap; the others climbed through the clouds to 25,000 feet. They patrolled for half an hour before they got word that Japanese fighters were over the field.

Again the 64th Sentai had come in below them—a potentially fatal error. Lieutenant Hinoki, on his second trip of the day into China, saw four Tomahawks fall out of the clouds upon the flight led by Lieutenant Endo Takeshi. Hinoki turned toward the Tomahawks and opened fire at the nearest pair, which dove away with Hinoki and Sergeant Misago Aikichi following them. Their opponents were R. T. Smith and Bob Brouk. As R. T. recalled the clash, he bounced several retractable-gear fighters but dove out when he found himself hard-pressed by two more. He then went after one of the intruders while Brouk chased the other. Wrote Brouk: "I made three passes at the enemy ship hitting him each time. On the fourth pass, a head on attack, I hit him and he turned to my left; went over on his back, and flames shot from under his left gas tank. He started down and I followed him for several seconds, thousands of feet, while he was in flames." The stricken Hayabusa was almost certainly Sergeant Misago's.

Meanwhile, R. T. dueled Hinoki. As the Japanese lieutenant recalled, they went into the clouds, dodging in and out of the murk at ever-lower altitudes. At one point, Hinoki saw a ghostly wing in the clouds. He fired at it, only to have R. T. open fire at the same moment, and to better effect. Hinoki heard bullets tearing through his fuselage, and his face turned warm and sticky with blood. Worse, gasoline was spilling out of his right wing, turning to vapor as it met the air. R. T. saw the white cloud and naturally assumed it was smoke: "After firing at one," he wrote, "I observed heavy smoke pouring from his engine as he dove down."

Believing himself too badly hit to make it home, the Japanese lieutenant "decided to die in the mountains." He turned toward the nearest peak. The Tomahawks kept after him but were intercepted and driven off by two other Hayabusas, to whom Hinoki signaled thanks and farewell. ("I fought two of them for 7 or 8 minutes," R. T. wrote, "and finally had to dive out as they both got the advantage.") Again a liquid-cooled fighter came at Hinoki, and more bullets tore through his plane. The Hayabusa's wingtips disintegrated, but at last the enemy broke off. Then Hinoki looked down and saw a river—the rendezvous for the flight home. Death no longer seemed inviting; so instead of diving into the mountains, he set out for Chiang Mai, where his tanks ran dry just as he was gliding down to the grass field, after a total of nine hours in the air. Hinoki had twenty-one bullet holes in his Hayabusa and one in his back, obliging him to spend the next month in an army hospital.

Hinoki put in no claim, but a Tomahawk was credited to Colonel Kato and another to Sergeant Yasuda Yoshito. The sergeant had suckered an enemy plane into a dogfight, only to have his guns jam; clearing them, Yasuda soon ran out of ammunition . . . whereupon his opponent nosed up, fell off, and dove into the jungle. In both cases, the Allied fighters were actually Hurricanes of 17 Squadron, one flown by Tex Barrick (now an ace as a result of his service in Burma) and the other by Gordon Peters, a South African lieutenant. The two RAF pilots were evacuated to India for medical treatment.

Recalling that Japanese pilots tended to go slack when the heat was off, Chuck Older and Duke Hedman flew south for twenty minutes, hoping to intercept the enemy fighters as they headed for home. Seeing nothing, they turned back toward the field—and spotted a radial-engine fighter. The Americans pulled up, made a positive identification, and dove on the enemy's tail. "He went wild," Older recalled in 1962. "He went into a flat loop and went right over our heads. I could look right up and see him go by—upside down in the cockpit."

This was Sergeant Yasuda, fresh from his victory over the RAF. His first warning of danger was the sight of red fireballs dancing on his cowling—flashes from the American incendiary bullets. His Hayabusa shook, and for a moment he thought its nose guns had spontaneously begun to fire. Then he did go wild, trying to survive close combat with two enemy fighters when he had no ammunition. "All I can do is turn, turn," he recalled years later. "Oil is coming out of the exhaust pipes like white smoke, and oil is on the fuselage and windscreen." He opened the canopy, but the oil fouled his goggles, too, and he had to throw them away. At one point, he gave up and tried to ram his tormentors.

"For the next half hour," Chuck Older wrote in his combat report, "Hedman and I engaged the enemy in a twisting and turning dogfight. We lost altitude and ended up right over the mountain tops. . . . We both got in several good burst after this, and finally saw the enemy going down steeply toward a hill side, apparently out of control, with black smoke streaming to the rear. We lost sight of the enemy after this, but after circling I noticed smoke rising from a spot on the hillside near where the enemy seemed to be falling."

But Yasuda was still airborne, though exhausted, his eyes and throat burning from the 300 mph blast of air. Like Hinoki, he limped back to Chiang Mai and made a dead-stick landing at the home field.

R. T. Smith had also gone on the prowl for the retreating enemy fighters. "I looked south and saw three of them heading for home," he reported. "I chased them and after about 5 minutes caught up with the last one. Closed to about 100 yards and opened up. He went into a dive and I followed, shooting on the way down. He crashed in a rice paddy on the side of a mountain about 30 to 40 miles down the valley." Killed in the crash was Sergeant Goto Chikara, credited with two Hurricanes over Singapore on December 31.

Bus Keeton of the AVG and Tex Barrick of the RAF were also credited with victories in this battle. That raised the Allied claims to five "Zeros," as against two Hayabusas actually shot down. The over-claiming doesn't obscure the fact that Chennault's pilots were besting

Kato's whenever they met. The 64th Sentai had lost thirty pilots in four months of almost continual combat, including several accidental deaths; of that number, eight had fallen to the guns of the AVG, and in just three encounters. In return, the Japanese pilots had shot down Eddie Overend and spoiled Parker Dupouy's day on December 25, with both Americans living to fight again. Stretching a point, the 64th Sentai might also take credit for Jack Newkirk's death and Mac McGarry's capture on March 24, but even that would leave the laurels on the other side. In five years of war—against Chinese, Russian, British, Dutch, and American pilots—this was the first time the 64th Sentai had come out second-best.

On Saturday evening, April 11, the pilots and ground crewmen at Loiwing gathered at the American Club to hear Chennault on the subject of induction. He'd softened his pitch since the lecture at Hostel Number One. If anyone decided not to join the U.S. Army in China, he assured them, he could serve out his year with CAMCO, then go home.

Tex Hill, Pete Wright, and John Croft of the Panda Bears missed this talk, having flown down to Lashio to prepare for the next day's mission. They spent the night at the CNAC hostel, and at sunrise warmed up their Kittyhawks on the red-clay runway. The plan was to follow the road and railway south to Pyinmana, make themselves known to the defenders, then scout Toungoo to see if the JAAF had moved into Kyedaw airfield. Wright told what it was like, showing the twelve-pointed sun on the Burma front: "We hit our checkpoints without fail and in about an hour and a half the ranges of mountains dropped away and we were over a lush green valley floored with rice paddies. Running down the center, crisscrossing each other every few miles but never more than a few hundred yards apart, were the Rangoon-Mandalay railroad and the Burma Road. Ahead of us we could see the village of Pyinmana smouldering in the distance. We went into a shallow dive . . . [and] made two quick turns around it to make sure [the Chinese soldiers] recognized us. . . . We climbed as quickly as possible and started south down the railroad. By the time we reached 15,000 feet we could see the aerodrome of Toungoo."

As they watched, a twin-engine plane landed on the asphalt and taxied off to the side—probably a Kawasaki Lily of the 8th Sentai, which had moved to Kyedaw to support the army around Pyinmana. Radioing Wright and Croft to fly top cover, Tex Hill dropped his wing and dove on the airfield, where he claimed a bomber destroyed on the ground and another shot down in the act of landing. Then a shell from an antiaircraft cannon hit the Kittyhawk, tearing a hole in its wing and almost flipping the aircraft on its back. Hill was able to nurse it back to Lashio.

Wright had followed him onto the field. "I was scared to death," he recalled. "I had my eye on the plane that had just landed. As I came over the field at about 200 feet, I saw it parked out to the side with its engines still turning over. I eased over a bit to get it in my sights and squeezed the trigger. Pulling back on the stick, I flashed over it and made a steep climbing turn to the left. I looked back to see the results. As I did so . . . huge black balls exploded all around me. One went off under my tail. I gave my plane full throttle and did a series of violent maneuvers and miraculously got away." He, too, was credited with two kills, one on the ground and another ten miles north of Toungoo. None of these victories can be confirmed in Japanese records.

Stilwell was directing the Burma missions, virtually on a day-to-day basis. "Request you arrange air recon road and railway Rangoon to Toungoo," he radioed Chennault on April 14, "with mission: are reinforcements from 40 ships reported Rangoon moving to Chinese end?"

Of the original invaders, Sakurai's 33rd Division was advancing up the Irrawaddy Valley against the Commonwealth army, while the 55th under Takeuchi battled the Chinese along the the Sittang River. Meanwhile, Watanabe's tank-equipped 56th Division—its supplies carried in British trucks and passenger cars from Singapore—swung east into the Shan Highlands, flanking the Chinese with an end run to Lashio. This was "the hook," a favorite tactic of the Japanese army. The idea was to set up a roadblock to the enemy's rear, draw off his forces to meet that threat, then hammer him on the original front.

Stilwell's radiogram referred to yet another division, the 18th under General Mutaguchi Renya. As a colonel in 1937, at the Marco Polo

Bridge near Beijing, Mutaguchi had commanded the regiment that fired the first shots of the Sino-Japanese War.* His troops were former coal miners, most of them, and in Malaya they'd earned a reputation for brutality. As Stilwell feared, they were indeed moving up the Sittang Valley to reinforce the 55th at Pyinmana. In other words, while a single division dealt with the Commonwealth army, three were now aimed at the "Chinese end."

Chennault dutifully sent the Panda Bears to scout the Sittang Valley below Pyinmana, and next day he sent them all the way to Pegu, 150 miles into Japanese-held territory. On the Pegu mission, John Petach lost his way, ran out of gas, and made a wheels-up landing in a dry riverbed. He was rescued by Major Gordon Seagrave, an American missionary doctor serving with the Chinese army. Meanwhile, Chennault finally sent that radiogram to Chongqing, accepting a commission as colonel in the U.S. Army. Twenty-four hours later, six Douglas transports flew in from India with supplies for him. It was as if the Old Man had sold the AVG for a mess of props and tires, and himself for a pair of silver eagles.

At Loiwing, the rebellious mood was spreading. "It is believed," Dan Hoyle wrote, "that about 10 or 15 members of the Group at Kunming . . . resigned a few days ago probably to work for Pan American Airways, Ferry Command. Pilots are disagreeing over some of the missions they go on as to the necessity and valuation of them."

Seven ground crewmen had indeed decamped for India. They included Glen Yarbery and Frank Metasavage, the crew chiefs who'd been put under house arrest. Clayton Harpold, the redoubtable mess sergeant from Eighteen Mile Ranch and Magwe, also quit at this time. Of the pilots, none had yet left, but George Burgard was planning to join Pan Am as soon as the AVG disbanded, and perhaps some hoped to change employers before that. Certainly Chennault was worried, to the extent that he asked Bissell to put his finger in the dike: "Please issue instructions to

*In 1943, trying to hold Burma against the British, Mutaguchi instructed his troops: "If your hands are broken, fight with your feet. If your hands and feet are broken, use your teeth." Among the 30,000 Japanese who died in obedience to his order was Shimura Kikujiro, whose piss-call at the Marco Polo Bridge had led to the first skirmish of an eight-year war.

CNAC and Pan American not to employ former AVG personnel. Many AVG men quitting hoping to take better pay jobs with these companies. Also issue orders that U S Army air transports may not carry AVG personnel except by written request."

And on Saturday, April 18, the Old Man called a meeting in the American Club. He began by blustering: "If you want to show the white feather," he said, according to several reports, "you can all quit." They knew what he meant: the white feather was a token of cowardice, presented by Englishwomen to young men in civilian clothes during World War I.

Then he reasoned with them. He'd accepted a commission in the U.S. Army, he said, so he had no choice but to schedule the morale missions if Stilwell asked for them. Finally, he appealed to their love of country: "You fellows have to remember, that's an American general with his staff down there directing these Chinese armies, and we owe him all the support we can give him."

The pilots were astonished to hear that Chennault was back on active duty—and relieved, too, for if the hated orders were coming from Stilwell, then perhaps the Old Man's judgment was as sound as ever. But however much they loved and respected him, they despised the morale missions more. "The pilots are bitter," Pappy Paxton wrote in his diary. "They feel Chennault is bloodthirsty and will sacrifice the AVG to the last man. . . . He keeps telling us the most important thing is to beat the Japs. That is more important than any of us personally, including himself."

Caucusing afterward, they voted to strike—or so they termed the event that became known as the Pilots' Revolt. Actually, the letter they drafted was less a strike call than a mass resignation: "We, the undersigned, pilots of the American Volunteer Group, hereby desire to terminate our contracts with the Central Aircraft Mfg. Co. and our services with the AVG."

Tex Hill unhinged himself, got to his feet, and urged them not to sign. Of all the squadron leaders, Tex was the most popular: raw-boned, shambling, dispenser of one-liners that could be sidesplittingly funny. Curiously for a man from the Southwest, he didn't tan, but burned and peeled under the tropical sun, until "his cherubic face glowed like a ripe tomato." What motivated him at Loiwing was a mix of patriotism, affection for the Old Man, and an understanding that a soldier had to go along to get along. "Look," he told them, as he recalled his speech years later. "I don't like these missions any more than y'all do. . . . [But] y'all need to remember something. We came over here as mercenaries—there are no bones about that. . . . But our country is at war now, and if you're part of the country, then you're at war too—uniform or not. These missions are the orders we've got, and the Old Man is giving 'em. I think we ought to follow them. I'm going to fly where I'm told, when I'm told. I'd say, with that guy, we're in pretty good hands."

Only four men—Eddie Rector from his own squadron, Frank Schiel from the Adam & Eves, and Duke Hedman and Catfish Raine from the Hell's Angels—followed Tex's lead. That left twenty-four names on the letter.

At this lowest hour of the American Volunteer Group, a group of U.S. Army airmen reached China by a route that had been closed since December 8. Early in the morning of April 18, sixteen stripped-down B-25 Mitchell bombers under the command of Colonel Jimmy Doolittle roared across the deck of the carrier *Hornet,* lifted off with an ease that astonished their crews, and skimmed at low altitude toward the Japanese main island of Honshu. After bombing Japan, one B-25 diverted to Siberia, where its crew was interned. (Though allied with the United States in Europe, the Soviet Union maintained a cynical neutrality in the Pacific until the last week of the war.) The remaining bombers reached China at nightfall and out of gas, and one by one they ditched offshore or crashed in Japanese-held territory. Three airmen were killed; eight were captured. Chinese partisans guided the others to safety, but not one B-25 survived to become the nucleus of Chennault's long-promised bomber group.

Nor was the AVG entirely out of action that Saturday: Bob Prescott and Bob Brouk claimed a "white-painted Army 98" shot down near Loiwing. There is no Japanese record of this plane, which was probably a Ki-46 Dinah.

The mutineers handed their document to Chennault on Sunday

morning. He never said how much it burned his fingers, but he could count. Of the men he could depend upon to fight the JAAF, half were now at Loiwing, and most of those had just vowed to quit. The rebels included a squadron leader (Oley Olson) and six aces (Bob Prescott, Dick Rossi, Whitey Lawlor, Ken Jernstedt, Chuck Older, and R. T. Smith).

The Old Man called a meeting that night in the American Club and told the pilots he wouldn't accept their resignations. If you want to go

A war-weary Tex Hill in flying helmet, leather jacket, and coveralls, with the trademark jug ears and dangling cigarette. The most popular of the squadron leaders, he stayed in China as a U.S. Army major and eventually commanded the 23rd Fighter Group for Chennault. (Alicia Schweizer collection)

home, he said, you must go as deserters. The distinction between desertion and resignation (which of course brought a "dishonorable discharge" with it) might be hard for a civilian to grasp, but it was clear to these proud young men. "There wasn't much we could do but stay," Bus Keeton wrote in his diary. "Here we have fought tremendous odds and done a good job. Desertion would ruin everything." There was a lot of brave talk among the pilots about calling the Old Man's bluff, but in fact he'd called theirs. Chennault's only concession in the Pilots' Revolt was to pretend it had never happened.

Tex Hill and three of his loyalists—Eddie Rector, Duke Hedman, and Catfish Raine—missed the Sunday showdown at the American Club, having flown down to Lashio for Monday's morale mission. After a 6:45 AM takeoff, they made the bread run to Pyinmana. They arrived over the village an hour later. "We had circled for twenty minutes at 9,000 [feet]," Rector reported, "when I observed an enemy ship approaching from the south and two thousand feet above us. I informed Hill by radio then turned toward the plane and started climbing. The plane turned west on sighting us and poured on all gun to escape. . . . I gave him three bursts in the turn [and] one more long one as he straightened out eastward and started in a dive toward the ground. Hedman had meanwhile made a pass at him, and gave him a final burst setting him on fire." The plane was a Ki-15 Babs of the 8th Sentai, whose enlisted pilot died in the crash along with Lieutenant Fujimori Akira, probably a reconnaissance officer. Rector and Hedman shared the credit for its destruction.

Reporting the shoot-down to Skip Adair at Kunming, Chennault added what was even better news: "Situation here normal today with all hands working." But it's worth noting the pilots on this mission were all drawn from the five who'd refused to join the Pilots' Revolt.

Chennault now sent a detachment to Namsang, the British airfield nearest the Thai border, in the continuing effort to mount a joint AVG-RAF raid on Chiang Mai. General Obata also repositioned his forces, sending the 77th and 31st sentais to Magwe, to keep the pressure on the Commonwealth army, and moving his two heavy-bomber groups into Burma, the 12th Sentai to Mingaladon airport and the 98th to Kyedaw airfield. This last was a bit risky, since the AVG had been active around Toungoo in recent days. So, to protect the Sallys, Obata stationed the 64th Sentai there as well.

Colonel Kato's Hayabusas were on the prowl Tuesday morning, April 21, and ten of them buzzed Namsang just as Bob Brouk was landing there. "As they approached the field they dropped to about 5,000 feet," Frank Schiel reported, "and three of them peeled off to strafe Brouk who was landing. He was caught by surprise and hit by the first burst. With his airplane still rolling he jumped from the cockpit and dived head first into a trench. His airplane rolled a short distance and stopped. The Japs made about four passes each until the plane began to burn. It was completely burned, and Brouk was shot three times in the legs."

Major Seagrave, who'd earlier rescued John Petach, drove to Namsang with a Karen nurse and operated on Brouk in the RAF billet. "One bullet had gone right through the thumb," Seagrave recalled. "Two others were in his legs, and I recovered several bits of airplane metal from various parts of his body." The AVG Beechcraft happened to be at Loiwing that day, having delivered a cargo of drop-tanks for the Kittyhawks, so John Hennessy and Einar (Mickey) Mickelson flew the battered transport to Namsang to evacuate Brouk. The other pilots flew back to Loiwing under their own power, and the AVG ground crewmen pulled out of Namsang by truck.

Next day—Wednesday, April 22—Chennault achieved his life's ambition, becoming a brigadier general in the U.S. Army. His pleasure may have been dimmed by the knowledge that Clayton Bissell's star was twenty-four hours older than his. Furthermore, as a serving officer, Chennault now had to route all his radiograms through the U.S. Military Mission in Chongqing. Thus, under date of April 22, Bissell sent the following message to the War Department: "Following from Chennault: 'Urge immediate appeal by president to all members of AVG to remain on duty here with promise early reinforcement. Group literally worn out—nerves and morale shot. Pilots quitting.'" Even as he forwarded Chennault's request, Bissell was able to ensure that news of the Pilots' Revolt was spread around Washington: "Another reliable

report states: 'Three or four individuals refused to go on scheduled mission. Twenty-four of best pilots have served notice of termi-
nation of contract.'" The radiogram concluded with a damning
assessment: "Many of AVG pilots are wild, undisciplined lot unsuit-
able for command of squadrons at present. They fight well but are probably overrated."

Bissell was responding to a War Department suggestion that Chennault's best pilots be sent to other theaters as squadron leaders, thus
spreading their experience and panache throughout the air force. It's a
pity this scheme didn't go forward. Bissell was no fool, and what he said
about Chennault's pilots was unarguable: they were wild, they were undisciplined, their exploits were much exaggerated—and they fought
well. Bissell simply didn't have the imagination to realize that many of
these men, including some of the wilder specimens like Greg Boyington,
would soon prove their worth as squadron leaders and group commanders in U.S. service.

In any event, their ranks were shrinking. More or less recovered
from the injuries that had followed Freddie Hodges's wedding, Boyington was flying "slow time" in Tomahawks whose engines had been replaced at the CAMCO factory in Loiwing. Evenings he got drunk and
perhaps courted Olga Greenlaw. (Most AVG veterans I interviewed were
convinced that Greenlaw bedded Boyington and most of the other pilots
mentioned fondly in her book—each assuring me, however, that he himself had never been so favored. As with combat reports, there was no
doubt some wishful thinking with respect to the exec's wife.) Of his few
friends, Ralph Gunvordahl had quit in January and Percy Bartelt in
March. Now Boyington, too, threw in the towel, flying on a CNAC
Douglas to Calcutta, then a British flying boat to Karachi, where he tried
to get a flight to the U.S. He was refused—apparently the first to be
caught by Chennault's request that AVG returnees not be allowed on
military aircraft unless they had orders from him. Boyington finally took
passage on SS *Brazil*. His shipmates, he said, included several hundred
CAF cadets and some of the same missionaries who'd come out with him
on *Boschfontein*.

Then Cliff Groh got lost while ferrying a plane from Loiwing to
Kunming. He landed on a sandbar in the Mekong River. After the usual

confusion—was he Japanese?—he was taken to the local magistrate, who allowed him to compose a message to be sent by runner to the nearest telegraph office. The most important information must have been omitted, for the AVG never learned his location. After waiting two weeks for an answer, Groh destroyed his Tomahawk and set out on horseback for the long trek to Kunming.

And on April 24, Frank Swartz died in India. Charlie Bond had visited the injured pilot not long before, while on a ferry mission to pick up some Kittyhawks and the first of the Republic P-43s that Lauchlin Currie had acquired in 1941 for the 3rd AVG. Swartz had then seemed in good health and reasonable spirits, for a man who'd lost part of a thumb, was undergoing skin grafts, and faced surgery to repair his mouth. It was a hospital-borne infection that carried him off. Twenty-six years old, he was buried at St. Sepulchre church in Poona.

Of ninety-nine combat pilots who'd sailed for Asia in the summer and fall of 1941, seventeen were now dead or missing and nineteen had gone home. That left Chennault with sixty-three names on his pilot roster. However, ten of those were now assigned as staff officers or noncombat pilots—jobs they'd drifted into in large part because they were unwilling or unable to fly a Tomahawk in combat.

A more promising replacement pool was the flight school at Yunnanyi, where Butch Carney still had six former army flight instructors serving as check pilots. Their work was now finished—the Chinese cadets aboard SS *Brazil* with Greg Boyington were presumably their graduates—and one of their companions, John Blackburn, had already made the transition from instructor to Tomahawk pilot. Chennault now asked the others to join the combat squadrons, which all six did at the end of April.

He picked up a seventh pilot in the person of Captain Ajax Baumler, who'd twice been frustrated in his attempts to serve with Chennault in Asia. After his close call at Wake Island on December 8, Baumler was pressed into duty with the 45th Pursuit Squadron in Hawaii, but in February was once again sent on his way to Kunming, this time by way of Rio de Janeiro and the South Atlantic ferry route. From Takoradi on the east coast of Africa, he led a flight of eight P-40E Kittyhawks through the Persian Gulf and India, reaching Kunming on April 20. He was attached to the AVG as the first uniformed U.S. Army officer to serve under Chennault's command. It would be a long time, however, before he saw combat. Instead, Chennault used him for a miscellany of jobs, pushing paper in the AVG office and ferrying P-43 Lancers from India. By all accounts, Baumler also drank more than was good for him.

Chapter 15

Auction Sale at Loiwing

The focus of the Burma campaign now shifted to Lashio, the dusty town where the railway ended and the mountain road to China began. On April 16, Lashio was so far behind the lines that Harvey Greenlaw felt it safe to park Olga there, at the CNAC hostel, while he ran errands for Chennault. (Among other chores, he coaxed Colonel Homer Sanders to Kunming. The colonel had brought three P-40 squadrons to India, and Chennault hoped to winkle one of them away, on the half-promise that Sanders would command the nascent 23rd Fighter Group.) The front that day was 200 miles southwest, with Commonwealth troops holding at the Yenangyaung oilfields on the Irrawaddy, and the Chinese at Pyawbwe on the railroad line.

East of Pyawbwe, a Chinese half-division guarded the Shan Highlands, and it now reported that it had met the Japanese vanguard. Stilwell assumed that it was being prodded by a battalion-sized force, but in fact it faced "the hook"—Watanabe's 56th Division, reinforced with tanks, heavy artillery, and 400 British vehicles from Singapore. Watanabe's first obstacle was the Karen guerrillas led by Chester Klein, the missionary who'd treated the AVG to Saturday-night beans and conversation at Toungoo. After routing them, Watanabe fell upon the Chinese troops, and for three days a desperate battle raged at a place the Japanese identified as Tzuchien. The tanks broke through on the night of April 18, advancing twelve miles "through continuous enemy fire" before finding themselves on a clear road to the north.

"Disaster at Loikaw," Stilwell wrote in his diary. "Wild tales of Jap tank division . . . Aiming at Lashio? Jesus. This may screw us completely." Indeed: in one of those audacious gambles that served Japan so well during the opening months of the war, Watanabe ordered that his trucks be used only to carry troops, leaving food, fuel, and ammunition behind. For resupply, the division would trust to "Churchill stores." The gamble paid off: running out of gasoline on April 22, the Japanese tank crews found seven hundred drums abandoned by the Chinese at Taunggyi. Next day they rumbled into Loilem, *north* of the Allied armies, giving Stilwell no option but headlong retreat. "All fade for Mandalay and its one bridge," he wrote. "I hope it's still there."

On the road to Mandalay, Stilwell experienced a sudden conversion to the merits of air power, as the only weapon he could bring to bear against Watanabe's rogue division. The campaign began on Friday, April 24. Five Blenheims flew down from Lashio to bomb the Japanese truck convoys. From Loiwing, Chennault dispatched five Tomahawks and six Kittyhawks, the latter carrying antipersonnel bombs in their under-wing racks. This was the AVG's first actual bombing mission, and Tex Hill flew tail-end Charlie to assess the results. "I could see bombs landing in a nice string about 50' apart," he reported, "some on the convoy and some to the right of road which was ideal for [hitting] the people who had left the trucks to take cover in the field. I came down the line of trucks straffing after the last man had bombed. The trucks were probably carrying gas as they burned readily. I counted 8 burning."

A Japanese plane then blundered onto the scene—probably one of the fixed-gear aircraft attached to ground units for observation and straffing. "We overtook him immediately and shot him down," Tex wrote, with the credit shared by him, John Petach, Pete Wright, and Eddie Rector.

The air attacks did nothing to delay Watanabe's advance, and the RAF moved its Blenheims back to Loiwing for fear they'd be captured. The last plane out of Lashio seems to have been the AVG Beechcraft. Before leaving, John Hennessy and Mickey Mickelson broke into the post office and made off with a bag containing mail for the AVG. "Perhaps someone got to sleep that last night in Lashio," Olga Greenlaw recalled of the general collapse, "but I didn't . . . The activity going on all over the dirty little town was frenzied and noisy: people shouting and running around in the rain, repairing tires and motors, loading trucks and all sort of vehicles in frantic haste and confusion. This was the last chance to escape. In a few hours it would be all over." On Saturday morning, April 25, she stripped the curtains from the CNAC hostel, then escaped with them in a truck driven by Henry Olson, the crew chief.

Meanwhile, the Kittyhawks and Tomahawks were bombing and strafing, and no sooner did they return to Loiwing than Chennault sent them out again. Five more Kittyhawks had arrived from Kunming, bringing his detachment to seventeen planes—the most any AVG combat commander had had at his disposal since December 20. They took off at 3 PM, and near Konghaiping they spotted two fixed-gear Japanese scouts, probably Ki-51 Sonias. Bombs still hanging from their wings, the lead Kittyhawks went after the enemy aircraft. "Hit him with a burst from about 250 feet," Link Laughlin reported; "he turned under me and I noticed two or three other P-40's making runs on him. I caught him in a shallow turn close to the ground. . . . The rear gunner quit firing at me and I am certain he was killed. . . . My plane had been hit eight times by the rear gunner's return fire. . . . I got behind him and two P-40's. The first P-40 hit him with a short burst and the EA skidded from a 50 ft. altitude into the ground, cartwheeled, and burst into flames. The pilot was thrown clear of his plane, his chute opened on the ground. Pilot apparently dead."

When Catfish Raine came on the scene, he saw six Kittyhawks making runs on one of the scouts, so he went after the other. "The Jap burst into flames," he reported. "As I pulled over him about 30 ft. the Jap looked as though he was trying to jump. The plane crashed just about 500 ft. from where he caught fire." Mysteriously, the two scouts became three in the AVG record, Raine credited with one and all seven pilots dividing the credit for two more.

The April 25 scrap was witnessed by a Japanese war correspondent, and it got a dramatic write-up in a Tokyo newspaper. According to his account, the two scouts had just finished strafing a Chinese column when they came under attack from Allied fighters. The rear gunners—Corporals Nakayama and Sora—were killed at their posts. "Determined to avenge the death of their comrades," the story continued, the pilots supposedly replaced them at the rear of the greenhouse canopy. "Captain Maruyama and Sergeant Major Uyeda manned the machine guns and fired furiously at the enemy planes, shooting down several of them. But the two Japanese machines were badly hit and becoming completely disabled were dashed to the ground by the pilots in heroic acts of self-destruction." Increasingly, in the Japanese press, elegiac tales were replacing the earlier accounts of easy and overwhelming victories.

G eneral Mao Pang-chu offered nine of his Russian bombers to support the Chinese army in Burma. Mao and Chennault exchanged radiograms on the subject for a week, and at one point the curly-haired general flew to Loiwing for further talks. But the Tupelov SBs didn't move, so Chiang Kai-shek turned again to Chennault: "Use all available AVG strength to strike enemy trucks, troops, etc. in Lashio-Namian region. Establish close liaison with [Chinese commanders] and report daily operations to me." A few hours later, he asked for *two* reports per day.

Chennault replied that Loiwing had become untenable. "Enemy reported in Lashio," he told the Generalissimo, requesting permission to quit Loiwing and set up a new base deeper into China. On Sunday morning, he sent the Hell's Angels to see if the reports were true. From the air, they reported, Lashio seemed deserted, and the road leading out of it was crowded with trucks heading north. (They belonged to the retreating Chinese, though the Hell's Angels seemed to think they were Japanese.) The Tomahawks then flew down to Hsipaw, a few miles southwest. Circling at 8,000 feet, they saw that the town was on fire, with twenty-eight twin-engine bombers heading away from it. Then the Tomahawks ran into the 64th Sentai. After some skirmishing, the Hayabusas left the scene. They'd been on their way to attack Loiwing but had dropped their auxiliary fuel tanks when they met the Hell's Angels; the weather was deteriorating, so they turned for home. Clouds and rain moved in at noon, forcing the opposing air forces to shut down for the day.

That option wasn't available to the men on the ground. At dawn on Monday, April 27, Stilwell crossed the Mandalay bridge in a balky command car. In the charred city, he held a bad-tempered conference with the British. ("Reconnaissance? No got. Limeys as usual knew nothing.") Chennault meanwhile was having his ears boxed by Madame Chiang: "Your urgent message of 26th just received. At this moment twelve o'clock midnight we are still receiving messages from Lashio radio station . . . Carry out morning bombing mission as usual. If by tomorrow enemy entrance into Lashio confirmed then Generalissimo consents that you change to whatever fields you think best."

That was good enough for Chennault. He told the 3rd Squadron ground crews to drive to Mangshi, eighty miles into China, and there prepare a fallback field for the AVG. The British, too, were winding down their operation on the China-Burma border, sending all but one of their Blenheims to India. About the same time, a U.S. Army transport landed at Loiwing on its way to Kunming—the first Ferry Command plane to make the trip into China. (Based at Dinjan, the easternmost airfield in India, the Ferry Command had been cobbled together from army C-47s and Pan Am DC-3s, flown by ferry pilots and former Doolittle raiders.) Among those who hitched a ride on the army Douglas were Olga Greenlaw, Lucy the dog, Ma Davidson from the American Club, and two Anglo-Indian women put aboard by Moose Moss and consigned to Ray Hastey in Kunming.

On April 29 the Japanese emperor would be forty-one years old. In 1938, his admirals had chosen his birthday for a spectacular raid on Hankou, and Chennault expected history to repeat itself in western China. At Wujiaba airport, Don Rodewald recorded the Old Man's warning: "We got as much done as possible today as we expect a birthday greeting from the Jap Emporer tomorrow. He will probably want to celebrate his birthday joyusly but we intend to have 18 planes to upset his plans." Rode went on to note that John Blackburn "took off about 4 P.M. and hasn't been seen since. . . . We fear for the worst. He was testing the guns for me on one of the new E's." The former flight instructor dove into Lake Kunming, evidently a victim of the Kittyhawk's reluctance to pull out of a dive.* The Japanese did have a birthday spectacular in mind, though not what Chennault expected. Instead, Watanabe's 56th Division was scheduled to capture Lashio with the help of parachute troops. To protect the airdrop, General Obata wanted to neutralize the American air force at Loiwing, and he planned a raid for Tuesday, April 28—a day early, by Chennault's reckoning. It consisted of twenty Hayabusas and twenty-four Sallys. Like the AVG, the 64th Sentai had received some replacement fighters in the spring of 1942, apparently including the Nakajima Ki-44 Shokis of the 47th Independent Chutai, whose pilots went home at the end of April to protect Tokyo from another Doolittle-type raid.

By coincidence, Chennault sent fourteen fighters down to Lashio that morning to support the Chinese troops defending the city against tanks and artillery. He didn't have enough oxygen for so many planes, and most of the Hell's Angels did without. Oley Olson led eight Tomahawks at 10,000 feet, with two oxygen-equipped Tomahawks guarding them at 12,000 feet. Higher still, at 18,000 feet, were four Kittyhawks under Tex Hill.

This three-step formation was southwest of Hsipaw when Hill spotted the Japanese formation on the reciprocal course. He called Olson but got no answer, so Tex told another Hell's Angel to relay the warning and himself led the Panda Bears toward the bombers. At the same moment, half a dozen Hayabusas dropped their auxiliary tanks and turned out to meet him. They were led by Captain Kuroe Yasuhiko, a 47th Chutai pilot who'd replaced the squadron leader killed at Loiwing on April 8. The Japanese "tried to get into some semblance of a formation," Tex recalled, "but I couldn't tell exactly what type. They were apparently trying to work in threes. I fired four short bursts at my first opponent before I got him. In the 4th burst he started off in a shallow dive [and] crashed into the jungle. From then on the fight was a rat race with 0s and P-40s on

---

*Blackburn's body was recovered a month or so later. In 2003, a Chinese-American salvage team found an airplane in the silt at the bottom of the lake, which the Americans called Lake Kunming and the Chinese know as Danchi. Very likely this is Blackburn's P-40E, though at this writing, the salvors still haven't managed to raise it to the surface.

each others tails. I got my second 0 on a head on approach with him having a slight altitude advantage. . . . The range was closing so fast that I
had to haul back on the stick violently in order to [target] him."

Lew Bishop shot a Hayabusa off Tex's tail and saw the Japanese pilot
bail out. Bishop was climbing so steeply that the recoil of the Kittyhawk's
guns caused it to stall; he fell off in a spin, recovered, and chased after a
Hayabusa that seemed to be leaving the fight. As he told the story, his bullets chopped a wing off the Japanese plane, which then burst into flame.
(Almost certainly, in the adrenaline rush of combat, Bishop had spun one
event into two: the plane that lost its wing was the same one whose pilot
bailed out.) Back in the fight again, he saw a "Zero" going down under the
guns of Tom Jones. Bishop laced another Japanese fighter, which "fell off
on one wing and started spinning." He followed his quarry down to 3,000
feet but was unable to set it afire.

Oley Olson was alerted to the fight by a Japanese voice in his earphones. "I heard a strange tongue on the radio," he reported, "and looked
about more intently. About two minutes later one of the planes in our formation sighted enemy [bombers] above about twenty miles away. I turned
to an interception course and called for the planes without oxygen to join
on me and advised the others to join on R. T. Smith who had the enemy located and who was supplied with oxygen."

Olson's radio must have strayed off the AVG frequency. He hadn't
received Tex's warning, and his instructions evidently went unheard by
the Hell's Angels, who went after the Japanese in flights of two or three.
"I saw [Chuck] Older give the attack signal but I did not see any enemy,"
Ken Jernstedt reported. "He changed his course a little and struck out
ahead of [our] formation. I then saw a large formation of planes a great
distance away that I judged to be bombers. By this time Older was some
distance ahead of [Eddie] Overend. . . . I saw some enemy fighters coming up from behind and below Older. Overend dove on 3 of them. They
split up and one pulled up sharply and apparently stalled as I made a run
on him from above. I gave him two short bursts. He burst into flames
and headed down."

This was Captain Kuroe and his men, returning to the formation
after skirmishing with the Panda Bears. As Eddie Overend recalled the

encounter, there were four Hayabusas, and two of them "pulled up and away." He closed on the other pair and gave the righthand plane a long burst at point-blank range. The Hayabusa burst into flame, clawed straight up, then dove for the ground. Following it down, Overend realized that the other Hayabusas were on his tail. He shook them by running the Kitty-hawk's indicated airspeed to 330 mph, but in the process lost sight of his quarry. Chuck Older claimed two of the retractable-gear fighters in the same skirmish.

Parker Dupouy and Tom Haywood had almost overhauled the bomber formation when another Hayabusa turned back to give fight. The two Hell's Angels went after it. "After about three passes each," Haywood re-ported, "the fighter started breaking up and crashed into the jungle out of control." They resumed their chase after the Sallys, catching them just as they reached Loiwing. Haywood made several runs on the bomb-ers before running out of ammunition, with no better result than to take several bullets through his Tomahawk.

R. T. Smith and Paul Greene (the oxygen-equipped weavers) began the chase with an altitude advantage over the other Tomahawks. They, too, went after the bombers, but before catching them met several retractable-gear fighters in a "large sloppy Lufberry"—a squirrel-cage for-mation, with each pilot protecting the tail of the man in front. "The two of us went into the Lufberry on the tail of one Jap," R. T. reported. "We both shot at it, and then Greene had to break off as another Jap came up. I fol-lowed the first one. . . . He pulled up sharply in a steep chandelle, and I followed. Got a good rear quarter shot at him and he flew right thru a burst. He caught fire around the engine immediately, and crashed out of a long spiral."

Greene squared off with the intruder, but the Hayabusa refused the challenge. "I still had speed enough to get on his tail," Greene reported. "After several bursts he caught on fire." By this time the Sallys had fin-ished their bombing run, and the two Hell's Angels set out in hopes of intercepting them on their way home. They gave up when they realized they didn't have enough fuel to follow the bombers downcountry.

After the Tomahawks and Kittyhawks had taken off from Loiwing, but before the Sallys came over, several more Douglas transports arrived from Dinjan, including an army C-47 and some Pan Am DC-3s. Chennault ran across the runway and ordered them to take off again. At the controls of the C-47 were colonels Caleb Haynes and Robert Scott of the Ferry Command, carrying two Ryan trainers for the CAF, food and ammunition for the AVG, and a bottle of whiskey for Chennault. As Scott recalled the incident, the Old Man drawled: "Guess we're going to have some Japs—you-all had better get those transports off the field."

Scott was desolate to leave the combat zone, or so he told the story. "I'd have given anything," he wrote in a wartime memoir, "to trade my colonel's eagles and that 'delivery wagon' that I flew for the gold bars of a second Lieutenant and one of those shark-nosed pieces of dynamite! But we started the Douglas up and took off for China. . . . Even as we cleared the field and climbed towards the Salween, I heard the call 'Tally-Ho' from the AVG. . . . Every now and then we could hear one of the AVG say to some unlucky Jap, 'Your mother was a turtle—your father was a snake,'—and then the rattle of fifty-caliber guns over the radio." One DC-3 failed to clear the field and had its tail blown off. Chennault's bottle of whiskey was another casualty, blown up with the jeep where Scott had put it for safekeeping. The runways were damaged, though not heavily enough to prevent the Panda Bears and Oley Olson from landing there.

The rest of the Hell's Angels flew on toward Mangshi, their new home. They landed safely except for R. T. Smith, who ran out of gas while following the directions of the Mangshi radio station. (The operator talking him down was looking at another Tomahawk.) R. T. made a wheels-down landing, collapsed his gear in a gully, and hitched a ride into Mangshi with a truckload of Chinese casualties.

W hat are we to make of this carnage? The Panda Bears and Hell's Angels claimed no fewer than thirteen Japanese fighters: two each for Tex Hill, Lew Bishop, and Chuck Older; one each for Tom Jones, Ken Jernstedt, R. T. Smith, Paul Greene, Eddie Overend, and Frank Adkins; and a final one shared by Parker Dupouy and Tom Haywood. Yet of twenty Hayabusas taking part in this battle, only two failed to return to Toungoo.

The first to go down was an enlisted pilot of Kuroe's squadron, a corporal named Hirano who was "shot up by a P-40 and then collided with another pursuing P-40." Probably Hirano was winged by Tex Hill and finished off by Lew Bishop, who then claimed him a second time; he bailed out when his wing came off, causing his companions to imagine a collision. In any event, the corporal landed safely, walked south until he met the 56th Division, and six days later turned up at Toungoo.

The second pilot to go down was Lieutenant Kataoka Tadashi, who left the main formation and went out by himself to meet the enemy. As Captain Kuroe recalled, his squadron's final brush with the enemy involved two fighters, which then turned away in favor of Kataoka's Hayabusa. The likeliest candidates were Parker Dupouy and Tom Haywood (who met and attacked a lone Hayabusa) or Paul Greene and R. T. Smith (who were skirmishing with several fighters when Greene broke off to battle an intruder).

In any event, it was two-for-nought for the AVG, and the 64th Sentai was again obliged to count its dead. Kuroe was especially morose, because he was the one who'd broken formation and caused (as he believed) the death of Corporal Hirano. His commander didn't console him. "We knew you were battling the enemy," Kato said, "but we did not come to help because the principle was to protect the bombers. . . . Forget those pilots," he said. "Work for the group."

While this epic and confusing battle was underway, the Japanese army's 1st Parachute Brigade moved up to Toungoo by train. Before dawn on April 29, at the former AVG training base, 440 paratroopers filed into twin-engine Lockheed Electra transports built under license by the Kawasaki company. At the old RAF dispersal field, meanwhile, their supplies were loaded into nine Sallys from the 98th Sentai. They'd be accompanied to Lashio by Colonel Kato's fighters and the light bombers of the 8th Sentai. The escort consisted of sixteen Hayabusas, suggesting that in addition to the planes shot down the day before, two others may have been damaged.

The weather deteriorated as the raiders flew north. At 8:42 AM, 50 miles from the drop zone, the brigade commander gave the order to turn back. Of one hundred planes that had set out for Lashio, five were lost, including the Ki-43 flown by Sergeant Yasuda Yoshito, who'd dueled with Duke Hedman and Chuck Older on April 10. (The other planes lost were scouts that collided on takeoff from Toungoo, and Sally transports trying to find their way home in the storm.) Only four Anns managed to reach the objective, which they did by flying below the storm. They were on hand to support the 56th Division when it swept into Lashio at noon. In the nine days since Stilwell learned that he'd been flanked by a motorized division, General Watanabe had advanced 300 miles, doubling the Japanese penetration of Burma.

"Burma reporting net collapsed," Chennault radioed Skip Adair next day. "Steady rains [and] low clouds prevent operation. Field here and [at Mangshi] very muddy and unusable after few more rains. . . . Am sending 2nd Squadron to Kunming today." To the Generalissimo, Chennault sent a brief and bleak report: "Jap took Lashio noon 29 April. Situation here very bad."

Stilwell was in Shwebo, sixty miles north of Mandalay and beyond the point at which his army could have wheeled eastward into China. Still, he wanted to know about the situation at Lashio, and he asked Chennault to send a plane so he could reconnoiter that "front." But there was no front at Lashio, only a hundred-mile traffic jam of refugees and soldiers bound up the Burma Road toward China. It must have been with a private smile that Chennault radioed his boss that the Chinese staff had already left Loiwing and that the AVG would soon follow.

Colonels Haynes and Scott had spent the night in Kunming, and Bissell asked them to rescue the American generals—Chennault, Stilwell, and Frank Sibert—who were stranded in Burma. No better crew for the mission could possibly be imagined. Haynes, as the saying went, "looks like a gorilla and flies like an angel," and Scott's dream was to escape the Ferry Command and join Chennault as a fighter pilot. (The bottle of whiskey had been meant to lubricate this process.) They "took off about 0545 and went to Loiwing," as Haynes described the flight, "but there was a heavy rain in the vicinity and I couldn't get into the field. While I was circling Loiwing I was in contact with Gen. Chennault and told him of my instructions to pick up . . . the 'Double-O

Man.'" He meant Stilwell, whom the Americans in China called the Old-Old Man to distinguish him from Chennault. "He caught on at once and said he guessed maybe I should go take care of that job. I was beginning to run low on gas, so I told him I was going into the place I had been the day before [Myitkyina] and would come back for him."

Chennault replied that he'd have "an auction sale"—would leave Loiwing—at two o'clock; if Haynes couldn't return before then, not to bother. Haynes refueled at Myitkyina and headed south. "The Japs had just bombed Myingatha," he recalled, "and it was a blazing inferno, with people jumping out of houses, animals running everyplace and masses of people streaming out of town." He landed at Shwebo and went to Stilwell's headquarters, where the Americans were burning their files. "I told the General that I was prepared to take practically all of them to Calcutta," Haynes wrote, "and that I would take him to China if he so desired. He agreed to the latter, providing we stopped by Loiwing and picked up Chennault." Haynes radioed Loiwing, but the station had gone off the air. He then loaded twenty-nine officers for the flight to India, but Stilwell wasn't among them. He'd decided to stay with the Chinese army—an act of great courage and even greater folly. Once the C-47 lifted off from the dirt airfield at Shwebo, the highest-ranking American officer in Asia ceased to have any influence on events beyond the sound of his voice.

That was Friday, May 1. Another transport had picked up Chennault at Loiwing, leaving Harvey Greenlaw to demolish the CAMCO factory and twenty-two Tomahawks awaiting repair. They nearly had more aircraft to contend with: Tex Hill and some other Panda Bears were ready to abandon their planes and board the trucks when the fog lifted and they were able to fly out. Greenlaw and the wrecking crew followed them by road. With Loiwing abandoned, the Mangshi airfield was also perilously exposed, and Chennault called the Hell's Angels back to Kunming. They landed late in the day on Friday, not having washed or shaved for the past three days.

To support the troops in Burma, Chennault established a new base at Baoshan, 125 miles from the China-Burma frontier, on the high ground between the precipitous gorges of the Mekong and Salween rivers. He gave the assignment to the Adam & Eves, and Bob Neale took eight Toma-hawks to the soggy grass airstrip on Saturday, May 2. Before their engines cooled, they took off in a rainstorm to escort nine Tupelov SBs to Lashio. This was the CAF's first mission in Burma. The target was a highway bridge near Lashio, but the SBs passed it by and bombed the railroad yards instead. The bombers then returned to Kunming, and the Toma-hawks to Baoshan.

The Adam & Eves' new post was an ancient city jammed to the walls with refugees. Trucks were parked bumpers-touching in the streets, with their occupants sleeping in and under them. The Americans were as-signed to a monastery built against a mountain on the other side of town from the airfield. Dinner began with soup, which they gulped straight off, without pausing to wash their hands.

The Japanese advance had become a pincers. In the west, Sakurai sent a detachment up the Chindwin River, to prevent the Com-monwealth army from escaping to India. In the center, Takeuchi and Mutaguchi marched their troops along the main road, the divisions tak-ing turns so they could "advance by bounds." On the east, Watanabe's motorized units took advantage of the Burma Road, smoothed and hard-ened by Chinese labor. ("The Japanese," wrote radioman Smith in his diary, "are making better time up the road than we did in convoy.") Be-fore the 56th Division reached China, however, Watanabe diverted his main force toward Myitkyina, over the route used by the refugees from Lashio.

By Japanese estimates, 150,000 Allied troops were caught in this great trap. Chief among them was General Stilwell, who'd refused the last flight from Shwebo so as to stay with his army, but who now had no army to command. There was only a rabble, as terrified of the approach-ing monsoon as of the Japanese. Stilwell decided to head for the wilds of North Burma, far enough and fast enough that when he turned west for India, he'd brush past Sakurai's reaching fingertips. Thus the senior American officer in Asia—arguably one of the great fighting generals of all time—was unable to do more than save himself and his immediate party. It included three generals (Stilwell, Sibert, and a Chinese brigadier) and Major Seagrave's hospital unit with its Karen nurses and British Quaker drivers.

The scene was a nightmare. "British stragglers walked aimlessly about, haggard, shocked, frightened," as one of Stilwell's officers described it. "Punjabi soldiers twisted and turned through the mob, snatching food from helpless, unarmed families. . . . Turbaned, black-bearded Sikhs, aloof and sullen, their pride humbled, stumbled through the crowd. A dozen men of the Burma Rifles bickered over the loot of a house they had set afire, while the owners clustered in a silent knot of misery. Fighting for the possession of a truck, gray-clad Chinese troops hauled the Burmese driver from the cab and pistol-whipped him until he lay bloody and still in the dust. Mountain tribespeople stealthily explored the sprawled body of a Chinese soldier with bare toes to be sure the man was dead before they stripped him."

Japanese engineers and native conscripts rebuilt Lashio airport, and the Anns of the 27th Sentai—newly arrived from China—moved in to occupy the red-clay field. Also based there was the 71st Independent Chutai, attached to the 56th Division for reconnaissance. Presumably it was one of the squadron's Ki-51 Sonias that ran afoul of the AVG on May 3.

The weather that Sunday was too thick for bombing, so Chennault sent the Adam & Eves down to Loiwing to see if the CAMCO facilities had indeed been destroyed. Bob Neale led the six-plane flight to the border. At Loiwing, he reported, "no fires were noted except one at the west end of the long runway." Then Bill Bartling spotted a Japanese warplane through the clouds and chased after it. "I followed on a slightly different heading," Neale wrote, "and after diving thru a cloud ended up to my surprise on the tail of a Jap observation plane." All Neale had to do was press the firing button. "My second burst was at very close range, after which he started a diving turn to the left finally ending in an inverted dive in which attitude it crashed on the edge of a small river approximately 10 to 15 miles NE of Lungling." That was victory number fifteen for Bob Neale, making him the first American triple ace.

The Japanese entered Loiwing on Sunday evening, to find "a great many stores," including twenty-six planes. Most were Tomahawks, accumulated by the Pawley brothers at Loiwing and never repaired. A Tokyo newspaper published a photograph of the strange-looking aircraft.

"Note the peculiar design painted on the wreckage," said the caption— "a shark's bared teeth. If these markings were found on a submarine, the significance could perhaps be understood; but on a plane? Suffice it to say that Japan's 'Wild Eagles' will rule the skies regardless of what freaks the enemy may send up in his futile attempts to continue resistance." Clearly, Harvey Greenlaw's demolition had been something less than total.

Next day, General Obata sent his heavy-bomber sentais—the 12th from Mingaladon and the 98th from Toungoo—thundering north to the Burma-China border, then east to Baoshan. They were escorted as usual by the 64th Sentai. It was Magwe all over again, and most of the Adam & Eves jumped for the nearest trench. Charlie Bond ran in the opposite direction and was in his cockpit before realizing he was the only pilot on the flight line. Deciding it was safer to go forward than back, he started his engine and took off without pausing to don his flying gear. By this time the 12th Sentai had finished its bombing run. At least one bomb hit the monastery on the other side of town. Ben Foshee, an off-duty pilot, was caught in the blast, along with an AVG crewman, a CAMCO employee, and some Chinese hostel workers.

Climbing to 18,000 feet, Charlie Bond found himself in a position to make runs on the 98th Sentai. He watched his tracers lick through a Sally, but it wouldn't burn. Instead, two nearby bombers gave off streams of blue-gray smoke. Deciding that this was a decoy—oil injected into the engines—Bond kept after the original target: "On my third attack I saw his right engine disintegrate and ignite into a flaming torch. He went down and through the overcast. I turned on the bomber at the tail of the vee, but suddenly my guns quit firing. . . . Hell, I was out of ammunition!" He'd made plenty of hits, nevertheless. The 98th Sentai lost one Ki-21 on the raid and three others came home damaged, and Bond was the only Allied pilot in the air.

Meanwhile, the 64th Sentai had abandoned the bombers in order to settle its account with the AVG. The Hayabusas screamed down upon Baoshan airfield, strafing seven Tomahawks on the ground. Before they were done, Charlie Bond blundered into the line of fire. Hearing a rattle in his cockpit, and believing that his hydraulic system had burst, he reached down to operate the landing gear manually . . . and put his left hand into flames. "I swung my head around and looked to my rear," he wrote in his diary. "Three Jap Zeros right on my tail and firing like mad! The explosions were their rounds of ammunition hitting my armor plate behind my seat. . . . The fuselage tank had exploded, and the fire was whipping into my lower rear cockpit and then up around my legs." Bond opened the canopy, unhooked his seat belt, and rolled the plane over. The airstream yanked him free, and his parachute popped moments before he hit the ground in a Chinese cemetery, where he hid behind a burial mound until the Hayabusas finished strafing the airfield.

Bond had burns on his hand, torso, and head, and machine gun bullets had laid open his helmet and the skin beneath. Doc Richards gave him first aid and a shot of morphine, then friends bundled him into a jeep and drove him to the monastery. "There were bodies lying everywhere,

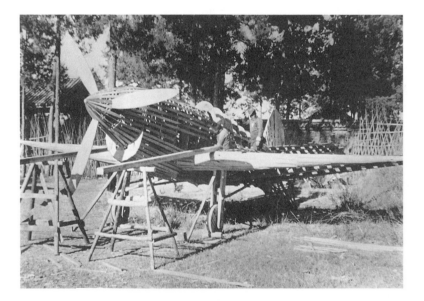

Chinese workmen built decoys from bamboo and canvas, so convincingly that Japanese pilots reported that they destroyed several Tomahawks at Baoshan airfield, several days after it was abandoned by the AVG. (National Air and Space Museum)

in and under charred debris," he wrote of the carnage in Baoshan. "Some were completely dismembered, and others were burned so badly the teeth were showing from fleshless faces. . . . Once Bob Little had to get out of the jeep to move a timber from our path. When he heaved it aside, a human head rolled across the road."

At the monastery, a Chinese doctor tried to amputate Ben Foshee's leg. The pilot drove him away, calling for Doc Richards, but died before the flight surgeon reached the hostel. A former navy pilot, Foshee had been attached to the Adam & Eves for his first combat tour.

The AVG ground crews worked feverishly to repair the damaged Tomahawks. Four planes were flown off to Kunming that afternoon, and another was made ready overnight. In the end, two fighters were written off and stripped of their guns and other gear, which were loaded aboard a U.S. Army transport that was sent over from Kunming on Tuesday morning. Also into the Douglas went Foshee's body, the wounded men, most of the pilots, and some ground crewmen. The transport was so heavily loaded that the pilot had to bounce it off the runway.

They never knew what a narrow escape they had. A few hours earlier, while the 12th Sentai was warming its engines for a return visit to Baoshan, B-17s from India had bombed Mingaladon airport. Two Sallys went up in flames and others were damaged, delaying their mission. That was the AVG's first stroke of luck for May 5. The second came when six Kittyhawks, assigned to escort the Douglas, were delayed at Yunnan-yi. Led by Tex Hill, they didn't reach Baoshan until noon—just as the Japanese raiders crossed into China. Frank Schiel recalled how radioman Ralph Sasser, who was still at the airfield, talked the Panda Bears into attack position: "Through the calm, accurate directions of the BC-5 crew we were able to quickly find the enemy. They consisted of 16 [Nates] circling at an altitude of about 18,000'. [Whitey] Lawlor led the flight into attacking position and started the first run. Lawlor got a flamer on his first run . . . On my first rear attack I got in a good burst. When I looked back the plane was burning in a spin."

Schiel's count was exactly right, and the Panda Bears' claims nearly so. Whitey Lawlor was credited with two Nates, and everyone else—Tex Hill, Frank Schiel, Matt Kuykendall, Freeman Rickets, and Gil Bright—with one apiece, for a total of seven. The Americans described the Japanese fighters as reddish brown on their topside, light gray beneath. Those were the markings of the 11th Sentai, whose commander had been killed at Magwe by the still-missing Cliff Groh. The group had moved up to Mandalay to support the raid on Baoshan. According to Japanese records, it lost four Nates on May 5—a quarter of its strength—and the 27th Sentai lost two Anns, which were no doubt included in the claims submitted by the Panda Bears.

Chapter 16

Piss on Bissell

On May 7, after five months of resistance, the starving remnant of General MacArthur's army raised the white flag in the Philippines—the largest capitulation in U.S. military history, as Singapore had been for the British. There was no resolute last stand in Burma. "The brave and gallant officers and men of the Japanese Forces are scoring overwhelming victories," boasted a Tokyo newspaper, "leaving in their wake the mercilessly scattered remains of the [Allied] forces to scatter in all directions." The Commonwealth army escaped to India, leaving 412 tanks, 8,254 cars and trucks, 420 heavy guns, 11,248 rifles and machine guns, 14,856 artillery shells, and 3,462,302 rounds of small-arms ammunition to be inventoried by the Japanese. (As each Southeast Asian country fell to the Imperial army, Tokyo newspapers ticked off the weapons and raw materials captured there, like a corporate report to the stockholders.) The Chinese abandoned 44,000 tons of lend-lease supplies, along with 30,000 soldiers.

To harry the lost Chinese army, General Obata kept his light bombers and the 77th Sentai Nates on the line in North Burma. The rest of his air force moved to the rear—heavy bombers to Vietnam, a fighter group to Japan, and the other fighters to Magwe and Rangoon.

The JAAF generals didn't have much reason to congratulate themselves on their victory. Between them, Obata and Sugawara had lost 117 aircraft—a quarter of the planes they'd committed to Burma, and far more than they'd lost in any other campaign. The Allies, of course, believed the total to be much higher. Air Vice Marshal Stevenson estimated that 291 Japanese planes were destroyed during the Burma campaign, with the Americans accounting for 217, while CAMCO paid 268 combat bonuses in Burma, Thailand, and along the China-Burma border. (Stevenson presumably didn't include the Loiwing combats in his estimate.) Though a considerable exaggeration, the Allied figures at least didn't dwarf the number of enemy aircraft taking part in the campaign. The same can't be said of the JAAF, which claimed no fewer than 554 Allied planes destroyed in the conquest of Burma!

The JAAF's difficulties in Burma were glossed over by the Japanese press. Individual pilots might die heroically from time to time, and combat losses were reported with reasonable accuracy, but Burma overall was presented as another unsullied victory for the Wild Eagles. The British air force had been defeated yet again, along with an American unit whose name evidently seemed too menacing to publish. "Last autumn," reported one newspaper, "American airmen calling themselves the 'Flying Corps' [sic] reached Kunming and temporarily relieved the Chinese fear by their tall talk. But before long, when the efficient Japanese airmen went into action, they proved to be no more than 'Flying Cats.'" As censored, the jeer made no sense unless the reader happened to know something about the Flying Tigers.

General Obata's units in North Burma would also support a stab into Yunnan province by a motorized regiment under Major General Sakaguchi Shizuo. In AVG mythology, this outfit is called "the elite Red Dragon Division," but it was neither a division nor did it have such a grandiose name. Sakaguchi Detachment was just one of three regiments in the 56th Division, and its assignment—to "pursue the enemy to the

Salween River and if possible destroy him in one blow"—was only an extension of the mop-up in Burma. But Chennault didn't know that. To him, the enemy column seemed a spear aimed at Kunming . . . and if Kunming fell, China would be out of the war. The Douglas transports of CNAC and the Ferry Command could reach "over the Hump" of the Himalayas from Dinjan to Kunming, but Chongqing was beyond their range.

Chennault therefore ordered the AVG and the CAF into action against Sakaguchi Detachment. The work began on Wednesday, May 6, with six Tupelov SBs bombing truck convoys moving toward the Salween. Meanwhile, in the deep river gorge, Japanese troops forced a crossing against the Chinese 36th Division. Tex Hill led the first AVG strike on Thursday morning, accompanied by Eddie Rector, Tom Jones, and Whitey Lawlor. They were "to destroy the Burma Road by blowing it up at a point where a landslide would result or repairs of the road would be difficult." AVG armorers had adapted the Kittyhawk's centerline shackle—intended to hold a fuel tank—to accommodate a 250-kg (550-lb) Russian demolition bomb. Tex, at least, was so equipped on May 7. The other Kittyhawks may have carried demolition bombs, too, or perhaps only the 35-pound "weed cutters" the Panda Bears had deployed on the Burma front. However that may be, the AVG romances relate that landslides wreaked havoc among the "Red Dragons," who retreated pell-mell for the Burma border.

In fact, Sakaguchi Detachment was still at the Salween. On Friday, May 8, Tom Jones and three other Panda Bears flew back to the gorge, armed with weed cutters and escorted by eight Tomahawks. They saw Japanese trucks still massed on the west bank of the river, while engineers worked on a pontoon structure to replace the bridge that had been dynamited by the Chinese. To get at them, the Kittyhawks had to thread their way between the steep walls of the gorge, in single file, unable to deviate from the one straight line. This was sweaty-palm time, as Lew Bishop reported: "Made first pass at an angle of about 50 degrees, speed 300 mph. Dived to within 100 ft. of trucks releasing [fragmentation] bombs in string. Continued on down gorge gaining altitude and turned back. Noticed results of attack as 4 bombs burst amidst line of trucks [and] other two slightly beyond but close enough to do destruction by

fragmentation. Made three straffing passes. . . . On third and fourth attacks drew fire from anti-aircraft gun stationed near road. By the time I
completed my last straffing attack, I noticed one extremely large fire and
two smaller fires amid trucks." Bishop estimated that the Panda Bears
had destroyed fifty trucks and inflicted two hundred casualties.

His dive angle and airspeed weren't radical by navy standards, but
his plane wasn't designed for dive-bombing. Nose-heavy and without
dive brakes, the Kittyhawk wanted to pick up speed without limit.
Bishop had throttled the engine back to idle, forcing the airstream to
turn the big, three-bladed propeller, and the prop to drive the engine—a
fairly effective brake, but one that caused the plane's built-in rudder trim
to pull it to the right. To fly a straight line, Bishop had to *stand* on his left
rudder pedal. Then there was the Kittyhawk's tendency to mush: when
he pulled back on the control stick, to bring the nose up, Bishop could
only hope that he wouldn't keep plunging toward the water, as had happened to John Blackburn on April 28.

On Saturday, rain put a stop to dive-bombing, but the Chinese 36th
Division crossed the river to the north of the Japanese bridgehead,
threatening Sakaguchi's supply line and sending his trucks retreating toward the Burma border. It was Chinese ground troops who broke the
Japanese advance, not the AVG.

At Wujiaba airport, meanwhile, a plot from the warning net caused
the Adam & Eves to scramble. At 18,000 feet Bill Bartling attacked a twin-
engine reconnaissance plane over Lake Kunming. "His first burst caused
the rear cockpit to blow up," Bob Neale reported, "and the Jap started
down making gentle spirals." Two other Tomahawks then joined the
fight. "I circled the fight area," Neale wrote, "and watched the 3 P-40's
making individual runs for about 5 minutes at approximately 16,000
feet . . . after which the plane went into a spinning dive and crashed about
60 miles southwest of the southern tip of the South Lake." Bartling was
credited with the kill—a Mitsubishi Dinah of the 18th Independent
Chutai, which for four years had reconnoitered China without loss. Before
crashing, Captain Takeuchi Hideharu managed to radio Hankou that he'd
seen twenty-seven enemy planes at Wujiaba.

The weather cleared on Sunday, so Chennault sent the Panda Bears
winging back to the Salween. Eddie Rector led the mission, but before

reaching the gorge he heard over the radio that Chinese troops had succeeded in crossing the river. He therefore pushed on to Mangshi, the
soggy airfield used by the Hell's Angels in the last days of Loiwing. He
saw a Japanese reconnaissance plane on the ground, but kept going west
until he found a truck convoy to strafe: "The trucks were so scattered
that I directed the flight to make individual attacks. I dived down, levelled out at 300 ft. . . . and released my bombs at three trucks parked in
a small village. They missed by twenty yards and hit in the village. We
were back to the airdrome by then and I straffed the Jap reconnaissance
plane setting it afire."

Two of the Kittyhawks were equipped with auxiliary fuel tanks, and
they carried on to the border. Here Frank Schiel and Harry Bolster (one
of the flight instructors who'd joined the combat squadrons) found and
strafed another convoy. "Two or three [trucks] were set on fire," Schiel
reported, "indicating that they were carrying gasoline. A few minutes
later we saw the head of the column on a straight stretch of road. . . .
Bolster and I each made two passes, raking the whole line and setting
some of them on fire." The dirty work of ground attack, which in Burma
had brought the AVG to the edge of mutiny, had by now become
routine.

On Monday, May 11, Chiang's 2nd Reserve Division also crossed
the Salween. In a reversal of the situation in Burma, the lightly armed
Chinese now put "the hook" on Sakaguchi Detachment, road-bound by
its vehicles and tanks. In the confusion, AVG crew chief Gale McAllister
made his escape from the refugee horde. Caught on the west bank when
the Salween bridge was dynamited, McAllister took advantage of the
fighting to walk upriver, cross over, and hitch a ride to Kunming, the last
AVG ground crewman to straggle in from Loiwing.

Tom Jones was the very model of an all-American lad, with curly
hair, wide eyes, and open features. In the navy, he'd been a dive-bomber
pilot on *Yorktown*. He'd missed the Panda Bears' tour at Rangoon, having contracted malaria on a tiger hunt with Moose Moss; in April, stationed at Loiwing, he'd suffered from dizzy spells that he concealed from
Tex Hill and Doc Richards. Believing himself to be fully recovered, he
now became one of the AVG's most enthusiastic dive-bomber pilots. On
May 12, Chennault assigned him to take six Kittyhawks to Hanoi to

drop propaganda leaflets, then to bomb and strafe Gia Lam airport. Long after, Link Laughlin recalled the briefing in the ready room at Wujiaba: "Chennault lays the raid out like a football plan in his terse, flat matter-of-fact briefing. . . . *and take-off from [Mengzi] at 1630. Cruise at 14,000. Your ETA over Hanoi will be around 1740. Twenty minutes out, start your letdown to come over the city at 1,000 feet. Drop your leaflets . . . then hit the field. Approach will be from the north at 300 feet. Maintain a two-hundred yard separation. Bomb and strafe on the first pass. If ground fire is minimal, come back for a second strafing run.'"*

Reality seldom matches the ready-room briefing. As soon as they crossed the border, Laughlin's engine began to grumble. ("It always does that when we get into enemy territory.") One pilot turned back to Mengzi, and clouds forced the others down to 3,000 feet, causing them to be spotted from an auxiliary airstrip. Nates came up and chased them to Hanoi, where the Americans ran into a firestorm of antiaircraft fire. Nevertheless they opened their canopies and pitched leaflets over the side. (Addressed *aux Français d'Indochine,* they appealed to the white population to rise against the Japanese.) In string formation, the Kittyhawks then swept down on Gia Lam with the sun behind them, strafing and dropping fragmentation bombs.

Link Laughlin was fourth in line: "I follow [Frank] Schiel down to 300 feet and over the airfield. [Tom] Jones and [John] Donovan are scudding down the runway unloading their fifty-calibers and dropping weed cutters like they were going out of style. The field is erupting like it was the end of the world. Donovan's hit! He goes straight into the runway and skids clear off the end in a big rolling ball of flame. . . . I squeeze down in the cockpit looking for a place to hide. Retract my neck right down into my puckering rectal area."

Bringing up the rear, Lew Bishop saw Laughlin riddle "a DC-3 type Transport." In a cluster of eight parked fighters, he saw four burning. Bishop spotted another cluster beyond that, and he jinked toward it, spilling his six bombs as he swept over at 300 feet. When he pulled up, he saw Laughlin's "transport" on fire and his own bombs bursting among the fighters on the ground. Fifteen planes were destroyed, he thought, and thirty damaged. "All the time," he reported, "the anti-aircraft fire was very heavy and I noticed four [Nates] in our midst. One was on Schiel's tail and

I started after him when I noticed Jones roll over and go down on him. The Jap turned away then back at Jones, passing above him." Laughlin saw the Japanese fighter, too. It blew up "like a gas well," he recalled.

North of Hanoi, the Panda Bears went into a thunderstorm so violent they had to fly on instruments. Afterward, they picked up the Michelin and flew IFR to Lao Kai on the border, then up the green valley to Mengzi, where they landed at 6:43 PM. When Bishop taxied off the runway, his low-fuel light winked on. Laughlin, too, was out of gas, the result of a bullet through his right wing tank.

It appeared to be Chiang Mai all over again, with the better part of a Japanese fighter group destroyed at the cost of one man shot down, and was so reported in the American press. But as with the 64th Sentai, the death of the JAAF at Gia Lam was greatly exaggerated. The airport was occupied by one squadron of light bombers and another of fighters. Most of the fighters were Nates, but Nagano Force (as the 81st Independent Chutai was called) also had received the first nine Ki-45s off the Kawasaki assembly line. The Ki-45 Toryu (Dragon Killer) was a twin-engine interceptor with twice the heft of a Hayabusa, and it was probably one of these that Laughlin flamed on the ground. The Japanese noted only that one Nate was shot down and that "three or four planes"— type unspecified—were destroyed on the ground by incendiary bullets and fragmentation bombs.

In Chongqing, the more optimistic estimate prevailed. "If we destroy fifteen Nippon planes every day," Madame Chiang exulted, "soon none will be left." The Generalissimo promoted Jones, Schiel, and Bishop to vice squadron leaders, and Laughlin was bumped up to flight leader. Curiously, John Donovan wasn't mentioned in the dispatch, though it was traditional to promote those killed in action.

It was also traditional that a pilot should know when he was flying his last mission. After all, if we are guaranteed a premonition of death, then without premonitions we can live forever. Among Donovan's belongings, the Panda Bears found support for this comforting fiction in a message addressed to his parents in Alabama: "Dear Folks You must not feel badly about my death the small part that I have played in the war though it has cost me my life I am glad to give that. Life has meant much to me but not so much that I am too distressed at leaving and neither must you be. I had only a few things planned for the future one of the most important was a nice home. Momma will please me much if she will live in a more comfortable home with many flowers and trees. I am happy and so must she be love to all—John Junior." They sent it as a telegram, without preamble or explanation. It reached Montgomery before his last letter home, in which Donovan had pondered his career options after July 4, and asked his mother to find out what rank he'd receive if he came home and returned to active duty. "If the Navy thinks that I would accept a commission as an Ensign," he warned, "after the experience that I have had over here, they are crazy."

In addition to the P-40E Kittyhawks that were trickling in, Chennault was responsible for fetching the Republic P-43 Lancers being assembled at Karachi airport by U.S. Army mechanics and AVG ground crewmen. He had to detach men from his combat squadrons to pick them up, even though the P-43s were intended for the Chinese. There were at least three such missions. The first took George Burgard, Jim Cross, Dick Rossi, and a dozen Chinese pilots to Karachi, where they spent two weeks on transition training. (Among the check pilots was Elwyn Gibbon, who in 1938 had flown a Vultee bomber in the CAF 14th Squadron at Hankou.) They spent another two weeks trying to fly the Lancers to China. One Chinese pilot was killed, four hospitalized, and six P-43s wrecked before Burgard led the survivors into Wujiaba on May 23.

Two Lancers, abandoned by their Chinese pilots at Dinjan, were commandeered by Colonel Caleb Haynes of the Ferry Command. He put them to use escorting his Douglas transports and scouting Japanese airfields in Burma. This was such a success that when Charlie Sawyer and Bob Layher came through Dinjan, ferrying Kittyhawks to Kunming, the colonel commandeered those planes as well. He'd have taken more, but the Old Man protested that he needed the Kittyhawks in China: "Thanks very much for the quart of Old Schenley [sic] which you sent me. It reminds me of home a great deal. . . . I regret very much that I am unable to send you six more P-40's. Our squadron strength now averages about eight P-40's and we are still conducting very active combat operations against our little brown friends." He took the opportunity to ask for more supplies, including cigarettes. Colonel Haynes did his best. From mid-April to mid-June, the Ferry Command hauled *two tons* of cigarettes to Kunming, along with 698 tons of fuel, ordnance, and miscellaneous stuff. Returning, the Douglas transports brought out Chinese tin, tungsten ore—and hog bristles, prized by the U.S. Navy for paintbrushes.

Chennault also mentioned that he was sending Harvey Greenlaw to India "to serve as our supervisor for distribution of supplies and as liaison officer to the 10th Air Force and the Ferry Command." He'd replace Robert DeWolfe, the navy commander who handled these jobs at the AVG Calcutta office, and who'd now return to Chongqing and his original assignment at the U.S. Military Mission. Sue Upfill, the Rangoon refugee who clerked for DeWolfe, recalled the Greenlaws' arrival in Calcutta. "We're closing the office and moving to Delhi," Harvey told her. "Olga and I leave tomorrow to make the arrangements." Upfill would follow on the overnight train, escorting the AVG records and Lucy the dog. She declined the dog duty, and got "a look of animosity" from Olga's green eyes.

In Delhi—"prostrate in the May heat"—the Greenlaws moved into the Cecil Hotel suite reserved for Bill Pawley. But what did Harvey do, to justify this billet? As liaison officer, he was nowhere near Dinjan, where the Ferry Command operated from a perforated-steel runway, or to Calcutta, where the 10th Air Force bombers were based. As for expediting supplies, Commander DeWolfe had managed that quite well from Calcutta, and Pappy Paxton also spent most of his time in India on supply matters. AVG veterans later speculated that Harvey had applied for a commission in the U.S. Army, was turned down, and therefore packed his bags for home. In any event, he and Olga never returned to Kunming, though the Cecil Hotel became a favorite rest stop for AVG ferry pilots. Duke Hedman, as Sue Upfill recalled, "could always be found in the music room playing on the grand piano."

M adame Chiang ordered the AVG to support the 30,000 Chinese troops cut off in Burma—eighteen sorties a day would do nicely, she thought. Chennault gave the assignment to the Adam & Eves, though by the time the orders were filtered through him and Bob Neale, the missions generally involved only two Kittyhawks, once a day. In the vastness of North Burma, the Adam & Eves rarely saw the Japanese army, let alone the Chinese. Chennault wrote a long and careful letter to Madame, explaining that the distances were too great, the weather too foul, and his planes too undependable for him to follow the letter of her instructions. In the five years since he'd enlisted in the service of the Chiangs, it was the closest he'd come to insubordination.

The Panda Bears, meanwhile, harassed the Japanese in Vietnam. On Friday, May 15, Gil Bright took four Kittyhawks to Lao Kai on the border in an attempt "to blow up the daily train that comes up from the south." They missed the train, but another flight managed to catch it on Saturday. "With steam squirting out of the boiler from fifty caliber holes, the engineer runs it into a mountain tunnel," Link Laughlin recalled. "'Hooo man!' hollers [Lew] Bishop, 'Let's catch him coming out the other side.' [But] that train crew is endowed with some sense of survival. They aren't about to come out the other side. Tunnels are security. But Bishop hops over the mountain and hangs around for ten minutes waiting for the engineer to come out and commit suicide."

They returned to Kunming to learn that Tom Jones was dead. He and Jim Howard had been practicing on the target range, a small plateau a mile or so from Wujiaba, using dummy bombs filled with white powder; on his second dive, Jones augered in. Perhaps he'd suffered another of his blackouts, or perhaps he was the second victim of the Kittyhawk's reluctance to follow its nose out of a dive. He was buried in the Chinese airmen's cemetery near Wujiaba, between John Blackburn and Ben Foshee.*

The Panda Bears returned to Lao Kai on Sunday, May 17. Bus Keeton had been scheduled for the mission, but when Robert Scott of the Ferry Command asked to go along, Keeton gave up his Kittyhawk to further the cause of melding the army and the AVG. The pilots had voted thumbs-down on Homer Sanders, whom Harvey Greenlaw had fetched from India to audition for command of the 23rd Fighter Group. Now Colonel Scott was trying out for the job.

*The bodies of most of the Tigers killed in China were eventually returned to the United States. Ben Foshee, for example, is buried at the church cemetery in Red Level, Alabama, where his gravestone is occasionally defaced because it bears a foreign flag and the information that he flew for China, which, ironically, is taken to mean he was a traitor to his country rather than one of its heroes.

Lew Bishop led the flight with two Panda Bears and the thirty-four-year-old colonel following him, while two Hell's Angels provided top cover. Fifty miles inside Vietnam, R. T. Smith spotted the elusive locomotive steaming north. He radioed Bishop, who told him to strafe the train while the Panda Bears took care of the railroad station. The Kittyhawks then dove on Lao Kai from out of the sun. "We approached the freight yard from South to North," Pete Wright recalled. "Bishop came down in a steep glide and released his bombs at about 500 feet. I was a few hundred yards behind him and just as I was releasing my bombs I saw him pull up in a steep climbing turn to the left. About four feet of flame was coming out of the tail of his plane. I called to him over the radio to jump and he rolled on his back and left the plane. His parachute opened immediately and his plane crashed and exploded a moment later. The wind drifted him towards the East. . . . He landed almost in the center of the town and was alive when he disappeared into the trees."

Lew Bishop was captured three days later. According to a Tokyo newspaper, he professed contempt for the Chinese and admiration for the Japanese fliers he'd faced in Burma. As for the AVG, he supposedly gave this report: "At the time when the war of Greater East Asia started, there were about 300 American volunteer fliers and ground crew men in the [Chinese] Air Force. However, at the time when I was shot down, there remained only about 50 American fliers and 100 ground crew members and there were only 45 Curtiss P No. 40 type planes left."

Bishop was the fourth AVG pilot to be lost in less than two weeks—not a run of luck calculated to encourage the others to join the 23rd Fighter Group. They were at the breaking point, many of them, worn down by combat, by the nightmares that preceded and followed it, and by the alien food and climate. Diarrhea was an almost constant companion, and most had been felled at one time or another with dengue fever or malaria. ("Even my eyelashes were sore," Jasper Harrington said of his bout with these tropical diseases.) Bob Neale had weighed 170 pounds when he reached Burma the previous August; now he was down to 138 pounds. As a rule, the more combat a man had seen, the more anxious he was to go home, or at least to settle into a billet that didn't oblige him to fly into the guns of the Japanese. In his diary, George Burgard wrote of Jim

Cross: "He is all through flying over here and nothing will change his mind. He is just plain scared—but so are we all." In Cross's case, it seems to have been the harrying journey with the P-43 Lancers that broke his nerve.

Chennault understood fear. He'd already found noncombat jobs for a half-dozen men who'd lost their nerve, and he now extended the same courtesy to Jim Cross and also to Hank Geselbracht, who'd refused to go on the most recent Lao Kai mission.

In their diaries and letters, the men voiced more mundane concerns: worries about health; concern for wives, sweethearts, and parents; and resentment against the army's policy of offering them commissions in the reserve rather than in the regular army. On May 18, Chennault took Bob Neale aside and asked him to become executive officer of the 23rd Fighter Group with the rank of lieutenant colonel. "Might do it," Neale allowed—"if he can get me a permanent commission."

On Thursday, May 21, Clayton Bissell flew to Kunming for a meeting in the auditorium of Hostel Number One. For the pilots and ground crewmen of the AVG, this was their first view of the man who'd command the U.S. Army Air Forces in China. They weren't impressed. The newly minted brigadier general struck them a womanish martinet, like the British officers they'd encountered at Singapore, Rangoon, and Magwe, whose manner and uniform Bissell liked to ape.

First Chennault explained the financial terms. Any man who wanted to go home would be released from his CAMCO contract on July 4 and be paid for leave not taken plus $500 travel expenses. If instead he agreed to return to U.S. service in China, he'd get the same cash settlements, and he'd also receive the difference between his army pay and what he'd have earned by serving out a full year with CAMCO, which for many of them was several months beyond July. That seemed fair to everyone.

Then Bissell took the podium to discuss an even more important matter: their military rank. Any ground crewman who stayed on in China would become a technical sergeant, entitled to wear four stripes. That was a blow to Don Rodewald, who'd expected to become an officer, and his disappointment was widely shared. "They didn't offer [the ground crewmen] a thing," he wrote disgustedly. "Looks like most of them will take their chances with the home draft board."

As for the pilots, anyone who accepted induction would become a reserve officer in the Army of the United States, probably with the rank of major. They, too, were disappointed, though reserve commissions were the norm in wartime—even the two brigadier generals, Chennault and Bissell, were still colonels in the regular army. To understand the pilots' anger, it may help to remember that they'd entered military service during the 1930s as reservists on four-year tours, and that many had joined the AVG precisely because the four years were running out and they expected to be unemployed thereafter. A regular-army commission had been the grail in 1941, and it remained so in 1942. Graduates of the Great Depression, they had no experience of a world in which jobs could be found for the asking.

Bus Keeton stood up and insisted on this point: he wanted a regular commission. Bissell lost his temper. Regulations were regulations, and if Keeton or anyone else hoped to get around the regulations by taking a civilian flying job with CNAC or Pan Am—well, forget it! That route was already closed. "And for any of you who don't want to join the Army," Bissell supposedly concluded, "I can guarantee to have your draft boards waiting for you when you step down a gangplank onto U.S. soil."

But of course they'd be drafted! Able-bodied men in their twenties, did they really think they could sit out the rest of the war? Perhaps a few did, but most wanted just a few weeks at home before returning to duty with the army, navy, or marines. Yet it was Bissell's mention of the draft that offended them more than anything else. "Instead of keeping us here," Keeton wrote in his diary, "he changed a few minds to the contrary. There will probably be 3 or 4 pilots stay." This was a very good forecast, as matters developed.

It was a tragedy that Bissell was so stupid, Chennault so uninvolved (or so pleased to see Bissell with pie on his face), and the men so prickly that they couldn't have compromised on this point. Stilwell was authorized to offer a commission "up to and including Colonel" to anyone he wanted to keep in China, even if that resulted in an organization top-heavy with oak leaves and eagles. Bissell knew this perfectly well, for he was handling the radio traffic while Stilwell trekked out of Burma. Even the matter of a regular-army commission was negotiable, as later events would show. Yet Bissell and Chennault hoarded rank as if the money was coming out of their own pockets, bidding four stripes for a ground crewman and a major's gold leaves for a pilot or staff officer.

As a matter of fact, behind his bluster, Bissell had undergone a change of heart with respect to the AVG. In his radiograms to Washington, he no longer sniped at Chennault and his men, but sang their praises in words like those the Old Man had been wont to use. "AVG has been at its best in past ten days," Bissell radioed the War Department earlier in the month, "and can do a job of work if kept supplied with planes and parts." And when General Marshall forwarded the president's congratulations to the AVG, as requested by Chennault, Bissell actually improved on the language. It was standard procedure to paraphrase radiograms, so an enemy agent couldn't break the code by comparing the original to what was distributed at the other end. Bissell's revisions seemed calculated to flatter the AVG. This was the first sentence of Roosevelt's message: "The conspicuous gallantry and daring of the AVG officers combined with their extraordinary efficiency is a source of tremendous pride throughout America." As touched up by Bissell, it read: "The *outstanding gallantry and conspicuous daring* of the American Volunteer Group, combined with their *almost unbelievable efficiency,* is a source of tremendous pride throughout *the whole of America* [my italics]." It was the hyped version, not Roosevelt's more austere original, that went onto the AVG bulletin board and into the Flying Tiger histories.

And Bissell continued to plead the AVG's case, even after the blowout at Hostel Number One. "Chennault and others have done wonders with very little," he radioed General Marshall toward the end of the month. "They cannot do the impossible. The wholesome effect of promises of help by the president and the [War Department] is wearing off due to our failure to deliver a single man to replace steady combat losses."

Bissell even supplied a star for Chennault's shoulder tabs, though he probably didn't know it. Early in May, Jimmy Doolittle had passed through Kunming on his way home, and he stopped for lunch at Hostel Number One. He noticed that Chennault still wore the silver eagles of a colonel. Doolittle, too, had just been promoted to brigadier, with Bissell doing the honors in Chongqing, pinning stars from his personal supply on America's latest hero. (Had he brought them to China, or were they

The Old Man in his office at Wujiaba airport. Chennault appears to be wearing a mix of U.S. Army and Chinese insignia, including (on his left shoulder only) a general's star given to him by Jimmy Doolittle. (National Air and Space Museum)

flown in with the typewriter ribbons and other necessities?) Doolittle unpinned one of his stars and gave it to Chennault, without mentioning where it had come from.

Part of Sakaguchi Detachment still clung to the west bank of the Salween, and on Friday, May 22, the AVG was ordered back into the gorge to blast them out. This time Chennault gave the job to the Adam & Eves, who'd received the latest batch of Kittyhawks to come in from Africa. It was their first attempt at bombing. The weather was clear when they took off, but deteriorated as they neared the Salween, and they had trouble spotting the cluster of tents on the west bank that was supposed to hide Japanese artillery. Bob Little led the attack echelon of four Kittyhawks. On his wing was Snuffy Smith. "After making several circles," Smith reported, "Little peeled off and following him I saw he was diving on the target. At about 1,000 feet, before Little had levelled off, I heard an explosion. Glancing at his plane I saw a burst of flame and black smoke midway of his left wing. He immediately went into a tight spin, I now noticed half his left wing was missing. He made no attempt to jump, or pull out, and was on fire when he hit the ground, when his plane exploded." A P-40 veteran from the 8th Pursuit Group at Mitchel Field, Little had built up his score in unspectacular but steady fashion, and at his death his bonus account credited him with 10.5 enemy aircraft destroyed.

On Sunday, May 24, Chennault took the 2nd Squadron off the Vietnam run and assigned it to the Salween. The target was a town in which three hundred Japanese troops were besieged by the Chinese 38th Division. The Panda Bears grumbled that they were drawing all the dirty jobs; Bus Keeton blamed "our two eager squadron leaders," meaning Tex Hill and Eddie Rector. Actually, Hill was in Delhi, enjoying the swimming pool at the Cecil Hotel with Duke Hedman, Olga Greenlaw, and Fred and Helen Hodges. It was Rector who assigned the missions, which were led in turn by himself, Frank Schiel, and John Petach. With twenty pilots and eight Kittyhawks, Rector filled the missions on a rotating basis. Butch Carney's flight instructors were blooded one by one: Arnold Shamblin on Monday, Van Shapard on Thursday, Lester Hall on Friday. Also flying his first combat mission was Ed Conant, the former PBY skipper who'd managed to wreck three Tomahawks at Kyedaw airfield.

The CAF joined this campaign with its SB bombers and I-15 biplane fighters, dating from the early days of the Sino-Japanese War. The weather was impossible, obliging the raiders to struggle over 12,000-foot peaks through clouds and blinding rain. More often than not, they turned back. On Thursday, May 28, Frank Adkins got through and dropped six weed-cutters on the Japanese. "Weather was very bad," he reported, "cloudy and raining. Found objective and only had 1200 ft. ceiling. I dove to 800 feet and released bombs. I saw all six bombs hit in the center of the town. The bombs hit about 50 feet apart causing quite a bit of damage to wooden buildings in the small town." And on Friday the AVG got through in force: eight Kittyhawks loaded with fragmentation bombs, with Tomahawks flying top cover. "We passed through some fairly bad weather," Bus Keeton noted in his diary. They found the walled town and attacked it in pairs. "Ed Rector and I laid all of our bombs in the middle of the town and started a fire." With this boost, the Chinese took the town—for the AVG, its last shot in the Salween campaign.

On Saturday, May 30, it was back to Vietnam. Gil Bright took the Kittyhawks down to Mengzi, then along the Michelin 70 miles into enemy territory, on what appears to have been another shakedown for inexperienced pilots. Bright's flight consisted of Lester Hall and Ed Conant—each flying his second combat mission—and Curt Smith, putting himself in harm's way for the first time since his inglorious retreat to Mingaladon on Christmas Day.

E ight pilots went ahead and took the tests that determined their suitability for commissions in the U.S. Army, though most didn't meet the posted criteria: four years of college, no older than twenty-six, and a graduate of army flight school, among other requirements. In Chongqing on June 4, they were interviewed by Bissell and took a battery of written and physical exams.

Bissell approved six of the applications. Regulations were regulations, he'd proclaimed at Hostel Number One, but behind the scenes he could bend regulations with the best of them. Thus he recommended Catfish Raine for a commission, though as a former navy pilot Raine had never been near an army flight school. He signed off on Charlie Sawyer, who'd failed the hearing test. And he approved George Burgard and Charlie Bond, who were too old, noting beside their names that the age requirement should be waived for them. Also passing muster were Frank Schiel and Ernest (Bus) Loane, formerly a flight instructor at Yunnan-yi. These six pilots, the induction board concluded, were "fully qualified and recommended for such commission." Each would become a second lieutenant in the regular army, while receiving a reserve commission as captain or major.

Incredibly, Bissell never told them that he'd support their applications. They flew back to Kunming believing they'd been turned down, for reasons varying from defective hearing to venereal disease— another insult, it seemed to them, from the officer who'd come to represent that most unloved creature in any organization, the son-of-a-bitch from headquarters. All the frustration, bitterness, disillusion, fatigue, and war weariness of the past year was now focused on this unfortunate man, who was only trying to do his best for the U.S. Army and (as he saw it) for the AVG. As the story is told, Chennault's men got their revenge by teaching the gas coolie at Wujiaba to chant: "Piss on Bissell!" Smiling and bowing, and believing it to be an American greeting, he shouted this pleasantry to the passengers of all incoming planes.

Chapter 17

Worse Than You Know

Forty-eight hours after Curt Smith's foray into Vietnam, he was put in charge of the 23rd Fighter Group—a civilian, commanding U.S. Army personnel, by order of a unit of the Chinese Air Force! His first pilots arrived the same day, June 1, and were distributed among the AVG squadrons for seasoning. Fresh from flight school and transition training, they nevertheless accomplished what the Flying Tigers had not, checking out in the Tomahawks with no worse mishap than a ground loop. "We had two Army Air Corp Pilots, 2nd Lt. Leonard M. Butsch, Jr., and 2nd Lt. Lee N. Minor, assigned to us and attached," wrote Dan Hoyle in the 3rd Squardon log. "They flew this afternoon in P-40 airplane and did very well. This looks like the army really means to take over very soon."

And a more formidable group was on its way: six twin-engine North American B-25 Mitchells, staging through India as the down payment on Chennault's long-promised bomber group. The flight into China was hazardous under the best of circumstances, but someone—the AVGs blamed

Bissell, of course, though General Brereton in Calcutta seems more likely—ordered the pilots to bomb Lashio en route. Burdened with cots, duffel, a full bomb load, and extra cases of ammunition, the Mitchells took off from Dinjan on Wednesday morning, June 3. To hit Lashio, they were on a flight path of 700 miles, rather than the customary 400 miles directly over the Hump. The first leg posed no great problem, and their bombs tore up Lashio's red-clay airfield and destroyed a Mitsubishi Dinah on the ground. Unfortunately, two Nates managed to take off and give chase. Four Mitchell pilots fled for China at full throttle, only to run out of gas and crash in the mountains before they reached Kunming.

The other pilots had the nerve to stay at cruising speed. The Nates shot up both Mitchells and killed Wilmer Zeuske, a radioman, but the B-25s limped into Wujiaba airport—two out of six. As always, Chennault believed that a bit more attention to detail would have prevented the disaster, as he radioed Caleb Haynes in Dinjan: "Please forward following to [General Brereton:] *Request all B-25's be equipped auxiliary tanks giving minimum one hour additional endurance before coming China. Better bomb sight also required for flight leaders at least.* Thanks. Please advise future bomber crews [about] AVG radio setup, frequency, call letters etc. Also need for getting frequent weather reports. . . . Sergeant Zeuske killed in action June 3. Require replacement urgently."

M eanwhile, thousands of miles to the east, two naval task forces were groping for each other, toward a combat that was arguably the turning point of the Pacific War. The Battle of Midway was inspired by Jimmy Doolittle's raid upon Japan: captured in China, some of his airmen claimed they'd taken off from "an island 500 kilometers west of Midway." The island was a fiction, but the threat was real enough. Fleets of four-engine bombers could indeed be launched from mid-Pacific, to strike Japan on a one-way flight, landing in China or Siberia. So the Japanese set out to capture Midway. Losses were huge on both sides, but in the end U.S. dive-bombers sank all four Japanese aircraft carriers and thereby doomed their complement of 261 planes. It was the worst defeat ever inflicted upon the Empire of the Sun.

For the same reason, the Japanese army went on the march in China, moving inland to "destroy the air bases from which the enemy might conduct aerial raids on the Japanese Homeland." It committed nearly two hundred thousand men to Operation Sei-go. They captured Zhuzhou on June 6, finding an airfield with two crushed-stone runways and an "underground hangar" large enough to hold forty or fifty bombers—so impressive a piece of work that it was ascribed to American engineers. The Japanese trenched the runways, gave the same treatment to two other captured airfields, and executed tens of thousands of peasants who may or may not have helped the Doolittle raiders. Like the other great battles that had raged in East China since 1938, Sei-go was ignored by the American press: yellow men fighting yellow men, after all.

The Panda Bears were scheduled to move up to Beishiyi airfield outside Chongqing, to protect the capital during the summer bombing season. Sei-go convinced Chennault that he needed a squadron in East China, too, an assignment he gave to the Adam & Eves. Before the squadrons left Kunming, Colonel Wang Shu-ming gathered the Americans in the main hangar at Wujiaba. He decorated thirty-three pilots and three ground crewmen with the Chinese Cloud Banner for "bravery and outstanding combat performance." They included fifteen Adam & Eves: Bill Bartling, John Blackburn (dead), Charlie Bond, George Burgard, John Dean, John Farrell, Cokey Hoffman (dead), Bob Little (dead), Bob Neale, Bob Prescott, Joe Rosbert, Dick Rossi, Sandy Sandell (dead), Snuffy Smith, and Fritz Wolf. Among the Panda Bears, nine pilots were decorated: Noel Bacon, Gil Bright, Tom Cole (dead), Tex Hill, Jim Howard, Ken Merritt (dead), Moose Moss, Jack Newkirk (dead), and John Petach. The Hell's Angels came away with an equal number: Parker Dupouy, Tom Haywood, Duke Hedman, Ken Jernstedt, George McMillan, Chuck Older, Eddie Overend, Bill Reed, and R. T. Smith. Also decorated were line chief Harry Fox, radioman Alex Mihalko, and armorer Herb Pistole.

Colonel Wang then presented each ace and double ace with a Five Star or Ten Star Wing Medal. Chinese troops provided an honor guard, and a band played martial music.

When the ceremony was over, the Adam & Eves and Panda Bears took off for Chongqing. The Hell's Angels stayed behind to guard Kunming with eight Tomahawks and fourteen pilots—including the army lieutenants and Cliff Groh, who turned up that day after his four-week odyssey by horseback and train. "We of the Third Pursuit Squadron," mused Dan Hoyle, "are here alone with the Chinese air force of P-43 airplanes which do not go into combat." Neither did the Hell's Angels, come to that. If the JAAF bombed along the Salween, the heroes of Rangoon and Magwe sprinted to their Tomahawks as before, but only to maintain a protective umbrella over the airport. It was all their weary engines could manage. From time to time, more army pilots came from India, and the Hell's Angels checked them out in Tomahawks. When they had no better entertainment, they watched the CAF pilots crash their P-43s, as happened once or twice a week.

Chennault's planes were now scattered as never before, in a triangle 400 miles to a side. A CNAC Douglas flew the 1st Squadron ground crews to Guilin in East China. The airfield was located in a range of sugarloaf peaks, like 800-foot pylons sticking out of the paddy fields, so close together that a pilot couldn't fly a normal traffic pattern but had to thread his way among them. The mile-long runway was surfaced with crushed rock, and there were revetments large enough to hide a Boeing B-17. (For which purpose, indeed, Guilin and Zhuzhou had been built in the fall of 1940—the only tangible result of the Morgenthau-Chennault scheme to bomb Japan from bases in East China.) The men bunked five miles away in dormitories tucked against the mountains, each with a stone foundation and camphor-wood sheathing—like "a small camp in the north woods," Don Rodewald marveled. They had showers, dining hall, clubhouse with pool table, and an air-raid shelter in a cave.

After breakfast on Wednesday, June 10, the ground crews stepped outside to see a Nakajima Nate circling the airfield. "We could watch him well with our glass," Rode noted. He drove to the field with armorer Robert Neal (not to be confused with the squadron leader) and crew chief Robert Rasmussen, stopping at the radio station manned by Ralph Sasser. "He has his transmitter in one large cave and his receiver in a small one," Rode wrote. "While there we got word of bombers headed this way. We went down to the field where Neal, Rass and myself got perched up on the ledge of one of the bluffs ready for the show. We didn't wait long before we heard them. The AcAc [antiaircraft guns] started in on them and then we started our cameras going.

Three passed over on each side of us dropped their eggs and then left."

The raiders came from Canton on the coast: Kawasaki Lily medium bombers, fixed-gear Nakajima Nates, and—though nobody identified them as such—twin-engine Kawasaki Ki-45 Toryu fighters. They did little damage. As Chennault had long ago noted, an unoccupied airfield made a poor target, especially one built of native materials and maintained by coolie labor.

CNAC brought the Old Man to Guilin that evening, and the pilots followed on Thursday. Two planes were delayed by engine trouble, and another crashed midway, but before dark eleven Tomahawks and Kitty-hawks had reached their new station. Chennault anticipated a follow-up raid, so he scheduled reveille for 3 AM. Two hours later, the Adam & Eves were hunched over their cribbage boards when the usual scout came over the field. They ran for their planes, took off, and climbed to the positions Chennault had assigned: George Burgard's flight at 21,000 feet, Bob Neale's at 18,000, and Charlie Bond's at 15,000, circling like hawks to the west of Guilin. It was just before 6 AM on Friday, June 12.

The raiders came from Canton: five Kawasaki Lilys of the 90th Sentai, escorted by eight Nakajima Nates of the 54th Sentai and five Toryus of Nagano Force—the same 81st Independent Chutai that had opposed the AVG at Hanoi. The Toryus had moved to Canton under Sergeant Ie-iri Jiro to lend some muscle to Operation Sei-go. For a month his twin-engine fighters had escorted the Lilys to Liuzhou, Guilin, and other East China fields, and not once had the CAF come up to challenge them. Sergeant Ieiri therefore adapted the Ki-45s for ground attack, slinging 110-pound bombs beneath their wings and loading the 20-mm nose gun with explosive shells.

Droning in from the southeast at 16,500 feet, the Lilys bombed at 5:58 AM and turned for home. The Nates were supposed to stay with them while the Toryus dealt with enemy fighters. As so often happened with Japanese formations, however, the squadrons had drifted apart even before the Americans swept down on them.

In the top flight, George Burgard saw four Nates. He put his Toma-hawk into a screaming dive, dropping 9,000 feet in seconds. "I fired several long bursts from a good position," he reported. "However, I observed no results as I was forced to recover sharply to avoid another Jap who was practicing his deflection shooting on me. The melee lasted for several minutes during which I fired at three Jap planes several times." Then he saw another Nate, chasing an AVG fighter that was streaming smoke from its engine. The burning plane belonged to Allen Wright, formerly of the CAF flight school: his engine had been hit by the greenhouse gunner on a Lily, but he went on to attack three "light bombers." Luckily for Wright, the Nate drove him away before he discovered that he was chasing three cannon-equipped fighters.

Burgard took care of the Nate, firing bursts at long range until the Japanese pilot turned away. Then Burgard escorted Wright back to the airfield, where the ex-instructor bellied in, spraining his back and wrecking his plane. Burgard then set up a patrol to the south of Guilin, in which work he was joined by 2nd Lieutenant Romney Masters in what seems to have been the first combat action for the 23rd Fighter Group. Spotting a Nate and a Toryu, Burgard went after the fixed-gear fighter and left the young army officer to take care of what seemed the easier target. The Nate wriggled out of the way, however, so Burgard, too, made a run on the twin-engine plane. "The bomber was light, fast, and exceptionally maneuverable," he reported. "He dove sharply for the ground and made a sharp turn." Then the Nate returned, put a shot through the Tomahawk's left aileron, and dove away with Burgard after him.

"The [Nate] skidded badly and fell off on a wing," Burgard wrote. "I pulled up and saw he had run into the side of a sharp peak and blew up." Masters had vanished by this time, so Burgard decided to finish off the twin-engine plane as well. His nose guns were dead, however, and the "light bomber" proved strangely elusive. "I got back some altitude and picked up the bomber hedgehopping through the sharp hills," Burgard wrote. "Each time I got at him from the rear he would slip in and out of the peaks. . . . After about five or six runs I caught him in a valley and got right in behind him but he turned almost 90° and began making 360° vertical turns around a sharp cone. . . . We were never more than 150' from the ground. On a pass from above my right fifty started working and in a brief interval his left engine caught fire. . . . I throttled back and continued to shoot until he dragged his wing on a small knob and mushed in." This was the command Toryu. Sergeant Ieiri died in the crash, but his enlisted gunner climbed out and was captured by the Chinese.

Joe Rosbert, flying a Kittyhawk in the low-level echelon, also attacked a Toryu thinking it was a bomber. The plane looped up and over, then fled in the opposite direction. Rosbert used his dive speed to gain altitude for another attack. This time, as he recalled long after, "a quick burst of the six fifties tore off part of his wing and the Jap spun towards the sharp mountains below."

Charlie Bond tried the same tactic, only to have the Toryu's rear gunner put a bullet through the Kittyhawk's coolant system. The yellow overheat light came on and smoke poured out of the instrument panel. Then two Nates came after him. Bond put his plane in a power dive, made himself small in front of the armor plate, and wondered whether to bail out or make a dead-stick landing. The Japanese pilots must have believed it was a death dive, for they peeled off and left him to belly into a flooded paddy field. Bond was thrown against the gunsight, stunning him. After a minute or two he climbed out, gathered his flight gear, and made his way to a telephone. He was on the railroad twenty-five miles southwest of Guilin, and a missionary priest picked him up and took him into Yongfu. "The reverend told me that this was the greatest moment in the life of the village," Bond wrote in his diary. "The Flying Tigers are heroes to them, and now they had seen one." They expressed their pleasure by strewing firecrackers in his path, giving him fresh burns to go with those from his Baoshan shoot-down the previous month.

Bob Neale wasn't having a good morning, either. The squadron leader got a few hits on the Lilys, then found himself with a Toryu on his tail. "Thought it was a Me 110," he wrote, referring to the twin-engine German fighter that had helped inspire the design of the Ki-45. "Had a hell of a time getting away."

Altogether, the Adam & Eves were credited with nine Japanese planes that Friday. George Burgard, Bill Bartling, John Dean, and Dick Rossi each claimed a Nate shot down, though only one was actually lost. On the other hand, the damage inflicted on the twin-engine aircraft was actually higher than the AVG believed. Bartling, Burgard, and Dean were each credited with a bomber, and Joe Rosbert with two. Against these claims, one Lily medium bomber was indeed shot down at Guilin, plus two Toryus. Another Toryu crashed on the way home, and two Lilys that made it back to base were so badly damaged they had to be written off.

Worse, the two Toryus that did survive the combat had developed wrinkles on their sides, suggesting that the Ki-45 wasn't up to the high-g-force maneuvers favored by Japanese pilots. After assessing this dismal result, the JAAF called off its campaign against Guilin, and the Kawasaki fighters were switched to ground-attack duties until the airframe could be strengthened.

Japanese press coverage of this battle makes interesting reading. Until the Battle of Midway, Tokyo newspapers had reported losses with reasonable accuracy, but no longer. "Nine American aircraft of the Curtiss-Hawker P-40 type were downed by the Japanese Air Unit in a fierce combat," the *Japan Times & Advertiser* reported of the Guilin action. "In the breath-taking aerial duel, the Japanese lost only two planes."

The Adam & Eves were celebrating their victory when the Chinese brought in the gunner from the command Toryu. The prisoner identified himself as Corporal Honda Kei, a member of Nagano Force since February. Honda proved to be something less than a dedicated samurai. "What are you fighting for?" the Americans asked him through an interpreter.

"I don't know," he replied.

"Do you think the Japanese will win the war?"

"I have no opinion on that."

"What did you do before you went in the army?"

"Raised chickens," Honda said.

He went on to tell the Americans what he knew about the defenses at Canton and Hankou, and he identified his fighter as a "Model 45"—the first time the AVG learned the *kitai* (air frame) number of a JAAF plane. Honda also told them about the large-caliber gun in the Toryu's nose, and that every second 20-mm shell was explosive. The Adam & Eves were greatly sobered by this information. Not only had they attacked a fighter believing it to be a bomber, but they'd been up against cannon. "No more head on runs for me," Bob Neale vowed.

Victorious Adam & Eves at Guilin. Standing, from left: Snuffy Smith, Corporal Honda, Bill Bartling, and George Burgard, who shot down the Kawasaki Toryu in which Honda served as gunner-radioman. Joe Rosbert and Dick Rossi are kneeling on the wing of the Curtiss P-40E. (Flying Tigers Association)

The Adam & Eves introduced George Burgard to Honda as the man who'd shot him down. They posed with him in front of a shark-faced fighter, his crew-cut head scarcely reaching their shoulders, and treated him to coffee and cream puffs. Then they gave him back to the Chinese. Since the usual fate of a prisoner was to be paraded from village to village in a bamboo cage, taunted and stoned by the peasants, Corporal Honda probably didn't survive very long.

Chennault flew up to Chongqing on Sunday, June 14, for the conference that would determine the future of U.S. air power in China. Stilwell was back in town, having marched his party across the Arakan

Hills to India, then returned to China by air. He was sick with jaundice and worms, so General Brereton flew in from Delhi in his Consolidated B-24 to take charge of the proceedings. He announced that army policy permitted only one air force per theater of war, meaning that the Old Man would have to run his squadrons as a stepchild of the 10th Air Force in India. Furthermore, as Brereton envisioned it, Chennault's China Air Task Force (CATF) would consist only of the fighter squadrons. Caleb Haynes of the Ferry Command would be promoted to brigadier general and put in command of the bombers, meaning that Chennault's responsibilities would actually diminish after the AVG went out of business.

"Deaf as a post," Brereton wrote of this meeting, "Chennault would sit around in conferences like a cigar-store Indian. However, he was a good lip-reader and his agile mind followed everything." Those who knew him better believed that the Old Man heard what he wanted to hear and used his deafness as an excuse to ignore the rest. In this case, he heard about the CATF and not the bit about a separate bomber command. That settled— more or less—the conference turned to the problem of persuading AVG pilots and ground crewmen to join the U.S. Army. Toward this end, they set up an induction board consisting of Chennault, Haynes, Homer Sanders (whose India-based P-40s Chennault still coveted), and a navy officer to pitch the men who'd joined the AVG from that service.

That Saturday night, the Guilin authorities put on a "comforting party" at the AVG hostel. The refugee mechanic Gerhard Neumann remembered it fondly: "A bevy of beautiful, slim, English-speaking girls in slinky Chinese silk gowns and a flower in their black hair . . . took each of us by the arm and escorted us, one by one, into the large dining room to the applause of our hosts." The Americans were treated to cigars, souvenir tapestries (a flight of eagles attacking the rising sun), speeches, toasts, and a dramatic skit in Chinese. There were place cards, too, and a handbill celebrating the achievements of the pilots:

> *Guardians of the air, you heroes of the American Flying Tigers and*
> *the Chinese Divine Hawks: After our long expectation and to our*
> *great cheerfulness, you have annihilated eight Japanese vultures*
> *in the air above Kweilin (Guilin) on June 12. This is the most*
> *brilliant merit of air combat that has ever been achieved at*

Kweilin. You have once more created your great glory of extinguishing the enemy in the air. . . .

Today, we, the 300,000 citizens in Kweilin, are presenting you our heartiest congratulations and highest respects to your comfort. And we are expecting your continual achievements of greater and richer merits with your inexhaustible heroism and bravery.

Let us yell:

Long live the American Flying Tigers!

Long live the Chinese Divine Hawks!

Long live the co-operation between the U.S.A. and China!

With his flight cap crushed low on his brow, Caleb Haynes flew the induction board to Guilin on Sunday, June 21. It was not, perhaps, the best day to begin recruiting. "Everybody had a lot of party left in them yet," as Don Rodewald wrote. He went before the board first thing on Monday and asked for a commission as first lieutenant. "The board didn't like the idea," he wrote, "but [Chennault] recommended me so there wasn't much they could do about it." Line chief Jasper Harrington struck the same bargain. He recalled Colonel Sanders as the man most opposed to giving silver bars to the former sergeants, with the Old Man pointing out that otherwise they'd go to work for the Chinese as civilians. "Chennault was the one that decided what rank you were going to get," Harrington said. "The board was a formality."

Charlie Bond offered to stay in China if he were commissioned in the regular army, and the board responded with the usual offer of a reserve commission. Bond refused, and so did George Burgard when the offer was made to him. As for Bob Neale, the squadron leader felt whipped, and all he wanted out of life was to see his wife again. Still, he came away from the interview feeling that he'd let the Old Man down. "It was the hardest thing I have ever done," he wrote in his diary. Neale took to his bed with what he assumed was dengue fever, but which he later diagnosed as a nervous breakdown.

And so it went. Half a dozen ground crewmen at Guilin signed up for continued service in China—but no pilots.

Two hundred miles northeast was Hengyang, where in 1938

Chennault had perched on a garden wall and studied Japanese bombing tactics. After its defeat at Guilin, the JAAF turned its attention to this undefended airfield, so Chennault brought the Panda Bears down from Chongqing. They found another miracle of the Chinese base-building effort: a two-story hostel, formerly a girls' school, with sleeping quarters above and dining and recreational facilities below, nicely sited on a fast-moving tributary of the Yangtse.

On Monday morning, June 22, Eddie Rector—commanding the squadron while Tex Hill went to India on a ferry mission—led the Panda Bears from Hengyang to the Yangtse, where they strafed a Japanese gunboat and three smaller vessels. Their bullets killed ten sailors, including the gunboat commander, a Captain Sumida.

The JAAF struck back the same afternoon with two squadrons of Nates from the 54th Sentai at Hankou and Nanjing. They winged south over the great oxbow of the Yangtse, to be picked up by the Chinese warning net at 1:20 PM. Rector made the interception with six Kittyhawks and a mixed bag of pilots, including Charlie Sawyer of the Adam & Eves, Catfish Raine of the Hell's Angels, and Captain Ajax Baumler of the 23rd Fighter Group, flying his first combat mission since the Spanish Civil War. They took off, climbed to 20,000 feet, and circled Hengyang. "We spotted 14 [Nates] 8,000 feet below us and attacked," Charlie Sawyer reported. "My first attack was a headon run, after one good burst a large stream of smoke started coming out his motor. . . . Later I made a rear quarter attack on one and again smoke poured out of his engine. . . . Finally, I got in position to make a direct stern attack; I came upon him slightly below and directly from the rear. I opened fire at approximately 500 yards and closed into about 250 yards with pieces flying off and smoke coming out. He turned 90 degrees to the left and I got in a good burst at close range and he seemed to explode and disintegrate."

Sawyer was credited with the kill, his first. Captain Baumler also claimed a Nate, the first victory for a U.S. Army pilot in China. And Catfish Raine and Frank Schiel each claimed a victory, for a total of four, though only one Ki-27 actually went down over Hengyang. (Another was badly damaged and may have crashed on the way home.) As had happened twice at Rangoon, the crippled Nate made a *jibaku* dive onto Hengyang airfield, trying to take out a Kittyhawk on the ground.

Major Shimada Yasunari, the group commander, was discouraged by his reception at Guilin and Hengyang. "Surprise attacks were very difficult," a JAAF officer wrote after the war, because of "the enemy's precise anti-aircraft observation networks." The Nates were too slow to compete with American fighters, and their maneuverability was offset by the enemy's tactic of "coming-and-go." Shimada recommended that the 54th Sentai be sent home and refitted with Hayabusas. In a conference at Nanjing on June 24, the JAAF decided that the Allied airfields would be attacked only at night, by small groups of bombers. The idea probably came from the AVG's longtime antagonist, Colonel Onishi Hiroshi of the 62nd Sentai, which had now moved to China.

In North Africa, the German army was hammering on the gates of Cairo, to such effect that General Brereton and most of his 10th Air Force flew to Egypt to bolster the British army. The planes diverted from the Burma front included the Lockheed Hudsons that Lauchlin Currie had acquired for Chennault: with exquisitely bad timing, they reached the Middle East just as the German tanks began to roll. So the only bombers in view for China were the six B-25 Mitchells already in Kunming: the two survivors of the ill-fated raid on Lashio, plus four that arrived later. On June 23, Chennault ordered the twin-engine bombers to Guilin, thus settling the question of whether he or Caleb Haynes controlled their movements. (That was one motive. Another was to prevent their being sent back through the pipeline to North Africa.) On the same day, he sent seven Adam & Eves to reinforce the Panda Bears at Hengyang.

The induction board followed them, and with considerably better luck than it had enjoyed at Guilin. As Jim Howard recalled the interview, he was warmly greeted, praised for his services as combat pilot and administrator, and offered command of a fighter squadron with the rank of major. (It would be a reserve commission, of course. Bissell wasn't about to bend on that point.) Two days out of three, Howard was so sick with dengue fever that he couldn't fly, and he refused to sign up. But his roommate Frank Schiel accepted the offer, and so did Eddie Rector—gold leaves and the command of a squadron! Gil Bright also accepted induction as a major, and Charlie Sawyer, the late-blooming pilot attached to Panda Bears, agreed to stay in China as a captain.

Then there was Tex Hill, en route from India with a flight of P-43s and a suitcase of contraband consigned to him by Fred Hodges. He and Chennault must have talked it over before he left, and agreed that Tex, too, would become a major and squadron leader. That the induction board fared so well at Hengyang was almost certainly his work, much as he'd led the loyalist faction during the Pilots' Revolt.

Then the induction board went off to interview the Hell's Angels at Kunming, where it made the same dismal hit as at Guilin: a handful of ground crewmen but not one pilot.

Chennault understood perfectly, he assured the Tigers at the time and also in his memoirs: they were worn out, Bissell had handled them stupidly, and they deserved a rest. If genuine, it was one of the rare moments in his life that the Old Man found it in his heart to forgive someone who'd let him down. On the other hand, there was this radiogram to Stilwell: "From present observations I deem it imperative that induction of AVG be deferred until October first and that present contracts etc be continued. Otherwise our operations are in serious jeopardy." (Though signed by Caleb Haynes, the radiogram was logged into the War Diary as Chennault's, and that seems much more likely.) But Stilwell had been down that path before, and he didn't forward the proposal to draft the AVG for three months' involuntary service in China.

Eighteen radiomen, crew chiefs, and clerks agreed to be commissioned in China as second lieutenants in the U.S. Army, and Ed McClure took an equivalent offer as a navy ensign. Nine more agreed to join the army as enlisted men, including Gerhard Neumann and three Chinese-American mechanics who'd worked for Bill Pawley in Rangoon and Loi-wing, then followed the AVG to Kunming. The staff officers also answered the call. Skip Adair returned to active duty as a major, as did flight surgeons Tom Gentry and Sam Prevo. John Williams and Roy Hoffman were commissioned as captains, and Daffy Davis, the Anglo-Irish salesman from Hong Kong, became a first lieutenant.

But ground crews and staff officers couldn't fight a war. Nor could five Flying Tiger pilots, Captain Baumler, and a couple dozen green lieutenants. Some imaginative stroke was needed, and it was provided by the head of the induction board, Homer Sanders. The colonel flew to India on June 27 to fetch a squadron from his 51st Fighter Group. He led the eight Kittyhawks across the Hump the same afternoon, finding Kunming after a heated argument with AVG radioman Robert King about whether to fly north or south to find Wujiaba airport. "God damn it," King finally said, "who's lost, you or me?" The 16th Fighter Squadron then took up residence at Kunming under the command of Major John Alison.

Chennault was involved in two other projects that June. Larry Moore and Ken Sanger, former clerks and presumed lovers, had been hired by the Republic film studio to advise an AVG epic starring John Wayne. When he heard of it, the Old Man fired off letters to anyone who might intervene, and Republic obligingly fired Moore and Sanger. He would have done better to stay out of it. *Flying Tigers* gave a wildly inaccurate impression of the AVG as a collection of former transport pilots who fought in China before the outbreak of the Pacific War. Indeed, the movie *ended* with John Wayne and his sidekicks listening to news of the Japanese attack on Pearl Harbor.

Then there was Chennault's brothel. At a time when the only treatment was bed rest, sulfa drugs, and aspirin, venereal disease was the AVG's most serious medical problem, with up to seven men hospitalized at a time. (Sulfanilamide was among the contraband that Tex Hill, in all innocence, was carrying on his flight from India.) "The boys have got to get it," Chennault reasoned, "and they might as well get it clean as dirty." He asked the Ferry Command to fly twelve Indian prostitutes over the Hump to Kunming. Stilwell got word of the scheme and radioed Delhi: "No women to China." They arrived anyhow, though from the other direction. Thirteen women were recruited in Guilin, inspected by an army doctor, and airlifted to Kunming in a U.S. Army C-47. "I am afraid Chennault does not realize the difference between the AVG and the U.S. Army!" Stilwell wrote to General Marshall, as probably the only man who could appreciate the enormity of what Chennault had done.

A few days later, Stilwell radioed a spiteful assessment of how the transition from the AVG to the 23rd Fighter Group was shaping up:

"Recommend no publicity at this time reference replacement of seasoned AVG group by American unit devoid of combat experience. . . . Fact is AVG is quitting under fire and walking out on United States in an emergency. They are placing personal interests before those of their country. This wont stand publicity."

Hengyang was just 260 miles from Hankou, giving Chennault a chance to take the offensive against the Yangtse River port that in 1938 had served as interim capital for Nationalist China. On June 29, he ordered his B-25s to Hengyang, and next day he followed them on a CNAC Douglas. He took the opportunity to have a private word with Bob Neale: "He had information that the Japs were going to try and knock out the Army after the AVGs leave on the 4th," Neale recalled. To stave off disaster, Chennault said, the Generalissimo had authorized him to extend the tour of anyone who'd stay two extra weeks in China. Would Neale stay on? And would he put in a word with the other Adam & Eves? Neale was feeling better now, and he hated to disappoint Chennault a second time. He agreed to stay, as he noted in his diary with no detectable emotion.

Charlie Bond's diary entry was less guarded: "Bob Neale came into the alert shack from a meeting with the Old Man and called in all of the First Squadron. I immediately sensed something wrong. Bob asked, 'How many of you are willing to stay two more weeks beyond the fourth to permit the [U.S. Army pilots] to arrive here and get in shape to replace us?' There it was; I knew it! Several of the pilots and mechanics said, 'Hell, no!' I was mad as hell. I knew my conscience wouldn't let me do anything about it but say yes." Which he did, of course, along with a majority of the pilots and ground crewmen at Hengyang—arguably their most heroic act during their time with the AVG.

On July 1, the B-25s became the 11th Bombardment Squadron, which immediately set off on its first mission. One Mitchell aborted with a broken hydraulic line, and another bogged down in the mud at the end of the runway. That left four bombers to make the run to Hankou, escorted by Eddie Rector with five Kittyhawks. Twice the Mitchells went astray; twice Rector put them back on course. In the end, they dropped their bombs on a Yangtse River village. Next day the B-25s improved their navigation and managed to find and bomb the docks at Hankou.

That brought the AVG to Friday, July 3: its last service day. Wake-up came at 2:30 AM with the familiar *DOOM-da-da-DOOM* of unsynchronized Mitsubishi engines. The bombs missed the runway by several hundred yards. At first light, Don Rodewald and his helpers (including two RAF armorers who'd followed the AVG into China) loaded bombs into the airworthy Mitchells. They took off at noon to raid the JAAF field at Nanchang. The flight was made in a clear zone between two layers of clouds, with the undercast breaking just before the five Mitchells and four Kittyhawks reached Nanchang. The B-25s bombed from 2,500 feet, then turned for home.

At that moment, the Nates fell out of the sky upon them. "One I fired head on," Catfish Raine reported, "but never saw him after he rolled over to tell if I had hit him or not. Came on another one from behind that was trying to chase the B-25's. I fired a long burst into him at fairly long range. He rolled over and dove back under me trailing smoke. He pulled up in a steep turn off to one side and bailed out of his ship. There were other Japs diving on me so I ran for a cloud and came on home."

Harry Bolster was also in the escort. After the Mitchells dropped their bombs, the former flight instructor went down to strafe. He left a Nate smoking on the ground; then he set off after the B-25s, catching up as three Nates came down on them: "I opened up on one of the planes and noticed it start into a spin. I then dove out and a shell exploded in my cockpit and a model 0 zoomed off my tail. I finally lost the Jap, but oil was covering the cockpit and constituted a very dangerous fire hazard. So after flying to friendly territory I bailed out." Bolster was credited with both victories, though they show on his record as Ki-27s, and Catfish Raine was also credited with a Nate that day.

Bolster's "Zero" may have been the first sighting in China of a Nakajima Ki-43 Hayabusa of the 10th Independent Chutai, commanded by Major Takatsuki Mitsuru. The squadron was rushed to China after the sorry performance of the Toryus and Nates against the AVG at Guilin. Certainly it was Takatsuki who struck at Hengyang that afternoon. The Americans scrambled to intercept a plane approaching at high altitude from the north, but the intruders proved to be seven retractable-gear fighters coming in low. While the Americans searched the clouds, the Hayabusas laced the field with machine gun bullets, as Don Rodewald recorded: "While straffing one caught sight of [Dr. Sam] Prevo, [Morton] Bent and myself and he straffed us. The bullets really cracked around that hole we were in. I hope I don't come any closer. They got our No 22 [Tomahawk] which was out of commission and also our only good truck."

In Chongqing, meanwhile, Chiang Kai-shek gave his final order to Chennault as commander of the AVG: "You are directed to demobilize the American Volunteer Group and to discharge the personnel of that Group in accordance with plans which I have approved." Chennault sat down to write the group's valedictory in a letter addressed to Lauchlin Currie but intended for "the Boss"—President Roosevelt. It was a gentler version of the resignation gambit Chennault had used so often and so effectively with Madame Chiang:

After talking to General Brett here between December 16 and 24, I knew that the A.V.G. was doomed and that the entire program we had mapped out and worked so hard to put through was likewise doomed. . . . I accepted recall to active duty early in April in the hope of obtaining better coordination and more support. I regret this action now and believe that I should have returned to the U.S. and told the story of China to the public.

I believe that the conditions out here . . . are far worse than you know or even imagine. I don't believe that the Boss knows about the mistakes and failures. I am sure that the American people don't. The things I told you in Washington about Air Force employment are true and our young pilots and excellent equipment are being needlessly sacrificed. We are also losing a great deal of the confidence and admiration of the people out here—two things which I have worked hard to retain. . . .

My work with the A.V.G. has been the most wonderful experience of my life. Few individuals ever have the opportunity to do the things they want to do and be of service in such a great cause at the same time. . . . Despite bad health which continued until March, I have maintained long hours of work and have had no holidays. At the present time I am in excellent health but a bit fagged mentally.

He wrote a similar but more restrained letter to T. V. Soong, then went to bed.

The Fourth of July fell on Saturday. The fireworks began early at Hengyang and the Lingling dispersal field, each of which received a salvo of bombs from Colonel Onishi's Sallys. At first light, the warning net reported a third formation on its way. Bob Neale and another pilot had spent the night at Lingling, and they flew up to Hengyang to lend a hand. Arriving over the airfield at 13,000 feet, they saw a dozen enemy fighters. "Dove on fighters . . . when I reached altitude above and in the sun," Neale reported. "Hit fighter I was aiming at, but saw no reason to believe he went down. Made another diving attack and my target started to smoke and started down. Did not see any further results. Followed flight north and picked out lone enemy fighter about 5,000 feet below. Made diving attack from rear quarter and pulled up. 2nd attack was a front quarter after which fighter started to smoke and was losing altitude." Before he could confirm the kill, Neale was bounced by two other Nates. He dove out, spotted four fixed-gear fighters, and followed them 100 miles north before giving up the chase.

The Panda Bears were patrolling at 18,000 feet when the Nates came in below them. "We immediately attacked," Eddie Rector reported, "and had enemy planes outlined against a white cloud layer at 7,000 feet. I fired a 4 second burst at [a Nate] in a slight diving turn, and he burst into flames and bits of debris flew from his plane as he dived through the cloud layer. I climbed up to the outside and made several more passes. . . . One [Nate] forced me to dive out, but in doing so I got in a head on burst at two fighters in close formation coming up at me. I got a fleeting glimpse of a wingman's engine letting out a large burst of smoke as I passed over them."

Rector was credited with one Ki-27, as were Jim Howard, Charlie Sawyer, and Van Shapard, another of the newly attached flight instructors. That made seven Nates claimed on July 3 and July 4. According to Japanese records, the 54th Sentai lost four planes in these combats, the last before the group went home to be refitted.

Chennault spent July 4 at Beishiyi airfield outside Chongqing, catching up on paperwork. That evening, Madame Chiang put on a party for the AVGs. It was planned as a barbecue, but rain moved it indoors. The guests drank nonalcoholic punch, Madame led them in a game of musical chairs, and Chennault was presented with an oil portrait of himself and the Chiangs. At 11 PM, the Americans—with what relief can only be imagined—drove back through the rain and mud to their quarters at the airfield.

Chapter 18

Passing into History

"At midnight," the Old Man wrote of Independence Day 1942, "the AVG passed into history." But the Flying Tigers weren't so neatly written off. On Sunday, July 5, Chennault's irregulars still provided most of his combat strength. Even the men who'd agreed to be inducted in China were still civilians—including Tex Hill, who led nine Kittyhawks from Beishiyi to Guilin on Sunday afternoon. (Dropping off the P-43s at Kunming, Tex got ready for his new career by buying a set of khakis from R. T. Smith, the only man in the AVG with trouser legs long enough for him.) Chennault followed him to Guilin on Monday, to put Bob Neale in charge of the 23rd Fighter Group. The designated commander, Colonel Robert Scott of the Ferry Command, was in Kunming, organizing his group headquarters and transforming the Hell's Angels into an army squadron.

Among the Panda Bears who came down from Beishiyi with Tex was John Petach, the married man. Petach was a steady if unspectacular pilot, and Hill took him on a raid of Canton that afternoon. Five Mitchells made the run, bombed an oil refinery, and turned for home. A few minutes into the return flight, one of the bomber pilots radioed that he was under attack. "I dropped my belly tank," Petach reported, "and looked about quite violently, but could see nothing." Then he spotted three Nates below him. He passed the word to Hill, waggled his wings, and dove upon the Japanese fighters. "They must have seen me," he wrote, "because the last E.A. fired a burst and all 3 started to turn towards me. I opened fire at 500 yards but was shooting behind the last man so I pulled the nose of my plane well ahead of the E.A. and gave him a 1 second burst. Then the E.A. pulled into sight right in front of my nose so that my fire raked him as he passed. . . . I pulled away and saw two more [Nates] about 3 miles north of our combat. I turned towards them and this time they turned away and headed for a mountain. The first plane was just turning around the mountain top when I overhauled the second plane. I gave him about a one second burst and he burst into flame and was burning well. Just then Hill called all planes from combat, so I joined up."

He was credited with one Nate, bringing his CAMCO bonus account to $1,991.67—a nice shower present for Red Petach at Beishiyi, pregnant with their first child. Tex Hill also claimed a victory, bringing his total to 10.25 enemy aircraft destroyed in the air plus another on the ground, second only to Bob Neale as the leading American fighter ace of the war to date. Neither victory is confirmed in Japanese accounts.

On Tuesday, Bob Neale sent the newly arrived Kittyhawks to Hengyang, where Tex resumed command of the outfit that the AVG called the Panda Bears and army pilots called the 75th Fighter Squadron.

Japanese scouts meanwhile probed the East China airfields, trying to discover the state of the American air force. (Stilwell had ordered a press blackout on the transfer, but it was no secret that the Flying Tigers were going home.) On Thursday, July 9, Pete Wright and Lester Hall took off from Hengyang in pursuit of a "reconnaissance bomber," probably a 90th Sentai Lily from Canton. After a long search, Wright caught the twin-engine plane in a climbing attack. "I opened up at about 150 yards directly behind him," he reported; "at the first burst part of his tail came off and his left hand motor caught on fire. I gave two more burst and he rolled over and went down. I did not see him crash as oil from his engines covered my windshield." Wright was credited with the shoot-down—the last for the American Volunteer Group, bringing his personal score to 3.65 and the group's to . . .

And here I must grasp a nettle of my own. How many planes *did* the AVG destroy, in the air and on the ground? Different documents yield different figures, but when they're sorted out, it appears that the Chinese paid 296 combat bonuses, including four in the days after the group had officially gone out of business. But these are only claims. Fighter pilots of all nations, in all theaters of World War II, overstated their victories for a variety of very good reasons, and the overclaiming was most egregious in the circumstances in which the AVG did much of its fighting: over water, rain forest, or enemy-held territory, and in furballs with enemy aircraft greatly outnumbering the defenders. In many instances I've been able to disprove a specific claim to my own satisfaction, but not with such consistency that I can advance an equally precise figure of my own, for a variety of reasons.

In the first place, the JAAF didn't celebrate the feats of individual pilots. After an air battle, survivors were debriefed at group or squadron headquarters to obtain a consensus of losses and victories, which was recorded by an enlisted clerk. A sergeant-pilot might bestow one of his victories upon an officer, to show gratitude for his leadership. This system was very different from the personal and obsessive interest that western pilots took in their casualties and victory claims, and it surely worked to inflate the tally of presumed victories while diminishing admitted losses. Japanese combat accounts seldom give the names of pilots taken prisoner, for example, and they pass lightly over "forced landings" away from the combat zone. (I have attributed all such crashes to Allied action.) And the JAAF squadrons attached to ground units often fell through the cracks, as if the men flying ground support weren't really combat aviators, and their losses correspondingly less important.

Then too, records were lost in the great retreat of 1944–1945. Major Yoshioka's 77th Sentai—the AVG's regular antagonist in the campaign for South Burma—was destroyed as a fighting force in New Guinea, its pilots and mechanics either fighting as infantrymen or setting out on overland marches that ended in starvation. Nobody in those circumstances was worrying overmuch about preserving the squadron logs. As for the records kept behind the lines, at theater or general headquarters, the jest in Tokyo in August 1945 was that the smoke from the final

American air raid merged into the pall raised by military and civilian bureaucrats burning documents before the victors arrived.

But even in the case of the 77th Sentai, some records did survive, to be processed by the Allied Translator and Interpreter Service in the 1950s, and demobilized Japanese officers were debriefed by the U.S. Army and their recollections published in mimeograph form. As time went on, JAAF veterans wrote their memoirs (the market was especially good for books about the 64th Sentai). And, in the 1980s, the Japan Defense Agency produced a mostly excellent set of campaign histories.

Taken together, the Japanese accounts share two characteristics with their Allied counterparts: absurdly optimistic with respect to victories, but persuasive when it comes to losses. How could it be otherwise? A soldier, after all, *knows* when a friend goes missing or is killed: the friend doesn't return; letters must be written and personal gear disposed of; his bunk is empty in the barrack; his chair is vacant at the mess. . . . We know for a certainty that Neil Martin and Hank Gilbert—and only those two— were killed on December 23, 1941, despite the expansive claims of Japanese pilots and gunners. Similarly, we know that the 64th Sentai lost Lieutenant Okuyama and Sergeant Wakayama—and only those two—two days later. A pilot's loss is a fact burned into the memories of every man who served with him, grieved for him, and later wrote about him.

Necessarily, the JAAF tallies are less precise than those for the American Volunteer Group. Japan lost the war, after all, and lost a greater proportion of the men who might have memorialized the dead. But even when a unit was destroyed, its history survived in the memories of airmen who had earlier been transferred out or invalided home, and in the records of units that served alongside it. There are gaps, of course. But on the whole the Japanese figures stand up to scrutiny, and what they show is this: The JAAF lost about 115 aircraft to the American Volunteer Group in Burma, Thailand, and China—perhaps as many as 120, perhaps as few as 110.

The toll in lives was far higher. As the aggressors, Japanese airmen more often found themselves over enemy territory, so they had almost no opportunity to make their way home after a shoot-down. There were more men per plane (two in a Ki-30 Ann, six or seven in a Ki-21 Sally) and Japanese fighter pilots sometimes flew without parachutes, preferring a *jibaku* death to captivity. As a result, the JAAF probably lost about 400 men in operations against the AVG, including four group commanders—the equivalent of four Claire Chennaults.

It's not easy to explain why the Flying Tigers succeeded where other Allied combat groups failed. To be sure, their airplane was robust and heavily armed—but Japanese pilots had handily defeated U.S. Army pilots flying the Curtiss P-40 at Pearl Harbor and Manila. And Chennault's tactics were indeed suited to the occasion—but to read the AVG combat reports is to be astonished at how seldom his pilots followed his doctrine of "the fighting pair." Even the "boom and zoom" tactic favored by the Flying Tigers was hardly unique to them, having been used not only by the Russians in China but by British pilots in Burma. Similarly, the ground-observation network that he pioneered did prove its worth in China, but the AVG did most of its fighting in Burma, often without any effective warning at all.

More important, I suspect, were the intangibles of morale and group élan. Alone of the Allied air squadrons trying to stem the Japanese onslaught in the winter of 1941–1942, the Flying Tigers were triple volunteers. They'd volunteered to join the U.S. military in peacetime; they'd volunteered to fly for China in 1941; and for nearly a year they'd voluntarily stayed on, in Burma and in China, despite dismal conditions and steady losses of men, planes, and territory. It's not easy to fight in a losing cause, but the Flying Tigers did it brilliantly—in large part because the quitters actually did have an opportunity to quit. Those who stayed were those with the will to fight.

It's an especially pleasing irony. Japan went to war knowing that its enemies were larger and richer than it was, but believing it would prevail—and promising its soldiers and airmen that they'd be victorious—because a man's spirit was more important than the quality of his weapon. Yet Japan's first and most spectacular defeat was at the hands of a few dozen American pilots who embodied that very same principle.

As for AVG losses, those weren't finished. On July 10—a year to the day after *Jagersfontein* sailed under the Golden Gate Bridge—Tex Hill sent four pilots winging northeast from Hengyang to bomb the walled city of Linchuan (Fouzhou). John Petach led the mission, with Lieutenant Leonard Butsch flying on his wing. The second element consisted of Captain Ajax Baumler and wingman Arnold Shamblin, formerly of the CAF flight school. Petach followed a heading of 68 degrees, crossed the wide tributary south of Nanchang, and hit his checkpoint at 11:45 AM, an hour into the flight. Here he changed course to the southwest, ordering the others to trail out behind him. The formation reached Linchuan "in string" at 12:03 PM.

Baumler's combat report is much more formal than those filed by AVG pilots. "Careful scrutiny of air revealed no pursuit of enemy in vicinity," he wrote. "We started dive from 6,500 feet in formation. Mr. Petach had just reached the terminus of his dive at about 2,300 feet when his airplane burst into flames around the cockpit and main fuel tanks. His airplane went into a violent tumbling spin completely out of control and a portion of left wing separated from airplane. His airplane crashed in flames on river edge at north east side of wall around city. The pilot remained in plane and it is my opinion that his plane received several direct hits from 20 mm anti aircraft fire immediately after he had released his bombs." A former navy pilot like most of the Panda Bears, Petach had graduated from New York University in 1939 with a major in aeronautical engineering. In another five days, he would have celebrated his twenty-fourth birthday.

Baumler pulled out over the river and followed its twisting course until he was safely away from the antiaircraft guns. Butsch did the same. Not until the two army officers were reunited at Hengyang did they realize that Baumler's wingman was also missing. A red-haired former army flight instructor from Oklahoma, Arnold Shamblin had been hit by flak over Linchuan; he bailed out of his Kittyhawk and evaded capture for several hours before Japanese soldiers caught him. Apart from a contemporary report in a Tokyo newspaper, however, there was no further news of Shamblin. He may have been murdered on the spot, or he may have died in prison camp, as happened to 27 percent of Anglo-American servicemen captured by the Japanese.

Twenty-two American Volunteer Group pilots were now dead, captured, or missing in action. In absolute numbers, this wasn't an especially high toll—for every airman lost by the AVG in combat operations, the JAAF lost twenty-eight. But as a proportion of the men on the squadron and flight-school rosters at the outbreak of war, the loss was huge. Nearly one pilot out of four had been lost.

The AVG's material losses were also significant. By my best estimate, the group's inventory of fighter aircraft during seven months of war came to 116 Tomahawks and Kittyhawks. Of these, it had lost 86 planes to combat, accident, and abandonment, including upward of 20 wrecks accumulated by Bill Pawley at Loiwing and there captured by the Japanese.

That same day, July 10, Major John Alison and his 16th Fighter Squadron flew into Guilin with eight Kittyhawks—the planes "borrowed" by Chennault from Colonel Sanders's 51st Fighter Group in India. Bob Neale sent them up to the dispersal field at Lingling. Two more B-25 Mitchells reached Guilin on Sunday, July 12. The Old Man followed on Monday in a Douglas transport, bringing belly tanks for the Kittyhawks, food and mail for the men, and Colonel Caleb Haynes to take charge of the 11th Bombardment Squadron. Chennault wanted to go on the offensive before his AVG holdovers went home, but rain kept the Mitchells grounded until Thursday.

Thursday was rainy, too, but Haynes managed to get the Mitchells off to raid the docks at Hankou, guarded by a mixed escort of army and AVG pilots. "The flight was uneventful," Major Alison reported; "the bombs hit the dock area, no fighters were sighted and we all returned to [Hengyang]." Their engines were still ticking, the metal contracting as it cooled, when fighter control reported a formation north of the field. There followed a desperate race to fly the planes to safety. "Most of the P-40's on the field got in the air," as Alison told the story, "and all the B-25's got off but not without some near collisions as we were scrambling like a bunch of geese."

Freeman Ricketts was flying one of the Kittyhawks. A former army pilot with more than 900 hours in his logbooks when he reached Burma, he'd seen little combat with the AVG. Now he flew an aimless pattern over the field while fighter control told him of "bandits" north of Hengyang—

no, south—and finally told him to land. The alarm was false: fighter control had been processing delayed reports of the Mitchells and Kittyhawks just returned from Hankou.

Ricketts didn't know that, of course. Making his approach to the Hengyang runway, he saw a twin-engine plane to the west. He turned toward it, whereupon the stranger turned away, so Ricketts gave chase. "I overtook this ship from directly behind and a very little below," he reported. "I opened fire at approximately 350–400 yards. My guns jammed, then I pulled off to the left and recharged my guns. The airplane again turned away from me. Apparently I slowed the ship down with the first burst for I overtook very easily and fired another burst." Then he saw the U.S. Army star on his target's flank: he was shooting at one of the Mitchells, scrambled to the supposed safety of the air. "I watched the B-25 to see if it could continue flight," Ricketts wrote, "and about one or two miles later saw five parachutes. The ship was still under control and when last seen was flying towards Hengyang." The Mitchell crashed near Lingling, and its pilot telephoned Hengyang next day to report he'd been shot down "by two Zeros" but had survived. So did his crew, and so did Ricketts, though not without a board of inquiry ordered by Chennault.

That was Thursday, July 16. A U.S. Army Douglas flew down to Guilin that afternoon with ten pilots and four mechanics for the 23rd Fighter Group. Two more transports came down on Friday. Colonel Robert Scott was among the passengers, but if Bob Neale met his successor he didn't mention it in his diary, nor could he recall the meeting afterward. (Scott remembered waving to Neale through the cabin door.) The same transports carried the AVG holdovers to Chongqing on Friday and Saturday. "Had iced tea," Neale wrote in his diary. "What a treat." As a reward for their two weeks' extra duty in the combat zone, Chennault gave them letters requesting priority status on military flights heading toward the United States.

Back in Guilin, among the weird pinnacles, in the heat and the damp, Don Rodewald was also posting his diary: "All the rest of the boys left today so it is *A.V.G. Finish*. Sure rough to see them going home. Sometimes I wonder if I made a mistake. I only got two armorers and two Limey helpers. Sure hope the [U.S. Army] men get in." Indeed, the

Royal Air Force had made a significant but never recorded contribution to Chennault's forces in China. In addition to Rode's British helpers, at least two RAF radio mechanics—Wilf Jepson and Gerald Jones—had retreated into China with the AVG, and worked for the Americans for more than a year. Chennault never entered them on a squadron roster, but he rebuffed the RAF's attempts to get them back until ordered to release them in August 1943.

With the reinforcements trickling in, the AVGs who'd agreed to accept induction, and the odd helper hijacked from the RAF, Chennault carried on as if his boys had never left. He even called the new men "Flying Tigers," to the lasting annoyance of the AVG veterans.

On Sunday, July 19, three more Mitchells reached Guilin and went out to "bomb hell out of a town," as Rode noted. That same day, he and the other AVGs were formally inducted into U.S. service. The commissioning went off without ceremony. Jasper Harrington was walking to the dining hall when he was hailed by an army officer. "It was after sundown, about dark," the line chief told me. "He wanted to know, 'Is your name Harrington?' I says, 'Yup.' 'Jasper J.?' I says, 'Yup, sure is.' He says, 'Hold up your hand.' I held up my hand, and he swore me in and shook my hand and says, 'Now you are a lieutenant in the Army Air Corps.' And I never saw the character before or since. . . . It didn't change my work any. I was still a line chief with a tool box, working."

Tex Hill took the oath "in a muggy tent" with the army induction board looking on. A sergeant handed him a pen and a form containing the oath of allegiance; Tex read the paper, signed it, and handed it back. "Congratulations!" Colonel Sanders told him. "You're now Major Hill, commander, 75th Fighter Squadron." In addition to his mostly green U.S. Army pilots, he had Major Gil Bright to help enforce the standards of the Panda Bears. At Guilin, similarly, Major Eddie Rector took command of the 76th Fighter Squadron, with Captain Charlie Sawyer as his leavening from the AVG. These two combat squadrons had twenty-four fighters between them, mostly Kittyhawks. At Kunming, meanwhile, Major Frank Schiel took command of the 74th Fighter Squadron—the Hell's Angels reconstituted, right down to its ten weary Tomahawks.

In addition, John Alison had eight Kittyhawks in the 16th Fighter

Squadron, and Caleb Haynes had seven Mitchells. Chennault's China Air Task Force (CATF) thus began operations with a grand total of forty-nine aircraft—scarcely the infusion he'd been promised for bringing the American Volunteer Group into U.S. service. Indeed, the CATF had fewer aircraft than the AVG on the first day of the war.

To pay for the planes taken over from the AVG, the United States gave China a $3.5 million credit on its lend-lease account. This was more than generous, considering that China had paid only $9.3 million for one hundred Tomahawks (from funds provided in the first instance by the U.S.) and nothing at all for the Kittyhawks. In the end, the net cost to China for the services of the American Volunteer Group was $5.8 million for aircraft and $3 million for salaries and combat bonuses—roughly $75,000 for each Japanese plane destroyed. It was one of the rare instances in modern warfare where the instrument of destruction cost less than the objects destroyed.

The last AVG contingent to leave China consisted of Bob Neale, Charlie Bond, and the widowed and pregnant Red Petach. After a week's delay in India, Chennault's priority letter got them a flight to Khartoum in North Africa. At this desert base, they saw great quantities of aircraft, including the Lockheed Hudsons that had been sold to Britain, twice diverted to China by Lauchlin Currie, and twice repossessed by the U.S. Army. At 11:30 AM on August 7, the three travelers touched down at Miami airport—the last to leave China and the first to get home.

They were the lucky ones. Most of the AVG pilots, headquarters staff, and ground crewmen had the choice of paying $1,200 for a seat on Pan Am or a smaller but still considerable sum for transportation by sea. "The Army is out to get us," Bus Keeton wrote in his diary on July 11. A week later, his anger had become more pointed: "The Army has at least 15 transports sitting on the field here and won't [fly] us out, the bunch of bastards." A week after that, hearing about the priority letters Chennault had given to the AVG holdovers, he switched his anger to the Old Man: "If I ever had any respect for him I don't have any now."

In retrospect, however, the AVG veterans blamed their shabby treatment on Lewis Brereton or (their favorite goat) Clayton Bissell. I searched the files of the U.S. Military Mission for documents to support this belief, finding only the radiograms Chennault himself had sent to India throughout the spring, to block military flights for his men who'd quit early. Perhaps the army transportation officers thought that every AVG veteran came under this ban. More likely, they were simply unable to cope with the problem of processing men who had no uniforms, no travel orders, and no explanation for their presence in India except that they'd served a year in a foreign air force and now wanted to go home.

The largest number bought passage on *Mariposa*, an Italian passenger liner seized by the United States and converted to a troopship. The fare was $150 for a belowdecks bunk, $800 for a cabin in officers' country. (Among those who presumably paid the higher fare were Olga and Harvey Greenlaw, who needed room for Lucy the dog, a Karen drum, and eight Persian carpets, among other souvenirs of their four years in Asia.) *Mariposa* sailed from Bombay (Mumbai) on August 7. As on the Java Pacific liners that had brought the AVG to Asia, many of their fellow passengers were missionaries; as the story is told, the AVG veterans had a running poker game on one side of the ship, while the missionaries prayed on the other. They reached New York on September 6. They were agreeably surprised to be greeted as heroes, and (in the case of the pilots) to learn that their combat bonuses had indeed been paid. "I knew you were doing all right," Ken Jernstedt was told by his banker in Hood River, Oregon, "because the money kept coming in."

The Greenlaws and most of the pilots stayed at the Commodore Hotel, where airlines and airframe companies set up hospitality suites in hopes of recruiting useful talent. Ken Jernstedt for one had had a bellyful of war, and with his friend Parker Dupouy signed on with Republic Aviation as a civilian test pilot. They weren't alone. Bob Neale, George Burgard, and Pete Wright went to work for the airlines, ferrying planes for the military. Twenty pilots, including several of the former flight instructors, had already signed on with CNAC in Asia, or would return to China for this purpose, flying Douglas transports over the Hump at $800 a month, plus up to $20 an hour for overtime. Ironically, the hardest part of the transition to transport flying, for many of them, was to

In August 1943, a grateful Britain awarded the Distinguished Flying Cross to Charlie Bond, Tex Hill, and Eddie Rector for their services in the defense of Burma. The Flying Tigers had to wait fifty-three years to be similarly recognized by the United States. (Charles R. Bond Jr. collection)

keep the Douglas heading in the right direction without benefit of the P-40's long snout—the very feature that had given them so much grief at Kyedaw airfield.

Chennault remained in China until August 1945, rounding out eight years of war against the empire of Japan. He continued to work miracles of improvisation and to win the love of his men, while infuriating the brass in Chongqing, Delhi, and Washington. He was helped by many of the same people he'd recruited for the AVG. Foremost among them was Tex Hill, who was credited with shooting down five more Japanese planes in China, and who eventually took his well-deserved place as commander of the 23rd Fighter Group. He was a legend throughout the air force. A young army pilot, new to the theater, recalled his first combat briefing at Guilin. Expecting something on the order of *The Target for Tonight,* with jests, chalkboards, and weather reports, what he got was a tall, sunburned man who shambled into the briefing room and spoke three words: "Y'all follow me!"

Casualties among this cadre of loyalists were as high as for the AVG. Major Frank Schiel was killed in China in 1943 when his P-38 crashed on a reconnaissance flight. Captain Roy Hoffman, AVG armorer and staff officer who accepted induction in China, was killed as a crewman in a B-24. George McMillan rejoined the army and returned to China, where he was killed in 1944. Bill Reed did the same, chalking up seven more aerial victories before he, too, was killed that year. Three AVG veterans who remained in China as CNAC pilots were also killed in crashes: John Dean in 1942, Allen Wright in 1943, Mickey Mickelson in 1944.

As a colonel, Eddie Rector served a second tour in China and likewise commanded the 23rd Fighter Group. Chennault's clerical staff— Tom Trumble, Doreen Lonborg Davis, and a Rangoon refugee named Eloise Whitwer—continued to work for him as civilians. Joe Alsop, repatriated by the Japanese, made his way back to China as a lend-lease official and there finagled a transfer to Chennault's headquarters, where he served the Old Man as before. So did Paul Frillmann. Spoiled for the godly life by his year in the AVG, he joined the U.S. Army as an intelligence officer and was sent to China, where Chennault greeted him with his usual air of infallibility: "Hello, Frillmann. I thought you would be back." One of his missing pilots also turned up: in 1945, Lew Bishop escaped from the train that was taking him to a new prison camp, and he, too, made his way to Kunming.

Clayton Bissell meanwhile had moved to India as commander of the 10th Air Force, having stayed in China long enough to be decorated for his "especially meritorious performance" in activating the 23rd Fighter Group. (Chennault was similarly honored, but as usual Bissell got there ahead of him.) From a distance of 1,800 miles, he made life so miserable for Chennault that the Old Man sometimes came down sick when Bissell was scheduled to land at Wujiaba on an inspection tour. This humiliation ended in March 1943 when the CATF was upgraded to the 14th Air Force, with Chennault as its commanding officer. Independence brought a second star: Major General Claire Lee Chennault, one of the most colorful, controversial, and popular commanders in U.S. service.

The conflicts with Stilwell continued, though in a more dignified fashion than the guerrilla war with Bissell, stemming as they did from an honest difference about the best way to defeat Japan. "It's the man in the trenches that will win the war," the good soldier supposedly said, to which Chennault supposedly replied: "Goddammit, Stilwell, there *aren't* any men in the trenches." They were both right. Stilwell warned Chennault that if the "air boys" ever seriously threatened the Japanese, the latter would simply take his airfields away from him—and they did, in Operation Ichi-go, in the spring of 1944. Chennault predicted that long-range bombers would devastate the Japanese home islands—and they did, beginning with Operation Matterhorn that summer. (Chennault wasn't permitted to control the B-29s, however, and Hap Arnold eventually found a better base for them on the Pacific islands of Guam, Tinian, and Saipan.) Each in pursuit of his own agenda, Chennault and Stilwell kept quarreling until Chiang Kai-shek demanded and got Stilwell's recall in October 1944.

But George Marshall and Hap Arnold didn't allow a China maverick to triumph over the old-boy network. When the U.S. Army began to gird itself for the invasion of Japan, they set out to get rid of Chennault—a campaign simplified by his loyalty to some of his less-admirable associates. Butch Carney, "stoned out of his gourd," shot and killed an army sergeant in a poker game. Harry Sutter, another early China hand, was the subject of a messy investigation into the smuggling of gold, drugs, and other valuables between India and China. These two scandals were compounded by the widespread belief that Rose Mok (Carney's wife or girlfriend) and Kasey Sutter were romantically involved with Chennault, and that he'd fathered a child with Rosie. (Her son, Joe Chennault, lives in the San Francisco Bay area today.)

Altogether, army investigators developed files on three hundred smuggling cases involving members or ex-members of the AVG, CNAC, CATF, and 14th Air Force. Chennault stood by his friends to the point where his own reputation was tarnished, thus providing a lever to the men in Washington who wanted to remove him. After a four-month holding action, he accepted Hap Arnold's pointed recommendation that

he "take advantage of the retirement privileges now available to physi-
cally disqualified officers." He left China on August 1, 1945. Within a
fortnight, Japan had surrendered, with eighty of her cities so devastated
by American air attack that they weren't fit for human habitation.

Pappy Paxton calculated in 1945 that the AVG had 220 members
when it disbanded, and that 187—85 percent—returned to active
duty with the U.S. armed forces. Most of the others took jobs in war-
related enterprises such as CNAC, and one joined the British army.

The AVG veterans served on many fronts and in every conceivable capacity, but a remarkable number made their way back to Asia. Oley Olson
and R. T. Smith served in the air-commando units that helped recapture
Burma for the Allies. In 1944, flying the Hump for CNAC, Dick Rossi ran
into R. T. at a base in northeastern India, piloting a B-25 named *Barbie
III*. The turret gunner was Chuck Baisden, former AVG armorer. For old
times' sake, they took Rossi on a tour of the Japanese airfields in Burma,
allowing him to sit up front and enjoy the view through the Plexiglas bombardier's compartment. On the way home, R. T. bombed a railway yard
and Baisden tested his guns, whereupon some of the Plexiglas panels fell
out. Rossi was still recovering from this shock when R. T. announced that
Barbie had an unexploded bomb dangling from her belly. He put her
down as gently as he could, but the bomb broke loose, skittered along the
ground, and rolled into a ditch. Rossi thanked R. T. for an interesting day,
then went back to the infinitely more calming work of driving an unarmed
Douglas across the Himalayas.

After his China tour, Gil Bright moved on to North Africa, to become one of the few Allied pilots credited with shooting down planes
from each of the three Axis powers. (Counting his victories in Spain,
Ajax Baumler was another.) Jim Howard commanded the 354th Fighter
Group in Europe and won America's highest decoration, the Medal of
Honor, for breaking up an attack on a bomber formation. "I seen my
duty and I done it," he told the war correspondents.

Greg Boyington rejoined the marines and formed the Black Sheep
Squadron, VMF 214, a maverick outfit with many similarities to the AVG,
with Pappy Boyington as Chennault. He was credited with destroying

twenty-two Japanese planes before he was himself shot down. He, too, was awarded the Medal of Honor, but to the chagrin of the Marine Corps (as Boyington told the story) he emerged alive from prison camp in 1945 and mortified the Corps by drinking his way through the ensuing publicity tour. Boyington felt that he had been treated shabbily by the AVG, and his revenge took the form of a comic novel called *Tonya,* whose title character bore many similarities to Olga Greenlaw.

The accident-prone former flying-boat captain, Ed Conant, returned to the U.S. Navy and finally became an outstanding fighter pilot, winning a Silver Star and credited with three Japanese aircraft on a sweep over Kuroe Bay, Japan, in March 1945. Postwar, he became one of the navy's first helicopter pilots, still under his *nom de guerre.* His identity as John Perry wasn't discovered for years, until a sharp-eyed clerk noticed that two men with the same name, born on the same day in the same town, had applied to renew their driver's licenses.

Altogether, of 109 pilots and flight instructors who sailed for Asia in the summer and fall of 1941, 36—nearly a third—lost their lives or freedom before the end of World War II. So much for Red Probst's theory that joining the AVG would be good for one's health.

Ten former ground crewmen went to flight school and became pilots. Ed McClure, commissioned in China, returned to the U.S. for flight training and has a good claim as a U.S. Navy ace, credited with five Japanese aircraft over the Japanese home islands. (McClure's squadron leader on the carrier *Lexington* was Lieutenant Commander Whitey Lawlor of the AVG.) Crew chief Henry Olson ran for Congress in Minnesota as a former Flying Tiger, supposedly shot down twice, wounded, and invalided home—then became an actual hero, who won the Distinguished Service Cross for his bravery as a P-47 pilot in Europe. After his U.S. Army tour in China, Don Rodewald earned his wings and returned to the 23rd Fighter Group as a Mustang pilot. These men became casualties at about the same rate as the pilots they'd formerly supported: Bill Sykes, killed in a crash on the day he graduated from flight school; Robert Rasmussen, killed in action in North Africa; Carson Roberts, likewise killed in North Africa; and Jesse Crookshanks, shot down over Germany and a prisoner of war for eighteen months, weighing 120 pounds upon his release.

Whatever their later service, they received no official recognition for their time in the AVG. Charlie Mott escaped from a Japanese compound in 1945 and joined a covert force building an airstrip in the Thai backcountry; the first plane to land brought the news that the war was over. Mott made his way to India, where, like the AVG returnees of 1942, he was classified as a civilian and denied military transport. It was the same for all the Flying Tigers. Their AVG victories didn't count toward qualifying them as fighter aces in the army, navy, or marines. Their CAMCO year didn't count as time-in-grade for promotion, retirement, or the "points" that determined a man's priority for discharge at the end of the war.

There was one exception: the U.S. Army awarded the Distinguished Flying Cross to John Petach for his mission to Linchuan, on the theory that he was serving with the 75th Fighter Squadron at the time of his death, but it neglected to deliver the medal. More than forty years later, the Air Force made good the oversight, and Joan Petach Randles—the daughter he never saw—was among those who attended the award ceremony at McGuire Air Force Base in 1984.

After the war, Chennault continued in the service of the Chiangs, organizing Civil Air Transport with Whitey Willauer and others of the AVG "Washington Squadron." CAT started with mercy flights and evolved into a paramilitary force during the civil war that ended with Chiang Kai-shek's ouster by the Communists in 1949. Chennault even tried to form a new AVG for service in China, but the scheme was vetoed by his old nemesis, George Marshall, then serving as President Truman's secretary of state.

Exiled with the Chiangs to Taiwan, CAT became a contract airline for the U.S. government, supporting American troops in Korea and French colonial forces in Vietnam. Among its pilots were Erik Shilling of the Hell's Angels and Randall Richardson, a clerk who quit the AVG to train as a navy pilot. Dropping supplies into Dien Bien Phu in the spring of 1954, Shilling and Richardson flew forty-five missions to that deadly valley—"hell in a very small place"—whose sides bristled with

Vietnamese guns. Chennault's plan to raise a group of F-84 Thunderjet fighter-bombers for service in Vietnam was quietly shelved by the Eisenhower administration.

There was another airline, too. In California, AVG veterans headed by Bob Prescott created the Flying Tiger Line, which in time became the country's largest air-freight carrier (eventually merged to create the FedEx empire). Among its pilots was John Leibolt, son of the man who'd disappeared over Rangoon in February 1942.

With his connection to the Chiangs, there was no doubt where Chennault would stand in the anticommunist scapegoating of the 1950s. He had an unwanted ally in the person of Bill Pawley, a millionaire from his aviation dealings in China and India, who used his wealth to fight the Cold War as ambassador to Peru and Brazil, sponsor of commando raids on Cuba, and perennial witness before the U.S. Congress. On the other side, Lauchlin Currie was accused of complicity in the "Silvermaster spy ring." He left the country, took up residence in Colombia, and had his American citizenship revoked in 1954, probably because he'd been fingered as an agent for the Soviet Union. Many of the old China hands—Paul Frillmann among them—were similarly tarnished by their association, real or imagined, with the Chinese Communists.

Lieutenant General Claire Chennault died of lung cancer on July 27, 1958. (He was awarded the third star a few weeks earlier.) Among the last visitors at his bedside was Madame Chiang Kai-shek. With the Old Man gone, his airline was reorganized as Air America under the control of the Central Intelligence Agency. Its gray planes, civil and military, with no national markings, carried out CIA missions all during the Vietnam War. Thus the covert air action proposed by Chennault in 1940 finally became an accepted instrument of American foreign policy. There were other guerrilla airlines in Southeast Asia, including Bird & Son, which specialized in missions in Laos and Cambodia, and whose chief pilot from 1962 to 1966 was Erik Shilling. Call him the last Flying Tiger.

Chennault was buried in Arlington National Cemetery. At Lake Charles, Louisiana, an air force base was named in his honor. In Taipei, Taiwan, in a park where hundreds of citizens gather for their dawn exercises, the Republic of China erected a bust of a jut-jawed Chennault, the only westerner so honored in Chiang's capital. In 1987, he became the last

A "first day of issue" envelope bearing a U.S. Postal Service stamp with Chennault's likeness, along with a Flying Tigers commemorative stamp from Taiwan. The Old Man's birth year is wrong by three years. (Author's collection)

major World War II figure to be dignified with a biography—and then there were two. (As if to confirm him as a man of contradictions, one gave his birth year as 1890, the other as 1893.) For a generation, Chennault's admirers made a commemorative stamp the litmus test of his place in history. He got that, too, at a "first-day" ceremony at Monroe, Louisiana, on September 6, 1990, on what was wrongly believed to be the centenary of his birth. The denomination was forty cents, a suitably maverick sum.

Since the 1950s, veterans of the AVG have met every year or two for a reunion, usually on July 4, most often in Southern California. (Until the FAA put a stop to it, Bob Prescott transported them gratis on the Flying Tiger Line.) Of the pilots, headquarters staff, and ground crewmen who served till disbandment, about one hundred were alive in 1989, when I was writing the first draft of this book. Half attended the reunion that year at Ojai, along with wives, children, grandchildren—and sweethearts. Eddie Rector turned up with Dorothea Dunsmore (nee Wilkins) on his arm, plump and beautiful, her voice as sweet as an English nightingale's. It was their first meeting since Rangoon in January 1942. Paul Greene was there, curly-haired and outrageous, flashing a photograph of *his* current project, a P-51 Mustang replica. And Parker Dupouy, hobbled slightly by a stroke—it was wondrous to recall that his hand–eye coordination was once so precise that he landed a fighter at 142 mph with a section missing off the wing. And Charlie Mott, an amiable Buddha with a briefcase of documents with which he hoped to persuade the U.S. Navy that it wouldn't set an undesirable precedent if it recognized him as a former prisoner of war. And R. T. Smith and Bob Neale. . . . Some were in wheelchairs, including Don Rodewald, who'd lost the use of his legs when he crashed an air force trainer, but who wasn't grounded by that: he outfitted a small plane with hand controls and flew it around the world, regretting only that the Burmese authorities didn't allow him to land at Mingaladon airport.

Three years later, in time for their fiftieth reunion in July 1992, the U.S. Department of Defense made an official determination that each "honorably discharged" member of the American Volunteer Group was a World War II veteran on the basis of his or her service from December 1941 to July 1942. At the same time, the AVG was awarded a Presidential Unit Citation—an admission that its members had behaved with "extraordinary heroism" on behalf of their country in Burma and China. And in 1996, each nonflying veteran was awarded a Bronze Star, and each pilot a Distinguished Flying Cross, awards that probably meant more to them than any other recognition, especially for those who hadn't returned to military service after their AVG tour.

The reunions continue, on an annual basis now, and over a wider geographical area. Most of the men I met in 1989 have since died— Rector, Greene, Dupouy, Mott, Smith, Neale, and Rodewald among them—casualties in a combat more deadly than the war for the Burma Road. At this writing, only six pilots are still alive who flew the Curtiss Tomahawk in combat for the American Volunteer Group. Of the ground crew and headquarters staff, the survivors number twenty-one men and one woman.

For some, the reunions are the best part of their year, and the AVG the organizing principle of their lives, one that has taken them back to China and Thailand, and even to visit the Japan they fought but never saw. (They were hosted by veterans of the JAAF 24th Sentai—which, in one of those misunderstandings that seem to cluster around the Tigers, flew against the 14th Air Force but not the AVG.) Because they've met so often, and because the moment they celebrate happened so long ago, the reunion has come to bulk larger than their months as Flying Tigers. Now they only tell war stories to outsiders. "That's five lies in five minutes," marveled a pilot of a ground crewman making his first appearance at one of these events. But who knows any longer what's true, what's imagined, and what's only wished for?

When someone asks, they oblige with the same stories that were told in the winter and spring of 1941–1942: that the Flying Tigers shot down 300 (or 600 or 1,000) Japanese planes, that they met and outfought the Mitsubishi Zero, that they stopped one Japanese army in the gorge of the Salween River and another in East China. (All wrong, save possibly the last. Operation Sei-go did indeed evaporate after the AVG reached Guilin.) What they don't say is that for a few months, more than sixty years ago, in their incandescent youth, they were heroes to a nation that needed heroes as never before and never since.

Yes. They fought magnificently, and their achievement isn't at all diminished by the fact that they believed their accomplishments to be greater than they were.

They were there. Mercenaries, gamblers, innocents, black-marketeers, romantics, war lovers—they were there when the British Empire was falling, and when America's future seemed nearly as bleak. "Did you ever regret joining the AVG?" a reporter once asked R. T. Smith. R. T. glanced off to the side, put his tongue in his cheek, and said: "Only on those occasions when I was being shot at." Yes. Frightened men in fallible machines, they fought against other men as frightened as themselves. All honor to them.

Identifying
Japanese Aircraft

Each Japanese warplane, like other military equipment, got a numerical designation based on the year it went into service with the Imperial army or navy. The calendar used for this purpose was based on the mythical founding of the emperor's dynasty in 660 BC. The western year 1940 was thus the Imperial year 2600—hence the navy's Zero fighter, which was formally adopted that year. Similarly, the army's numerous "Type 97" warplanes were so designated because they went into service in 1937, the Imperial year 2597.

Each Japanese navy plane also got an alphanumeric designation, similar to those used by the U.S. Navy. Thus the G3M: heavy bomber, third such in Japanese navy service, manufactured by Mitsubishi, and otherwise known as the Type 96 Land-Based Bomber. In this system, the "Type Zero" fighter was the A6M, with additional numbers to indicate modifications and improvements.

The Japanese army used a different system, based on the *kitai* (airframe) number given to a plane while it was being designed, without regard to type. Thus the Ki-27, otherwise known as Type 97 Army Fighter; and the Ki-43, otherwise the Type One Army Fighter. Beginning with the Ki-43, the army also gave fighting names to its warplanes, as was done in most western air forces, with the retractable-gear fighter becoming the Hayabusa, or Falcon.

Western pilots could make nothing of these designations. Claire Chennault, for example, guessed that the numerals referred to successive models, so he referred to the Type 96 fixed-gear navy fighter as the I-96, with the "I" standing for interceptor. The equivalent Type 97 army fighter became the I-97; and when the Zero made its appearance, he reported it as the mythical I-98. During the Pacific War, Allied pilots cut through the confusion by bestowing proper names on Japanese warplanes—male for fighters, female for other aircraft. The Ki-27 (Type 97 Army Fighter) became the Nate, and the Ki-21 (Type 97 Heavy Bomber) became the Sally. I use these western code names unless a better one is available in Japanese, as is the case for the Hayabusa and Toryu fighters.

Appendix 2

Warplanes Used in Burma and China

The figures are at the extremes (weight with full combat load; maximum one-way range with internal fuel; best speed at any altitude) for the model most often seen in the combats described in the book.

Brewster Buffalo As the F2A, this tubby warplane was the U.S. Navy's first monoplane fighter but was soon phased out in favor of the Grumman F4F Wildcat. The Buffalo had continual problems with its guns, radio, landing gear, and engine valves, and as delivered had no pilot armor. *Engine* 1,100-hp Wright Cyclone air-cooled radial; *weight* 6,500 lb; *range* 650 miles; *speed* 325 mph; *weapons* four .50-cal machine guns, 400-lb bombs.

Curtiss H-75 Though a sweet plane to fly, and durable beyond compare, the H-75 was slow in comparison to European fighters of the day. The U.S. Army took it into service as the P-36, and Curtiss sold hundreds to the French, British (who dubbed it Mohawk), and Dutch air forces. Other countries bought a cheaper version with fixed landing gear and less powerful engine, including the "M" model assembled in China

Appendix 2

by Bill Pawley. *Engine* 875-hp Wright Cyclone air-cooled radial; *weight* 5,300 lb; *range* 900 miles; *speed* 280 mph; *weapons* one .50-cal and three .30-cal machine guns.

Curtiss P-40B (Tomahawk) When the H-75 airframe was fitted with a liquid-cooled engine, it became a much more formidable fighter. At low altitudes, it proved equal to such rivals as the Messerschmitt Bf-109 and Mitsubishi A6M Zero, though only if a pilot refused to match the Japanese fighter turn for turn. Curtiss built 524 early-model P-40s for the U.S. Army and 1,180 Tomahawks for the Royal Air Force, including the 100 diverted to the AVG. Except for paint, "armourglass" windscreen, and caliber of the wing guns, the AVG's Tomahawk was substantially the same as the U.S. Army P-40B. *Engine* 1,040-hp Allison liquid-cooled in-line; *weight* 8,000 lb; *range* 700 miles; *speed* 340 mph; *weapons* two .50-cal and four 7.92-mm or .303-cal machine guns.

Curtiss P-40E (Kittyhawk) As compared to the small-mouthed P-40s, this later model of the Curtiss fighter had a more powerful engine, larger air scoop, shorter nose, and higher propeller shaft, giving it a distinctly jut-jawed appearance. Bomb racks and large-caliber wing guns made it immensely effective in ground support missions. Curtiss built more than 12,000, used to great effect in climates ranging from the tropical heat of Burma, through the dust of North Africa, to the frost of Alaska and the Soviet Union. The U.S. Army dubbed it the Warhawk, while the British knew it as Kittyhawk, which name was adopted by the AVG. *Engine* 1,150-hp Allison liquid cooled in-line; *weight* 8,840 lb; *range* 700 miles; *speed* 350 mph, *weapons* six .50-cal. machine guns, 210-lb antipersonnel bombs or 550-lb demolition bomb.

Douglas DC-3 Arguably the finest aircraft ever built, this twin-engine transport was one of the first all-metal passenger planes. Douglas built about 500 before 1942, when it was adapted to military use, to a total of nearly 32,000 by the time the war ended. They served the U.S. Army as the C-47, the RAF as the Dakota, and many other air forces as well, including a Nakajima-built copy flown by the Japanese navy. Intended for 21 passengers, the transport sometimes carried 70 out of Burma; designed to haul 2,500 pounds on civilian routes, it regularly lifted more than 7,000 pounds of cargo "over the Hump" to China. (The earlier DC-2 had a narrower fuselage and smaller capacity.) *Engines* two

1,200-hp Pratt & Whitney air-cooled radials; *crew* two or more; *range* 2,125 miles; *speed* 230 mph.

Hawker Hurricane The mainstay of the RAF at the outbreak of World War II, the Hurricane was slower than most front-line western fighters, but it was maneuverable, tough, forgiving of pilot error, and suitable for night fighting as a result of its exhaust shields and stable undercarriage. However, its record in Southeast Asia was poor. About 120 Hurricanes saw service in Burma, with 109 lost to accident, combat, and Japanese bombing. *Engine* 1,280-hp Rolls-Royce liquid-cooled in-line; *weight* 8,000 lb; *range* 470 miles; *speed* 340 mph; *weapons* eight .303-cal machine guns, 500-lb bombs.

Kawasaki Ki-45 Toryu Aware that the western powers had developed long-range, twin-engine escort fighters, the JAAF decided to build a similar plane. Kawasaki's prototype was lovely to see, with a needlelike nose, two neatly enclosed radial engines, and a rear-facing gunner. Production began early in 1942, so it went into service as the Type 2 Army Two-Seater Fighter, nicknamed Toryu (Dragon Killer). The June 12 shootout at Guilin seems to have been its baptism of fire. Disappointed by its performance, the JAAF thereafter used it against ground targets and Allied shipping. *Engines* two 950-hp Nakajima air-cooled radials; *crew* two; *weight* 11,600 lb; *range* 1,400 miles; *speed* 340 mph; *weapons* one 20-mm cannon, two 12.7-mm and one 7.92-mm machine guns, 1,100-lb bombs.

Kawasaki Ki-48 (Lily) Encountering Russian bombers in the fall of 1937, Japanese commanders were astonished by their speed, and they asked for a similar aircraft. The Ki-48 had a slender tail section behind the bomb bay, making room for a rear-facing gunner (otherwise the navigator) on a platform that swung down from the fuselage step, giving him a better range of motion than the porthole belly gunner on other bombers. It went into service in the Imperial Year 2599 (1939) and was therefore designated Type 99 Light Bomber. *Engines* two 950-hp Nakajima air-cooled radials; *crew* four; *weight* 13,000 lb; *range* 1,500 miles; *speed* 300 mph; *weapons* three 7.7-mm machine guns, 880-lb bombs.

Mitsubishi Ki-21 (Sally) The standard heavy bomber of the Japanese army, the Ki-21 was adopted in 1937 and saw service over Hankou, Chongqing, and the Burma Road. The wings were mounted at midpoint on the fuselage and had a distinct dihedral, giving it the look of a soaring though overweight hawk. The rudder was huge. By the outbreak of the Pacific War, most bomber groups had converted to the Ki-21-II (Sally-2). *Engines* two 1,500-hp Mitsubishi air-cooled radials; *crew* seven; *weight* 16,500 lb; *range* 1,500 miles; *speed* 300 mph; *weapons* one 12.7-mm and four 7.7-mm machine guns, 2,200-lb bombs.

Mitsubishi Ki-30 (Ann) This workhorse of the Japanese army was likewise introduced in 1937 and saw combat in China starting in October 1938 and against the Russians in the summer of 1939. It boasted an internal bomb bay but seemed old-fashioned in its use of fixed landing gear, rifle-caliber guns, and long greenhouse canopy; production ended in 1940, and Burma was its only significant deployment in the Pacific War. *Engine* 950-hp Mitsubishi air-cooled radial; *crew* two; *weight* 7,320 lb; *range* 1,000 miles; *speed* 260 mph; *weapons* one fixed and one flexible 7.7-mm machine gun, 900-lb bombs.

Nakajima Ki-27 (Nate) This gnatlike aircraft was the JAAF's first monoplane fighter. To meet army requirements, Nakajima produced a fragile craft with fixed landing gear and no starter motor, tail wheel, pilot armor, or self-sealing fuel tanks. The Ki-27 also went into service in

The Hayabusa's radial engine and clean lines fooled the AVG pilots into believing they were fighting the infamous Zero. The army plane was longer than the navy's, and the tail was rounded instead of being drawn out to a point. Note the weight-saving, non-retractable tail wheel, typical of Japanese fighters. (National Archives)

1937 and was therefore known as Type 97 Army Fighter. From China, Claire Chennault warned U.S. authorities that it "climbs like a sky rocket and maneuvers like a squirrel." It was the AVG's most frequent opponent both in Burma and in China. *Engine* 650-hp Nakajima air-cooled radial; *weight* 4,000 lb; *range* 500 miles; *speed* 290 mph; *weapons* two 7.7-mm machine guns, 220-lb bombs.

Nakajima Ki-43 Hayabusa For the JAAF's first retractable-gear fighter, Nakajima again delivered a comparatively fragile plane with no pilot armor, self-sealing fuel tanks, or internal starter. Butterfly combat flaps increased the wing area and transformed a sluggish fighter into one that could turn inside a Zero. It went into service in July 1941, by which time the JAAF was giving pet names to its warplanes, to oblige journalists who found it difficult to write about aircraft identified only by number and function. Thus the Ki-43, officially Type 1 Army Fighter, became the Hayabusa (Falcon). *Engine* 1,050-hp Nakajima air-cooled radial; *range* 750 miles; *speed* 305 mph; *weight* 5,000 lb; *weapons* one 12.7-mm and one 7.7-mm machine gun, 132-lb bombs.

Victories Credited
to AVG pilots

AVG pilots were paid $500 for each Japanese plane destroyed—the rough equivalant of $10,000 today. Unlike the practice in most air forces, aircraft destroyed on the ground were given the same weight as those claimed in air-to-air combat. The AVG tally was further muddled because pilots sometimes shared bonus payments among all who took part in a mission. (This most often happened when a pilot was lost.) In 1986, aviation historian Frank Olynyk worked through the AVG records, tossing out claims against aircraft on the ground and restoring air-to-air credits to the individuals who actually scored the kills, as shown in combat reports and other documents.

	Bonus Account	*Olynyk Air-to-Air*
Frank Adkins	1.00	1.00
Noel Bacon	3.50	3.00
Percy Bartelt	7.00	5.00
William Bartling	7.27	5.00

	Bonus Account	*Olynyk Air-to-Air*
Lewis Bishop*	5.20	2.20
John Blackburn*	2.00	2.00
Harry Bolster	2.00	1.00
Charles Bond	8.77	7.00
Gregory Boyington	3.50	2.00
J. Gilpin Bright	6.00	3.00
Robert Brouk	3.50	3.50
Carl Brown	0.27	—
George Burgard	10.79	10.00
Thomas Cole*	1.00	1.00
James Cross	0.27	—
John Dean	3.27	3.00
John Donovan*	4.00	1.00
Parker Dupouy	3.50	3.50
John Farrell	1.00	1.00
Henry Geselbracht	1.50	—
Paul Greene	2.00	2.00
Clifford Groh	2.00	2.00
Ralph Gunvordahl	1.00	1.00
Raymond Hastey	1.00	1.00
Thomas Haywood	5.08	4.00
Robert Hedman	4.83	6.00
David Lee Hill	11.25	10.25
Fred Hodges	1.00	1.00
Louis Hoffman*	0.27	—
James Howard	6.33	2.33
Kenneth Jernstedt	10.50	3.00
Thomas Jones*	4.00	1.00
Robert Keeton	2.50	2.00
Matthew Kuykendall	1.00	1.00
C. H. Laughlin	5.20	2.20
Frank Lawlor	8.50	7.00
Robert Layher	0.83	0.33
Edward Leibolt*	0.27	—
Robert Little*	10.55	10.00

	Bonus Account	Olynyk Air-to-Air
William McGarry*	10.29	8.00
George McMillan	4.08	4.50
Kenneth Merritt*	1.00	1.00
Einar Mickelson	0.27	1.00
Robert Moss	4.00	2.00
Charles Mott*	2.00	—
Robert Neale	15.55	13.00
John Newkirk*	10.50	7.00
Charles Older	10.08	10.00
Arvid Olson	1.00	1.00
Edmund Overend	5.83	5.00
John Petach*	3.98	3.98
Robert Prescott	5.29	5.50
Robert Raine	3.20	3.20
Edward Rector	6.52	4.75
William Reed	10.50	3.00
Freeman Ricketts	1.20	1.20
C. Joseph Rosbert	4.55	6.00
J. Richard Rossi	6.29	6.00
Robert Sandell*	5.27	5.00
Charles Sawyer	2.27	2.00
Frank Schiel	7.00	4.00
Van Shapard	1.00	1.00
Eriksen Shilling	0.75	—
Robert H. Smith	5.50	5.00
Robert T. Smith	8.73	8.90
Fritz Wolf	2.27	4.00
Peter Wright	3.65	2.65
TOTAL	296.00	229.00

An asterisk (*) follows the names of pilots killed, captured, or missing in action. The CAMCO list is based on what seems to be the final accounting; other records suggest that Hill and Boyington each had one more victory than they were paid for. Individual claims don't add to whole numbers because I've rounded them off to two decimal places.

Sources

In what follows, I generally cite a source only on its first appearance. A bibliography and detailed chapter notes can be seen online at www.flyingtigersbook.com. With one exception, Japanese-language books were translated with Miyuki Rogers, who reviewed the text, summarized it orally, and finally made a word-for-word translation of critical sentences. The exception was Umemoto Hiroshi's *Burma Air War*, translated with Difei Zhang. I read numerous documents at the National Air and Space Museum (NASM) and the San Diego Aerospace Museum in collections that afterward were acquired by the Flying Tigers veterans' group; I cite these documents as located in the AVG Archives even though I read them elsewhere.

Chapter 1: Presenting Colonel Chennault

Chennault published his autobiography as *Way of a Fighter* (Putnam, 1949); the manuscript was written by Robert Hotz from material supplied by the ostensible author, and without his close supervision. Martha Byrd wrote a more reliable biography, *Chennault: Giving Wings to the Tiger* (University of Alabama Press, 1987). Other sources were Anna Chennault, *A Thousand Springs* (Eriksson, 1962); Robert Hotz, *With General Chennault* (Coward McCann, 1943); and Jack Samson, *Chennault* (Doubleday, 1987). Chennault presented his tactical ideas as "The Role of Defensive Pursuit," serialized in *Coast Artillery Journal*, 1933–1934. For the China years, I drew heavily on Chennault's unpublished diary, supplied by Jack Samson; all of Chennault's unattributed quotes came from this source.

I conducted scores of interviews in person, by telephone, and by letter; the audiotapes are located at the Museum of Naval Aviation, Pensacola, Florida. For this chapter, the interviewees included Joseph Alsop, Anna Chennault, Nancy Allison Wright, A. L. Patterson, John Williams, Shah Konsin, Fu Jui-yuan, Lee Cheng-yuan, and Wang Shu-ming. I found other personal accounts at the Air Force Historical Research Agency (AFHRA), Maxwell Air Force Base, Alabama; and in the Columbia University Oral History Project files, which alas are no longer accessible, though transcripts of some are in the AVG Archives.

Useful studies of air operations in China included Ray Wagner, *Prelude to Pearl Harbor* (San Diego Aerospace Museum, 1991), and William Leary, *The Dragon's Wings* (University of Georgia Press, 1976). The *Foreign Relations of the United States* volumes from 1937 onward provided much information about Chennault and China, as did the Morgenthau Diaries at the Roosevelt Library, Hyde Park, New York. Japanese sources included Hata Ikuhiko in *The China Quagmire* (Columbia University Press, 1983); Hata Ikuhiko and Izawa Yasuho, *Japanese Naval Aces and Fighter Units* (Naval Institute Press, 1989); and Hisazuma Tadeo, "Air Operations in the China Incident," one of the invaluable Japanese Monographs published by the U.S. Army of Occupation in Japan in the 1950s. Also Paul Frillmann, *China: The Remembered Life* (Houghton-Mifflin, 1968); Royal Leonard, *I Flew for China* (Doubleday, 1942); Olga Greenlaw, *The Lady and the Tigers* (Dutton, 1943); Theodore White, *In Search of History* (Harper, 1978); Theodore White and Anna Jacoby, *Thunder out of China* (Sloane, 1946); and copies of the McHugh documents at Cornell, supplied by William Leary and David Dunlap.

Chapter 2: The Special Air Unit

For the formation of the AVG, I drew heavily on John King Fairbank's monograph, "Air Program," written for Lauchlin Currie in 1942, and supplied by William Leary. Thomas Corcoran wrote a memoir, "Pacific Wars," about his role in China Defense Supplies; the typescript of it was supplied by Anna Chennault. For the Curtiss fighters, I relied on Daniel Whitney, *Vee's for Victory* (Schiffer, 1998); Francis Dean, *America's Hundred Thousand* (Schiffer, 1997); Terrill Clements, *American Volunteer Group Colours and Markings* (Osprey, 2001); and Chuck Baisden, *Flying Tiger to Air Commando* (Schiffer, 1999). I am indebted to Corey Jordan and Erik Shilling for their letters, e-mails, and Internet postings about the planes sent to Burma. For their assembly at Rangoon, see Byron Glover in *Aviation* (Dec 1942) and Walter Pentecost in *American Aviation Historical Society Journal* (Summer 1970).

The Chennault Papers at Stanford University are a trove of information about the AVG; I used the microfilm copies at the Library of Congress. Also useful were James McHugh's monograph, "The History and Status of the First American Volunteer Group" (1941), Cornell University Library; Arthur Young, *China and the Helping Hand* (Harvard University Press, 1963); and many of the sources cited earlier.

AVG armorer Chuck Baisden recalled that the majority of the AVG's rifle-caliber machine guns were chambered for the U.S. .30-caliber cartridge, with a smaller number of 7.92-mm guns. The available documents support the version presented here.

Chapter 3: Too Good to Be True

This chapter was based in large part on my interviews with Skip Adair, Allen Fritzke, Emma Jane (Foster) Hanks, Paul Perry, Eddie Rector, Doreen (Lonborg) Reynolds, Lew Richards, and Olga Greenlaw's sister, Alicia Schweizer; and on the Columbia University interviews with Tex Hill, Joe Jordan, Matt Kuykendall, Bob Layher, Bob Neale, and Tom Trumble. Charlie Mott's diary is in the AVG Archives. Published memoirs include Gregory Boyington, *Baa Baa Black Sheep* (Putnam, 1958); Charles Bond and Terry Anderson, *A Flying Tiger's Diary* (Texas A&M University Press, 1984); David Hill and Reagan Schaupp, *Tex Hill: Flying Tiger* (Honoribus Press, 2003); James Howard, *Roar of the Tiger* (Orion, 1991); Frank Losonsky and Terry Losonsky, *Flying Tiger: A Crew Chief's Story* (Schiffer, 1996); Robert M. Smith, *With Chennault in China* (TAB Books, 1984); and the invaluable facsimile diary of R. T. Smith, *Tale of a Tiger* (privately printed, 1986). The Tex Hill memoir is written in the third person, and it's impossible to know if the words he attributes to Chennault are his or his coauthor's—and if the former, whether they owe more to Chennault or to Tex's own considerable combat experience. At the very least, the sentiments are consistent with what we know about Chennault.

The RAF's understanding of the AVG came from Robert Brooke-Popham's post-campaign dispatch in *Supplement to the London Gazette* (22 Jan 1948). Other published sources were Wanda Cornelius and Thayne Short, *Ding Hao* (Pelican, 1980); William Pawley, *Americans Valiant and Glorious* (privately printed, 1945); Michael Schaller, *The U.S. Crusade in China* (Columbia University Press, 1979); and Duane Schultz, *The Maverick War* (St. Martin's Press, 1987). The story of John Perry's impersonation of Edwin Conant was told by Joseph Brown in *Argosy* (Sep 1963); the story of Chuck Baisden's enlistment, by Thomas Cleaver in *Flight Journal* (Jun 2004); the story of Baumler's passport, by Lauchlin Currie in a cover letter for the Fairbank manuscript mentioned earlier; the story of the Chengtu Zero, by William Leary in *Aerospace Historian* (Winter 1987).

Latter-day historians have argued that the AVG's existence and plans for the 2nd AVG prompted or even justified the Japanese attack on Pearl Harbor—or, alternately, could have prevented that attack, had the bomber group moved to Asia in time. The first case was made by an ABC-TV documentary in December 1991, fifty years after the Pearl Harbor attack; the second, by Alan Armstrong in *Preemptive Strike: The Secret Plan That Would Have Prevented the Attack on Pearl Harbor* (Lyons Press, 2006). Armstrong's book contains many verbatim documents about the AVG's formation.

Chapter 4: Looks Mean as Hell

Unpublished sources for the Toungee training program included Arvid Olson's memoir, "A Story of the American Volunteer Group"; Olson's training notebook; Wilfred Schaper's diary; and Erik Shilling's memoir, "Origin of Shark Teeth" (all in the AVG Archives); Don Rodewald's Columbia University interview; and my interviews and correspondence with Noel Bacon, Ken Jernstedt, Harold Klein (the missionary's son), and Charlie Mott. I read the British and Japanese manuals in the Chennault Papers, and the radio traffic of the U.S. Military Mission in China (AMISSCA) at the National Archives branch at Suitland, Maryland.

J. Gilpin Bright's letters to his parents appeared in the *Atlantic* (Oct 1942). Other published sources included Neil Frances, *Ketchil: A New Zealand Pilot's War in Asia and the Pacific* (Wairarapa Archive, 2005); Ikari Yoshio, *Shinshitei* (Sankei Shuppan, 1981); Eriksen Shilling, *Destiny: A Flying Tiger's Rendezvous with Fate* (privately printed, 1997); U.S. 79th Congress, Joint Committee on the Investigation of the Pearl Harbor Attack, *Hearings* (GPO, 1946); Muriel Sue Upfill, *An American in Burma, 1930 to 1942* (Arizona State University Program for Southeast Asian Studies, 1999); Richard Ward, *Sharkmouth, 1916–1945* (Arco, 1979); and *Illustrated Weekly of India* (2 Nov 1941).

Chapter 5: Flaming Till Hell Won't Have It

For Japanese activities in Burma, I used Izawa Yasuho and Hata Ikuhiko, *Nihon rikugun sentokitai* (Kantosha, 1977); the excellent Japan Defense Agency history, *Nanpo shinko rikugun koku sakusen* (Asagumo Shimbunsha, 1970); Kasuya Toshio, *Yamamoto jubakugetai no eiko* (Futami Shobo, 1970); and Umemoto Hiroshi, *Burma Air War* (Dai Nippon Kaiga, 2003). An especially valuable English-language source was the *Japan Times & Advertiser*, published daily in Tokyo throughout the war, including Kato Tateo's posthumous diary (25 Jul 1942). Other English-language sources were Izawa Yasuho in *Aero Album* (Summer 1970, Fall 1971); Hata Ikuhiko et al., *Japanese Army Air Force Fighter*

Units and Their Aces, 1931–1945 (Grub Street, 2002); Tomioka Sada-
toshi, "Political Strategy Prior to Outbreak of War," and Yamaguchi
Shiro, "Malaya Invasion Naval Operations," both in the Japanese Monograph series; and the typescript of a television interview with Suzuki
Goichi (1992), supplied by Frank Christopher.

Olga Greenlaw kept the AVG's War Diary from December to March,
taking a copy with her when she left China; there are copies of this version
at AFHRA and in the AVG Archives. When Doreen Lonborg took over
the diarist's job, she retyped most of Greenlaw's entries, and the two versions differ slightly. Lonborg's diary was kept by Chennault and appears
in the Chennault Papers. I drew from both versions, as well as from a 31
Dec 1941 briefing paper, "Activities of Third Pursuit Squadron"; the 3rd
Squadron log (written by Daniel Hoyle); and Robert Keeton's diary, all in
the AVG Archives.

For the activities of British Commonwealth squadrons in Burma, I
relied on Christopher Shores and Brian Cull with Izawa Yasuho, *Bloody
Shambles: The Drift to War to the Fall of Singapore* (Grub Street,
1992). Other published sources included British General Staff, *ABDA-
COM* (Government of India, 1942); James Cross in *Mechanix Illus-
trated* (Dec 1942); Larry Moore and Ken Sanger in *Cosmopolitan*
(Aug–Sep 1942); Gerhard Neumann, *Herman the German* (Morrow,
1984); C. Joseph Rosbert, *Flying Tiger Joe* (privately printed, 1985);
U.S. Strategic Bombing Survey, *Japanese Air Power* (GPO, 1946); Don
Whelpley in *Ex-CBI Roundup* (May 1989); and Fritz Wolf and Douglas
Ingells in *Air Trails Pictorial* (Oct 1942). The RAF 67 Sq log is at the
Public Record Office, London.

For the origin of the Flying Tiger name, I relied on *Time* magazine
(29 Dec 1941); Thomas Corcoran's "Pacific Wars" memoir cited earlier;
the Chennault Papers; and my interview with Joan Corcoran.

Chapter 6: Such a Bright Red!

After each mission, AVG pilots were expected to file a combat report,
and these were an invaluable source of information. I read some at
NASM, in a collection now part of the AVG Archives, and others in the

Chennault Papers. In addition, these reports were often excerpted in the Group War Diary, and for some combats I found flight-leader summaries in the Chennault Papers. Frank Olynyk broke out individual AVG claims in "AVG & USAAF (China-Burma-India Theater) Credits for the Destruction of Enemy Aircraft in Air-to-Air Combat" (privately printed, 1986); I've used his figures throughout.

Tsuji Masanobu provided a useful introduction to Japanese tactics in *Singapore: The Japanese Version* (Constable, 1962), including an appendix translating his pamphlet given to troops in the Malaya invasion force. Ishikawa Shin et al described the Burma campaign in "Southwest Area Air Operations Record" in the Japanese Monograph series. Other Japanese-language sources not cited earlier included Hasegawa Naoyoshi, *Rikuwashi nanpo sakusen* (Nihon Gunyo Tosho Kabushi Kigaisha, 1943); Hayashi Iwao in *Shichi jusan butai kaisoki* (Reimeisha, 1980); and Izawa Yasuho, *Nihon rikugun jubakutai* (Gendaishi Shuppankai, 1982). For the 77th Sentai, see Richard Dunn's monograph at www.warbirdforum.com/lucky.htm. Some Japanese names—Lieutenant Shingansho's in particular—are approximations.

For Allied activites, I drew on H. R. Dean, *The Royal New Zealand Air Force in South-East Asia 1941–42* (War History Branch, 1952); Emile Foucar, *I Lived in Burma* (Dennis Dobson, 1956); O'Dowd Gallagher, *Action in the East* (Doubleday, 1942); M. I. Omar in *Rangoon Guardian* (Dec 1960); Archibald Wavell's dispatch in *Supp. London Gazette* (5 Mar 1948); and sources cited earlier.

New to this chapter were my interviews with Parker Dupouy, Paul Greene, Duke Hedman, Chuck Older, and R. T. Smith; Older's Columbia University interview; a report from Arvid Olson to D. F. Stevenson (1942) in the AVG Archives; and an undated audiotape by Erik Shilling, supplied by Martha Byrd.

Chapter 7: He Just Went Spinning Away

The 64th Sentai veteran Hinoki Yohei wrote two memoirs of his Burma service, *Hayabusa sentotai cho Kato* (Kojinsha, 1987) and *Tsubasa no kessen* (Kojinsha, 1984). He supplied additional information by letter, as did the historian Hata Ikuhiko. In their Columbia University interviews, Don Rodewald and Wilfred Schaper told how AVG crewmen rebuked Olson. Joe Alsop described his capture in *Saturday Evening Post* (9 Jan 1943). The to-and-fro with the War Department came from documents at the Roosevelt Library at Hyde Park.

Chapter 8: Leaning Forward

Donald Stevenson's campaign dispatch appeared in *Supp. London Gazette* (11 Mar 1948). For the AVG, I used Jack Newkirk's "Report on Activities of This Squadron" (13 Jan 1942) in the Chennault Papers, and a USAAF "Informal Report on A.V.G. Activities" (1942) at AFHRA. Published recollections included Noel Bacon in *N. Y. Sunday News* (2 Aug 1942); C. H. Laughlin in *Foundation* (Spring 1983); and Peter Wright in *Flying* (May 1944). Tanaka Masa related Japanese ground operations in "Burma Air Operations Record," Japanese Monograph series. Japanese-language books included Kubo Yoshiaki, *Kyunana jubakutai kusanki* (Kojinsha, 1984), and the Japan Defense Agency history of air operations in China, *Chugoku homen rikugun koku sakusen* (Asagumo Shimbunsha, 1974).

For this chapter, I also used the RAF 113 Sq log at the Public Record Office London; a 1949 interview with Sato Shoichi at the National Archives; my interviews with Dick Rossi and Dorothea (Wilkins) Dunsmore; my correspondence with Charlie Mott; John Donovan's letters in the AVG Archives; and recollections by Frank Losonsky, posted on the AVG veterans' Internet forum in 2006.

Chapter 9: They Fell in a Straight Line

Several RAF 17 Squadron pilots published their memoirs, including M. C. Cotton, *Hurricanes over Burma* (Titania, 1988); Hedley Everard, *A Mouse in My Pocket: Memoirs of a Fighter Pilot* (privately printed, 1988); and Kenneth Hemingway, *Wings over Burma* (Quality, 1944).

Colin Pinckney's letters home were published by Roger Cooke and Ann Gresham Cooke, *Your Uncles* (privately printed, 1950). Additional information from John Rawlings, *Fighter Squadrons of the RAF* (Macdonald & Jane, 1976). In the Japanese Monograph series, Terakura Shore et al., "Burma Operations Record," and Hattori Takushiro et al., "History of Imperial General Headquarters," provided details of ground tactics and strategy. George Rodger's photo appeared in *Life* magazine (30 Mar 1942).

Chapter 10: Hoffman Down and Dead

For George Burgard's diary, see the AVG Archives; for Robert Prescott's wonderful yarn, see his Columbia University interview; for the change in Sandell, see J. Richard Rossi in *Foundation* (Spring 1995). The Commonwealth army's withdrawal is from T. J. Hutton's campaign dispatch in *Supp. London Gazette* (5 Mar 1948). Robert Keeton's story, from his diary and my interview with him. For RAF activities toward the end of the Burma campaign, I used the second volume of Christopher Shores's campaign history, *Bloody Shambles*: *The Defence of Sumatra to the Fall of Burma* (Grub Street, 1993). Additional information from Wilfred Burchette, *Trek Back from Burma* (Kitabistan, 1943).

For Lieutenant Yamamoto and *jibaku,* I drew on Tagata Takeo, *Hien tai Guramen* (Konnichi no Wadaisha, 1973); Kuwahara Yasuo and Gordon Allred, *Kamikaze* (Ballantine, 1957); the translator's note by Don Cyril Gorham in Hata and Izawa, *Japanese Naval Aces*; and the Japanese edition of Izawa and Hata's book, *Nihon rikugun sentokitai.* I also had the benefit of an unpublished English-language essay on this subject by Dr. Izawa, "Japanese Fighter Units and Aces," supplied by John Fredriksen.

Chapter 11: Get the Heck Out of Here

In addition to sources cited earlier, for this chapter I drew upon S. W. Kirby's history of the Burma campaign, *India's Most Dangerous Hour*

(His Majesty's Stationery Office, 1958); Thomas Hughes, *The Burma Campaign* (privately printed, 1943); the Toho Motion Picture Company documentary, *Biruma* (1942), supplied by John Fredriksen; Kuroe Yasuhiko, *Aa Hayabusa sentotai* (Kojinsha, 1969); and my correspondence with Dick Rossi.

Christopher Shores addressed the contentious subject of the Moulmein strafes in the second volume of *Bloody Shambles,* pages 279–282. Hedley Everard's implausible claims appear in *A Mouse in My Pocket,* pages 170, 183. My interview with Vic Bargh is posted at www.flyingtigersbook.com.

Chapter 12: Did You Have Any Warning?

For Stilwell's epithets and journal entries, see Joseph Stilwell and Theodore White, *The Stilwell Papers* (Sloan, 1948). Also useful in writing this chapter were the "Chronology of 10th Air Force" at AFHRA; Frank Dorn, *Walkout* (Crowell, 1971); Philip Moyes, *Bomber Squadrons of the RAF* (Macdonald & Jane, 1974); A. J. Young and D. W. Warne, *Sixty Squadron* (Eurasia, no date); British Air Ministry, *Wings of the Phoenix* (HMSO, 1949); and sources cited earlier, especially the AMISSCA radiograms. The U.S. Army's campaign history was written by Charles Romanus and Riley Sunderland in *Stilwell's Mission to China* (GPO, 1953), with additional material in *Stilwell's Personal File* (Scholarly Resources, 1976).

Chapter 13: Like a Movie Only Better

Additional information for this chapter came from Bruce Gamble's biography of Greg Boyington, *Black Sheep One* (Presidio, 2000); Sekigawa Eiichiro, *Pictorial History of Japanese Military Aviation* (Allan, 1974); Yasuda Yoshito's chapter in *Eiko Hayabusa sentai* (Konnichi no Wadaisha, 1978); Robert Mikesh, *Japanese Aircraft Equipment 1940–1945* (Schiffer, 2004); and an interview with Robert Andrade, at that time keeper of the AVG Archives.

Chapter 14: The Pilots' Revolt

Peter Wright told the story of the Toungoo strafe in *Sportsman Pilot* (May 1943). Other sources included Hata Ikuhiko's chapter in *The China Quagmire,* cited earlier, Gordon Seagrave, *Burma Surgeon* (Norton, 1943); a 1981 letter from Greg Boyington to the USMC historian Robert Sherrod, in the AVG Archives; the *Army Directory* for 20 Oct 1942; Kirk Setzer at www.warbirdforum.com/baumler.htm; and the usual combat reports, diaries, memoirs, and especially AMISSCA radiograms. Hinoki Yohei listed all 64th Sentai combat deaths in the appendix to *Tsubasa no kessen.* I found the AVG pilots' resignation letter in the Chennault Papers, while Tex Hill's speech to the pilots appears in the memoir he wrote with his grandson, Reagan Schaupp. Chennault's U.S. Army personnel file contains no documents relating to his induction and promotions. Some AMISSCA radiograms give the induction date as April 8, but I follow the chronology laid out in a July 17 radiogram from Stilwell to the War Department.

Chapter 15: Auction Sale at Loiwing

Caleb Haynes gave his account of the Burma rescue flights in a 1943 letter to the U.S. Army historians Romanus and Sunderland, supplied by Martha Byrd. Other sources included Robert Scott, *God Is My Co-Pilot* (Ballantine, 1956); Jack Belden, *Retreat with Stilwell* (Knopf, 1943); an unattributed article in *Ex-CBI Roundup* (Jul 1989); and my interview with John Hennessey.

Chapter 16: Piss on Bissell

For Japanese mop-up operations in Burma, I used the unattributed volume "Southern Area Air Operations" in the Japanese Monograph series. JAAF losses in the campaign were detailed in a British Military Intelligence report, "Japanese Air Losses" (Tokyo, 1953), at the Imperial War

Museum, London. For the Red Dragon division, see Hill and Schaupp (*Tex Hill,* pages 158–160) and James Howard (*Roar of the Tiger,* page 146). The fiction's creator seems to have been Robert Hotz (*With General Chennault,* page 224).

McAllister's odyssey was related in the AVG 3rd Squadron log; the Gia Lam strafe, by C. H. Laughlin in *Foundation* (Spring 1983). Donovan's radiogram and his letter home are in the AVG Archives. For the story of the Lancers, I drew on my interview with Jasper Harrington and an unattributed article in *Ex-CBI Roundup* (Nov 1989). Chennault's letter to Caleb Haynes was supplied by Martha Byrd; Kenneth Jernstedt told me about Harvey Greenlaw's quest for a commission; Little's death was described in "Statement of Peter Wright" in the AVG Archives; George Burgard wrote about Jim Cross's refusing further combat missions in his diary entry of 10 May 1942; and Martha Byrd told the story of the gas coolie in her biography of Chennault.

Chapter 17: Worse Than You Know

For the Japanese moves against the East China bases, I drew on Kori Katsu, *Nihon no koku gojunen* (Kantosha, 1960); Wei Ju-lin et al., *History of the Sino-Japanese War* (U.S. Army Military Assistance Advisory Group, Taiwan, 1967); Shiba Takejiro, "Air Operations in the China Area," Japanese Monograph series; and Carroll Glines, *Doolittle's Tokyo Raiders* (Van Nostrand Reinhold, 1964). The introduction of the Kawasaki fighter was described in Watanabe Yoji, *Toryu* (Sankei Shuppan, 1983), and the reaction to the Guilin battle by Nonaka (no first name), "Southwest Area Air Operations Record," Japanese Monograph series. I found Corporal Honda's debriefing in the Chennault Papers.

Lewis Brereton told the story of the CATF's creation in *The Brereton Diaries* (Morrow, 1946). For the attempted induction of the AVG, I drew on a U.S. Military Mission report, "American Volunteer Group" (1942) at AFHRA, and the usual AVG diaries, interviews, and memoirs. Chennault's whorehouse from Theodore White, *In Search of History;* Jack Samson, *Chennault;* and AMISSCA radiograms.

Chapter 18: Passing into History

Shamblin's capture was reported in the *Japan Times & Advertiser* (18 Jul 1942). AVG aircraft losses were tallied in an AMISSCA radiogram (2 Jul 1942); the count was 82, to which I added 2 shot down on July 10. The AVG had 62 Tomahawks in service when the war began; 6 out-of-service aircraft were subsequently repaired at Toungoo, 1 was assembled at Loiwing, and 47 P-40E Kittyhawks were delivered in the spring of 1942, for a total of 116.

Geoffrey Ellis documented the service of RAF radio mechanics with the AVG. The Tigers joining CNAC were Frank Adkins, Bill Bartling, Carl Brown, John Dean, Cliff Groh, Lester Hall, Duke Hedman, Fred Hodges, Link Laughlin, Bus Loane, Mickey Mickelson, Moose Moss, Bob Prescott, Catfish Raine, Joe Rosbert, Dick Rossi, Van Shapard, Erik Shilling, Allen Wright—and Lew Bishop after his return from captivity. Doc Richards and four former ground crewmen also worked for CNAC. Tex Hill's leadership style, from my interview with Donald Lopez, who served under Tex in the 23rd Fighter Group. The Chennault-Bissell feuds described by Robert Scott, *The Day I Owned the Sky* (Bantam, 1988), and in the Byrd and Samson biographies. The account of Butch Carney's homicide, from my interview with Carl Brown. Jack Samson tells the story of Rose Mok's son, pages 289–90, and in 2005 I exchanged correspondence with Joe Chennault himself. Kirk Setzer wrote about Ed McClure's navy service at www.warbirdforum.com/mcclure.htm.

George Paxton summarized the AVG's wartime service in Flying Tigers Inc., *Bill of Rights Requesting Veteran Recognition by Congress* (privately printed, 1945). Henry Olson's Congressional campaign described in *Life* (24 Aug 1942) and his later combat service at www.368thfightergroup.com. For CAT, I drew on William Leary, *Perilous Missions* (University of Alabama Press, 1984); and for Erik Shilling's Vietnam War career, on Sterling Seagrave, *Soldiers of Fortune* (Time-Life Books, 1981), and my interview with Shilling. R. T. Smith's concluding comment from the Anscorp video, *The Flying Tigers and 14th Air Force Story* (Army Air Forces Museum, 1985).

Appendices

For Japanese aircraft data, I drew on Baba Kazuo, *Nihon gunyoki no zembo* (Kantosha, 1956); Ogawa Toshihiko, *Nihon hikoki daizukan* (Kodansha, 1980); and Sekigawa's *Pictorial History of Japanese Military Aviation*, cited earlier. CAMCO bonus account, from documents in the Chennault Papers; Olynyk's figures, from his monograph cited earlier.

Index

Planes are indexed under *Aircraft*, by manufacturer, with profiles in heavy type. Illustrations in italic type. Military units are indexed under the parent service.